Small Nations in Times of Crisis and Confrontation

Small Nations in Times of Crisis and Confrontation

Yohanan Cohen

***

*Translated from Hebrew by
Naftali Greenwood*

State University of New York Press

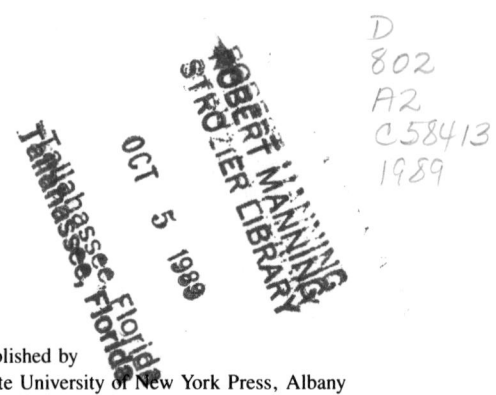

Published by
State University of New York Press, Albany

© 1989 State University of New York

All rights reserved

Printed in the United States of America

First published in Hebrew
under the title:
"Umoth ba-Mivhan"
by Maarachot/MOD, Tel-Aviv 1985

No part of this book may be used or reproduced
in any manner whatsoever without written permission
except in the case of brief quotations embodied in
critical articles and reviews.

For information, address State University of New York
Press, State University Plaza, Albany, N.Y., 12246

Library of Congress Cataloging-in-Publication Data

Cohen, Yohanan.
    Small nations in times of crisis and confrontation.

    Translation of: Umoth ba-mivḥan.
    Bibliography: p. 379
    Includes index.
    1. Czechoslovakia—History—1938–1939. 2. World
War, 1939–1945—Czechoslovakia. 3. Poland—History—
Occupation, 1939–1945. 4. World War, 1939–1945.
5. Finland—History—1939–1940. 6. World War, 1939–
1945—Finland. I. Title.
D802.A2C58413   1989   940.53′437   88-24871
ISBN 0-7914-0018-2
ISBN 0-7914-0019-0 (pbk.)

10 9 8 7 6 5 4 3 2 1

To my son, Danny

Contents

Illustrations	ix
Acknowledgements	xi
Introduction	1

Part One: Czechoslovakia 1938–1939

Chapter One: An Obstacle on the Road to Lebensraum	7
Chapter Two: In the Crucible of Appeasement	15
Chapter Three: Munich	31
Chapter Four: Surrender	39

Part Two: Poland and Her Neighbors

Chapter Five: Poland Between the Two Wars	55
Chapter Six: The War	81
Chapter Seven: Under the Yoke of Occupation	97
Chapter Eight: The "London Government"	105
Chapter Nine: The Teheran Conference	135
Chapter Ten: Between Teheran and Yalta	153
Chapter Eleven: The Yalta Conference	185

| Chapter Twelve: Potsdam and Its Implications | 207 |

Part Three: Finland—"The Winter War"

Chapter Thirteen: The Thunderhead Looms	237
Chapter Fourteen: Talks in the Kremlin	247
Chapter Fifteen: War	263
Chapter Sixteen: The Course of the Battles	273
Chapter Seventeen: World Sympathy and its Expressions	277
Chapter Eighteen: Peace Feelers	289
Chapter Nineteen: The Front Collapses	297
Chapter Twenty: The Affair of the English–French Expeditionary Force	307
Chapter Twenty-One: The Fateful Decision	315
Chapter Twenty-Two: The Winter War Saved Finland's Independence	323

Final Remarks and Reflections	325
Notes	345
Select Bibliography	379
Index	389

Illustrations

Maps by Ziv Bashan

Map 1: Czechoslovakia, 1938   33

Map 2: Poland's Frontiers 1939, 1946   57

Map 3: Curzon Line and Ribbentrop-Molotov Line   149

Map 4: Proposed Annexations by Poland   190

Map 5: The Russian Offensive in February 1940   299

Map 6: Finnish Territory Annexed by the Soviet Union in 1940   317

Photos

Photo 1: Lord Runciman received by President Beneš   21

Photo 2: Munich Conference—Chamberlain, Daladier, Hitler, Mussolini, Ciano   31

Photo 3: Czech policeman changing a sign from "Freedom Avenue" to "Adolf Hitler Plaza"   36

Photo 4: Marshal Jozef Piłsudski   66

Photo 5: German Foreign Minister on a Visit to Warsaw   71

Photo 6: Foreign Minister Beck Received by Hitler   73

ILLUSTRATIONS

Photo 7: Hitler in the Wehrmacht's HQ with Reich's Marshal
Goering and Field-Marshal Keitel   76

Photo 8: Molotov—with Ribbentrop and Stalin looking on—signs
the Nazi-Soviet Friendship Treaty   78

Photo 9: Molotov arriving in Berlin, November 1940   109

Photo 10: Churchill and General Sikorski with Polish troops in
Great Britain   130

Photo 11: Polish PM, Mikołajczyk   142

Photo 12: The Big Three in the patio of Livadia Palace, Yalta   195

Photo 13: Truman and Churchill at the Potsdam Conference   208

Photo 14: Polish President, Bierut   215

Photo 15: Marshal G. C. Mannerheim   240

Photo 16: The Finnish delegation leaving for talks in Moscow   247

Photo 17: Hella Wuolijoki   294

Photo 18: Finnish soldiers on the Summa front   298

Photo 19: Finnish ski-troops on the move   300

Acknowledgements

I take this opportunity to express my gratitude to my friends, who in various ways encouraged me to begin and to proceed with the writing of this book.

My special thanks go to those of them who read the original manuscript, in whole or in part:

> General (Ret.) Meir Amit, former government minister; Prof. Hedva Ben-Yisrael, Dept. of History, the Hebrew University of Jerusalem; Professor Jakob Goldberg, Dept. of History, the Hebrew University of Jerusalem; Prof. Dan Horowitz, L. Davis Institute for International Relations, Hebrew University, Jerusalem; Mr. Moshe Kol, former government minister; Mr. Gideon Rafael, former Ambassador to the United Nations.

I greatly benefited from their incisive suggestions, remarks and kind advice.

The original Hebrew version of this book was published at the beginning of 1986 by Maarachot/MOD, Tel-Aviv. I am indebted to the MOD Publishing House and its Director-General, Mr. S. Seri, who made the publication of this book in its English version possible.

I wish to extend my thanks to the translator, Mr. N. Greenwood, who did his share with great skill and understanding.

I express my gratitude to Mr. William D. Eastman, Director of State University of New York Press, to Ms. Diane Ganeles, Production Editor, and to Mr. Joseph Blackman, the literary editor, for their indispensable and faithful help in editing and publishing this work.

Last but not least, my deepest thanks to my dear wife Miriam, who gave me the inspiration to start the work and the patience to complete it.

***

I am also grateful to the various publishers/copyright owners, who have kindly permitted me to incorporate in the book quotations from the following books and articles:

ACKNOWLEDGEMENTS

Foreign Relations of the United States: The Paris Conference, 1919; The Conferences of Cairo and Teheran, 1943; The Conferences of Malta and Yalta, 1945; and The Conference of Berlin (Potsdam), 1945, as well as other official publications of the U.S. State Department by permission of the United States Department of State.

Documents on Polish-Soviet Relations—by permission of the Polish Institute and Sikorski Museum, London.

Documents on the British Foreign Policy 1919–1939—by permission of Her Majesty's Stationery Office.

Soviet Documents on Foreign Policy (ed. by Jane Degras)—by permission of Oxford University Press.

E. Beneš: *Memoirs*—by permission of Allen & Unwin Hyman, Ltd.

J. Bishop: *FDR's Last Year*—by permission of William Morrow & Co.

J. W. Bruegel: *Czechoslovakia before Munich*—by permission of Cambridge University Press

E. H. Carr: *The Bolshevik Revolution*—by permission of Weidenfeld & Nicolson, London.

Winston S. Churchill: *The Second World War*—by permission of Cassell, London.

J. Ciechanowski: *Defeat in Victory*—by permission of Doubleday, division of Bantam, Doubleday, Dell Publ. Inc.,

R. Conquest: *The Great Terror*—by permission of Curtis Brown.

A. Eden: *Full Circle—The Reckoning*—Copyright The Times, Publ. Company, reprinted by permission of Houghton Mifflin Co.

A. B. Fox: *The Power of Small States*—by permission of Chicago University Press.

S. Haffner: *The Meaning of Hitler*—by permission of Curtis Brown, London.

A. Hitler: *Mein Kampf*—by permission of Houghton, Mifflin Company.

S. Hoffman: *Duties beyond Borders*—by permission of Syracuse University Press.

M. Jakobson: *The Diplomacy of the Winter War*—by permission of the author.

M. Jakobson: *Substance and Appearance: Finland*—by permission of Foreign Affairs.

L. B. Johnson: *The Vantage Point*—by permission of Henry Holt and Company, Inc.

J. Karski: *The Story of a Secret State*—by permission of Houghton Mifflin Company.

Acknowledgements

G. F. Kennan: *Russia and the West under Lenin and Stalin*—by permission of Little, Brown and Company.

N. Khrushchev: *Khrushchev Remembers*—by permission of Little, Brown and Company.

H. Lauterpacht: *International Law*—by permission of Cambridge University Press.

V. S. Mamatey: *The United States and East-Central Europe, 1914–1918*—by permission of Princeton University Press.

R. Medvedev: *Let History Judge*—by permission of Alfred Knopf Inc.

S. Mikołajczyk: *The Pattern of Soviet Domination*—by permission of Macdonald Publishers, London.

H. Morgenthau: *Politics Among Nations*—by permission of Alfred Knopf, Inc.

J. Nevakivi: *The Appeal That Was Never Made, 1978*—by permission of C. Hunt & Co., London.

O. Odlozilik: *Edward Beneš on Munich Days*—by permission of East European Quarterly, University of Colorado.

L. Oppenheim (ed. H. Lauterpacht): *International Law*—by permission of Longman Ltd., UK.

H. Ripka: *Munich and After*—by permission of Victor Gollancz, Ltd. (all attempts made by the publisher to trace the heirs of the late author and the copyright holder were unsuccessful).

T. C. Schelling: *The Strategy of Conflict*—by permission of Harvard University Press.

W. C. Shirer: *The Rise and Fall of the Third Reich*—by permission of Secker and Warburg (covering the British Commonwealth, excluding Canada only), and by Simon and Schuster (covering USA and Canada).

J. Talmon: *The Myth of the Nation and the Vision of Revolution*—by permission of Secker and Warburg (covering the British Commonwealth, excluding Canada only) and by the University of California Press.

V. Tanner: *The Winter War*—by permission of Stanford University Press.

L. Thompson: *The Greatest Treason*—by permission of William Morrow and Company.

M. Truman: *Harry S. Truman*—by permission of William Morrow & Company.

B. Tuchman: *Practising History*—by permission of Random House and Alfred Knopf, Inc.

A. Ulam: *Expansion and Coexistence*—by permission of Henry Holt and Company.

D. Vital: *The Survival of Small States, 1971*—by permission of Oxford University Press.

J. Wheeler-Bennett: *Munich—Prologue to Tragedy*—by permission of Lady Ruth Wheeler-Bennett.

E. Wiskeman: *Czechs and Germans, 1938*—by permission of Oxford University Press.

D. Yergin: *Shattered Peace, 1977*—by permission of Houghton Mifflin Company.

I wish to thank the following institutions for their kind permission to reproduce illustrations: The Yad Vashem Archives; the Jerusalem Post Archives; the Embassy of Finland, Tel-Aviv; the Polish Institute and Sikorski Museum, London; Maarachot/ MOD Publishing House, Tel-Aviv.

Introduction

This book, presented to the English-speaking reader, is a revised edition of a book originally published in Hebrew in early 1986, in Israel, under the name *Umoth Bamivhan (Nations Under Trial)*. The publisher was Maarachot, MOD Publishing House, Tel Aviv.

The book describes the behavior of three nations—Czechoslovakia, Poland, and Finland—which, at frequent intervals, especially in the dramatic days of World War II, found their fate as small nations under trial. Although the circumstances and reactions of each of these nations were different, they shared this characteristic and various elements related to it.

The crises that beset them during that period; their confrontation with enemies of superior strength; the disappointment caused by lack of support from faraway friends; the wars into which they were thrust—these are the central themes of this book. Although its essence and content identify it as a history book, it also addresses itself to the fundamental, complicated, and difficult circumstances of small nations as such, and contends with several questions deriving from these circumstances:

What can a small nation do to further the cause of its own survival when, by historical fate and geographic location, it finds itself up against a terrifying neighbor?

What is the most effective way to prevent confrontation? Putting the stress on a policy of accommodation and co-existence with its neighbor, or fostering the nation's internal prowess—in the broadest sense of this term—on all of its components?

Should a small nation aspire to restore its historical borders, or is ethnic homogeneity a preferable objective?

To what extend should it rely on its own military strength, and what role does diplomacy play in its struggle for peace and sovereign existence?

Can it prevent bloodshed and sacrifice and, at one and the same time, survive as an independent national entity?

To what extent can a small nation rely on the commitment of a friendly power, and what should it do to amplify this commitment and partnership?

***

If we are to deal with small nations, how shall we define them? Is it a matter of so many people or square miles?

Today, of the United Nations' 157 member states, 35 are "small nations" by any measure, inasmuch as their population falls below one million (including some with only several tens of thousands). But how shall we classify other countries? True, it is widely accepted that Finland and Czechoslovakia are "small nations." In fact, however, some of this is an "optical illusion" or a perceived image. After all, Finland is the fourth-largest country in Europe, while prewar Czechoslovakia had the considerable population of 14,000,000. By contrast, many will raise their brows at the inclusion of Poland in the concept under discussion. After all, prewar Poland had a population of no less than 30,000,000, and its own leaders and citizens considered it a large, strong country, capable of contending successfully with its mighty neighbors. But within a month—a most tragic month for Poland and the world—its fortunes suffered such a reversal that it became a defeated, shattered "small nation."

The concept "small nation" therefore transcends geography and demographics. Those are parts of it, as are other objective factors, such as GNP, economic and military dependence on other nations, etc. In the main and above all, however, the concept is relative. It is the outcome of a nation's geo-strategic location, a given political constellation, and the overall—not only military—balance of forces between the "small" nation and its mighty neighbor or neighbors.

It is therefore more a matter of a situation than of a formulation.

If so, we have good reason to consider Czechoslovakia, overrun by Germany; Poland, occupied by Germany and the Soviet Union; and Finland, cast into a showdown with the Soviet Union, as small nations.

***

Volumes have been written about the period reviewed here, and they shed light on the events from various angles. I allow myself to add this book to them, under the assumption that my vantage point is unique in some way.

As the reader will easily discover, I belong to a nation which is admittedly large in terms of history, problems, and threats to its security and existence, but small by any other conventional measure—territory, population, water, natural resources, etc. In view of this background, it is natural that I have taken an interest in the fate of Czechoslovakia, Finland, and Poland. This is so although my country is far different from them—in time, conditions, ways of meeting danger, results, and the extent of reliability and solidity of relations with a friendly power.

Motivated by this interest of mine, I examined a large number and wide variety of sources and committed my findings to writing. I remain faithful to factual truth throughout. Nevertheless, I assume and even hope that my particular point of view adds a dimension of experience and understanding—the experience of a nation contending with threats to its existence, and understanding of the pressures and constraints it must often face.

Thereby, I believe, I will have made my modest contribution to the great collection of historiography on the World War II period.

Yohanan Cohen

PART ONE
***
Czechoslovakia 1938–1939

Chapter One

An Obstacle on the Road to Lebensraum

"What's Munich?"

Ask people in their twenties or thirties what the name "Munich" means to them, what feelings it evokes. A newspaper reader will certainly reply with scraps of information. A lover of world travel will praise the handsome capital of Bavaria. Very few, maybe one in a thousand, of the young generation will link this name with a historical-political concept. Only a few will identify it as a symbol of surrender to aggression, an emblem of appeasement and betrayal.

The events occurred fifty years ago—quite an interval for those born in the 1960s and 1970s, although very recent in the course of human annals. Perhaps it would thus still be appropriate and useful to retrieve forgotten events which, however remote in time and space, are of interest to our generation as well.

"A Malignant Thorn in Germany's Side"

One of the stumbling blocks in Hitler's path to securing lebensraum ("living space") in Eastern Europe for the German race was the Republic of Czechoslovakia.

Its geographic status, democratic government, well-developed industry, military strength, alliances with both France and the Soviet Union—all these, from Hitler's point of view, made Czechoslovakia the caretaker of one of the gates to Eastern Europe. In addition to these factors, he had developed an apparent aversion to his little neighbor. He had often expressed himself to his confidants that he "could not tolerate an inimical Czech thorn in the German flesh."[1]

As early as November 5, 1937, Hitler had made up his mind. In a meeting with his generals he announced resolutely that the aim of German policy was to secure lebensraum and security for the German race, and that Germany's entire future hung in the balance. Hitler's actions in the matter of Czechoslovakia were pursuant to and further development of the strategy and tactics he had invoked in his previous operations—invading the Rhineland on March 7, 1936 (thus abrogating the Locarno Pact) and annexing Austria on March 11, 1938.

A three-stage method was adopted for Czechoslovakia: An outcry over the "injustice" that had ostensibly been done to ethnic Germans and the need to set it right, a threat to use "desperate measures" if this imperative were not addressed, and a solemn assurance that this was the "last demand."

The first step, then, was a series of anguished expressions of profound "moral shock" in view of the "repression" of the German minority in Czechoslovakia.

The Birth of Czechoslovakia—Historical Background

One of the major results of World War I was the crumbling of the Russian, German, Austro-Hungarian, and Ottoman Empires. On their ruins, flying the banner of "the right to self-determination," new national states came into being. The ideological and political foundations for this development were established by President Wilson and by Lenin.

In a speech on May 27, 1916, Wilson asserted that the United States would act to bring about a peace based on three principles. The first of these, he said, was

> . . . that every people has a right to choose the sovereignty under which they shall live. Second, that the small states of the world have a right to enjoy the same respect for their sovereignty and for their territorial integrity that the great and powerful nations expect and insist upon. And third, that the world has a right to be free from any disturbance of its peace that has its origin in aggression.

On November 15, 1917, the Soviet Government issued the following order confirming:

> The rights of the Peoples of Russia to self determination . . . even to the point of separating and forming independent states.

Less than two months later, in January 1918, Wilson delivered the famous address subsequently known as "the Fourteen Points" before a joint session of both houses of Congress. While he did not say so in so many words, Wilson implicitly repeated his demand for self-determination:

> An evident principle runs through the whole program I have outlined. It is the principle of justice to all peoples and nationalities and their right to live on equal terms of liberty and safety with one another, whether they be strong or weak.

The peoples of Eastern Europe and their leaders drew brave encouragement from these declarations, and went to considerable lengths in the war's last stages to become active partners and fighters in bringing down the old empires, liberating their peoples, and establishing a "new order" in Europe.

One of the most active entities in this struggle was undoubtedly the Paris-based Czechoslovakian National Council. Led by Thomas G. Masaryk, a professor of philosophy at the University of Prague and a man of uncommon personality and political aptitude, he earned the recognition and admiration of both the Czechs and the Slovaks, as well as great prestige among the leaders of other nations. His right-hand man was Eduard Beneš, a professor of sociology and economics endowed with rare diplomatic skills. Alongside them was Milan Stefánik, representing the Slovaks. When the Czar and his regime fell, Masaryk was given the opportunity to go into Russia and organize a military force of 40,000 Czechs and Slovaks who had been taken POW by the Czar's army. From there, via Japan, he headed for the United States, where he won Wilson's recognition and support. A conference he chaired in Pittsburgh on May 20, 1918, resolved to establish a state shared by the Czechs and the Slovaks, with autonomy assured for the Slovakian area.

On October 18, 1918, Masaryk, Beneš, and Stefánik declared Czechoslovakia an independent state and announced the establishment of its government. The Allies recognized this move—a great political victory, but still a far cry from consolidating and stabilizing the state.

Borders and Population

Delimiting the borders of Czechoslovakia and the other new states, and basing them on the principle of ethnic affiliation, were not the easiest things to do. The Czechoslovak leadership struggled tenaciously to extract what it wanted from the new heirs of the vanquished empires—Germany, Austria, Hungary—and from its new neighbor, Poland. Furthermore, the principle of self-determination occasionally clashed with other considerations no less weighty.

For reasons of topography and defense, the mountainous area in the north and west had to be left within Czechoslovakia, because it was a natural barrier between it and Germany. No less important in the same way was the historical consideration—the desire to restore the territorial continuity of the Old Bohemian Kingdom, the "Lands of the Crown of St. Wenceslas." However, as stated, this intention clashed with the population's ethnic composition, because some 3 million Germans had been dwelling in Bohemia and Moravia for hundreds of years. The outcome of a historical development, different national populations were living alongside one another, in proximity but apart, in relations that verged at times on hostility. This phenomenon stood in stark contradiction to the intent of establishing a national or bi-national state called Czechoslovakia.

The Czechoslovak leadership treated the demographic consideration as subordinate to the historical and defense-topographic one. It believed it could overcome the demographic menace by means of an enlightened democratic regime that would assure equality of rights and obligations for all citizens, and lay a solid foundation for joint coexistence. This leadership believed it had a mission to right a historic injustice, incorporating within the borders of the new Czechoslovak state all the territories which once "had formed part of the historical kingdom of Bohemia."

This perception was reinforced and confirmed in the international arena. Third-party states were interested in preventing Germany's military recovery, and the Allies were favorably impressed by the security and historical reasoning. The principle of the Czechoslovak national revival won full recognition in the Treaties of Versailles, St. Germain, Trianon, and Neuilly, while the committee for Czechoslovakian affairs at the peace conference ruled unequivocally in 1919 that:

> Bohemia forms a natural region, clearly defined by its fringe of mountains. The mere fact that a German population has established itself in the outlying districts at a relatively recent date did not appear to the committee a sufficient reason for depriving Bohemia of its natural frontiers. . . . The chain of mountains which surrounds Bohemia constitutes a line of defense for the country. To take away this line of mountains would be to place Bohemia at the mercy of Germany.[2]

As a result of these developments, a Czechoslovakia of 87,299 square miles (140,493 square kilometers) came into being, comprising three major provinces: Bohemia, Moravia, and Slovakia. According to results of a census taken in February 1921, the country had 13,374,364 residents, including

An Obstacle on the Road

more than 3 million Germans, nearly all concentrated in the Su Bohemia and Moravia), bordering Germany and Austria, and million Hungarians, Ukrainians, and other minority groups.[3]

This demographic makeup was of no concern at first, as stated, to the heads of state. As the years passed, it became clear that they should have been worried.

Czechoslovakia and the German Minority

Czechoslovakia's democratic regime, one of the most progressive in Europe, guaranteed full equality of rights to all national groups. There may, of course, have been exceptional instances, and life among the Republic's constituent national groups may not always have been idyllic. However, in the words of Elizabeth Wiskesman, a British researcher of that period:

> The Czechs had observed their obligations to the German minority seriously enough to allow its members liberty to arm world opinion against them—no other minority in inter-war Europe had such freedom.[4]

The ascent of German Nazism infused the Sudeten-German SDP party, chaired by Konrad Henlein, with new momentum. This party was in fact the Nazis' fifth column in Czechoslovakia. At first it camouflaged its irredentist intentions in a stream of legalistic-sounding and seemingly moderate demands. However, Henlein's real method, as he described it himself, was to "always demand so much that we can never be satisfied."[5] (In this, he was faithfully carrying out instructions from Berlin).

The banner waved by Henlein and his followers—actively serving Hitler and Goebbels, of course—was the "right to self-determination." How could it be, Hitler howled in one of his staged eruptions of rage and lunacy, that millions of German ethnics, "those tormented creatures,"[6] could come under the rule of inferior races and thus be denied the elementary right to national self-determination?

To express the magnitude of the injustice, the Nazi propaganda machine started to churn out concocted "atrocity" stories with unprecedented speed and intensity. Hair-raising accounts of brutal Czech repression and "abominations" against the poor Germans began to influence all of Europe.[7]

When Henlein's followers staged an illegal demonstration in the city of Teplice-Sanov in October 1937, and one of its leaders was arrested for a few hours, the Sudeten-German press raised a hue and cry about "terrifying police brutality." The German newspapers added a dash of their own to the wave of incitement. The following is an example of rapportage in *Völkischer Beobachter* on October 19, 1937:

> At the cradle of the Czech State lies and hatred, murder and terror stood as sponsors. . . . In Siberia during the war Czech deserters led by a crook began to murder and plunder unarmed German prisoners and a defenceless population. When these gangsters, honoured as heroes to-day, were brought back to their home . . . they continued their blood-thirsty handiwork. . . . In Prague they had better observe that the days of German impotence are over.[8]

German propaganda never failed to exploit or inflate to the magnitude of atrocity the slightest of incidents, friction, or any squabble in order to present the Czechs as a nation of oppressors and murderers. Even Nevile Henderson, Great Britain's ambassador to Berlin and a conspicuous proponent of the "appeasement policy," acknowledged in his memoirs:

> There was a constant influx of German press telegrams about incidents in the Sudeten lands. One, I remember, reported that forty Germans had been killed in a clash somewhere with Czech gendarmes. A British observer . . . who was immediately sent to verify the facts of the case, subsequently ascertained that there had, in fact, been one death.[9]

The Right to Self-Determination

The conclusion begging to be drawn from all these "facts," was, of course, unequivocal: three million ethnic Germans could hardly be denied the right of all peoples—self-determination.

No, the Germans had no territorial demands, Hitler proclaimed. "The period of surprises is over. Peace is now our highest aim."[10] However, the injustice had to be set right; the Sudeten Germans had to be given back their legitimate national right to self-determination.

This propaganda—applied to accepted principles in order to exploit them for its own devices, representing a small democratic nation as the epitome of tyranny and repression, and portraying nationalists as deprived of rights—landed on fertile soil.

Europe of the 1930s was psychologically ready to acquiesce to the creeping advancement of Nazism and Fascism, and to seize upon an illusion that peace could thereby be saved. Shortly before Hitler took over the Rhineland in 1936, he was visited by Arnold Toynbee, who purported to understand the processes of world history. British Prime Minister Stanley Baldwin's secretary noted in his memoirs that Toynbee returned from his visit to Germany after having interviewed Hitler for an hour and 45 minutes, "convinced of Hitler's sincerity in desiring peace in Europe and close friendship with England."[11]

Unwillingness to stop the wave of aggression and unpreparedness for war against Hitler—when this still entailed little risk—laid the foundation for "a whole period of deliberate 'appeasement' by the Western Powers at the expense of their friends at the very moment that Hitler was preparing for war against them and planning the destruction of his weaker neighbours one by one."[12]

As Nazi propaganda flooded Europe, public opinion and its shapers—intellectuals, authors, artists, parliamentarians and journalists, economists and politicians—first began to rub their eyes in puzzlement and disbelief. As time passed and the propaganda effort gained strength, and as the proof ("It was in the newspaper!") appeared more frequently, skepticism began to yield to other reactions. First came the "balanced approach"—by which "both sides are right and the truth must lie in the middle." Then, however, even these sentiments gave way to reservations about the behavior of "repressive" Czechoslovakia. Whenever it was reported that a Czech had accidentally jostled a German off a sidewalk, Nazi supporters in England and France raised a cacaphony of protest.[13]

The German demand for "the right to Sudeten self-determination" was especially well-received. After all, what could sound better to all fair-minded Europeans than this just demand, which, since World War I, had been considered a sort of Magna Carta of the oppressed peoples,[14] on whose basis Lenin and Wilson competed for world moral leadership?[15]

However, it is worth mentioning that even during the glory days of "self-determination"—the period of the Wilson euphoria—this slogan was penetratingly criticized by many, including American Secretary of State Lansing. His argument was that it was politically unfeasible, misled the national minorities, and was liable to generate unending instability and hostilities:

> When the President talks of "self-determination" what unit has he in mind? Does he mean a race, a territorial area or a community? Without a definite unit which is practical, an application of this principle is dangerous to peace and stability. . . . The phrase is simply loaded with dynamite. It will raise hopes which can never be realized. It will, I fear, cost thousands of lives. In the end it is bound to be discredited, to be called the dream of an idealist who failed to realize the danger until too late, to check those who attempt to put the principle in force. What a calamity that the phrase was ever uttered! What misery it will cause![16]

The controversy reflected the nearly permanent gap between a realistic, cold perception based on (and, to a great extent, trying to perpetuate) existing reality as well as diplomatic experience, and an overview which, in addition to pragmatic political considerations, also takes account of ideological-moral ones. As we know, it was Wilson's idealistic conception, which strove to remake reality, that won the battle. It is nevertheless worth mentioning that the triumph of "the right to self-determination" did not nullify Lansing's arguments and fears, but at the very most swept them under the rug. The stinging criticism he expressed after his resignation stressed the internal contradictions and intrinsic dangers of the "self-determination" slogan, as it was presented and as attempts to realize it were made.

His weighty apprehensions came to pass about twenty years later, on a scale that exceeded his bleakest dreams.

In the meantime, however, self-determination had won the hour. Thomas Masaryk's great achievement was the recognition he obtained from Wilson for the establishment of independent Czechoslovakia on the basis of this principle. Now, the naïve asked, how dared the Czechs deny the oppressed Germans this self-same right?

These innocent questions of "principle," however, were not necessarily rooted in virgin conceptual soil. They were produced in a milieu saturated with fear of a militarily ascendent Germany and willingness to accede to its demands. Many good Europeans fell for the idea that if the Nazi beast were appeased and stroked, it would calm down and behave itself.

The appeasement-supporters did not take the trouble to look past the demands of Konrad Henlein and his activists. They did not want to understand that Hitler wanted neither the attainment of self-determination for the Sudeten Germans, nor even territorial adjustments, but the destruction of Czechoslovakia—and this, too, only as a first step toward a takeover of all Europe.

Myopically, they failed to understand that behind the Germans' "innocent" and "legitimate" demand for Sudeten self-determination lurked Hitler's unequivocal intent "[to wipe] Czechoslovakia off the map"[17] (as he told his generals on May 28, 1938.)

Furthermore, the shapers of the appeasement policy considered the fulfillment of this demand a political measure that would promote understanding and peace. British Ambassador Nevile Henderson wrote:

> Some objective sympathy on the part of Britain for Germany's comprehensible and not even unworthy aspirations for unity might, moreover, have served the useful purpose of showing the Germans that it was not Britain's sole policy to stand in their way everywhere, regardless of whether their aims were legitimate or not.[18]

Chapter Two

In the Crucible of Appeasement

The Origins and Perpetrators of Appeasement

Perhaps Hitler's threat could have been dealt with in good time by military means. The Czechoslovak Army comprised more than thirty-five divisions and was well-equipped and trained. Much of its equipment, including light arms, artillery, motor vehicles, and aircraft, was locally manufactured. The western border zone was well-fortified.

As early as March, 1936, when Hitler marched into the Rhineland, Czechoslovakia and, by all indications, Poland as well, would have been ready to go to war if France, their ally, were to participate in such action. The balance of forces between Germany and these allies assured the latter a decisive victory at the time. However, France and, with her, England, were not willing to pursue a military solution. This line of thinking was rooted in the pacifistic tendencies that had flooded Western Europe after the horrors of the First World War. "Combat fatigue," the wish to view WWI as "the war to end all wars," the aspiration of individuals to pursue a workaday life, enjoying all its beauty and wealth, spawned deeply-rooted popular opposition to any military trend—even if purely defensive—in the European democracies, especially those considered "victorious" or "affluent." Even when Fascism and Nazism surfaced, spread, and engulfed Italy, Germany, and Spain, entered into alliance with Japan, and chalked up conquests in Europe, Africa, and Asia, pacifist sentiment continued. It received conceptual, organizational, political, and financial encouragement from both the Right and the Left.

Despite the growth of Nazi power and the menace this presented, the Soviet Union did not perceive itself as having any interest in strengthening the two capitalistic powers, France and England.[1] Stalin assumed that they were strong enough to engage Hitler in a protracted war, if and when it broke out, and—erroneously—that this war would emasculate both the democratic and the Nazi-Fascist versions of capitalism. Guided by this perception, the Comintern and the Communist parties in the Western countries waged an extensive campaign against the military build-up of those countries. The Seventh Congress of the Comintern, held in Moscow in July–August 1935, vociferously denounced Nazism and Fascism but also saw fit to resolve that the Communist parties of all capitalist countries should fight against the military expenditures and steps toward militarization—especially with respect to youth—taken by capitalist governments.[2]

On this basis the French Communists waged an energetic campaign against rebuilding the French Army and augmenting the military budget. When Germany reinstated the draft, it became clear that France, a country of smaller population, could maintain the balance of forces only by lengthening its conscript soldiers' tour of duty. In view of this prospect, French Communist leader Maurice Thorez declared it an imperative to continue to fight in the name of the French working class against the enslavement of the people, and against a return to the two-year term of military duty.[3]

The one and only Communist member of the British Parliament proclaimed his belief that the war spirit that had remained in Germany could never be countered by a buildup of armaments; therefore, "We say, not a penny for armaments."[4]

The Communists' influence in this field—weakening military preparedness and fomenting popular resistance to anything that smelled of "militarism"—exceeded their actual electoral weight.[5]

However, "patriotic" circles and the reactionary Right, too, steered clear of confrontation with Nazism. They were especially influential in France, where deeply-rooted opposition to Bolshevism, resistance to socialist ideas, and anti-Semitic thoughts were openly and conspicuously expressed during the short life of Prime Minister Leon Blum's "Popular Front." "Better Hitler than Blum" was the slogan that united the successors of the anti-Dreyfusard tradition, and it was only quite natural to move from this to "Better Hitler than Stalin." France floundered in a tidal wave of Nazi propaganda, and the forces of reaction came around to the view that a German defeat in a future war was no less dangerous than the defeat of France herself. The following quotation shows how far the distorted logic of some had travelled:

> Not only was defeat and devastation of France possible, but a German defeat would mean the crumbling of the authoritative systems which constitute the main rampart to the communist revolution, and perhaps the immediate Bolshevization of Europe. In other words, a French victory would really have been a defeat for France.[6]

Paris' bookstores and newsstands sagged under the weight of Nazi literature and propaganda. Vitriol in the right-wing press against Georges

Mandel and Jean Zay, two Jewish members of the Cabinet, grew more frequent (both were murdered in 1944 by Vichy Government police). Any call to prepare for war against Nazi Germany was smothered in a hoarse cacophony and presented as Bolshevik-Jewish propaganda.

> The history of France between 1919 and 1939 (Sebastian Haffner wrote), the history of a victory obtained in a harsh and bitter struggle and thereafter utterly lost, and a gradual decline from very proud self-confidence to nearly total self-obliteration, is the story of a tragedy.[7]

Thus France was primed for its surrender. On April 9, 1938, a new Government took office under Edouard Daladiėr. Its Foreign Minister was George Bonnet, one of the architects of the political position others labelled "appeasement." Beneš described him as follows:

> George Bonnet was known as ever ready for compromise. To him, any means was good enough provided it helped him to get what he wanted. He was, in the worst sense of the word, a typical politician. . . . Afraid of the social and revolutionary consequences of war in France, Bonnet was a priori against any decided or war-like resistance to Hitler's policy of expansion.[8]

Bonnet's personality and politics did much to strengthen the trend of appeasement in the West. The kinds of thinking mentioned thus far, caused the West to accede to and to appease the rising power of Nazism. The trend provoked cuts in military budgets, standstill in the production of war materiel, and in the main, unwillingness of governments to use military force even when the risk was still slight and the advantage theirs. In hindsight, of course, this thinking brought the world no closer to Isaiah's vision of the end of days, when "nation would not lift up sword against nation." On the contrary: it seems merely to have whetted the despot's appetite. Only a daring few, such as Churchill, saw what was coming and sounded the alarm[9]—but these were voices in the wilderness at first.

"Sacred" Guarantees

The Government and people of Czechoslovakia failed to heed the ominous omens. They still innocently and firmly believed that once the truth became known, once their information efforts (which were accused of "blunders" and "poor professional quality") improved, once the Nazi atrocity propaganda was refuted and the facts brought to light—the ship of state would sail into calm waters.

The Czechoslovak Government also relied on the strength of its democratic regime, the country's industrial and military might, the League of Nations, and—last but not least—the guarantees of its allies.

For the peoples in little states whose independence had been restored, the establishment of the League of Nations instilled trust in the new international order and the validity of the principle of collective security, which would lead to peace and serve as the normative basis of international relations.

The Government of Czechoslovakia was one of the most loyal and consistent proponents of this trend. It also believed in the durability of signed treaties and agreements. Nor was it exceptional in this sense. Agreements and alliances among European states so proliferated during the 1920s as to represent a fad, a "pactomania."[10]

Czechoslovakia's political leadership was aware of the new state's weakness—surrounded on almost all sides by neighbors who bode it ill will (Germany, Austria, Poland, Hungary)—and sought a strong crutch to lean on. In 1924 and 1925, Czechoslovakia concluded mutual defense agreements (Locarno) with France against German attack. Her 1935 accord with the Soviet Union required the latter to rush to Czechoslovakia's aid upon effectuation of the France-Czechoslovakia accord. Czechoslovakia secured its southeastern flank by means of the "Little Alliance" embracing itself, France, Romania, and Yugoslavia. Its trust in the strength of these alliances, its fealty to the League of Nations and its Charter, and its adherence to the "peace-is-indivisible" principle were the foundations of its policy.[11]

However, the collective security that the League of Nations purported to represent, lead, and even impose if necessary (under Article 16 of its Charter) was soon fated to become a dead letter.

International conflicts became more frequent. Lights went on in war rooms around the world. Surging Fascism, Nazism, and Bolshevism threatened the entire established order. Slowly but surely, *realpolitik* took over the world of political thought. The totalitarian regimes cultivated an ideology of "might is right," and applied it in both domestic and foreign policy.

As the situation worsened, the League of Nations stood paralyzed and helpless. It neither undertook enforcement nor imposed real sanctions when Japan aggressed against China in 1931 and 1937, when Paraguay attacked Bolivia in 1934, when Italy assaulted Abyssinia in 1935, nor when Germany invaded the Rhineland in 1936 and annexed Austria in 1938.

If it was widely believed in the League's early years that collective security would deter aggressors and that states would unite to help one another and preserve the status quo, it became clear within several years that this idealistic conception was detached from international reality.

This reality demonstrated—as noted by Professor H. Morgenthau—that "Collective security cannot be made to work in the contemporary world as it must work according to its ideal assumptions."[12]

Nevertheless, it was still possible, the Czechoslovak Government believed, to rely on one's allies. Indeed, in March 1938, two important pronouncements were uttered on this topic:

British Prime Minister Neville Chamberlain, addressing Parliament, spelled out his perceptions with respect to Britain's commitments to its ally. Although most of his remarks seemed designed to appease, he did see fit to add a more unequivocal assertion:

> Our armaments may be used in bringing help to a victim of aggression. . . . That case might, for example, include Czechoslovakia.[13]

Then French Foreign Minister Paul-Boncour informed his parliament that his Government meant to honor its commitment to its Czechoslovak ally "instantly and effectively."[14] His successor, Bonnet, repeated this proclamation a month later, and Prime Minister Daladiėr reaffirmed that French guarantees were "sacred" and inviolable.[15]

Even then, the Germans continued to lull Europe. Hitler proclaimed that Germany had no territorial claims to press against Czechoslovakia, while Henlein, in May 1938, set out on an "informational" mission to London. He succeeded in depicting himself as "eager to give the impression of moderation driven desperate by frustration and oppression, yet ever ready to listen to reason."[16] He also convinced his audiences that he could not even conceive of harming Czechoslovakia's territorial integrity, since he had sworn allegiance to its flag as an officer (in fact, he had never served in the Czech Army).[17] To defuse the gathering tension, the Czechoslovak Government decided to open negotiations with Henlein and display willingness to make far-reaching concessions. The contacts began in May, but led nowhere. This, of course, was a consequence of the Sudeten Nazis' tactic: "Always demand so much that we can never be satisfied." Meanwhile, on May 19, 1938, both the Czechoslovak Government and the British intelligence services were informed of suspicious movements by four mechanized Wehrmacht divisions toward the Czech border.

Although the fact of the matter was not altogether clear, the Czechoslovak Government preferred not to overrely on its optimistic assumptions. To avert all risk, it declared and efficiently implemented a partial mobilization. Within 24 hours, 170,000 reservists reported for duty,[18] and the German military movements stopped. Hitler, unable to stomach the "humiliation," ordered his envoy in Prague to make sharp representations about the mobilization to Czech Chief-of-Staff Krejči. The latter rejected the protestation and claimed that he had proof of the concentration of eight to ten German divisions in Saxony.[19] Receiving the envoy's report, Hitler exploded. The fact that members of this "inferior race" dared offend his prestige, put up a resolute stance, and demonstrate willingness to defend themselves, kindled his rage.

On May 28, 1938, he resolved once and for all that the Czechoslovakia problem had to be "solved" by year's end, even at the price of a general European war. Two days later, on May 30, 1938, the Wehrmacht commanders were given the Case Green (Fall Grün) order. During those 48 hours, the goal changed significantly. Instead of general talk of "wiping Czechoslovakia off the map," the matter was now stated brutally and directly: "It is my unalterable decision to smash (*zerschlagen*) Czechoslovakia by military action in the near future."[20] The order also set the date: October 1, 1938.

Negotiations with Henlein

Hitler was not the only one who fumed at Czechoslovakia for calling up its reserves. The Western appeasement-supporters considered this mobilization, as Neville Chamberlain said, a gesture of arrogant provocation. Henderson, the British ambassador in Prague, added his own measure of appeasement by commenting that:

> The defiant gesture of the Czechs in mobilizing some 170,000 troops, and then proclaiming to the world that it was their action which had turned Hitler from his purpose, was equally regrettable.[21]

H. M. Government dreaded the possibility of an escalation into war. Such a development would require France to come to Czechoslovakia's aid, and this, in turn, would drag Britain into the conflict on France's side. Both Paris and London now believed there was only one way to prevent such a prospect: maximum concessions by Czechoslovakia to the Sudeten Germans.[22] It was widely assumed that negotiations leading to autonomy would satisfy Henlein and Hitler alike. In order to apply "friendly persuasion" to the Prague Government, and to bring the sides to the negotiating table, H. M. Government offered its Czechoslovak counterpart its "good offices" in July 1938, in the form of Lord Runciman. Runciman reached Prague in early August—with the blessings of Paris—and began to mediate as if the Czechoslovak Government and Henlein and his comrades were equals in status and rights. Like the direct negotiations of May that led nowhere, Henlein's people again obstructed any progress toward agreement.

Lord Runciman (left) received by President Beneš

President Beneš intervened in the talks on September 4. In a daring diplomatic gamble, he presented the Sudeten Germans' representatives with a white piece of paper and called their bluff: "Please write down all of your demands for the German minority. I promise you in advance that I shall fulfill them immediately."

Henlein's henchmen were stunned. Noticing their astonishment, Beneš took up the paper, reached for his pen, and said: "Very well. If you won't write, I will. Spell out your demands."

Thus, apart from a paragraph devoted to Czechoslovakia's foreign policy, Beneš recorded all the Sudetens' demands in his own hand, including full rights to live in accordance with "the Nazi worldview," which would establish for one section of the population a totalitarian system within a democratic Czechoslovak republic.[23]

Beneš was fully aware that even his consent and signature would not pacify the Germans. All he meant to accomplish with his diplomatic gamble was to prove to the British and the French that concessions and appeasement had exhausted their utility, and that his Western allies had to be ready to meet their commitments. As he expected, the Germans rejected his acquiescence and broke off the talks. Henlein's orders from Ribbentrop were to reject all compromise and conclude no agreement. Hitler was out to destroy Czechoslovakia, not to reach arrangements with her.[24]

Hitler's diatribe in the Nuremberg Party Rally on September 12 served as a further example of his demagogic talent. One of his confidantes says that it had been his practice to play the role of an enraged national leader so as to frighten other nations' leaders and convince them that he would not shrink from war.[25] This is precisely the impact his speech made. It also sparked demonstrations, violence, and manifestations of armed insurrection throughout Czechoslovakia, organized by Henlein's stooges.

The Republic's forces effectively put down the Nazi terror, and Henlein fled to Germany with several thousand of his men. Nazi propaganda blew the matter out of all proportion, screaming of "a quarter of a million miserable refugees," and describing in terrifying color the abominations carried out during the repression. Many of these "refugees" were mobilized in Germany into the "Frei Korps" (Free Corps) and slipped back into Czechoslovakia for terror and sabotage.

Even with his diplomatic ruse, Beneš could not persuade Chamberlain and Daladièr that he was right and that the Germans were up to no good. Hitler's speech actually strengthened their commitment to the appeasement policy, while the Czechoslovak Government's repression of Nazi terror frightened them all the more.

"How to Save Czechoslovakia from Herself"

It was already clear to the leaders of the two powers that the Czechoslovak Government was being "intransigent" and inflexible, and that the "despair" and "frustration" forced upon the Sudeten Germans, so long as they were denied the right to self-determination, would ultimately ignite Herr Hitler's terrible temper.

Chamberlain and Daladièr always had the danger of a European war in mind, and understandably and deliberately meant to prevent it at any price. And if the price was the security, the independence, and the very existence of a little state—too bad for Czechoslovakia. Why throw Great Britain, France, and all of Europe into the throes of a terrible war? Why, the French press asked, should three million Frenchmen die so that three million Germans be kept under Czech rule? Why, asked Lord Ponsonby during a debate in the House of Lords, should Britain fight for Czechoslovakia, when perhaps one man in a hundred in his country knew where the place was?[26] Why couldn't the world demand a little concession from a balky little state which, contrary to the spirit of the times, refused to recognize its national minority's right to self-determination? Why did Czechoslovakia refuse to relinquish part of its territory to spare the world from war?

The principles of the arrangement and the nature of the "concession" were disclosed and spelled out on the pages of the highly prestigious London *Times*. In an editorial on September 7, 1938, the *Times* suggested that Czechoslovakia dismantle itself, or, in more elegant terms:

> "The advantages to Czechoslovakia of becoming a homogeneous state might conceivably outweigh the obvious disadvantages of losing the Sudeten German districts of the borderland. . . ."

This editorial—which, cognoscenti knew, reflected the Government's positions—drove the French Government to demand clarifications. The French Premier instructed his ambassador in London to obtain a direct reply as to Britain's response if France took up arms for Czechoslovakia. "We are marching. Will you march with us?"

The British answer was evasive, asserting only that "While H. M. Government would never allow the security of France to be threatened, they are unable to make precise statements of their future action."[27]

Asking practical questions, the French ambassador was told that England could mobilize two non-mechanized divisions and 150 aircraft during the first six months. In this context, Churchill commented later that if Bonnet had been looking for an excuse to leave the Czechs to their fate, he found one.[28]

Against this background, the British Prime Minister announced in no uncertain terms that with all Great Britain's sympathy for Czechoslovakia, it would not go to war for her: "If we have to fight it must be on larger issues than that."[29] With each passing day, the leaders of Britain and France became increasingly convinced of the justice of their stance and the intransigence of the Czechoslovak Government, which had dared to step out of line. Chamberlain and Daladiėr began to fashion a decision to "save" Czechoslovakia from herself and salvage the peace of Europe.

Chamberlain goes to Obersalzberg

For this noble purpose Chamberlain was ready to spare no effort. Aged 69, the Prime Minister of Imperial Britain, upon which the sun still never set, considered it no diminution of honor to scale the heights of Hitler's mountain fortress in Obersalzberg, above Berchtesgaden.

When he arrived, after an exhausting flight—the first of his life—in a small plane through rain and fog, he found Hitler waiting for him symbolically at the top of the staircase, in uniform and black boots, without troubling himself to come down and greet his guest.[30] They held their talk on September 15. After tea was served, they exchanged a few polite sentences, including Chamberlain's appreciation of Hitler's activity on behalf of English-German understanding. Once formalities were out of the way, Hitler launched a vicious offensive against his counterpart, and then, as his interpreter testified, put his standard trick to work once again, "in one of those sudden changes from raging to complete calm and collectedness."[31] Hitler must have been greatly surprised when Chamberlain, instead of responding vehemently, posed a question: In which parts of the Sudetenland was Herr Hitler interested? Hitler replied with feigned humility: those areas where 80 percent of the population is German.[32] To emphasize his moderation he added:

> If, in considering the Sudeten question, you are prepared to recognize the principle of the right of peoples to self-determination, then we can . . . see how that principle can be applied in practice.[33]

Immediately he intoned solemnly that this was his last territorial aspiration, and that he had no desire to incorporate aliens, non-German racials, into the Reich.[34]

Pressure of the Western "Friends"

Three days later, the Governments of Britain and France (which had received Hitler's "final" demand) coordinated their stance and, on September 19, sent it on to Prague for approval. When the "intransigent" Czechoslovak Government responded in the negative the next day, her Western "allies" refused to take no for an answer. At 2:15 a.m. on September 21, the British and French envoys roused President Beneš from his sleep and handed him their governments' ultimatum. The two diplomats explained to Beneš that, with all due respect and friendship, if his Government did not agree to cede the Sudetenland, Czechoslovakia's "friends" would leave her to the fate "which she had brought upon itself." They added that they "certainly would not go to war with Germany just to keep the Sudeten Germans in Czechoslovakia."[35]

Time was short, the British envoy said. "The Prime Minister must resume conversations with Herr Hitler not later than Wednesday, September

22. . . . We therefore feel we must ask you for your reply at the earliest possible moment."[36]

To add insult to injury, the French Government—after having evaded its commitment—now promised to guarantee Czechoslovakia's "new borders." To be on the safe side, however, it limited this undertaking to the case of an attack "not caused by provocation."

The Czechoslovak Government now entered into feverish deliberations. That very day the Soviet Commissar for foreign affairs, Litvinow, declared in Geneva that the Soviet Union would keep its promise to Czechoslovakia. When the report reached Beneš, he summoned the Soviet envoy, Alexandrovsky, for a more explicit account. He discovered that the Soviet Union would indeed keep its word—but only if France did so, and if France obtained the explicit consent of Poland or Romania for the crossing of Soviet troops and airforce. The Soviet commitment, too, was therefore conditional and packed with hypothetical terms.[37] The Government meeting went on for hours, and culminated in the evening with a decision to surrender to the ultimatum of its "friends."

Its official communiqué read: "We had no other choice, because we were left alone."[38]

The Godesberg Meeting and the Reaction in Prague

Paris and London sighed with relief. On September 23 Chamberlain set out again, this time to Godesberg, near Cologne, to bring Hitler the good news. Hitler asked: "Am I to understand that the Governments of England, France, and Czechoslovakia have agreed to transfer the Sudetenland to Germany?" Chamberlain, pleased with the great success and his role in it, answered emphatically in the affirmative. How stunned he was when Hitler now announced coldly that "I am exceedingly sorry, but that is no longer of any use" (*"Es tut mir fürchtbar leid, aber das geht nicht mehr."*)[39] What he demanded now, he said, was the annexation and immediate military occupation of all territories with a majority, however small, of Germans, between September 26 and 8:00 a.m. on September 28—two days! Hitler rejected Chamberlain's claim that this was a diktat. "It is not a diktat," said the insulted tyrant with innocent righteousness. Clutching a piece of paper in one hand and motioning at it with the other, he added: "Look, the document is headed by the word 'memorandum.' "[40]

As a "special gesture" to Chamberlain, Hitler finally designed to make the "concession" of postponing the deadline several days, but no more than five.

"You are the only man," he said, throwing a sop to the old gentleman's ego, "to whom I have made a concession."[41]

During this bargaining in Godesberg, the burghers of Prague made an impressive attempt to prove that the Czechoslovak people wished to determine their own fate and future. From the evening of September 21 and into the next day, hundreds of thousands demonstrated in the capital. Streaming through the narrow streets of ancient Prague, via the Karl Bridge—adorned with a double row of baroque effigies of saints on either parapet—the mass of people reached Hradčany Hill and the plaza of the Presidential Palace.

"We won't hand our country to the Wehrmacht. We want to fight!" "Better fight than surrender!" "Down with the Government of surrender"—shouted the demonstrators, demanding the Government's resignation and the appointment of the Army's Inspector-General, General Syrovy, as Prime Minister of a new one.[42]

Hodža indeed resigned, and Syrovy was installed at the head of a government that rejected the Godesberg ultimatum. A general mobilization was broadcast on September 23, sparking a rise in morale. Word of it emptied the cafés and cinemas. Crowds thronged into the streets to vent their emotions. Taxi drivers and owners of private cars volunteered to transport the reservists to their units. The nation wanted to defend its independence.[43] More than a million men were called to the flag, and they reported. Civilians went out to dig trenches and prepare shelters. On September 27, the German attaché in Prague informed his Government: "Calm in Prague. Last mobilization measures carried out. . . . According to the estimate . . . the total call-up is 1,000,000; field army 800,000. . . . "[44]

"Because of a Quarrel in a Far-Away Country"

The developments in Prague threw the French and British Governments off-balance. If war indeed broke out and the Czechs fought, could the French and English really remain bystanders? In a last effort to appease Hitler, moderate his demands, and prevent war, Chamberlain sent his right-hand, Sir Horace Wilson, to Berlin.

Hitler received him with an eruption of fury and an unequivocal assertion: the Czechs had to accept the Godesberg conditions, thus sparing themselves a crushing defeat. Their affirmative answer must arrive by September 28, two days off. "At midnight?" asked Wilson, a man of precision. "No," Hitler ruled. "By 2:00 p.m."[45]

Chamberlain wasted no time. Once informed of the results of Wilson's mission, he sent an urgent cable to Beneš, advising him to agree to a "limited" German occupation and the establishment of a German-British-

Czech committee that would decide which further territories would be appended to the Reich. Otherwise, the British Prime Minister threatened, Czechoslovakia faced invasion and dismemberment. To dispel any doubts about where he stood and how he felt, Chamberlain took to the airwaves that very evening:

> How horrible, fantastic, incredible, it is that we should be digging trenches and trying on gas-masks here because of a quarrel in a far-away country between people of whom we know nothing.[46]

Black Wednesday

September 28, 1938, has gone down in history as "Black Wednesday." It began with the first tremblings of threshold-of-war fever, which spread through Europe and even spanned the Atlantic Ocean. The menace appeared inevitable, and dread was rife.

Hitler's confidantes, too—including Goering and the senior army command—were apprehensive, confused, and reluctant to mount an invasion. Tension peaked when Ribbentrop accused Goering of cowardice. The latter, Chief of the Luftwaffe, could not tolerate the insult. Solemnly he declared that if the Führer ordered war, he, Goering, would lead the Luftwaffe offensive in his plane—provided that Ribbentrop flew with him.[47]

At 4 a.m., the French ambassador in Berlin was awakened by his telephone. From the Quai d'Orsay (the French Foreign Ministry) he was instructed to request an urgent meeting with Hitler, in order to present him with another compromise plan. The King of Sweden urged Hitler to reschedule the ultimatum. The Spanish dictator, Franco, proclaimed that if war broke out, his country would declare itself neutral.

President Roosevelt, too, cabled Hitler urgently with a request to refrain from hasty action and keep the talks going. He sent Beneš a similar telegram.

Notwithstanding Hitler's contempt for and hate of America, its "Jewish plutocracy," and its crippled President, he apparently decided that the appeal could not remain unanswered. The mantle of protocol and pertinence in his response fails to conceal its author's cunning and astonishing deceit:

> Your Excellency,
> Be assured that I can fully appreciate the lofty intention on which your remarks are based. . . . Precisely for this reason, however, I can and must decline all responsibility of the German people and their leaders if the fur-

ther development, contrary to all my efforts up to the present, should actually lead to the outbreak of hostilities. . . . The origin of this problem . . . was the founding of the Czechoslovak State and the establishment of its frontiers without any consideration for history or nationality. . . . Thus the right of self-determination which had been proclaimed by President Wilson as the most important basis of national life, was simply denied to the Sudeten Germans. . . . From day to day it became more evident that the Government in Prague was not disposed seriously to consider the most elementary rights of the Sudeten Germans. On the contrary, they attempted by increasingly violent methods to enforce the Czechization of the Sudetenland. . . . Political persecution and economic oppression have plunged the Sudeten Germans into untold misery. . . . We reckon at present 214,000 Sudeten German refugees who had to leave house and home in their ancestral country and flee across the German frontier, because they saw in this the last and only possibility of escaping from the revolting Czech regime of force and bloodiest terror. Countless dead, thousands of wounded, tens of thousands of people detained and imprisoned, and deserted villages, are the accusing witnesses before world opinion of an outbreak of hostilities . . . carried out for a long time by the Prague Government. . . . The possibilities of arriving at a just settlement by agreement are therefore exhausted with the proposals of the German memorandum. It now rests, not with the German Government alone, to decide if they want peace or war.[48]

This letter is a succinct and perfect example of the "Newspeak" depicted so ably by George Orwell in *1984*. This language began to develop long before 1948, when Orwell wrote his novel. The Communist, Nazi, and Fascist propaganda machines (similar to Orwell's "Ministries of Truth") drained conventional terms and values of their real content, replacing them with distortions and brainwashing people with a relentless flood of propaganda—not only in the countries they controlled. Day in, day out, they proclaimed Orwell-style that:

War is peace.
Freedom is slavery.
Ignorance is strength.

Using this method, Hitler argued in his letter to Roosevelt that the aggressor had been the victim, that a liberal democracy was a repressive regime, that self-determination for the Sudeten Germans was more important than the existence of Czechoslovakia, and that responsibility for the war would be the Prague Government's alone if a "just solution" were not found. There it was: Teutonic justice and tolerance on the one hand, and repression and mass expulsion by the rapacious Czechs on the other.

One might assume that now, fifty years after the letter and the events in its wake, we would no longer hear "Newspeak," double-talk, and selective morality throughout the world. But this is not the case. Abuse of the term "self-determination" is still being practiced. The demands for it come quite often from those who seek the complete suppression of the self-determination of another group; from those who claim for themselves the right not only to self-determination but also the right to exterminate an existing democratic nation.

In this context, Stanley Hoffman's assertion bears repeating:

> A community of vocabulary is not the same thing as a community of values. When people with very different values use the same vocabulary, it debases both the vocabulary and the values hidden behind the vocabulary. This is what has been happening to notions like self-determination. . . . [49]

Chapter Three

Munich

The Munich Conference

The Nazi terror and extortion campaign on the one hand, and the Western powers' policy of appeasement on the other, resolved the crisis and ultimately gave rise to the solution Hitler wanted. The "redeeming angel" appeared in the guise of the Italian Duce, Mussolini. The road to war in Europe was not one he found particularly attractive, and when the British Ambassador to Rome, Lord Perth, suggested to him that Wednesday morning that he sponsor a peace initiative, the Duce leaped at the opportunity.

Munich Conference—(from left) Chamberlain, Daladier, Hitler, Mussolini, Ciano

From that moment on, matters proceeded with dizzying speed via ambassadors and cables between Rome and Berlin.

As a result of these contacts, Chamberlain received a message from his ambassador in Berlin: the Führer was willing to convene a four-party summit—Germany, Italy, France, and England. It was 3:00 p.m. In the House of Commons, as the political situation was being debated with crackling tension, the Prime Minister stood up and asked for the floor.

His thick eyebrows trembling, he waved the cable and informed the MPs of its contents. His announcement was accompanied by hurrahs and eruptions of jubilation. An overwhelming majority of the MPs considered Hitler's invitation a victory for the policy of peace and appeasement. Almost everyone breathed sighs of relief. They overlooked just one little detail, perhaps simply ignoring it altogether: The invitation did not include a representative of the very country whose fate would be adjudicated. No one queried this.

The man who issued the invitation and, it seems, those who accepted it, thought it sufficient to lay Czechoslovakia on the negotiating table. Nevertheless, for reasons of diplomatic protocol, the Czechoslovak Government was asked to dispatch two officials to be nearby and materialize when so requested.

Thus we arrive at that conference which, for its humiliating essence and tragic outcome, has become notorious. It opened in Munich on September 29 at noon, and the agreement was signed at 2:00 the following morning. The accord established procedures for the transfer to Germany of territories with a German majority. October 7 was chosen as the date by which this process would be completed (apart from one region, which was given another three days).

The Prime Ministers of Britain and France felt no shame when they affixed their names to the document, nor when they signed a declaration of their readiness to guarantee Czechoslovakia's new borders. However, the humiliation, betrayal, and looting of Czechoslovakia did not end there. Like a wolf declaring himself willing to watch over some sheep after he has already disembowelled them, so did Germany and its Italian ally express willingness to guarantee Czechoslovakia after the minority problem was solved.

Now there remained only one "technical detail"—to communicate the content of the agreement to the representatives of the Czechoslovak Government. The task was entrusted to the Prime Ministers of Britain and France. The "verdict" was read to Dr. Mastny, who could not restrain his tears. Daladiėr was slightly embarrassed but purposeful as he bluntly presented the information. Chamberlain, however, could not stifle a yawn. He merely apologized for his exhaustion but noted that he was "pleasantly tired."[1]

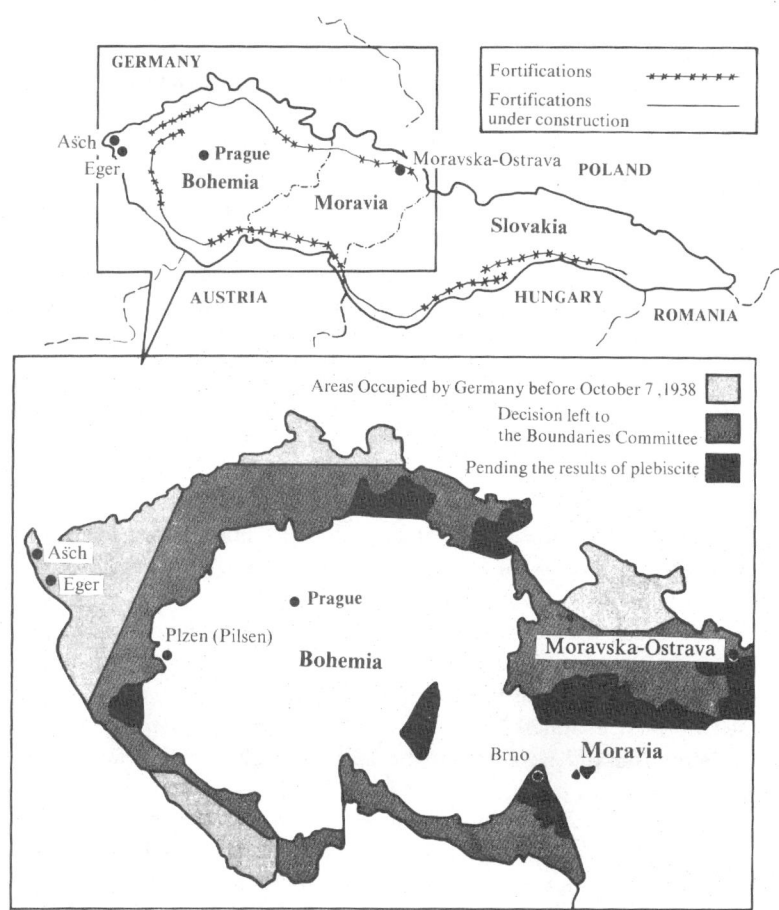

MAP 1: Czechoslovakia, 1938

On the afternoon of September 30, the Czechoslovak Government decided to surrender to the Munich diktat. "We were deserted," said an exhausted Prime Minister Syrový in a radio broadcast to the nation. "We stood alone."[2]

"Peace with Honor"

Hitler was still not satisfied. The total capitulation, arranged with help of Chamberlain and Daladiėr, temporarily thwarted his aim of fully occupying and destroying Czechoslovakia. Hitler told Schacht at the time (according to the latter's testimony at the Nuremberg trial) that "That fellow has spoiled my entry into Prague."[3]

Such sentiments, however, were still off the record, and the streets of Berlin hummed with jubilation. The Führer and the German people had chalked up a great victory without a single shot being fired. But Paris and London were no less jubilant. Daladièr and Chamberlain were greeted upon their return from Munich as victors.

The German Ambassador in London wrote: "The newspapers are not exaggerating when they say that men and women wept with joy in the streets."[4] A shouting, cheering throng of thousands greeted Chamberlain, who appeared that evening on the balcony of 10 Downing Street. Excited from head to toe, he promised them:

> My good friends, this is the second time in our history* that there has come back from Germany to Downing Street peace with honour. I believe it is peace in our time.[5]

For a long time after he retreated into the house, the streets echoed with cheers of joy, cries of "For he's a jolly good fellow," and "God Save the King."

The French parliament greeted Daladièr's report with a short, dreary debate. The Premier elegantly avoided any mention of the guarantees and the alliance that had once linked his subjects to Czechoslovakia. Neither did he see fit even to tell the MPs about the meetings in Berchtesgaden and Godesberg. Nor did he mention the ultimatum the French had communicated to Prague.

Both parliaments approved their respective Governments' actions and "achievements." In Great Britain, however, not only the Labour MPs but even Churchill and Duff Cooper vigorously attacked the Government's stance and policy of appeasement.

Churchill, in his speech, implored his colleagues neither to view the problem as touching just upon Czechoslovakia, nor to consider it only with respect to the strategic difficulties connected with the circumstances of this small state. Instead, he told them to remind themselves that a moment might come when, because of the invasion of Czechoslovakia, a European war would erupt. When that moment came, Britain would have to enter the fray, and everyone knew on whose side. Churchill said he bore no grudge against his loyal, courageous people, which was always ready to do its duty

---

*The reference being to Disraeli's return from the Congress in Berlin in 1878.

at whatever price, and which had given expression to a natural, spontaneous outburst of joy and relief upon hearing that it would not have to face this demanding ordeal at that particular moment. However, Churchill continued, the people had to know the truth: the preparations for their defense had been a fiasco. England had suffered a defeat without a war, and the results would accompany her the whole way. This was only the beginning, a first taste of the bitter dregs England would be served year after year . . . unless she made tremendous efforts to recover morally, to marshal her fighting spirit, and to take up position once again for the cause of liberty, as she had done in the past.[6]

The Government met the opposition's wrath with hypocrisy, its spokesmen falling over one another to lament Czechoslovakia's fate and laud the country posthumously. The Czechs had preserved the peace of Europe, Chamberlain proclaimed; it had been their sacrifice that prevented war. In the House of Lords, Lord Halifax, "eulogizing" President Beneš, said: "Without his help it would have been impossible to prevent a European war."

With its customary courtesy, H. M. Government announced that it was very sorry about the Czechs. It would do its best to honor its guarantees of the new borders, and it proposed, as consolation, an immediate grant of 10 million pounds sterling (whereas the Czechoslovak Government had applied for 30 million pounds in credit).[7]

The Government's reasoning convinced the majority that there was no other way to prevent war, appease Hitler, and bring about peace in Europe. No matter that the price was "self-determination" for the Sudeten Germans and the amputation from Czechoslovakia of a region vital to her defense.

When Parliament voted on "Peace with Honour," the ayes won, 366 to 144.

The Price

The price Czechoslovakia paid for this ersatz "Peace with Honour" was onerous in the extreme. Territory of 28,000 sq. km. was transferred to the German Reich, together with a population of 2.8 million Germans and 800,000 Czechs. The well-equipped fortification system fell into German hands, and Czechoslovakia was left torn, vulnerable, and defenseless.

Like vultures, the Poles and Hungarians—actively encouraged by Germany and Italy—fell upon Czechoslovakia and came away with additional border districts. In addition to population and territory, Czechoslovakia lost most of its natural resources and highly valuable industrial centers, including coal (66 percent), iron and steel (70 percent), textiles (80 percent), china (90 percent), glass (86 percent) chemicals (86 percent), lumber (40 percent), and electricity (70 percent).⁸

"Czechoslovakia has Ceased to Exist"

Hitler, however, had only just begun. "It was clear to me from the first moment," he informed his senior commanders, "that I could not be satisfied with the Sudeten-German territory.⁹

The next step was taken on October 16, when, on the basis of German demands, the Slovakian area was granted autonomy. On October 23, Hitler ordered the commander of the Wehrmacht to draw up a plan "for the liquidation of the remainder of Czechoslovakia."¹⁰

Czech policeman changing a street sign from "Freedom Avenue" to "Adolf Hitler Plaza"

Just half a year later, on March 14, 1939, Slovakia was granted its "independence." The Wehrmacht marched into Czechoslovak territory the next day, bringing it totally under the Third Reich's "patronage." Again, France and England did not lift a finger to keep the promises and "solemn" guarantees they had given upon concluding the Munich agreement.

"That remained the position until yesterday," Chamberlain declared blandly. "But the position has altered since the Slovak Diet declared the independence of Slovakia."[11]

"Czechoslovakia has ceased to exist," Hitler trumpeted, embarking that very evening on a triumphant visit to the Hradcany Palace in Prague. Czechoslovakia descended into a long and dark night of occupation and brutal oppression.

Chapter Four

Surrender

Troubling Questions

World War II began less than half a year after Czechoslovakia was dismantled.

It could be argued that the peoples of Europe and the United States paid a terrible price in blood for the Munich policy, that of appeasing the aggressor and betraying a loyal ally.

It is conventionally claimed that Czechoslovakia was torn apart by the force of two factors: Nazi aggression and the West's treasonous appeasement. But this analysis is puzzling on several grounds. Where did Czechoslovakia, its people, and its government fit in? Was Czechoslovakia really a passive actor in this drama, and, if so, why? Did it have no will of its own, or had it no way to express this will? Was it too weak to frustrate the schemes it faced? Could it not defend itself? Did France and Great Britain's policy of appeasement truly justify its own surrender, too?

We submit that the Czechoslovak Government, and more precisely, its President, bear much of the responsibility for the Republic's collapse and downfall. Admittedly, the picture would not be objective if it failed to include the general background of the events: the winds of pacifism that had become rife in Europe in the 1930s; Hitler's campaign of terror; his dizzying success in annexing the Rhineland and Austria; Germany's massive rearmament; and the democracies' paralysis and reluctance to enter into any confrontation. If mighty nations like France and England were driven into a state of fear and appeasement, how can Czechoslovakia be criticized, when it found itself isolated and betrayed?

The question Britain and France faced was essentially political: how to save world peace, even at the price of a third state's existence. This question has far-reaching moral, economic, military, and political implications. But the existence and fate of France and England would not have come under challenge in the circumstances prevailing in 1938 even had they chosen to meet their obligations to Czechoslovakia and stand up to Hitler's diktat.

For Czechoslovakia, however, it was a matter of life or death. Any decision its Government reached could have sealed its and the nation's fate. The Czechoslovak Government faced an impossible dilemma: either surrender to the Munich diktat—i.e., dismantle the state, permitting the Germans to take over until Czechoslovak independence became a dead letter—or fight alone.

No responsible government—and we are speaking, of course, of the government of a democratic state—is exempt from painful soul-searching and serious doubts when faced with this kind of decision. This is especially true when, in the government's opinion, a decision to fight under conditions of political isolation may result in annihilation and the destruction of the fiber of national life.

In this context, Prime Minister Syrový said the following:

> We have had to choose between making a desperate and hopeless defence, which would have meant the sacrifice of an entire generation of our adult men, as well as of our women and children, and accepting without a struggle and under pressure, terms which are without parallel in history for their ruthlessness.[1]

The Czechoslovak Government may therefore be viewed as justified in the decision it finally took, or in being deterred from taking a stance. Nevertheless, its leadership cannot be relieved of responsibility for the Republic's demise.

Czechoslovakia, during its years of existence, had succeeded in establishing a handsome example of democratic government and an industrially and militarily competent state. She was one of the two most industrialized states in Europe;[2] the output of her heavy industry exceeded that of the eleven Eastern European states together. The Czech automobile industry was one of the continent's most advanced and developed. Nor did Czechoslovakia lack defensive power.

Beneš has the following to say in his memoirs:

> It is a fact that in the late summer of 1938, our army, in spite of all its deficiencies which I did not conceal from myself, was at the time of the Munich discussions, one of the best in Europe, and that it was fighting fit in its morale as well as in its equipment—as our two mobilizations, in May and in September, demonstrated. Our officers' corps was in no way inferior in technical ability.[3]

Lest we write this testimony off as subjective—because Beneš credits these achievements to his own political support and momentum toward building the army—we have ample proof that the Czechoslovak Army was indeed a powerful deterrent force.

The Czechoslovak Army

Czechoslovakia succeeded in organizing and maintaining a relatively large army, as the statistics below (from various sources) demonstrate. By estimate of French Chief of Staff Gamelin, Czechoslovakia fielded 27 divisions.[4] Most sources, however, speak of 35 divisions or more.[5] The *London Times'* correspondent wrote about 40 divisions at the time of the 1938 mobilization,[6] and the British military attaché in Czechoslovakia, a professional observer who had undoubtedly researched the matter thoroughly, mentioned 38 divisions.[7] It was assumed, too, that the country had additional manpower potential, and could mobilize another ten divisions or so as backups.[8]

This army, about a million and a half strong during the September call-up, was quite modern for the time. It had substantial mechanized capabilities (30,000 motor vehicles), armor (700 tanks, 16 armored trains), and appropriate light weapons, automatic weapons, and artillery (2,200 field cannon of all kinds, and 2,500 anti-aircraft guns).

The equipment was better than adequate. Many observers considered Czechoslovak armor and heavy artillery better than their German equivalents. Moreover, much Czechoslovak equipment was of local manufacture. Skoda alone employed 50,000 workers, and another 25 factories produced light and heavy arms.[9] The country's arms industry turned out all kinds of weaponry, combat vehicles, aircraft, and engines.

The Czechoslovak airforce had about 1,700 planes of all types, including 500 first-line craft.[10]

Czechoslovakia's defense was largely based on a line of fortifications permanently manned by 70,000 soldiers. The line was technically well provisioned, protected by high tension current, ample war matériel, anti-tank obstacles, automatic doors against gas attack, underground hangars for aircraft, concrete blockhouses buried in the ground, etc. Experts considered this line better provisioned than the French Maginot Line.[11]

Years later, Albert Speer, a confidant of Hitler's, the man responsible for Germany's construction enterprises, and later the Reich's Minister of Armaments, wrote that the Czech border fortifications caused general amazement. Surprised experts found in a test bombardment that the Germans' weapons would not have overcome them. Hitler himself went to the former border to inspect the fortifications and returned impressed. He said they were astonishingly massive, were designed with extraordinary skill, and made optimal use of the lay of the land. If defended resolutely, they would have been very difficult to overcome, and would have cost a great many German lives.[12]

The Czechoslovak Army also had important strategic advantages.

In the event of war, it would have operated on very familiar territory, taking full advantage of relatively short internal transportation, supply, and communication lines. The Germans had forfeited the element of surprise, and the Czechoslovakian Army had completed its mobilization and deployment as planned.

Foreign experts also concurred that the Czechoslovak Army was professionally and operationally adept, and that its morale was high. The superb efficiency of the mobilization was further proof of this.

The German Army in the Autumn of 1938

The Wehrmacht, by contrast, was still undergoing rearmament in 1938, and had not yet become the overwhelming, self-confident force that would crush Poland, France, and other countries under hammer blows a year or two later.

In September 1938, the Germans had 37 infantry divisions, organized and equipped much as they had been in 1918. There were also three armored divisions, four light reconnaissance divisions, and four armored infantry divisions—a total of 48 regular divisions. In addition to these, the Germans were able to mobilize another eight reserve divisions and 21 garrison divisions (*Landwehr*), comprising WWI veterans at least 40 years of age.[13] It was also assumed that the Germans could "scrape together" additional manpower after the fighting had begun—another 15 divisions each month by General Gamelin's estimate, which was no doubt exaggerated.[14] In any event, the Germans had fewer than 80 divisions at their disposal in September 1938.

The Luftwaffe, too, had not yet reached the dimensions it would attain a year or two later. In fact, it was not prepared for war. In September 1938, it had about 3,000 aircraft—1,128 bombers, 773 fighters, 513 reconnaissance craft, and 308 transport craft. According to its manning table, it should have had 3,714 pilots, but its actual strength was 1,432.[15] Obviously, too, even the airforce could not have been deployed only on the Czechoslovak front in the event of war.

German General Staff plans allocated 37 regular divisions to the Czechoslovak front. On the Western front, five regular divisions and several reserve and Landwehr divisions were to be placed in a defensive posture.[16]

Another three divisions were stationed in Eastern Prussia. The rest of the forces remained in the rear as a strategic reserve. At that time, the German defense line (the Siegfried Line) was in much less than satisfactory condition. Of the 10,000 fortified positions called for under plan, only 517 had been completed. This, of course, was of concern to the German command, which Hitler disregarded.

At the end of August, when Gen. Wilhelm Adam, in command of the western front, remarked that if war broke out, the Wehrmacht could not hold the Western line more than three weeks, Hitler flew into a rage.[17]

Summing up, even if the Germans threw their reserves into the campaign, they would not come away with a swift victory. It can be surmised that Germany, nearly six times as populous as Czechoslovakia (seven times excluding the latter's national minorities) and having greater industrial potential, would eventually come out on top—although the victory would be neither easy nor quick. (All this presupposes that no other states would enter the fray.) The widespread assumption today is that Czechoslovakia could have held out for at least three months, inflicting heavy losses on the Germans.[18] Because the German General Staff held much the same view in 1938, some generals resisted the Führer's designs, entered into friction with Hitler, and even gave initial thoughts to a putsch. In July 1938, the Wehrmacht Chief of Staff, General Ludwig Beck, resigned for these reasons, lambasting the intentions of invading Czechoslovakia as "a mad dream."[19] However, the German generals' main professional concern was not so much a direct and exclusive confrontation with Czechoslovakia, with all this implied, but the possibility of active French, British, and perhaps even Soviet intervention. The French Army was considered Europe's largest and strongest at the time, and its plan called for pitting 56 divisions against the meager German divisions in the West.[20] Bitter recollections of the battles of World War I had not yet faded, and the German generals feared a new Battle of the Marne and a new Verdun. They assumed that France would be ready, as she had been in 1914, to sacrifice her sons' blood in riverlike quantities.[21] Testifying after the defeat, they spoke frankly about the prevalent assessments and trends of thought in the German General Staff during the period under discussion. Field Marshal Keitel, head of the High Command (OKW) during the war, testified at Nuremberg:

> In the autumn of 1938 the number of divisions was probably equal. . . .[22]
>
> We were extraordinarily happy that it had not come to a military operation because . . . we had always been of the opinion that our means of attack against the frontier fortifications of Czechoslovakia were insufficient. From a purely military point of view, we lacked the means for an attack which involved the piercing of the frontier fortifications. . . .[23]

Neither our western nor our Polish frontier could really have been effectively defended by us, and there is no doubt whatsoever that had Czechoslovakia defended herself, we would have been held up by her fortifications.[24]

As for the situation at the Western front, General Jodl, head of OKW Operations, had the following to say:

It was out of the question, with five fighting divisions and seven reserve divisions in the western fortifications . . . to hold out against 100 French divisions. That was militarily impossible.[25]

When a Czechoslovak representative at Nuremberg asked whether Germany would have attacked Czechoslovakia had the Western countries come to its aid, Field Marshal Keitel answered unequivocally: "Certainly not. We were not strong enough militarily."[26]

But all the German generals' reasoned, professional assessments were flawed. They failed to take account of France's unwillingness to fight. They did not know that Gamelin quashed any thought and practical proposal that would have involved the French Army. Presenting his assessments to Daladièr and Chamberlain, he went no further than a vague promise that if war broke out it would be the democratic states that would dictate the terms of peace. He planned no real offensive against Germany in the event of war; his major intent was to deploy along the Maginot Line, hold it through the winter, and wait for the arrival of large-scale British reinforcements.[27]

The German generals did not know how to read Daladièr and Chamberlain's political minds, but Hitler undoubtedly did. Assuming that the "rotten democracies" would not fight, his demonic intellect successfully deciphered and influenced the Western state of thinking. He knew how to frighten the Western statesmen, cultivate illusions with meaningless promises, manipulate them with tricks, deter them from embarking on war, and induce them to betray a friend. In September 1938, he was totally convinced that his ruse would work. He was correct.

Beneš: A War Initiative Will Cause a Slaughter in Czechoslovakia

The most intriguing question, extending beyond the domain of ex post facto wisdom and concerning Europe's political and military existence, is: why did a small but courageous and well-armed nation not make a risky but not-hopeless attempt to take its fate in its hands? Why did it not utilize all its ability? Why did it not take up arms? Were the Czechoslovaks cowards, unwilling to fight?

Victory-drunk, euphoric generalissimos or amateur "historiosophers" occasionally proclaim boldly, after the initial triumph, that their enemy is immeasurably inferior to their glorious army, and cannot fight as their soldiers can. Such ignorant, racist declarations are usually received at first with enthusiasm—and years later with painful silence brought about by the belittled enemy's hands and artillery.

At the time, historiosophers of this type associated the Czechoslovaks with "Schweikism," as portrayed in the mocked character of Soldier Schweik. The Czechs—the critics asserted—were a nation of Schweiks, thickheaded cowards who would use the best of their cunning to evade the honorable duty of bearing arms. Some of these historiosophers even go back a thousand years, imputing the original Munich precedent to the first Czech king, Wenceslaus. Legend recounts that when his army confronted that of Henry the Fowler, king of the Saxons, he dismounted from his horse and surrendered to the German, preferring this to battle.[28] Czechoslovak history also abounds in examples of the opposite kind, but for the "historiosophical" rationale discussed here, "Schweikism" is convenient in the extreme.

Yet everything that occurred in Czechoslovakia immediately before the Munich agreement refutes this theory. The Czechoslovakian people was ready to fight for its independence, and expressed its willingness by demonstrating *en masse* in Prague. Political leaders and shapers of public opinion insisted that the country face its enemy. Eight party leaders came before President Beneš as the crisis reached its climax and forcefully urged him to fight.[29] Jaroslav Stránský declared that:

> We cannot believe that a state which has such a disciplined and self-sacrificing people, such a magnificent army, would voluntarily give up. . . . We should defend ourselves.

Gottwald, the Communist deputy, said:

> Barefoot, unarmed Ethiopians defended themselves, and we yield. Look at the Spanish people, how they defended themselves. We have a great army; the nation is united!

Josef David reminded the President that:

> The President Liberator taught [the nation] that death was better than slavery. People cannot understand why we give away part of our territory without fighting.

Monsignor Stăsek challenged President Beneš:

> In this castle, Czechoslovak kings reigned in an independent state and frequently determined the history of Europe. No one in this castle ever retreated. We should have defended ourselves. . . . Future generations will condemn us for having given away our lands without fighting. . . .

But the people of Czechoslovakia engaged in more than fervent demonstrations and rhetoric in expressing its desire to exist as a free nation. The two military call-ups—in May and September—demonstrated its battle-readiness, discipline, and performance. We should perhaps mention remarks written during the mobilization period by the Czechoslovak author Karl Čapek:

> Throughout our Czechoslovakia there prevails an absolute calmness which is born of our certainty, of our decision, and of our realization that there is no way of avoiding what is inevitable. Calmly and soberly our menfolk have come forward in answer to the summons to perform their supreme duty. . . . They look as though they were simply going to their normal work, for it seems as natural to our men to defend their country as to earn their daily bread. It is a historic effort which is being made without any pomp and ceremony. Indeed, ours is a great people.[30]

The army's senior commanders bluntly demanded of Beneš an order to fight. On September 21, Fourth Army OC Gen. Lev Prchala went to the President's palace for an order to launch a defensive war.[31] He came away disappointed and embittered. But the matter did not end there. About a week later, on the fateful 29th of September, a dramatic meeting was held in the Hradcany Palace between the President and the commanders of his army: Chief of Staff Ludwig Kreici, three District OC's—Wojcechowsky, Loza, Prchala and the Inspector-General of the Army and at that time also Prime Minister Gen. Jan Syrovy. Everyone in attendance, Beneš subsequently wrote, insisted that he give the order. The atmosphere crackled with tension and the generals were vehement: "We must go to war regardless of the consequences. The population of the Republic is united, the army resolute, anxious to fight. And even if we are left alone we must not yield; the army has the duty to defend the national territory; the army wants to go and will go to war."[32]

But Beneš, as President and Commander-in-Chief of the Republic, turned his generals down for his own reasons. I cannot, he said, consider only the people's and the army's emotions and moods; I must weigh the total picture. Under the present conditions, he argued—with France having shirked its duty, thereby releasing the Soviet Union from its commitment as well, and with Poland and Hungary threatening Czechoslovakia from its flanks—a Czechoslovak war initiative will elicit a slaughter. However, Britain, France, and others will soon be forced to go to war. Then Czechoslovakia's time, too, will come.[33] The meeting was traumatic—for the generals, who left the palace bitter and disappointed, and for Beneš, who was disturbed by what they had said. Contemplating the tears in their eyes, he ruminated and reconsidered: "Have I made the right decision?"[34] Ultimately, his resolve overcame his doubt, his view prevailed over others', and, by force of his status, personality, and prestige, he tipped the scales.

A Small Nation Defends Itself

Every nation, large or small, has the unassailable right—even the duty—to use every means to defend itself against the encroaching aggressor. Only a people willing to defend its rights also by force can survive. However, this rule, shaped over millennia of human history, has exceptions and limitations. It is hard, for example, to fault a leader who, faced with a balance of forces liable to destroy the fabric of his nation, prefers surrender over armed resistance. A responsible and sane leader will not sanction an act that will leave posterity nothing but an epic saga for the tattered remnants of his nation to contemplate. So much for exceptions. As for limitations, the right and duty of self-defense do not legitimize lust for battle, saber-rattling, and irrational decisions to rush to arms. On the contrary: a national leader's highest imperative is to invest his very heart, thought, and talents in a supreme effort to spare his people the agonies of war. He must exhaust every political and diplomatic possibility and seek out every avenue toward resolving an international dispute without bloodshed. Only when all these have been exhausted, when the political path is going nowhere, auguring not a peace with honor, independence and sovereignty, but an imposed peace, a quiet surrender, an "arrangement" tantamount to a loss of independence, a "friendship" that spatters the nation's dignity with mud—only when the nation's leader has verified that resistance and self-defense are viable despite the imbalance of forces—only then is he permitted, and even obliged, to lead his people to war. Then, however, he is assured the support of a united nation, which has witnessed his efforts and realizes there is no alternative. At a fateful hour such as this, the great hour at which his leadership is tested, the national leader throws his full moral and political weight into the war, exhausting all his resources to maintain morale, bolster it at difficult moments, seek international support, and terminate the war in a manner that will prevent its future resumption.

This is not how President Beneš behaved as head of a nation which, though small, was ready and able to defend its independence.

A Concept Crumbles

The president's views and decisions were not entirely the products of moral or pacifistic concepts, although these, too, played an important role. National responsibility and assessment of the balances of forces shaped his outlook as well. The decisive factor, however, was the disintegration of the conception on which he had built and consolidated his policy over the years. "We were left alone," he said in explaining his decision to the people, and this utterance best explains the decision. Beneš believed that Czechoslovakia, in order to survive, had to be a "light unto the nations" in its conduct, its adherence to democratic ideals, and its foreign policy— which had to be based on "the principle that European peace is indivisible, and on collective security as expressed in the existence of the League of Nations."[35]

It should not be adduced that Beneš believed blindly in the League of Nations' effectiveness. As a practical statesman contemplating the ascendancy of Fascism and Nazism, he recognized the need to consolidate his country's peace and security by alliances and guarantees. Principal among these was the Small Entente which embraced Yugoslavia and Romania, with France at its center. The best way to stop Nazism, he thought, was to effect a rapprochement of the democratic West and the Soviet Union. Such a development, pacts signed by Czechoslovakia with France and the Soviet Union, and the League of Nations' blessing, were viewed by Beneš as "a pre-requisite of international security and the very existence of our state."[36]

Though Beneš did strengthen the army, his personal background, experience, and propensities led him to view pure diplomacy as the major vehicle for resolving international disputes. Czechoslovak diplomacy aided by friendly powers, he believed, could bridge the political abyss. He dismissed the possibility that Czechoslovakia could influence political developments by its own initiative and deeds. Moreover, he maintained that only such a concept and policy could foster Czechoslovak security.

Events disproved all the above.

Nazism proceeded from strength to strength. The West folded into a cocoon of appeasement, yielding to Mussolini and Hitler. France and England's military preparedness diminished drastically, while Germany grew ever stronger. Treaty violation and evasion of commitments and guarantees apparently became more common in international relations.

As early as the first years of the 1920s—certainly reflecting the demoralizing effects of the World War—new, stinging tones and voices began to be heard. Moreover, their message was wrapped in a mantle of legalism. The international jurists, so familiar with the polished phrasing of agreements, friendship treaties, alliances, and guarantees, with stipulations in large print and substipulations in small print, sanctioned certain departures from the letter of the law. Thus, for example, the following became a norm in international law:

> The duty of the guarantor to render, even by force, the promised assistance to the guaranteed state depends upon many conditions and circumstances. Thus, first, the guaranteed state must request the guarantor to render assistance. Thus, secondly, the guarantor must at the critical time be able to render the required assistance. When, for instance, its hands are tied through waging war against a third State, or when it is so weak through internal troubles or other factors that its interference would expose it to serious danger, it is not bound to fulfill the request for assistance. So too, when the guaranteed state has not complied with previous advice given by the guarantor as to the line of its behavior, it is not the guarantor's duty to render assistance.[37]

In 1924, the League of Nations General Assembly explicitly gave every member state the right to determine for itself how far it really had to go in implementing the undertakings in its guarantees.[38]

This devaluation of international commitments undermined the foundations of international morality. In place of "the sanctity of pacts," the principle of *pacta sunt servanda*—which purported to establish the foundations of stability and security—a new principle began to take shape: *Clausula rebus sic stantibus*. Under this tenet, any alliance becomes null and void if the circumstances and conditions that led to its establishment have changed.[39]

Beneš was not blind to these developments; he saw his concept collapsing:

> Europe was hastening to its doom as a result of universal selfishness. . . . Everyone in Europe was spinelessly, if resignedly, running away from the fight for the defense of democracy and was "safeguarding" himself alone by means of blind negotiations with perfidious Hitlerite Germany and dictatorial Italy. . . . I sensed how, step by step, the life work of Masaryk and myself was collapsing and the world was sliding into an abyss.[40]

If the giants were toppling, what could Czechoslovakia do? Collective security, alliances, guarantees, and solidarity among the democratic states were Czechoslovakia's cornerstone, its foundation, a "prerequisite" for its very existence. If this concept were collapsing, if everyone had abandoned Czechoslovakia, then the use of military force would only provoke a national cataclysm—"the sacrifice of an entire generation," in General Syrový's words.

***

Some believe that Beneš's decision was "rational" under the circumstances. It seems to us that the topic under discussion does not yield to a dichotomy of "rational" as opposed to "emotional" decisions. One of the most important researchers of international conflicts was right when he asserted that:

> Decision makers are not simply distributed along a one-dimensional scale that stretches from complete rationality at one end to complete irrationality at the other.[41]

People, including leaders of nations, rarely conform with psychological stereotypes. "Emotional" types invoke rational motives in their actions, and "rational" types are not devoid of emotions. Fear, defeatism, and despair lurk behind a "rational" attitude, just as an "emotional" approach can include many elements of precise thinking. The various labels and generalizations are merely the results of subjective assessments; they fail to encompass the entire, far more complicated truth.

When two wills and forces collide, the resulting set of considerations and resolutions is usually an admixture of instinctive reactions, rational thinking, willpower, and a collection of impulses, emotions, and desires—"fight or flight"—all in varying degrees of intensity. When two groups of people confront one another, the greatness of the decision makers and leaders is tested by their ability to strike a balance between all these factors, examine the situation soberly, draw correct conclusions, and drive their peoples to action.

The dividing line does not run between "rational" decisions (of positive connotation) and "emotional" ones (of negative connotation), but rather between those that end in success and those that end in failure.

Historians, commentators, writers, and café politicians—i.e., everyone who does not have to make history, who is absolved from fateful, life-and-death decisions—can sit at a desk or coffeehouse table, comfortably analyzing the annals of people, the demise or success of little nations, and "establishing" where and how the fatal mistakes were made. They can pinpoint where "blatant illogic" occurred, and where "balance and sagacity" won the day. But those who cannot afford to demonstrate ex post facto wisdom—those whom history, destiny, circumstances, and chance entrust with the responsibility of making decisions and leading nations—never find success in their tuxedo pockets. For them, chances are always slim: they are deterred by their enemies' might, sorely tempted to avoid a dangerous confrontation, certain only that uncertainty is certain. Every decision they must take is fateful, at times verging on lunacy. The makers of history cannot afford the luxury of Monday morning quarterbacking. Theirs is the task of coping—every moment—with the need to decide between evil and greater evil, between almost inevitable disaster and possible hope. Every decision and measure adopted is like taking a step along the divide between the miracle of victory and the abyss of disaster. Nevertheless, the issues are theirs to decide and resolve—and only the outcome determines whether they were right or horribly wrong.

The aforesaid requires us to treat Beneš's actions with extreme caution, appreciating his motives and understanding the tragic situation in which he found himself.

This does not mean we have to assess all his actions positively.

Beneš's decision to keep the Republic's Army in its barracks during the German aggression may seem to have been based on rational considerations. In fact, however, it was more the result of despair, frustration, and dread—understandable in and of themselves—than of reasoned weighing of risks and prospects. The decision can be criticized on rational grounds, and attacked in view of the actual balance of forces in 1938. It can also be justified if account is taken of the emotional pressure thrust upon the president of a small nation whose every friend had left her to her fate. In the main, however, it should be judged by its results: the negative impact it had on the Czechoslovak people's morale, fate, development, and behavior in the ordeals it underwent in and after 1938.

A nation willing and able to defend its independence and sovereignty in 1938 had to grow accustomed after Munich to accepting the yoke of aliens and adapting itself to a coercive regime.

In a democracy, the army is a tool of national leadership. If the leadership is irresponsible and adventurous, it can lead to national catastrophe. If the leadership is hesitant or frightened, it becomes an empty vessel, a mere arsenal, and a symbol of humiliation. Because Beneš did not want to use the force he had helped build, Czechoslovakia's willingness to defend its independence, land, and sovereignty was unexploited. Instead of capitalizing on the nation's fidelity and capability, Beneš policy did not prevent German aggression or a sellout by foreign powers. Once Czechoslovakia relinquished her independent military option, it forfeited her sovereignty as well.

PART TWO
***
Poland and Her Neighbors

Chapter Five

Poland Between the Two Wars

A Sonata for Three Matches

Sunday, November 28, 1943: although it was late at night, the lights were still ablaze in the vast Soviet Embassy building in Teheran. An enormous crystal chandelier dangled from the middle of the ceiling in the cavernous dining hall, and stubs still flickered in the silver candelabra.

The dinner marking the end of the first day of the summit conference had just ended. Here, in this mid-war conclave, the strategic trail to victory over the common Nazi enemy would be blazed, and the world's fate would be decided.

The host—a visibly fatigued American President Franklin Delano Roosevelt—parted from Stalin, Churchill, and a host of senior advisors, and went off to his special wing in the Embassy.

Now came the time for an informal, lighter, even jocular exchange of remarks and ruminations. Lest the reader misinterpret this as a stage of idle chatter, Churchill considered talks of this kind no less significant than the formal ones. Thus Churchill and Stalin seated themselves on a sofa in a corner of the oval room, the former with his cigar and the latter with his pipe, and began to converse. Joining them were Molotov, the Soviet Commissar for Foreign Affairs, and Anthony Eden, the handsome British Foreign Secretary.

At first the talk focused on the disposition of Germany and the Germans after the victory. Stalin expressed his apprehension that Germany would recover its industrial and military capabilities within fifteen to twenty years. This, he said, they had to prevent.

Churchill concurred and then some: to secure world peace, they would have to strip Germany of its arms, control its industry, denude it of air power, and redraw its borders radically.

"All that is very good, but not enough," Stalin ruled. After they continued in this vein for a few more minutes, Churchill suggested that they address themselves to the matter of Poland. As a gesture of courtesy, Stalin permitted his British colleague to open the talk. Churchill lit up a new cigar and presented his opening gambit in a cloud of aromatic smoke:

Poland was important to Britain, he asserted; H. M.'s Government had gone to war for her. Just the same, he hastened to add, nothing mattered more than the security of the Soviet Union's western border.

The Soviet leader's eyes lit up, and Churchill knew he had hit home. He continued to strike the iron while it was hot. Would the Marshal be inclined to reveal his thoughts as to the Soviet Union's defense needs in the west? They could then talk it over and reach an accord.

Stalin merely continued to draw on his pipe silently. He would let the representative of British imperialism disclose his position first.

Churchill hesitated for a moment, finally deciding that the decision should not be put off. The ground for the fateful reckoning had to be prepared. Though neither he nor Roosevelt had a mandate from their legislatures to act on Poland's borders, he ventured, the three heads of state would do well to adopt a policy which they could present and recommend to the Poles. To make matters clear, he added that he personally thought Poland, the whole country, could move westward, just as a squad of soldiers takes two steps "left close." This would involve stepping on some German toes, but what of it? Poland had to be strong; it was a key player in the European orchestra.

The scion of Russian imperialism took on a satisfied look; the fringes of his mustache twitched momentarily as if concealing a thin smile. However, he did want to ascertain that the talks would take place without Polish participation.

Churchill's laconic and unequivocal answer was, "Yes." Somehow he considered it unnecessary to hear out the representatives of the nation whose fate and future were about to be rendered. The "Big Three" would serve the issue adequately by arriving at an informal arrangement, which would be brought before the Poles ex post facto with advice to accept it.

Here, Eden commented that he was highly impressed by something Stalin had said during the banquet: the Poles could advance as far as the Oder River in the west, recovering there whatever they would lose in the east.

Stalin asked if they had really thought he was about to swallow up Poland. Eden replied that he did not know just how much the Russians were prepared to bite off . . . Stalin repeated his slogan about not coveting anyone else's territory, although a nibble of Germany was not out of the question. When Eden reiterated Stalin's postulate about offsetting Polish losses in the east with gains in the west, Stalin cautiously replied that it could indeed come about, but that he was not sure.

Now Churchill picked up three matches (representing the Soviet Union, Poland, and Germany) and illustrated how the process might work.

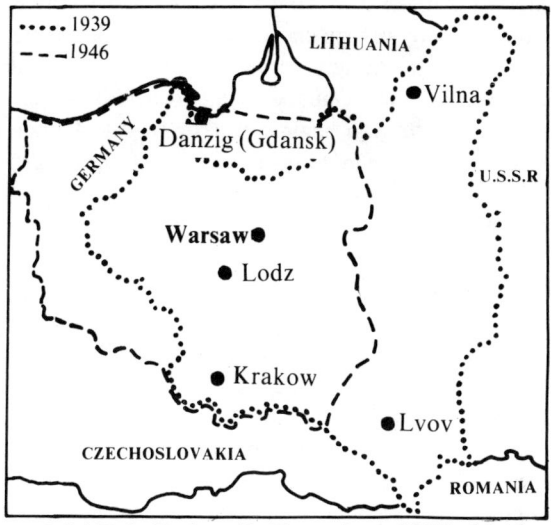

MAP 2: Poland's Frontiers 1939, 1946

Stalin seemed quite pleased, and the foursome parted for the night.

As fantastic as it sounds, this account is not a figment of the author's imagination. The conversation described here, about shifting an entire state and, with it, millions of people, really took place. One of the participants described it in his memoirs.[1]

Redrawing the Borders

Furthermore, it came to pass. Anyone who undertakes even a hurried comparison of the maps of pre-1939 and postwar Poland will easily notice the tremendous differences. Prewar Poland's general outline changed from a hand with splayed fingers to a clenched fist. Its borders—formerly long, winding, protruding in every direction, and wide open to enemy invasion—were drawn in, straightened out, and tightened on all sides. A narrow corridor previously running through two sections of Germany to permit access to the Baltic Sea vanished as if it had never existed. The Prussian enclave in the east disappeared, too, and its lengthy shoreline was now Poland's. Furthermore, a mighty hidden hand seems to have grasped prewar Poland and shoved it a considerable distance to the west. Study of the differences between the two maps bring the following facts to light:

Poland's pre-1939 territory of 389,700 square kilometers decreased to 312,500. Almost half of prewar Poland (about 46 percent, or 179,800 square kilometers) had been torn from it and annexed to the Soviet Union. In compensation, Poland was given 103,000 square kilometers of former German territory to the north and the west, thus confining Poland's loss to 77,200 square kilometers. The country's land borders had been shortened—5,534 kilometers before the war against 3,067 now—and made more defensible. Its prewar maritime border of 140 kilometers had grown to about 581.[2]

Demographic Changes

As Poland's borders moved and their contours changed, a large-scale migration of people took place: more than two million Poles moved from the east into the newly-acquired territories.[3]

Of the eight to nine million Germans in these territories before the war, no more than 100,000 remained. Some, of course, had died during the hostilities.[4] Others were expelled to the west, and opinions and statistics are divided as to their number. German sources seem to abide by the rule that "the more, the better." Even Polish statistics, however, place the number of German refugees in 1946 at some 5.7 million.[5]

As early as 1946, 4,375,000 Polish "repatriates" from the east and other Polish citizens from other parts of Poland supplanted the Germans in the "liberated (or, in Polish, the 're-redeemed') territories."[6]

The ethno-demographic changes in Poland were no less drastic and substantial.

More than six million Polish nationals—including three million Jews—had perished during the war. The Ukrainians and Belorussians remained in territories subsequently annexed to the Soviet Union, while the Germans, as stated, were evicted to Germany. Thus the population of Poland dwindled from 35 million (1939) to 24 million (1946). Its ethnic makeup, too, underwent significant change. While less than 70 percent of Poland's population was Polish before the war,[7] this proportion reached 98 percent afterwards.

Rid of its minority groups, postwar Poland was a homogeneous nation.

Background

It would certainly be an oversimplification to assume that an informal conversation between two major leaders was enough to wreak the upheaval that occurred in Poland following the war. Notwithstanding the personal strength and might they represented, only the tempest of the war could have moved borders and millions of people; only the revolutionary situation that had come to pass in its wake—in this war against the unprecedentedly evil forces of Nazism—could have produced the psychological and practical terms for a change equally revolutionary.

But we will never fully appreciate the event without taking account of the historical, demographic, geopolitical, social, and political background of the times, as well as the Poles' political and military struggle for the future of their land.

Only if we add this background portrait to the occurrences acted out during the war can we understand the basis for the Churchill-Stalin talks and the development of the twisting, dramatic political negotiations on the subject of Poland at the Big Three summit conferences at Teheran, Yalta, and Potsdam.

Between Germany and Russia

Peoples and states can select their friends, but not their neighbors. Neighbors are not always a source of pleasure.

Poland's neighbors, especially to its east and west, had caused Poland anguish and peril for generations. Poland was sandwiched between two large, expansion-minded peoples—the Russians on one side and the Germans on the other—and this left a special imprint on its thousand-year history.

In relatively recent memory alone, Poland's mighty neighbors had carved her up three times (1772, 1792, 1795).

Excluding the short lifetime (1815–1832) of the independent rump-state of "Congress Poland," Poland was off the map of Europe from 1795 until her resurrection in 1918. World War I marked the end of her partition and enslavement. The defeat of monarchist Germany, the weakening of Russian imperialism due to the Bolsheviks' victory, and the dismantling of the Austro-Hungarian empire permitted the reconstitution of independent Poland.

However, this did not do away with mutual hostility, suspicions, and intrigues. Treaties and exchanges of letters cannot eradicate enmity of generations and historical memories drenched in blood and tears.

To the Poles, the Germans were and remained the offspring of the Teutons and the Crusaders*—a mighty and ruthless folk, yearning to enslave

---

*See H. Sienkiewicz's monumental work, *The Crusaders*.

the Polish people and make off with its land. The Russians, in turn, were the spiritual and actual successors of Genghis Khan. The years of oppressive Czarist rule in Poland were like an unhealed wound, and Poland considered herself Christian Western Europe's bulwark against the Russian savages. The Bolshevik ideology and its aggressive, revolutionary, expansionist element that strived to spread the gospel of redemption to the proletariat of all peoples, further intensified Polish anxiety and enmity.

It has been said (e.g., by Henry Kissinger) that even paranoids can have real enemies. One could go so far as to justify an element of paranoia, if there was one, in the Poles' apprehensions.

Although the German monarchy had metamorphosed into the Weimar democracy and the Czarist empire into the USSR—and although both had been weakened—they still presented a potential threat to Poland. It suffices to compare the quantitative disparity of their populations to appreciate how serious this threat was. In the summer of 1939, Germany had a population of more than 86 million, the Soviet Union 190 million . . . and Poland 35.8 million.

Germany and Russia reacted to the resurrection of Poland. Political and military actions taken by the new state merely intensified their intentions to "settle scores" with her until she was off the map again.

Poland therefore had good reason to be wary and ever concerned about having its borders breached and its independence stripped once again.

Aspiration to Restore the Historical Borders

The end of World War I laid foundations for a free Poland. This is not to say that the border issue had been settled. In November 1918 the Polish government controlled no more than 140,000 sq. km. and population of 14,500,000.[8] These results were not satisfactory from the Polish point of view. After 150 years of partition and subjugation the Poles strived to restore the bygone glory. They did not settle for the area densely populated with Polish ethnics and set their sights also on territories to the west and to the east which had been under Polish rule for centuries, and where now a mixed population existed. They considered Pomerania in the north and Silesia in the west as basically Polish territories. These provinces had been the nation's cradle. Prince Mieszko laid there the foundations of the Kingdom of Poland at the end of the tenth century, and from this region his successor, Boleslaw Chrobry expanded the country's borders from the Oder and Elba Rivers in the west as far as Kiev in the east. The fact that these territories* were populated—in the west by Germans and in the east by Ukrainians, Belorussians, Jews and other nationalities—did not bother them in the least; the territory was no less "Polish" for all that. Does a house change hands because it was let or sublet to a foreigner?

As a result of these tendencies, between 1919 and 1923, the Poles vigorously waged political and armed struggle—to the extent of actual war—against both the Germans and the Russians to restore Poland's sovereign territory to its "historical" dimensions.

The Western Border

The outcome of this activity, and of resolutions taken at the Versailles conference, was a Polish "corridor" (80 km. wide on the average) between Eastern Prussia and parts of German Pomerania. If this were not enough of a complication, another one developed in the form of the "free city" of Danzig (Gdansk). The Allies recognized Poland's vital interest in access to the Baltic Sea and use of the Danzig port. The city, German in character and population, was designated to become "free," giving Poland the responsibility for handling, under restricting conditions, Danzig's foreign affairs and limited responsibility for internal order. To complicate things even more, the League of Nations' representative was stationed in the city to resolve future eventual disagreements. In 1921 Upper Silesia was partitioned between the two countries and Germans regarded all these arrangements as a severe blow to their national pride and a further step in the "humiliation" process of Germany by the Versailles Treaty.

The Eastern Border

After a protracted war between the Poles and the Russians—a war which progressed like a see-saw (bringing the Poles in the spring of 1920 to the shores of Berezina and Dniepr and to the gates of Kiev; and the Red Army to the suburbs of Warsaw in August 1920)—the Poles appealed to France and Britain for military help or diplomatic mediation.

Experts of the two powers worked up a detailed plan to end the war, and delivered it to the governments of the Soviet Union and Poland on July 11, 1920. The proposal, bearing the name of the British Foreign Minister, Lord Curzon, included an immediate cease fire, detailed demarcation of the cease-fire line (later known as the Curzon Line), Polish withdrawal from Soviet territory to this line and deployment of the Red Army fifty km. east

---

*Including in the east the areas of Kovno, Vitebsk, Mohilev, Homel, Berdicheva and as far as Braclav in the south. West of this line were the areas of Vilna, Minsk, Pinsk, Lvov and Tarnopol.

of it. The suggested cease fire line stretched from Grodno in the north (leaving Vilna outside of Poland), eastward to Bialystok, along the Bug river as far as Belz, turning there to the southwest. In that sector, with Przemysl on the Polish side of the line and Lvov to its east.[9]

The Russians, whose offensive at that time was widening, were in no hurry to quit. Lenin believed that a communist revolution would erupt once the Red Army approached the gates of Warsaw. On July 17, 1920 Foreign Affairs Commissar Chicherin sent to Curzon a negative response. (Only some twenty years later did the Soviet Union display resolute "adherence" to the Curzon Line, and this became the major bone of contention between the Soviets and the Poles.) Another two months of fighting left both sides spent and brought about the opening of direct negotiations between them.

They convened in Riga and an accord was signed on October 12, 1920. Six days later the 18-month war ended. The two sides forfeited any demand or claim to redress as to the territories across the border established in the agreement. Essentially it was a compromise between the two peoples' intentions and reflected the balance of forces as this proved to exist during the war. The war did not result in the dismantling of the Soviet Union, nor in the establishment of a "federation" in which Poland would play a dominant role.* Neither did it restore the borders of 1772. To the Polish way of thinking, this "concession" amounted to 311,007 sq. km. of territory. By the Soviet perception, the war's "cost" resulted in the loss of 180,000 sq. km. with population of 10,700,000 who had become Polish citizens.[10]

Poland's borders Before World War Two

When the dust of war and diplomatic activity faded away, Poland's borders, as they were finally set in 1923, exceeded the contours of the Curzon Line, including Vilna and Lvov. They were very long, convoluted, hard to defend, and apart from the Pripet Marshes to the east and the Carpathian mountains to the south, they were not based on significant natural obstacles. Of 5,534 km. of land frontier, 1,412 km. abutted Poland the Soviet Union and 1,912 km. (including 607 km. at Eastern Prussia) with Germany. Add to these 984 km. with Czechoslovakia, 507 km. with Lithuania, 349 km. with Romania, and 109 km. with Latvia.[11]

---

*For a certain period of time Piłsudski entertained the notion of establishing a federation between Poland, Lithuania, Belorussia and Ukraine with Poland as the dominant factor. Another attempt of Piłsudski to create a Baltic alliance including Lithuania, Latvia, Estonia and Finland failed too.

When Reach Exceeds Grasp (Including National Minorities)

The sovereign Poland ruled now over a large territory. Even if her historical borders had not been restored in full, the new borders signified a considerable achievement. However this came with the seeds of disarray. Her far-reaching goal, rooted in historical perceptions, weakened her sensitivity and alertness to the intrinsic danger of the security drawbacks of the new borders and the demographic threat they presented. The latter timebomb went by the name of "national minorities."

According to the 1921 census relating to January 30 of that year, Poland's population stood at 27,176,717, out of which ethnic Poles were 69.2 percent, Ukrainians 14.3, Jews 7.8, Belorussians 3.9, Germans 3.9, others (Lithuanians, Russians, Czechs) 0.9.[12]

This ethnic composition—the result of historical developments and the positioning of the new borders—hindered the internal consolidation of the Polish state, created a complicated tapestry of relations rife with contradictions, tensions, suspicion and mutual enmity, and, on the eve of World War II, led to national irredentism by the German, Ukrainian and Belorussian minorities.

The Minorities in the Eastern Territories

The vast area of 180,000 sq. km. between the Curzon Line and the Lithuanian and Russian borders, as demarcated in the Riga Agreement, was home to roughly 12 million people—Poles, Lithuanians, Russians, Belorussians, Ukrainians and Jews. Precise figures as to their ethnic breakdown are hard to come by. Be this as it may, we may sum up the general picture by saying that the population of these territories in 1939 included 3.5–4 million Poles, more than 5 million Ukrainians, 1.5 million Belorussians, and 1.3 million Jews. To the Poles, who considered the Riga border a concession and compromise relative to their historical aspirations, the ethnic breakdown issue was of secondary importance. They regarded the eastern territories as parts of ancient Poland above and beyond anything else. The fact that other peoples were dwelling there, as they had in the past, made this land no less "Polish" than a house would be less "owned" by its owner after a guest or tenant had spent time there.

As seen by the Poles for generations these territories had served as front-line positions and buffer zones between "Christian" Poland and "Asiatic" Russia; a Polish presence there would thus do the bidding of "civilization." Poland therefore tried to strengthen her foothold in these territories and overcome the matter of the minorities' national separatism by enforced assimilation, by cultural and economic activities. This intent, fundamentally unsound—especially when applied brutally—further exacerbated the rift between the Poles and the Slavic minorities. The eastern population of 6.5 million Ukrainians and Belorussians rapidly turned into an irredentist factor and a time bomb ticking away at Poland's integrity.

The two sides—the Poles on the one, and the Ukrainians and Belorussians on the other—were embraced in an inescapable trap. Clashing national aspirations and interests, one side's secessionist tendencies and the other's will to repress them, fueled mutual enmity, acts of violence and suppression.

The late 1920s and the 1930s were marked by incessant sabotage of railroads, communication facilities and government offices. Estates of Polish noblemen and upper class were attacked; Sejm delegates, educators, and officials were assassinated. The most showy operation of all was an attempt to assassinate the President of Poland, Prof. Wojciechowski, while he was visiting Lvov in 1924. These operations, carried mainly by the UWO (Woiskowa Organizacja Ukrainska) were met, as might be expected, by punitive reactions by the Polish authorities.

Ukrainian (and to some extent, Belorussian) nationalism sought out the Germans as a source of support. This was met with a positive response. The role Hitler envisaged for the Ukrainians was to pave Germany's way to the dismantling of Poland and the inevitable drive into Russia. In August 1939, a satisfied German consul in Lvov was able to deliver the following report to his superiors:

> The Ukrainians have seen the opportunity approaching for which they had longed for many years, namely of realizing the aim of a free Ukraine. In their national aspirations the Ukrainians count on, and firmly believe in, help from the Führer and Germany.[13]

The German Minority

More than a million Germans lived in Poland between the two wars, but their economic and political influence exceeded their numbers. More than a quarter of a million had settled in central Poland, mainly in the great industrial city of Lodz. After the plebiscites were held and the border was demarcated for good, more than half a million ethnic Germans remained in the northern and western frontier areas, the "corridor," the Poznan area, and Silesia. The remainder were dispersed in other parts of the country.

Their feelings of "injustice" and "humiliation," after the despised Poles have become their rulers, were amplified by their superiority complex and by economic, social and cultural power in these areas.

These trends of thought of course, were assiduously nurtured by the Nazi propaganda machine, and the territories involved became bastions of Nazism within a few years.

***

Summing up thus far, we may therefore say that Poland's revived independence and territorial integrity were threatened from its very beginning by two mighty neighbors; its hard-to-defend borders; and its own minorities. If all of these were not enough, the Polish people were saddled with a regime whose foreign policy took Poland's stature to even greater depths in the 1930s.

From Democracy to the "Colonels' Junta"

Poland's young democracy collapsed after few years of existence. Marshal Piłsudski, the undisputed hero and redeemer of the nation, lost faith in the virtue of the democratic system. His social-democratic past and background did not prevent him from mounting, in 1926 a military coup d'etat, and installing a de facto, if not de jure, authoritarian regime. His contempt for Polish democracy coincided with his disillusionment with the Western democracies. The trends of pacifism and appeasement that spread in the West strengthened his assessment that democracy was rickety crutch. In March 1933, when the Nazis came to power, Pilsudski approached Daladier and proposed a preventive war against Germany—with French, Polish and British collaboration—while Hitler was still too weak to be dangerous. Daladier refused. Pilsudski let a month go by and tried again. This time he received no answer.*[14]

As long as Pilsudski was alive, Poland's foreign policy tried to maintain the delicate equilibrium in her relations with each of her two mighty neighbors. On January 26, 1934 Poland signed a non-aggression pact with Germany, and on May 5, of that year, extended its treaty with the Soviet Union to December 31, 1945. But Pilsudski's death (in May 1935) upset this equilibrium, just as it undermined the delicate, tense balance that had

---

*Subsequently Goering admitted to the Polish ambassador Lipski, that had the French and the Poles attacked in concert at that point, Germany's situation would have been catastrophic.[15]

Marshal Józef Piłsudski

been maintained during his rule between the military ruling cliques. His autocratic regime rested on popular sympathy for the army, and in practical terms, on a cadre of senior officers—generals and colonels. With the abolishment of democracy—though obfuscated by the nominal existence of several parties in the Sejm (Parliament)—and the establishment of the BBWR ("The Non-Partisan Bloc of Cooperation with the Government"), the army became politicized. Senior officers started to harbor political ambitions. With Piłsudski's death the Diadochi war began.

Several senior generals, such as Sosnkowski and Sikorski, were distanced from the centers of power. One of Piłsudski's closest aides, Col.

Slawek, took his own life.[16] Another former aide, Col. Koc, founded and led a Fascist organization. Gen. Smigły-Rydz, Pilsudski's successor as Marshal, began to maneuver for broader powers and the status of "number two" de jure and number one de facto in the governmental hierarchy. To obstruct this endeavor, President Moscicki appointed Gen. Slawoj-Skladkowski as Prime Minister. This did not bring the friction to an end, and the cabinet was in fact factionalized into two or three cliques that engaged in guerrilla warfare one against another around the Cabinet table.[17]

The set of concepts and values dear to Poland's new rulers, known by many as the "Colonels' Junta," had been shaped in army barracks and was narrow-minded, chauvinistic, and authoritarian. It was the colonels' clear intent to root out the remains of democracy, and their regime exacerbated the economic crisis and social disparities, fomented radicalization, persecuted political opponents, and worsened anti-Semitic tendencies. They were conceptually and emotionally torn between hatred of Bolshevik Russia and fear—mixed with admiration—of Nazi Germany.

Col. Beck and His Foreign Policy

One of the most prominent figures in the new cabinet was the Foreign Minister, Col. Jozef Beck. His policy lead to further alienation from the democratic western powers, and found a justification of sorts for this when these powers sank into the torpor of appeasement. Beck, like his mentor Pilsudski, had no illusions about Germany's intentions and aspirations. This often presented the question of whether the Soviet Union (with which, too, the Poles had a non-aggression treaty) should not become a source of support. Beck and his comrades dismissed this notion categorically. He hated the Russians, and "Combatting . . . Bolshevism was the primary aim of his policy."[18]

Furthermore, the practical meaning of such a connection was that in case of war with Germany, the Soviet Union would have to come to Poland's aid, crossing into Polish territory to do so. This was the last thing the Poles—not only the "colonels"—wanted, considering the distant and not-so-distant (1918–1921) past.

The third reason was the "colonels' " contemptuous underestimation of the strength and capability of the Red Army, while overestimating—out of nationalistic megalomania—the might of the Polish forces. As for the Red Army, this assessment, shared by many non-Polish actors, was the result of Stalin's "purges" during the "Great Terror" of the 1930s (chiefly between 1937 and 1938).

The "Great Terror"

Stalin and his regime elevated the triumph of communism to the status of an end that justified all means. "When you cut down trees, chips fall," cynics recited, explaining the need to offer human sacrifices to the Moloch of Communism. The number of "chips" ran into many millions. Many of those executed were Red Army leaders who had been accused of espionage, terror, Trotskyism, sale of state secrets to Fascist Germany, etc.[19]

An official Soviet publication in 1965 stated that the Red Army personnel swept up in the purges included most armies' commanders, all corps commanders, almost all division and regiment commanders, and about half of the brigade commanders.[20]

People—not only in Poland—asked themselves if it was worth entering into alliance with a rotting, crumbling power, whose heads, leaders and army commanders were either traitors—if one believed the Soviet courts—or victims of a savage, unreliable regime.

Even as the bells of war with Germany were clearly tolling, the Poles rejected the idea of Soviet assistance. The Polish Chief-of-Staff, Gen. Stachiewicz, and Foreign Minister Beck made explicit pronouncement to the effect that "The Russians are militarily worthless"; "Under no circumstances shall we agree to let Soviet forces set foot in Poland"; "We neither have nor want a military agreement with the Soviet Union."[21]

In the Web of National-Militarist Megalomania

In addition to this errant assessment, the "colonels' junta," and many other Polish leaders and pundits had a distorted and exaggerated view of the might and capabilities of Poland's own army. They believed that the armed force that had been established and which, drawing on a magnificent heritage and becoming one of Europe's greatest,* would represent sufficient guarantee of the country's independence.

Adopting a sardonic tone, the German ambassador to Warsaw, Moltke, reported to his superiors on August 1, 1939: "They still feel a certain security through . . . the legend of the 'invincible' Polish army."[23]

The kind of thinking that had overtaken Poland in those days was reflected in the saying, "With the Germans we risk our freedom, and with

---

*The Polish Army's manning table (in June 1939) stood in peacetime at 347,076 men, and in wartime it numbered 46,000 officers and 1,300,000 NCOs and soldiers. In addition, plans for the emergency call-up of reserves included 577,780 men. Total manpower planning in 1939 comprised 1,923,780 soldiers.[22]

the Russians—our souls." This combined with an over-reliance on the army's might, strengthened Beck's intent to navigate the ship of Polish policy between these two shoals. He believed that thus he could make Poland "the decisive factor in Eastern Europe." What he really accomplished, however, in fact, was to inject Fascism into Polish life, while his foreign policy facilitated the German build-up that ultimately cost Poland its freedom. Beck went far beyond the conception of his mentor, Piłsudski; not only did he consider the Soviet Union Poland's major enemy, but he believed Poland could arrive at a modus vivendi with Nazi Germany. Besides the anti-communism and underrating the potential of the Red Army; besides the megalomaniac and militaristic attitude of the colonels' junta—there were two other factors which weakened the all alertness of Poland's rulers towards the German threat. These were the anti-Semitism and Hitler's tactics, aimed at making his future victims to believe in his "peaceful" policies.

Anti-Semitism in Poland

Anti-Semitism was deeply rooted in all public strata of Poland—apart from a relatively narrow stratum of intelligentsia, liberals and some common people. Despite a thousand years of co-habitation, and the Jews' contribution to Poland's economy and culture, the anti-Semitism was an integral part of the Polish landscape. Drawing on various and sundry sources each generation bequeathed it to the next.

The re-emergence of the Polish state did not change the situation of the Jews for better. The Catholic clergy, bearing enormous influence on the Polish masses, sowed openly and constantly seeds of hatred towards the "Christ-killers." The rightist opposition, the National Democrats (hereinafter N.D.)—the largest party in the Sejm (140 of 394 representatives, or 35.8 percent) in 1919—made anti-Semitism a major plank in its platform. Its incitement found attentive ears and fertile breeding ground. The government, together with the ruling party (the "nonpartisan bloc" BBWR) increasingly tended—if with some hesitation—to introduce into its platform measures directed mainly against the Jews, although the intent may have been only to keep up with the ND and maintain popularity among the masses.

The situation worsened in the early 1930s when Poland slipped into an acute economic crisis. The mounting radicalization was diverted into a traditional channel—fingering the Jews, the Communists and . . . the Freemasons as the reason and root of all Poland's woes.

The death of Piłsudski on May 12, 1935 (his personality had kept antisemitism from running wild altogether) and the currents sweeping the country from Nazi Germany encouraged the Polish anti-Semites to stop confining themselves to N.D.-style incitement or measures which "merely" denied Jews their status and livelihood. Two political organizations came into being in 1937: The ONR (the National-Radical Camp) and the OZN (the National Unity Camp). The conceptual platforms of both drew on Nazi and Fascist sources and encouraged Poland to "cleanse" itself of its Jews.[24] The government, not wishing to be considered a laggard, tried to prove to the masses that it, too, was acting to hasten the Jews' departure from Poland and harass them in the meantime.

Prime Minister Slawoj-Skladkowski spoke in this vein in the Sejm:

> The Government will fight those who bring about riots, while it sees no crime in the economic struggle against the Jews. On the contrary: it may be waged by one and all.

This policy of "on the contrary" (*owszem*), therefore, became an official catchword of Government policy toward the Jews. Many among the masses caught the hint without excessive mental effort and with no reservations. The Jews now faced violent boycott and physical terror—on trains, in the universities, in city streets—that claimed hundreds of lives.[25] The Nazi propaganda mill made adroit use of these trends, and the German fifth column converted Poles to the cause of "Polish-German rapprochement."

The colonels' regime, and the anti-Semitic thinking nurtured under its inspiration, caused Polish public opinion to consider Nazi Germany a power from which to learn and with which to cultivate intimate relations.* No wonder, therefore, that the Nazis correctly regarded Polish anti-Semitism as

---

*Characteristic of the kinds of thinking that had come to dominate the Polish establishment and public were comments by Jozef Lipski, Poland's ambassador to Berlin. When Hitler told him of his ideas on how to solve the Jewish problem by expelling the Jews to colonies in Africa—in collaboration with the governments of Poland, Hungary and Romania—Lipski's reaction was: "I told him that if he finds such a solution we will erect him a beautiful monument in Warsaw."[26]

Lipski's colleague Jerzy Potocki, Poland's ambassador to Washington, reported to his minister in January 1939, that Jewish factors in the United States had nearly total control of all communication media and the film industry, and were fomenting hatred of Chancellor Hitler and everything Nazism stood for. Ambassador Potocki asserted in his memorandum that the anti-Nazi propaganda was meant to push the United States into a war that "world Jewry is striving to ignite in full cognizance."

a bulldozer which, if maintained properly, would pave their way into the hearts of the Polish people and Polish territory.

In the Web of Hitler's Charms

The other factor which made the colonels' junta to abandon more and more the narrow path of non-identification with one of its neighbors towards a growing admiration for the "achievements" of Hitler's Germany, were the latter's "peace-loving" tactics.

For years Hitler had been dripping anesthetics into the veins and ears of the European statesmen—reassurances, vows of peace, oaths of brotherhood. All he wanted was to "redress injustice," "rescue the German minorities," and "arrive at a peaceful solution to all the problems."

Europe thirsted for peace. Governments and the rank-and-file imbibed the false augury of peace that Hitler handed them from time to time. Whenever he spoke in the Reichstag, diplomats raced to cable to their governments the content of his rhetoric, and journalists hasted to describe his aspiration for peace.

> If present-day Germany is in favor of peace, it is neither through weakness nor through cowardice . . . —the Nazi tyrant proclaimed righteously in the Reichstag on May 21, 1935— . . . She is for peace by the very reason of the

German Foreign Minister on a visit to Warsaw—(from left) Marshal Smigly-Rydz, J. von Ribbentrop, Ambassador von Moltke, Colonel J. Beck

National-Socialist conception of the people and of the State. . . . Our racial doctrine regards any war undertaken to subjugate and decimate a foreign people as an event that, sooner or later, will modify and weaken the internal structure of the victor state.[27]

Beck and his cadre thirstily drank of Hitler's tendentious proclamations and promises, still not understanding that their turn would come. On January 14, 1938, Hitler received Beck and the two found a common tongue with respect to "the Bolshevik peril threatening Europe." Hitler lavished Beck with praise, and "promised" to withhold his support of any change in the status of Danzig.[28] In return, Beck adopted so conciliatory a stance that his German partners were taken by surprise.[29] He also enthusiastically concurred with Hitler's assessment that Czechoslovakia—because of its "intolerable" national structure and its policy—was liable to become a focus of Bolshevik menace.[30] Beck was jubilant, still believing that he was on the "right side." These steps taken by the Polish government and its domestic policy, together with the rising antisemitism and its policy on the Slavic minorities, caused a chasm to open and widen between Poland and the democratic powers. Poland now had a "bad press" in the West, and her political isolation grew as time passed.

Danzig on the Agenda

On February 20, 1938, again in the Reichstag—while concocting the stages of annexation and conquest—Hitler assured the Poles that:

Germany respects Polish rights in Danzig. . . . The way to friendly understanding has been successfully paved . . . transforming the relations between Germany and Poland into a sincere, friendly cooperation. Germany will not leave a stone unturned to save the ideal which provides the foundation for the task which is ahead of us—peace.[31]

These tactics continued as long as Hitler, before "solving" the Polish "problem," had first to "solve" the Austrian and the Czechoslovakia "problems." However, the ink had hardly dried on the Munich agreement when, on October 24, 1938, the Polish ambassador to Berlin, Jozef Lipski, was invited to lunch with the German Foreign Minister, Ribbentrop. The first topic in need of attention, said the host, was Danzig. Danzig had to "return to Germany," and connection between Germany and East Prussia had to be established by means of an autobahn and a railroad with extra-territorial status.[32]

From then on, German pressure on the Poles mounted with each passing day. Hitler considered "the solution to the Danzig problem" a logical

Foreign Minister Beck received by Hitler, Berchtesgaden, January 1939

step toward attaining his overall objectives. It was neither Danzig nor its status that concerned him; Danzig was only a first stepping stone toward the extermination of Poland and securing the Lebensraum in the east. On November 24, 1938, Hitler ordered the armed forces to prepare to take Danzig by surprise—not by launching war against Poland, but rather by "exploiting a political situation."

On January 5, 1939, Beck was received in Berchtesgaden by Hitler for another talk. Hitler, who had promised Beck a year ago that he would not support any change in the status of Danzig, now informed him in no uncertain terms that "Danzig was German, will always remain German, and will sooner or later be part of Germany." Nevertheless, he said, he was "still willing to settle for an autobahn and railroad through the corridor."[33]

On March 15, 1939, the Wehrmacht marched into dismembered Czechoslovakia and took over "independent" Slovakia for its "defense." On March 23, Hitler entered the "liberated" port city of Memel in a triumphant procession. Now Beck opened his eyes. German forces had closed on Poland from three sides—north, west and south. The ground on which he had built Poland's security thus far—fostering close relations with Nazi Germany and devouring crumbs dropped from the table of its conquests—was suddenly beginning to tremble under his feet.*

---

*Poland's short-sighted policy fell to a trough of lowliness and blindness when, together with Hungary it fell upon torn, anguished Czechoslovakia in October 1938, ripping the province of Teshen from its side.

Sobering Up

Now the "colonels' junta" realized that "solving the Danzig problem" was a first step toward slashing away at Poland's independence. The process of sobering up drew encouragement and courage not only from wellsprings of national pride and ability to conduct political analysis, but also—to no small extent—from a sharp turnabout in thinking that had occurred elsewhere.

When the German takeover of Czechoslovakia became final (March 15, 1939), Chamberlain's reaction surprised his followers and his opponents as well. This man who had placed his trust in Hitler and his promises; who considered himself the person who had saved world peace; who only three days earlier declared in Parliament: "Do not let us on that account be deflected from our course"—suddenly realized that he had been deceived. The outcome of this radical turnabout was the British Government's declaration—in concert with the French—that the Polish Government would be lent all possible support in the event of any action which clearly threatened Polish independence.[34]

Chamberlain's proclamation toppled Hitler into one of his eruptions of rage. On April 13 he phrased a top-secret operation order to his generals, bearing the code-name Fall Weiss (Case White). It called for the beginning of "military preparations" with the following aims:

> To destroy the Polish military force, and to create in the east a situation that will meet the national defense needs. The city of Danzig will be declared part of the territory of the Reich, and this upon the beginnings of the hostilities at the very latest.

As for tactics, the generals were ordered to plan a war that would proceed in such a way as to ensure "rapid success" by "a sudden attack . . . a sudden and heavy blow." Hitler believed in the possibility of securing convenient international conditions for a "limited war." His order continued as follows:

> The political leaders consider it their task . . . to isolate Poland if possible, that is to say, to limit the war to Poland only. The development of increasing internal crisis in France and the resulting British cautiousness might produce such a situation in the not too distant future. Intervention by Russia . . . cannot be expected to be of any use to Poland . . . Italy's attitude is determined by the Rome-Berlin Axis.

On the basis of these guidelines and goals, the commanders of the Wehrmacht's three services were ordered to present detailed plans to the

OKW (High Command of the Armed Forces) by May 1. The order went on to determine that "Preparations must be made in such a way that the operation can be carried out at any time from September 1, 1939, onward."[35]

The Unholy Alliance

Hitler spent the five-month period he had given his army drawing up operational plans and applying the political goal mentioned in the Case White order. His major concern was to ensure Poland's political isolation as the war broke out and progressed, in order to avoid a two-front war. The question that nagged at him was not only how to neutralize the West but also how to keep Russia from joining the camp of his western enemies.

The only way was one that contradicted all logic, every prediction, anything accepted as possible—an agreement between Nazi Germany and its greatest and most hated enemy, Soviet Russia.

This could not have been an easy decision for Hitler to reach. After all, he considered Bolshevik Russia, together with the "World Jewry," the very embodiment of evil and degeneracy.

> The Jew becomes the blood-Jew and a tyrant over peoples. . . . The most frightful example of this kind is offered by Russia, where he killed or starved about thirty million people . . . in order to give a gang of Jewish journalists and stock-exchange bandits domination over a great people.[36]

This conceptual contradiction, however, had to be put aside for the time being for the sake of military considerations. Furthermore, the agreement he sought, was meant as a historical interlude only, a tactical stage in which one of Germany's flanks would be secured. Bolshevik Russia's turn would yet come.

By the end of April 1939, hectic direct and indirect diplomatic activity began to culminate with a secret telegram, sent by Ribbentrop to his ambassador in Moscow, Count von Schulenburg, on April 14, 1939. The latter was instructed to meet with Molotov immediately and inform him verbally, word-for-word, that:

> There exist no real conflicts of interest between Germany and the USSR. . . . The crisis which has been produced in German-Polish relations by English policy . . . makes a speedy clarification of German-Russian relations desirable. . . . Therefore I am prepared to make a short visit to Moscow in order, in the name of the Führer, to set forth the Führer's view to Herr Stalin. . . . In my view . . . it should not be impossible thereby to lay foundations for a definite improvement in German-Russian relations.[37]

Hitler in the Wehrmacht's HQ with Reich's-Marshal Goering and Field-Marshal Keitel

In attached instructions, the ambassador was ordered to arrange a talk between Ribbentrop and Stalin. Ribbentrop would not visit otherwise.

An exchange of frantic letters ensued. The Germans were pressing, but the Soviets were playing a cool, coquettish game of "hard-to-get." Overcoming his disgust, enmity, and hubris, Hitler sent a personal telegram to Stalin on August 20, containing a half-request, half-demand: Would Stalin be so kind as to receive Ribbentrop on August 22, or, at the very latest, August 23? There was nothing further to gain by toying with vague formulations and small talk. It was time to lay the cards (at least a few of them) on the table. The telegram therefore contained a clear signal that war with Poland was imminent:

> The tension between Germany and Poland has become intolerable. . . . A crisis may arise any day. . . . A longer stay by the Reich Foreign Minister in Moscow that one to two days at most is impossible in view of international situation.[38]

On the evening of August 21, after twenty-four hours of unimaginable tension, Stalin's answer was received in Berlin:

> I hope that the German-Soviet non-aggression pact will bring about a decided turn for the better in the political relations between our countries. The

peoples of our countries need peaceful relations with each other. . . . The Soviet Government have instructed me to inform you that they agree to Herr von Ribbentrop's arriving in Moscow on August 23.[39]

What impelled Stalin to seek an agreement with Hitler? What did he have in mind? His major intent was to have the future war fought in places other than his adopted homeland. The "historiosophic" theory that explains the Nazi-Soviet agreement as originating in traits shared by the two totalitarian regimes does not seem to hold water, in our opinion. It was not similarity of character that had brought this agreement into being, just as the sharp ideological contrasts between the two did not prevent it. Stalin's considerations were devoid of conceptual sentiments. Stalin had no doubt that Hitler would attack Poland in the very near future, and that the offensive would end with Poland's defeat. His problem was how to keep the war away from Russia—in territory and in time—after Poland fell. The Poles' refusal to permit the Red Army to fight the Germans on their soil left Stalin with two alternatives: cooperate with the West or cooperate with Hitler.

Stalin's suspicions of England and France were deeply rooted. They drew on both conceptual sources and memories of the West's "siege" and "intervention" in the early stages of the Bolshevik revolution. Khrushchev, in his memoirs, reflects the thinking of senior Soviet leadership at the time:

> England and France would have loved to have stood by and watched Germany and the Soviet Union go at each other and finish each other off. The English and the French rubbed their hands in delight at the idea of lying low while Hitler's rampage took its toll of our blood . . .[40]

The Munich accord convinced Stalin that the democratic powers were not reliable. On the other hand, Stalin assumed that a deal with Hitler, notwithstanding the "dialectic contradiction" and conceptual "discomfort"—would allow the Soviet Union the possibility of staying out of the war, if only for a limited period of time.* That period of time and, perhaps, even the territory to be gained, were important to Stalin. The choice was clear. On the one hand, a commitment to enter the war, with all this implied, alongside untrustworthy partners. On the other hand, a fence-sitting posture with prospects of easy profit. It was clear to Stalin from the outset that his agreement with Hitler would be in effect a "gentlemen's agree-

---

*The threat from Japan, on the Soviet's far eastern front, also argued for the German option. This being outside the contrours of our study, we cannot speak at greater length of it.

ment" between two gangsters. However, he assumed, he would "fix" Hitler in the end, and not the other way around.

The Ribbentrop—Molotov Agreement

Ribbentrop's plane landed at Moscow airport on the afternoon of August 23. His meeting with Stalin and Molotov took place immediately after he reached the Kremlin. Within three hours, with no particular ado, the draft of the agreement was approved.

The non-aggression pact signed that evening established the following: neither of its signatories would attack the other. Should one of them become the object of hostile action by a third state, the other signatory to the pact would not be allowed to provide the third state with help of any kind. Similarly, neither Germany nor the USSR would join any constellation of other states aimed directly or indirectly against the other.[41]

Thus Hitler got what he wanted. Russia had been neutralized, and could not join up with England and France if either of these decided to keep her promise to Poland. But since a deal is a deal, he had to pay Stalin's price. Thus, a "secret protocol" was attached to the treaty, dividing the spoils between the partners. The major points follow:

Molotov—with Ribbentrop and Stalin looking on—signs the Nazi-Soviet Friendship Treaty

1. In the event of a territorial and political rearrangement of the areas belonging to the Baltic States (Finland, Estonia, Latvia, Lithuania), the northern boundary of Lithuania shall represent the boundary of the spheres of influence of Germany and the USSR;
2. In the event of a territorial and political rearrangement of the areas belonging to the Polish state, the spheres of influence of Germany and the USSR shall be bounded approximately by the line of the rivers Narew, Vistula and San. The question of whether the interests of both parties make desirable the maintenance of an independent Polish state, and how such a state should be bounded can only be definitely determined in the course of further political developments.
3. With regard to Southeastern Europe, attention is called by the Soviet side to its interest in Bessarabia. The German side declares its complete political disinterestedness in these areas.[42]

Thus, within a few hours, in a diplomatic move reflecting a cynicism almost unmatched in the annals of mankind, the ground was prepared for the Nazi war of aggression, the enslavement of peoples, and the dividing up of spheres of control and influence.

Nazi aggression and terrorism, Western appeasement, and perfidy had celebrated their victory in Munich. The Ribbentrop-Molotov agreement, by contrast, lacked any indication of the pacifist sentiment Chamberlain exhibited. A gang of hoodlums had papered over their differences, and the hope of dividing up fat booty temporarily weakened their mutual suspicion.

A few hours later, on August 24, Ribbentrop left Moscow "beaming with jubilation," bearing Stalin's go-ahead to Hitler to launch the war.

When Hitler received word of the success of Ribbentrop's mission, he set zero hour at 4:30 a.m., August 26. "There would be no further orders in this matter. Thereafter everything would proceed automatically."[43]

When Hitler's junior partner, the Italian Duce, found out that they were heading for real war and not a parade of arms, he looked for a way to wiggle out of the deal. On August 25 he informed Hitler that in view of his army's condition and state of arms, and in expectation that the entire West, including the United States, would rush to Poland's aid, he could undertake no military initiative unless Germany immediately provided him with equipment and war matériel. Mussolini was still hoping for a new Munich.

The British and the French, too, had not despaired of a "peaceful solution," and pressured the Poles to negotiate with Hitler in order to deny the Germans the possibility of holding Poland responsible for the conflict.[44] These developments, and enquiries by the President of the United States, the Pope, and other heads of state, held hostilities at bay for another several days. But Hitler had made up his mind, and his Foreign Minister, Ribbentrop, complained to British Ambassador Henderson that "The Poles are the aggressors, not we!"[45]

Zero hour was set for good at 04:45, September 1, 1939.[46]

The time of hesitation and delay was over. The deal had been nailed down on all sides.

Chapter Six

The War

The Course of the Battles

At dawn on Friday, September 1, 1939, the German forces crossed the Polish frontier. The invasion planned by Halder, the Chief of the German General Staff, and directed by Brauchitsch, the Commander-in-Chief, enriched the international lexicon with two new concepts that have since become idiomatic: "Blitzkrieg" and "total war."

The Luftwaffe took control of the skies, and, within two days, destroyed the Polish air force—most still on the ground. Bombardment of airports, concentrations of Polish armed forces, communications facilities, railroads, cities, and civilian installations sent the Polish army into a state of chaos and the civilian population into stark terror. Columns of German armor and divisions of mechanized infantry, with tactical air assistance, poured into the Polish heartland in a pincer movement from the north, west, and south. The Polish plain offered easy going for the German tanks. The Germans conducted the war with an intensity, speed, and brutality hitherto unknown, using new and innovative tactics of movement and fire; deep penetration of formations into the enemy heartland; close inter-arm cooperation; maximum exploitation of technological superiority; and use of three armed formations* belonging to the local fifth column.[1]

Within seven days the strategic outcome of the invasion had in fact been settled. Between September 8 and 17 the German army engaged in mopping-up operations, completed its encirclement of targets, and destroyed the last pockets of resistance. In a mighty pincer movement the 3rd and 14th Armies closed in on the territories west of the line formed by the San, Narew, and Bug Rivers.

On September 17, Poland was stabbed in the back.

---

*Kampf und Sabotage Organization; Freikorps Ebbenhaus; Selbstschutz.

At 2:00 a.m., Stalin received German Ambassador von Schulenburg to hear the good news that the Red Army would cross the Polish border in another four hours. Then he asked the Luftwaffe to stop operating east of the Bialystok—Brest-Litovsk—Lvov line.[2]

The same day, Molotov summoned the Polish ambassador to Moscow, Grzybowski, and read to him a letter that established the following:

> The Polish-German war has revealed the internal bankruptcy of the Polish State. . . . The Polish State and its Government have virtually ceased to exist. Treaties concluded between the USSR and Poland have thereby ceased to operate. . . . Poland has become a fertile field for any accidental and unexpected contingency, which may create a menace to the USSR. Hence, while it was neutral hitherto, the Soviet Government can no longer maintain a neutral attitude toward these facts. Nor can the Soviet Government remain indifferent when its blood brothers, the Ukrainians and White Russians living on Polish territory, having been abandoned to their fate, are left without protection. In view of this state of affairs, the Soviet Government has instructed the high command of the Red Army to order troops to cross the frontier and to take under their protection the lives and property of the population of Western Ukraine and Western White Russia. At the same time the Soviet Government intends to take every step to deliver the Polish people from the disastrous war . . . and to give them the opportunity to live a peaceful life.[3]

Once Molotov had completed his recitation, the Polish ambassador tried to lodge a vehement protest. The reply, "with all due respect," was that inasmuch as the state of Poland had ceased to exist, he and the embassy staff could no longer enjoy diplomatic immunity. Behind this assertion seems to have been Molotov's intent to arrest the ambassador and his aides, and only the intervention of the ambassadors of Germany and Italy averted this innovation in diplomatic procedure. Just the same, an embassy counselor named Matusinski vanished without a trace.[4]

***

Encountering little resistance from the remnants of the Polish army, the Russians advanced toward the line agreed upon by Ribbentrop and Molotov. The next day, September 18, advance units of Hitler and Stalin's armies met near Brest-Litovsk, and the commanders smiled at one another and shook hands.

Another politically decisive event took place on September 17. President Moscicki of Poland, Commander-in-Chief Smigly-Rydz and the "colonels' junta" fled to Chernovitz, with the approval of the Romanian Government. Even as he fled for his life, Smigly-Rydz nevertheless managed to dispatch an order to his army to continue fighting.[5]

The battles lasted until the end of September, but Poland's fate had been sealed.

On October 1, Molotov informed the Supreme Soviet about the Red Army's "liberation campaign" ("The Ukrainian and Belorussian population greeted our soldiers with indescribable enthusiasm. . . . Our soldiers came as liberators from the yoke of the capitalists and the Polish landlords"). He reported light Red Army losses in the campaign (737 dead, 1,862 wounded) relative to the achievements in the field (capture of 196,000 square kilometers with a population of 13 million).

Oozing contempt and self-aggrandization, Molotov bragged:

> One smart blow to Poland, first by the German army and afterwards by the Red Army—and not a trace remained of this ugly offspring of the Versailles Treaty . . . [6]

The Polish Embassy in London fiercely condemned the Soviets and ruled that:

> . . . By the act of direct aggression committed this morning the Soviet government have flagrantly violated the Polish-Russian Pact of Non-Aggression concluded in Moscow on July 25, 1932 . . . and prolonged on May 5, 1934 . . . until December 31, 1945. . . . Therefore, the Soviet Government stands self-condemned as a violator of its international obligations, thus contradicting all the moral principles upon which Soviet Russia pretended to base her foreign policy since her admittance into the League of Nations.[7]

The Soviets, of course, were not moved by the "compliments" and in fact ignored them altogether. Moreover, in the manner of true liberators, they quickly handed the reins of power to their "blood brothers." Like a true-blue democracy faithful to the doctrine of "self-determination," the Soviet regime rigged up a "plebiscite" in the territories they had occupied.

The people there were asked to decide "of their own volition" whether they wished to be annexed to the Ukrainian and Belorussian SSRs. Of course, information meetings were held first, as befitting a progressive regime. Below, Nikita Khrushchev—boss of the Ukraine, and the man responsible for Sovietizing the annexed territories—describes the meeting held in Lvov (which, it should be mentioned, was a Polish city with a solid Polish majority):

> The assembly in Lvov proceeded triumphantly. Representatives made speeches with tears of joy in their eyes. . . . History's injustice to the Ukrainian people was being set right. . . . Only now, in the Soviet era, was this dream at last coming true.[8]

It appears, however, that many others did not share this fervor with Khrushchev and some of the Ukrainians. Therefore, as if parenthetically, Khrushchev adds:

> At the same time we were still conducting arrests. It was our view that these arrests served to strengthen the Soviet State and clear the road for the building of Socialism on Marxist-Leninist principles.[9]

The arrests that Khrushchev and his leader thought so healthy and essential for socialism encompassed hundreds of thousands. Most were exiled to Siberia.[10]

After the Polish administration was swept aside and all its functions handed over to NKVD and Red Army personnel, "elections" were held on October 23, 1939, for the National Assemblies of the Soviet Republic of Western Ukraine and the Belorussian SSR.

Of 4,776,275 people with voting rights in the Western Ukraine, 4,433,997 voted—93 percent. Of 2,763,191 registered voters in western Belorussia, 2,672,280 voted—97 percent.[11] These "duly elected" Assemblies convened at the end of October and resolved "unanimously" to be annexed to the Soviet Union. "The injustice committed by the Riga Treaty of 1921 which was imposed upon the Soviet Union . . . was thus rectified," the Soviet Government proclaimed.[12]

Present-day Polish historical literature tends to adopt a rather laconic and discrete tone in its treatment of these dramatic and decisive events, which led to the enslavement and repartition of Poland. Thus, for example, a thick book on the topic devotes only three lines to the Ribbentrop-Molotov agreement, asserting that:

> The Soviet Union, facing danger in Europe from the Third Reich and in the Far East from Japan, agreed to conduct negotiations with the Reich Government. On August 23, 1939, a Soviet-German pact of Non-Aggression was signed for a period of ten years.[13]

Period.

Duraczynski writes about the invasion of the Red Army and the partitioning of Poland between the Soviet Union and Germany in much the same vein:

> On September 17 at 3:00 a.m., the Polish ambassador in Moscow was handed a letter describing the terms under which the Soviet Government

would order the Red Army to cross the border and take the lives and property of the populations of the Western Ukraine and Western Belorussia. That very day at 5:40 a.m., the Red Army crossed the border and moved west to carry out the order.[14]

This is undoubtedly a highly abridged bit of historical information.

The Causes of the Military Defeat

How did it happen that a proud and fighting nation, confident of itself and the ability of its army, fell victim to blitzkrieg? How could a state crumble and collapse so quickly?

In previous chapters we have identified the reasons and major factors that prepared the ground for Poland's defeat.

First among these was Hitler's aggressive policy; the deal between the Nazi Reich and Soviet Russia; Poland's hard-to-defend borders; the weakness of the West and its chronic credibility gap. We have also explored the causes of Polish domestic weakness—the country's ethnic composition, a reactionary domestic regime, and the inept, short-sighted policy pursued by the "colonels' junta."

We now briefly examine several military factors that led to Poland's demise. The first of these is the balance of forces.

As noted in previous chapters, the Polish army was numerically one of Europe's largest. The Poles were proud of their army and had faith in its capability. Morale in military and civilian circles was high to the point of megalomania.

Germany's ambassador to Warsaw, von Moltke, reported on March 28, 1938, about his conversation with M. Gluchowski, Polish Vice-Minister for War. The latter, expressing the prevailing sentiments and opinions, stated that:

> Germany's armed forces were one big bluff . . . When asked whether he seriously believed Poland to be superior to Germany from a military point of view, M. Gluchowski answered, 'Why, certainly.'

Some months later, in early August, Moltke wrote, quite sarcastically:

> Amongst the masses of the population the will to resist is obviously still unbroken. . . . Very wide circles are really convinced that Poland is on the side of the future victors. . . . They still feel a certain security, thanks to . . . the legend of the "invincible" Polish army.[15]

Furthermore, the Poles' regard for their army was shared by military leaders in other countries. When French Chief-of-Staff Gamelin was asked by his prime minister how long he thought Poland could hold out if attacked, he answered that Poland would resist "honorably" and would thereby stop the Germans from diverting their main strength against France until the spring of 1940.[16]* British Field Marshal Ironside, too, came back from a visit to Poland in late August with highly positive reports about the ability and morale of the Polish Army.[17] Furthermore, the British and the French guarantee to Poland in late March had taken on the contours of a formal agreement promising military aid in wartime. (A military protocol was signed with France on May 19, 1939 and with Great Britain on August 25).

Thus, Poland was not impotent and isolated in its confrontation with the German menace; the two great powers stood at her side. At the time, admittedly, the British army and airforce were still unprepared for war. Britain's major strength was still, traditionally, the Royal Navy, together with the country's economic and human potential. The French, however, were thought to have a mighty army. Fully mobilized, it numbered 110 divisions; of these, no fewer than 65 were active, including five of mounted cavalry, two mechanized, and one armored. The French could place 85 divisions on the German front.[18]

Theoretically and numerically, then, a joint operation by the Polish and French forces would have produced an impressive result. Together they could have thrown 130 divisions against the Germans, outnumbering them in pure numbers and in trained soldiers as well.[19] On the eve of the war, most of the German forces had not yet been properly trained and organized, and they were not yet organized for war in division formations. Germany had mobilized 98 divisions. Of them, 52 were active. Another ten divisions were composed mostly of raw recruits and soldiers already doing conscript service. Another 36 divisions were assembled by the mobilization of men aged 40 and over, World War I veterans who had not yet gotten used to the new equipment and the new demands of combat.[20]

To ensure French-Polish supremacy, however, three conditions had to be met:

A. Polish ability to impede the first German strike and enable the French to activate their forces; as stipulated in the French commitment, this would take fifteen days.

---

*We shall see that this opinion was influenced by Gamelin's perceptions. Nevertheless, it also expressed his assessment of Poland's military capabilities.

B. Coordinated deployment of the Polish-French forces.
C. The will to operate in this fashion, especially on the part of the French.

These terms were not met, of course, and the aforementioned combination of forces remained nothing more than an intellectual and numerical exercise.

Poland fought alone.

The German invasion force comprised 1,750,000 men, organized in 58 infantry divisions (17,700 men per division), 6 armored divisions, 4 divisions of mechanized infantry, 4 divisions of motorized infantry, 11,000 cannon, 2,800 tanks, about 2,000 aircraft, and naval formations. The rest of the Wehrmacht was placed in defensive positions on the Western front, or was kept as a strategic reserve.

The Poles managed to mobilize and deploy about a million men against this force.

The Polish Government refrained from calling a general public mobilization until August 30. This was much the doing of British-French diplomatic influence,[21] which sought to deny the Germans a pretext for embarking on war. A quiet call-up of reserves began in March, with partial success. When the blitzkrieg began, some of the Polish army had not been mobilized. The rapid advance of the German armored columns, and aerial bombardment of transportation arteries, trains, and communications facilities, severely hindered the call-up.

Thus, at the outbreak of war, the Polish force included 39 infantry divisions (16,500 men in each), 11 regiments of cavalry, several border patrol units, 4,500 cannon, about 700 tanks, and 400 aircraft. Small formations were positioned on the Eastern front.[22]

According to conventional doctrine, an army can conduct a defensive war when at a disadvantage of 1:2 or even 1:3. Thus, theoretically at least, the balance of infantry forces should have enabled Poland to hold out for quite awhile, thereby permitting the French to generate an offensive against the German forces and invade the Reich.

However, the equation is misleading, and our repeated emphasis on the theoretical nature of such assumptions and equations is well-placed. Such "accounting" ignores real differences—the composition of the fighting forces, their equipment, fire-power, their combat methods, and the motivation of those who put these to use.

The famous military commentator, Liddell Hart, regards the differences in attitude toward the tank and armored war by the Germans on the one hand, and the Poles and their Western allies on the other, as the major factor behind the German victory:

The incomprehension of the new idea of warfare and official resistance to it was even greater in France than in England, and greater in Poland than in France. That incomprehension was the root of the failure of both armies in 1939, and of the French again, more disastrously, in 1940.[23]

At the very same time that the German command acknowledged and absorbed the modern ideas, which placed greater value on armored and mobile war, the French, although amply equipped with tanks, considered the tank nothing more than a means of support for infantry.

The Poles were short on both modern military thinking and tools. The former disadvantage, to a great extent, also reflected social and cultural realities in Poland. The Polish army, like the armed forces of other peoples, was "prepared for the last war."

Polish military thought could not fathom the strength and fighting tactics of the Wehrmacht. It failed to appreciate the speed at which the German armor advanced, and Germany's methods of total war, built on sudden thrusts, deep penetration, and extensive use of armored formations, bombers and dive-bombers, parachuted forces, and a fifth column.

This failure to evaluate, and adherence to obsolete combat doctrines, affected the manner in which the Poles assembled their armed forces and failed to build armored and motorized formations.

According to Polish data,[24] a breakdown of their forces showed 49.4 percent infantry, 10.2 percent cavalry, 14.9 percent artillery, and 2.9 percent armor. The Germans, by contrast, were well on the way to mechanizing, developing a modern armored corps and airforce, and increasing land forces' firepower. As a result of these blunders, the Poles faced the Germans at the outbreak of the war with 700 tanks against 2,800 (a 1:4 ratio), 4,500 cannon against 11,000 (1:2.44), and 400 fighters and bombers against 2,000 (1:5).

According to the same sources, the disparity was even wider along the Wehrmacht's major attack routes: 1:8.2 for tanks, 1:4.3 for cannon, and 1:7.6 for anti-tank guns. The Poles still believed in the advantage of massing infantry and cavalry. The cavalry, the "flowers of the nation" as they were affectionately and proudly known in peacetime, in the days of showy parades, set out in September 1939 at a valorous and romantic gallop, armed with swords and spears, against the columns of German tanks.

The Germans' supremacy in armor, air power, and innovative tactics were invaluable, too, in view of Poland's terrain and the length of her borders.

Those 2,000 kilometers, obtained at such great toil in effort to restore historic luster to an old crown, now became a death trap. They simply could not be defended effectively, and the vast plains merely improved the mobility of German armor. Most of the Polish defense was based on aggregations of seven armies facing north, west, and south. Because of a manpower shortage (due to disruptions in mobilization), the great expanses, and an undeveloped transportation infrastructure, the armies were separated by vast "dead areas" and undefended territory.

Thus, for example, the Lodz and Cracow armies were separated by eighty kilometers of undefended territory. Here the German 10th Army (17 divisions, including two armored and two mechanized) staged its breakthrough.[25]

Lacking mechanized formations, the Poles could not move quickly into an alternative defense deployment in the rear. The German armored columns swept through the openings, and the Polish infantry forces soon found themselves totally surrounded.

Above and beyond all the objective, technical, and tactical factors, however, the fundamental cause of the rout was psychic, psychological, and conceptual. Liddell Hart suggests that the defeat of both the French and the Polish armies may have originated in a fatal measure of self-assuredness at the top. For the French, it had been fostered by victory in World War I; for the Poles, it had been nourished by their defeat of the Russians in 1920. In both cases, the military leadership had long proved itself impudently complacent about its forces and military techniques.[26]

***

Self-satisfaction and self-confidence, and the national and militaristic megalomania cultivated by the ruling junta in Poland, combined to cause an overestimation of Polish strength, a standstill in military thinking, failure to understand the Germans' innovations in the structure and activation of armed forces, and underestimation of the Red Army's strength.

The propensity to pat themselves on the back also served the self-serving and power-mongering interests of the "colonels' junta." It deluded much of the Polish public—and some foreign military leaders—as to the army's strength and ability. At times, too, recurrent media reports about foreign agreement with the Poles' own assessments further amplified their self-confidence and the magnitude of the illusion, while lending new prestige to the colonels' junta. Politization of senior army command, too, grew under the colonels. Commanders who did not identify with the "colonels" were deposed, while ambitious generals played to the political grandstand, developing "public relations" at the expense of military thinking. Their view, nourished on complacency, was that the Polish army was invincible.

The French Guarantee

We previously mentioned that the Polish and French forces together would have outnumbered the Germans. The British and French guarantee, had it been honored, could have changed the course of the war.

The Polish believed that because of the very existence of the guarantee, "Germany would probably never dare to pick a quarrel with Poland. . . . Even if war came and even if Poland were completely occupied by German troops, she would nevertheless in the end, thanks to the victory of the coalition, arise again even greater and more powerful than ever."[27]

The Poles assumed that the guarantee, and the military agreements to which they were signed, ensured "political agreement securing automatic intervention should the vital interests of either side be endangered."[28]

Things did not develop as the Poles expected. As a factor that might reduce the pressure of the German offensive and even result in an offensive against Germany, forcing the Germans to divert much of their forces to the West, the Western guarantee proved meaningless.

The Poles fought alone, and lost.

The assumption was that while the British guarantee had significant value in the longer term—once Britain's vast but somnolent potential was mobilized—France's loins were girded, its forces ready for action.

This was not a mere assumption but an article of faith anchored in a signed protocol and an explicit promise. According to the agreement concluded in talks held in Paris in May 1939, between the French senior command (Chief-of-Staff Gamelin, Admiral Darlan, and Generals Dentz, Vuillemin and Georges), and General Kasprzycki and Colonel Jaklicz of the Polish army,[29] the French undertook gradually to mount offensive operations against limited enemy targets, starting on the third day of a general mobilization of the French army.

The heads of the French army also undertook that fifteen days after the mobilization began they would place three-fourths of its strength on the northeastern (German) front—and about half of this force—according to Gen. Gamelin 35–38 divisions—would take part in the offensive. Responding to an explicit question by Colonel Jaklicz, Gamelin announced that the reference was to an offensive in which French forces would cross into Germany.[30]

However, the military protocol that summarized this commitment, signed on May 19, began to lose its initial momentum within a few days. Prime Minister Daladièr and, in particular, his foreign minister, Bonnet, were in no hurry to give overly explicit commitments their political seal of approval. Though they were slowly sobering up to Hitler's charms, and although Czechoslovakia had been dismantled, the urge to appease had not been totally extirpated. Just as Chamberlain had asked during the Munich episode if the British ought rightly to fight "because of a conflict in a faraway country, between peoples we know nothing about"—so many people now asked, "Are we supposed to die for Danzig?"

These developments undoubtedly caused General Gamelin to retreat from his promise to the Poles during the talks. As one who had been known to take a chilly attitude toward France's Czechoslovakian ally, now, too, he found it neither psychically nor intellectually difficult to return to his basic strategic conception. This conception was fundamentally defensive, and relied on the "unbreachable" Maginot line.

Gamelin's memoirs make no mention of his commitments of May. However, he writes angrily about the Air Force commander, General Vuillemin, who dared proclaim in the presence of the Poles that "the French air force will be able to intervene energetically to alleviate Poland's task when the battles begin." Gamelin claims that he had promised no more than a maximum French effort to pin down as much of the Wehrmacht as possible on its borders.[31]

Indeed, in keeping with this line of thought, Gamelin, in a joint meeting of the government and the senior command (August 23, 1939), recommended that the French honor its commitment to Poland. The practical import of this commitment, however, was very flexible and a far cry from the protocol signed three months previously. The French Chief-of-Staff expressed the optimistic view that Poland could defend itself "honorably" for several months, during which time France would mobilize and train its forces properly, thereby pinning down part of the German Army in the west and alleviating the pressure on Poland. This would go on until the spring of 1940, when Britain, too, equipped by the United States, would enter the war.

> By the spring, . . . I hope we should be in a position to fight a defensive battle (of course if necessary)[32]*

Thus, while the Poles believed in the commitment given them on May 19—"automatically" triggering a French offensive on the sixteenth day of the war—the French Government was deliberating with its army commanders, several days before the war broke out, as to steps that would permit the French Army's one hundred divisions to wage a defensive (not offensive) half a year later or more (not fifteen days) after the outbreak of the war—and this only "if necessary."

---

*In the original: *Bien entendu s'il le fallait.*

The French, of course, did not communicate these resolutions to the Poles. They preferred to have the Poles "defend themselves honorably" and keep the German army busy in the meantime.

Paris and London's reluctance to enter into the heat of war—understandable in and of itself—persisted even after the Germans had invaded Poland. For forty-eight fateful hours the French and British kept up their diplomatic efforts (with the active participation of Italy). The French and British politicians still sat on the fence and considered whether to climb off it, and, if so, whether on the run or at a shuffle. The diplomats engaged in semantic exercises in search of a miraculous formula that would stop the war without requiring their governments to honor their guarantees.

After midnight on September 1, Churchill wrote impatiently to Chamberlain that he was deeply concerned, with the Poles having been under heavy attack for more than thirty hours, that people in Paris were talking about another note. He also expressed his trust that Chamberlain would be able to announce the joint declaration of war at no later time than the Parliament meeting that afternoon.[33]

Only on the morning of September 3 did the ambassadors of Britain and France present Ribbentrop with their Governments' ultimatum. It was rejected, and France and Britain found themselves at war with Germany.

Enthusiastic and vociferous mass demonstrations were held in front of the French and British embassies in Warsaw. Nothing on the battlefield suggested any real reason for this outpouring of jubilation.

The Polish people learned the bitter truth about the substance and dubious value of international guarantees—even when given in good faith and sincerely meant—the hard way.

"We promise in keeping with our hopes, and act in keeping with our fears," wrote Francois Rochefoucauld. When it comes time to honor guarantees given under certain conditions, those who gave them often suddenly find that conditions have "changed" in the meantime. Natural apprehension about the effort and sacrifice required to keep the promise overcame the virtues of honor and moral duty, and supplied ample reasons to justify the turnabout.

(A study of the extent to which international guarantees signed between 1815 and 1945 were invoked proves that only 48 percent of them [45 of 115] proved reliable.)[34]

The French English guarantee to Poland saved the world from the disaster of Nazism. Britain's proud and courageous stance (it would soon be left alone in the campaign) was a grand episode in human annals. However, the concrete and effective value of this guarantee for the immediate salvation of Poland was nil. Throughout the fateful month of September, in which Poland was vanquished and repartitioned, hardly a shot was fired in the West. The first English casualty, a corporal in the British expeditionary force, fell in France while on patrol on December 9.[35]

Between the autumn of 1939 and the spring of 1940, the situation in the West was one that the Americans called the "phony war" and the Germans called *Sitzkrieg*.

Molotov, Ribbentrop's partner, therefore had reason to report derisively to members of the Supreme Soviet on October 31, 1939:

> As we know, neither British nor French guarantees were of help to Poland. To this day in fact nobody knows what these "guarantees" were.[36]

Poland Repartitioned

A further step toward eradicating the Polish state was taken several days after the Soviet invasion.

While the Ribbentrop-Molotov agreement of August 23, 1939, left the future of politically truncated, shattered Poland open "to additional political developments," the Soviets now took an initiative to repartition Poland and exterminate it as a political entity.

Underlying this move were Stalin's fears and suspicions. He was impressed and terrified by Germany's swift victory, and was afraid that the German military momentum would continue into Russia.

We find the indications of this fear in his talk with German ambassador von Schulenburg, when Stalin asked if the Wehrmacht would indeed withdraw from the point it had reached in its momentum to the agreed-upon line.

> His concern . . . was based on the well-known fact that all military men are loath to give up occupied territories.[37]

The "phony war" magnified his suspicions all the more. Was it not clear indication of the conspiracy being concocted between the West and Hitler, aimed at opening an offensive against Russia? From now on, Stalin began to approach Hitler with proposals and measures meant to prevent possible friction. The Soviet media were instructed to refrain from doing Germany any offense:

> The Soviet press. . . . .is as though it had been transformed. Attacks on the conduct of Germany have not only ceased completely, but the portrayal of events in the field of foreign politics is based to an outstanding degree on German reports . . . [38]

Now Stalin strived for as much understanding with Hitler as he could muster, and labored to prevent unnecessary difficulties, inquiries, and "anything liable to create friction between Germany and the Soviet Union in the future." From this point of view he considered it a mistake to leave an independent Polish "rump state."[39] Based on these initiatives and ideas, the two accomplices concluded a new deal on September 28. The "German-Soviet Boundary and Friendship Treaty"[40] partitioned Poland once and for all, and included secret appendices. The territorial appendix and its map represented a response to Stalin's proposals. He did not find the prospect of having several million obstreperous and hostile Poles under his scepter particularly enticing. Therefore, the areas of Warsaw (up to the River Bug) and Lublin were handed to Germany, while Lithuania, Estonia, Latvia, and Finland were assigned to the Soviet sphere of "influence" in exchange.

(The Polish territories handed over to German control had a population of more than 22 million, including more than 2 million Jews. The eastern territories had a population of some 13.5 million, with 1.4 million Jews.)[41]

The second appendix promised mutual "repatriation": Soviet residents of German extraction would be returned to Germany, while Ukrainians and Belorussians residing in Germany could emigrate to the Soviet Union. (One of the results of this ostensibly humanitarian gesture was the delivery of German Communists, who had succeeded in fleeing Germany into the Soviet Union—into the hands of the Gestapo.)[42]

The third appendix gave expression to the spirit of "partnership" and "friendship" by which a joint and coordinated repression of the spirit of freedom and resistance might be undertaken. Thus:

> Neither side will tolerate in its territories any Polish propaganda liable to offend the other side. [The sides] will repress any beginnings of such propaganda, and will exchange information between each other.

Although Stalin, sure that he would "fix" the perfidious Germans, played his game in cold blood, the final partitioning of Poland and his acquisition of exclusive "influence" in the Baltic countries played into Hitler's hands. Now, in return, Stalin had to support Hitler's propaganda. This development comes to the fore in a joint declaration on September 28, 1939, calling for immediate peace and blaming England and France for continued hostilities.[43]

In keeping with accepted practice, the event was celebrated in a banquet in the Kremlin. The hosts went to every length to shower their guests with genuine friendship and a feeling that they were partners in dividing the spoils. The banquet was up to Czarist standards; the food and drink demonstrated the high-living style of the Soviet regime.

The impression was striking indeed, as attested by a senior member of the German delegation:

> At the Kremlin Palace entrance the Russian Chief of Protocol received the Foreign Minister [Ribbentrop] and conducted him into a reception room decorated in red and gold. Here Stalin, wearing his well known litewka, and Molotov, surrounded by Marshal Voroshilov, Commissar for Internal Affairs, Beria and other highest dignitaries, awaited the Führer's envoy and the other German guests. After the greeting, the door was opened to an oval room where the table was set. Richly decorated with flowers, set with costly porcelain and gilded cutlery, in the bright light of electric candles it presented a thoroughly festive appearance. The Foreign minister took his place next to Stalin and across from Molotov. An army of waiters dressed in white served a repast that did full honour to the reputation of Russian hospitality. . . . Among the many hors d'oeuvres they had of course not forgotten the famous Russian caviar. . . . After the official remarks Molotov addressed to each guest a special toast. Each time Stalin himself stood at the place of the person addressed to drink to his health. . . . How pleasant and relaxed the atmosphere was . . . is shown by the following utterance of Stalin, which he gave laughingly when Molotov had repeatedly toasted him: 'If Molotov really wants to drink, no one objects, but he really shouldn't use me as an excuse.' . . . It was clear that by this performance the Soviet Government wished to pay the Foreign Minister signal honor. This was shown . . . by the presence of Stalin, who very seldom participates in state banquets honoring foreign guests . . . [44]

Warsaw fell that very day.

***

A few Polish units kept up a desperate battle until October 5. The Polish soldier proved to be a courageous, stubborn fighter. In the coastal area at Westerplatte, 182 Polish soldiers confronted a German force of 4,000, backed by aircraft and 65 cannon. One might have expected them to fold within hours. Instead, they held out for a week.[45] The valor of the Polish fighting man, however, did not save Poland. She crumbled and was consumed by her two neighbors.

Chapter Seven

Under the Yoke of Occupation

The downfall and partitioning of the Polish Republic were accompanied by indescribable suffering of its population. About a million and a half Poles from areas captured by the Red Army were either expelled or exiled into the Soviet Union, mainly its Asiatic reaches. Throughout the war it was their fate to migrate from one labor camp to another amid grueling labor, starvation, and epidemics. A great many succumbed. Almost all (1,060,000) were imprisoned in camps or sent to distant areas. Of them, about 270,000 died during the next two and a half years (up to 1942).[1]* Soldiers and officers taken captive (about 200,000) were incarcerated in Soviet camps.[2]

Immeasurably worse was the fate of those who remained in Poland under German occupation. On October 2, Hitler issued unequivocal orders, which were recorded by Martin Bormann:

> The Government General represents a Polish reserve of manpower—a vast Polish labor camp . . . the Poles are specially born for low labor . . . it is necessary to keep the standard of life low in Poland . . . the Poles are lazy and it is necessary to use compulsion to make them work . . . There should be one master only—the German; two masters, side by side, cannot and must not exist. Therefore, all representatives of the Polish intelligentsia are to be exterminated. This sounds cruel, but such is the law of life.[3]

Indeed, the orders were carried out to the letter and in their spirit. During the combat, after the guns fell silent, and throughout the years of

---

*It should nevertheless be recalled that this, notwithstanding the suffering involved, saved the lives of *very many* of them. Had they stayed where they were, they would undoubtedly have fallen into the clutches of Einsatzgruppen, units attached to the Wehrmacht that engaged in the annihilation of Jews in the occupied Soviet territories.

occupation, Poland served as a reservoir of human beings exploited for forced labor, economic abuse, and relentless repression. Hundreds of thousands breathed their last in the labor camps, dying of disease and starvation.

In the first weeks of the occupation, German terror was applied against Jews, Communists, and members of the Polish intelligentsia and elite. Others consoled themselves with the thought that the terror and executions were invoked "only" against certain groups, and deluded themselves with the hope that when the initial fury had passed, life would go back to normal.

It was not to be. The terror and repression machine became more efficient and cut a widening swath of activity.

At the risk of putting the cart before the horse, let us note that World War II claimed the lives of 6,028,000 Poles—22.2 percent of the country's entire population.[4] No country in Nazi-occupied Europe matched this percentage.

According to Polish data,[5] 644,000 people fell in action (in the September 1939 invasion, and later in the underground and Allied ranks); 3,577,000 were put to death in extermination camps; 1,286,000 died of epidemics and exhaustion in the camps; and 521,000 died of disease and exhaustion outside the camps.

These dry statistics cannot be understood and will not be complete unless we stress that about half of the Polish victims were Jews. While the 3,000,000 non-Jewish dead—a terrifying figure in its own right—accounted for about 14 percent of all ethnic Poles, the disaster that befell Polish Jewry was immeasurably greater. Ninety percent of Poland's Jews—about 3 million out of 3.3 million—perished in ghettos, labor camps, and extermination camps.[6]

Thus, Hitler's terrible "prophecy" was almost fully realized (see his speech of January 30, 1939, and other speeches on January 30, 1941, January 30, 1942, September 30, 1942, and November 8, 1942). Consider the following sample (January 30, 1939):

> In the course of my life I have often been a prophet . . . Today I wish to be a prophet once more. Should international Jewry . . . succeed once more in plunging the nations into war, the result will not be the bolshevisation of the earth and through it the victory of Jewry, but the annihilation of the Jewish race in Europe.[7]

The Jews and Poles in occupied Poland not only faced brutal death as a regular fare, but had to contend with every other form of suffering, starvation, poverty, and humiliation that the Nazi mind could invent and implement.

The picture would still not be complete, however, if we failed to note the drama of audacious resistance that, alongside the terrible and tragic suffering, also characterized occupied Poland.

Resistance

Poland went down fighting—and continued to resist the occupier even after its defeat. Occupied Poland did not cooperate with Germany, as Romania and Hungary did. Nor did collaborators of national stature emerge there, as they had in France, for example.

Although the government and the senior army command had collapsed and fled to Romania, the Poles did not lay down their arms.

Polish soldiers who had succeeded in crossing the border, Polish emigrés in the Western countries, and Polish citizens—including many Jews—who had somehow found their way to the Soviet Union began to organize in military formations under the Polish flag. Such units, established in France, England, the United States, Canada, and the Soviet Union, fought heroically in various theaters of the war.

Though relatively small in number at first (about 150,000),* their very existence under the Polish flag was enough to mark the Polish nation's will and its right to political resurrection.

The Polish nation did not produce a quisling. On the contrary: the underground that came into being after the German occupation commenced was a supreme and daring manifestation of Poland's fighting spirit, adherence to freedom, and intent to re-establish its place in the family of free nations after Nazi Germany was defeated.

The Nazis' acts of savagery, repression, and devastation in Poland provoked profound hatred and a will to exact revenge on the part of the Polish nation. First dozens, then hundreds of fighting groups organized clandestinely in Poland proper, engaging in harassment and sabotage.

How strong the underground really was, of course, is hard to determine with precision. Data are inaccurate, documentation is understandably lacking, and the testimonies not fully objective. The definition of "under-

---

*According to recent official Polish data,[8] Sikorski's army (in the west) had 82,264 men in the spring of 1940; Anders' army (in the Soviet Union) had 73,425 soldiers in February 1942, and 83,000 when it left the Soviet Union.

ground fighters," too, is not clear-cut. Were these only those men and women who actually threw grenades, planted explosives, etc.? Or does this term also apply to those who pasted up underground posters and printed insurrectionist leaflets?

With respect to underground fighting units, too, the numbers do not express operational reality. For example, we know there were about 40,000 men in the underground in Warsaw at the time of the uprising in that city (August 1944)—but only about half of them were armed.[9]

Another difficulty in determining the actual strength of the underground was its political factionalization. The largest element in the underground was organized under the AK (*Armia Krajowa*—"Home Army"),[10] which represented a very broad range of Polish public circles that excluded only the far left. Politically, the AK was based mainly on members of four large parties (the Socialists [PPS], the Nationalists [SN], the Peasants [SL], and the Christian Workers [SP], and it was subordinate to the government-in-exile in London. This government was represented in Poland by commanders of the remnants of the defeated Polish army. The second underground faction, the AL (*Armia Ludowa*—"People's Army") did not begin to organize until 1942. It drew its inspiration from the Polish Communist Party, and about 5,000 Soviet nationals fought in its ranks.[11]

The rift between the two undergrounds was so deep as to preclude any coordination. Each criticized the other for inaction, belittled its value and strength, and accused it of conniving with the enemy. According to the AK, the leftist underground collaborated with the Soviet Union and was not fighting the Germans. The AL, in turn, accused the AK of cooperating with the Germans. Thus even the available numerical data are not objective. Each side tried to aggrandize its own strength "for the sake of historical truth," and understated the strength of the other side for the same cause. A certain indication (whose extent of accuracy and objectivity is hard to determine) of the strength of the AK can be found in the memoirs of Stanisław Mikołajczyk, head of the Polish government-in-exile, who claims that at its peak it had about 300,000 members.[12] Some other sources[13] support this assessment. But this number is devoid of operational meaning; its operational potential was constrained by an acute shortage of arms.

The AL was unquestionably a much weaker body, and its activity made almost no imprint until 1944. Official documents indicate that the AL developed its major momentum in the summer of 1944, and this only in the eastern and southern provinces (Lublin, Kielce). Basing ourselves on official data, we can estimate that the number of AL fighters did not exceed 30,000 (although certain sources mention 50,000–60,000).[14]

Despite the fragmentation and the relatively restricted activity of both undergrounds, both can justly boast of having maintained the torch of resistance that burned inexhaustibly in the heart of the Polish nation.

The Jews in the War and the Resistance Movement

In the context of the facts discussed thus far, we should briefly mention the role of the Jews of Poland in the campaign of resistance—the tens of thousands of Jewish soldiers in the Polish Army who took part in the 1939 war, the Jewish soldiers in Polish units that organized after the defeat in the West and the Soviet Union, and the Jewish partisans and underground fighters.

In the confines of this book, we cannot explore at length the vast difference between Polish gentiles, who were under German occupation, and Polish Jews, who were the targets of the Nazi annihilation campaign on the one hand and a hostile environment on the other.[15] The armed Polish underground, while relying on help from the government-in-exile, treated every Jewish attempt to join its ranks with suspicion, hostile indifference, and rejection. Its aid to the fighting Jewish organization, ŻOB (*Żydowska Organizacja Bojowa*) was negligible.

Only in late 1942 did the Polish underground extend some very limited help to a parallel fledgling Jewish movement. Most of this took the form of several dozen handguns (some non-functioning), instruction, and assistance in forwarding reports to London.

Several examples demonstrate the AK command's cold-shoulder attitude.

AK commander Gen. Stefan Rowecki, in a telegram sent to London on January 4, 1943, said the following:

> Too late Jews of various groupings, also Communists, appeal to us for arms, just as if we had full arsenals. As a trial, I gave them a few pistols. I am not sure they will use the weapons altogether . . . [16]

So great was the estrangement that even when the Warsaw Ghetto uprising—the first popular armed insurrection on Polish soil—was in full blaze in April, 1943, Itzhak ("Antek") Zuckerman, deputy commander of the ŻOB was told the following by a major AK figure:

> I can tell it to you straight: we don't believe you. We think the ghetto is nothing but a Soviet Russian base. A plan has been readied, and the Poles know what it is. It was the Russians who planned the Warsaw Ghetto rebel-

lion, and you've got much more weapons than you're letting on . . . The Polish man in the street is afraid that the rebellion will cross the Ghetto walls and that the Poles will rise up—and that's what the (Communist-influenced) AL wants. So I warn you: if this really happens, and if you collaborate with the AL and the AL comes to your aid, we'll move against the Ghetto.[17]

Even an appeal for help in reaching the Aryan side through sewers, by the last survivors of the Warsaw Ghetto fell on deaf ears. However, such aid was provided by the Communist underground, the AL.

After the war, spokesmen for the AK tried to describe, with considerable exaggeration, its contribution and help to the Jews in general and the Warsaw Ghetto rebels in particular.

One organization among the Polish population which did help greatly and with tremendous devotion was Żegota, which provided the Jews with help in a variety of forms. There were also some thousands of genuinely righteous Poles, of whom no few risked or gave up their lives to save Jews. Some of them were simple folk; others belonged to the nobility, the intelligentsia, or the priesthood. Their activity and heavy sacrifices will be remembered: an avenue of trees has been planted in their names in Yad Vashem, the Holocaust Remembrance Institute in Jerusalem. The bitter, brutal truth, however, is that these were only weak flickers of light in a general ambience of darkness.

Without dwelling on the instances of active collaboration by Polish nationalistic and criminal factors in the Germans' enterprise of annihilation, we must assert that the attitude of most of the Polish populace to the phenomenon was typified by hostile passivity.

As mentioned before, the AK underground shared this attitude. Although the AK's attitude stemmed mainly from deeply-rooted wellsprings of anti-semitism, there was also a real conflict of interests between the AK and the Jewish underground. It originated in the AK's resistance to expanding the field of combat "prematurely," in fear of brutal German reprisals against the population. The AK considered its major task one of information, the training of cadres, economic assistance, and fomenting civil rebellion, in addition to symbolic sabotage and attacks on Polish collaborators. Actual fighting, the AK leaders believed, should be delayed until the Germans' main force had been heavily attacked by the Allied forces, and when the front had moved into the Polish heartland or at least to the border.

Hence the AK was also afraid of "irresponsible" actions by the Jews. While the Polish underground considered its struggle a means of rescuing the nation and restoring its independence, for the Jews it was a desperate, final way of expressing and salvaging the honor of a people being led to slaughter.

Indeed, the pace of the extermination process disabused the survivors, especially members of pioneering Zionist movements, of any illusions they had harbored.

Jewish armed resistance erupted in the summer of 1942 in the ghettos of Nieśwież, Lachwa, Kleck, Kovno, Minsk-Mazowiecki, Krzemieniec, Lida, Miory, Slonim, Nowogródek, Luck, Braclaw, Glebokie, Zdolbunów, Adamów, and Kobryń. The Jewish resistance movement progressively spread and variegated. It embraced groups of fighters in the ghettos of Bendzin, Cracow, Bialystok, Brody, Częstochowa, Tarnov, and Vilna; the extermination camps of Treblinka and Sobibor, in the Ninth Fort, and the forests of Polesie. It reached its heroic and tragic pinnacle in the Warsaw Ghetto uprising, the first and greatest act of armed insurrection in Poland since its occupation.

The Right to Political Rebirth

Interviewed on May 4, 1943, Stalin was asked by writers of the New York *Times* and the *Times of London* whether the Soviet government wished to see a strong and independent Poland after the victory. His answer was terse and unequivocal: "Yes, without a doubt." During the war years, Poland and its people were showered with compliments and praise by Churchill and Roosevelt. Their support for its cause and its right to an independent and free existence was firm and sincere. However, the fact of this right, which Poland had earned with blood and tears, had nothing to do with the content or the final form of its independence.

The Polish government-in-exile toyed with the illusion that the Poles' suffering and resistance would by themselves cause their aspirations and demands, including those of territorial nature, to come true. It quickly found out that the Three Powers, especially the Soviet Union, Poland's next-door neighbor, would also have a say in these concerns.

Indeed, even as the fighting went on in the underground and on the battlefield, so did an extremely difficult and complicated war for the future of Poland begin to rage in the theater of diplomacy.

Chapter Eight

The "London Government"

The Sikorski Government

A Polish government-in-exile was set up in Paris in October, 1939, and moved to London after France fell.

Poland's military defeat brought the "colonels' junta" and its policy to their organizational and political demise. Everyone formerly affiliated with democratic opposition circles now joined ranks in Paris and London[1] to establish a new governmental framework. This was no easy task, in view of the broad party spectrum that embraced ND followers on the Right and Socialist Party (PPS) supporters on the Left. Nor were personal contradictions and friction lacking, and the long-standing Polish tradition of individualism (*liberum veto*) complicated the matter further.

However, the Government came into being, and General Sikorski was installed as its head. He proclaimed that:

> We do not want merely to re-establish the pre-war status quo . . . which was to some degree the cause of what had happened. . . . We are fighting not only for an independent Poland but for a new, democratic state assuring to all her citizens political and social freedom and progress.[2]

Shortly thereafter, the government-in-exile was recognized by the United States, France, England, and several other countries.

This government, organically weak because it was a government-in-exile, and largely dependent on the mercies of its hosts, was entrusted with three formidable tasks:

A. To organize the defeated people and the occupied country for a stance against the most brutal of enemies.
B. To develop relations with the major Allies in order to obtain their support for Poland's post-victory resurrection, and to obtain the tools necessary for war and survival.

C. To conduct diplomatic negotiations with the Allies leading to the restoration of Poland's territorial integrity, the creation of secure borders, and the consolidation of Polish independence and sovereignty.

Considering the conditions under which the "London government" worked during its five years of existence, its achievements were substantial. Cut off from its people and its country, shorn of genuine executive power, based solely on the voluntary response of the exile community in free Europe and the underground in occupied Poland, this government succeeded in holding itself together, obtaining the great powers' recognition, negotiating with them, mobilizing and organizing military formation, maintaining a permanent, executive legation (*Delegatura*) in occupied Poland, establishing an extensive political and military underground, and providing it with war matériel and support. All this under conditions that were harsh in every sense, and in an internal maelstrom of parties, factions, pressure groups, and individuals, in whom the tradition of *liberum veto* and the inbred pride of a rural gentry were still heavily entrenched.

The Polish government-in-exile considered its first and most urgent task the organization of a new Polish Army comprising formations and remnants of formations that had succeeded in fleeing to the West.

The goal of the army and the underground, and the government-in-exile's very *raison d'etre,* was to bring about Poland's liberation and political resurrection. At this point, then, we should explore the "London Government's" political goals and struggle—a protracted, convoluted, stubborn, and complicated struggle that it waged throughout the war years with its enemies and friends alike. This struggle and additional factors indeed resulted in the emergence of a postwar Poland—although not necessarily the same Poland envisaged and sought by the government-in-exile.

The "London government" presented the reconstitution of independent, sovereign Poland as its major demand. Its position was that once victory and liberation were achieved, all indications of occupation and annexation be erased. Thus the new Poland would first of all embrace the borders in effect on August 31, 1939. At the same time, however, the government-in-exile demanded rectification of these borders at points that had been foci of friction with Poland's neighbors (e.g., Danzig). It also demanded that Poland have ample and direct access to the sea, and borders guaranteeing lasting security.[3]

As for the major issue—the resurrection of independent Poland—and the western border problem, the Poles could only present their ideas and demands, wait for victory over the German enemy, and integrate themselves into the array of forces fighting against him. As for the eastern border, however, a dramatic change occurred on June 22, 1941, when Germany attacked the Soviet Union and the latter joined the Allied camp. This opened new horizons for Polish diplomacy. Before considering this affair at length, however, let us retrace our steps to the developments between the signing of the Soviet-German friendship agreement and the German invasion.

"Stalin the Infallible"

To this day, many reputable spokesmen condemn the Munich agreement and, in the same breath, find ways to rationalize, "understand," and defend the pact between Ribbentrop and Molotov.

All of them castigate the appeasement policy of Chamberlain and Daladiér, their hat-in-hand trips to Berchtesgaden, their surrender to the Nazi tyrant's *diktat,* their willingness to "save the peace" at the price of eradicating a small democratic state. Miraculously, though, they also tend to justify Stalin's policy, arguing that the Soviet dictator and the leader of international Communism had acted wisely, soberly, and correctly in striking a deal with the sworn and brutal enemy of Communism and humankind.

The German invasion of Russia destroyed Stalin's conception in one go. It took him almost two weeks to recover from the initial shock and approach his nation with an explanation. Broadcasting on July 3, 1941, he appealed apologetically to his people:

> It may be asked: how could the Soviet Government have consented to conclude a non-aggression pact with such treacherous monsters as Hitler and Ribbentrop? Was this a mistake on the part of the Soviet Government?[4]

These questions were merely rhetorical, of course. The experienced, cowed citizens of the Soviet Union did not ask them. They knew that Stalin and the Soviet Government were "infallible," and that unnecessary questions were by definition ill-advised. This was clear to them when the agreement was signed back in 1939, too. No one dared ask why a regime which, only two or three years earlier, had hanged its select leaders and senior commanders for "treason, espionage for Germany, and collaboration with the Fascist enemy" now signed a friendship and non-aggression agreement with the very same Fascist Germany.

Indeed, as expected, Stalin answered his own questions this time around, too:

> We secured for our country peace for a year and a half and the opportunity of preparing its forces to repulse Fascist Germany should it risk an attack on our country despite the pact. This was a definite advantage for us. . . .

All Stalin's actions, then, were products of his foresight, genius, and wisdom. All he meant to do by concluding the agreement was to buy the time he needed to prepare for war and acquire the territory that would distance the Nazi enemy from the Russian border.

From then on, Stalin's apologetics have been widely credited, and his justification of the treaty upheld.

Should this be so?

Stalin at the Service of the Nazi War Machine

Stalin indeed gained time and territory, the importance of which in defending Russia had been proved as far back as Napoleon's time. These factors, however, were of even greater benefit to Hitler. With the Soviet Union neutralized, Hitler no longer had to fear a two-front war, and could more easily capture Poland, the Low Countries, and France. When Germany attacked the Soviet Union and the latter repeatedly implored the West to open a "second front," Stalin conveniently forgot that his agreement with Hitler had facilitated the occupation, enslavement, and exploitation of those countries by the German war machine, including the harnessing of slave labor for war production. Yes, the Red Army did organize itself, and the wounds caused by the "Great Terror" slowly healed, during those eighteen months. At the same time, however, the Wehrmacht not only strengthened itself several times over but gained combat experience and self-confidence.

Stalin boasted about his sagacity and achievements in concluding the 1939 agreement as a means of covering up his mistakes and crimes. In fact, the agreement furthered the Nazi rearmament not only directly but in other, indirect ways. Ribbentrop and Molotov had also arrived at a trade agreement under which the Soviet Union had to provide Germany with raw materials in exchange for industrial commodities and war matériel.[5]

The very first stipulations of the agreement, signed on February 11, 1940, established the German advantage: the Russians had to deliver their goods within 18 months; the Germans had 27.[6]

When it came to implementation, the two nations' traditional roles and attributes were somehow reversed: the punctilious Germans discharged their obligations negligently, while the Soviets met theirs down to the last letter.

The Germans tried to toy with the Russians, to "lead them by the nose," and to procrastinate in forwarding the war matériel as long as possible. Fifteen months after the agreement was signed, German trade expert Schnurre reported to his superiors that the Russians were acting in full

Molotov arriving in Berlin, November 1940

compliance.[7] A month later, on May 15, 1941, he delivered a longer report, hinting at his satisfaction over Germany's success in duping the Russians.

> Difficulties arose, as in the past, regarding the execution of German delivery commitments to the USSR, especially in the field of armaments . . . [and] with respect to the execution of certain contracts covering supplies for the air force, as the Reich Ministry for Air will not release the aircraft promised and already sold. . . . However, the nonfulfillment of German commitments will only make itself felt after August 1941, since until then Russia is obligated to make deliveries in advance . . . The status of Soviet raw material deliveries still presents a favorable picture.[8]

By contrast, Khrushchev, with a mixture of naïve pride and inferiority feelings, recalls, "We made all our deliveries punctually."[9] Indeed, Maj. Gen. Georg Thomas, chief quartermaster of the Wehrmacht, reported just before the invasion of the Soviet Union that the Russian shipments were arriving on time and that rubber from India had actually been shipped by express train.[10]

Thus the following picture emerges: the Germans were diddling with the Russians, trusting that their deceit would not be detected until later; the Russians, for their part, worked feverishly to meet their commitments.

According to the trade agreement, the Russians undertook to ship to Germany millions of tons of commodities during the first twelve months—especially grain, mineral oil, cotton, phosphates, chrome ore, iron ore, scrap iron and pig iron, platinum, manganese ore, metals, lumber and other raw materials.[11] The Soviets also agreed to act as agents for the purchase of raw materials and metals from third countries (e.g., rubber from India) and their shipment to Germany. The total value of goods that the Soviet Union undertook to deliver to Germany at that period of time was about DM 800 million. Stalin himself repeatedly promised his "generous help."[12]

Stalin helped Hitler build his war machine in other ways too. One of the many examples was naval warfare: he provided German submarines with a base in the northern Soviet port of Murmansk. Thus the Germans acquired a refueling and maintenance port, broke the Allies' naval blockade, and established a takeoff point for raids and attacks.[13]

Thus Stalin had much to do with aggrandizing Germany's war strength, indirectly and directly. Had the Germans not invaded the Soviet Union, he would probably have persisted with this strategy and settled for partitioning Europe into two spheres of influence.[14]

Not only in economic and military affairs did Stalin honor all the provisions of the agreement, trusting that Hitler would do the same. One of his most significant contributions to the Nazi effort belonged to the domain of ideas and propaganda.

From September 1939 until June 22, 1941, the Comintern suspended all anti-Nazi and anti-Fascist propaganda, explaining instead that the war raging in Europe was a matter of capitalist states attacking one another for imperialist purposes. This war had nothing at all to do with the aspirations of the international proletariat.

Addressing the Supreme Soviet on October 21, 1939, Molotov proclaimed that the conventional concepts had to be reassessed in view of international developments. Thus, for example, it was manifest that Germany aspired to halt the war and bring about peace, while the English and the French were the true aggressors.[15]

Proclamations of this kind not only sowed confusion among the communist parties in Europe, but even forced the disciplined French party to wage antiwar propaganda.[16] By so doing, it aggravated the defeatist spirit among the public, which persisted until Germany invaded Russia. And when anti-German demonstrations erupted in occupied Prague in October 1939, the Czech Communist Party (an illegal body, of course) was ordered by the Comintern to use all its strength to paralyze the "chauvinist elements."[17]

All expressions liable to offend the new allies vanished from Soviet press and literature. "The doctrine of Marxism-Leninism-Stalinism" adjusted to the new political realities with dialectic flexibility.

The political lexicon, too changed, The NKVD chief Beria ordered the Gulag administration to forbid its jailers to use the term "fascist."[18] The term, hitherto considered an epithet and insult, was indeed taken out of use. After all, how could anyone invoke his friends' favorite attributes as nicknames for miserable prisoners or anti-revolutionary criminals?

Even though the Soviet public greeted this turnabout with understandable amazement (and this, "after years of propaganda aimed deliberately against German aggression," Ambassador Schulenburg explains in his telegram of September 6, 1939), its practical action did not exceed cautiously arched eyebrows. The reticent and disciplined Soviet public, still living under the traumatic impression of the show trials, preferred not to ask embarrassing questions. The German ambassador also added a satisfied and grateful comment: "The Soviet Government is doing everything to change the attitude of the population toward Germany."[19]

Thus, without a doubt, Stalin dulled the public's alertness to the menace lurking behind the Nazi banner. Had that been all, the distortion could probably have been rectified and the public's alertness honed as the German invasion drew near. But this did not happen. The fact that Stalin ignored intelligence warnings, even dismissing them outright, proves that he had undergone a strange psychological change: he had in fact duped himself, not Hitler.

Operation Barbarossa

On December 18, 1940, even as Stalin dutifully shipped war material to Germany, Hitler signed an operational command (Number 21) for the action subsequently known as Operation Barbarossa. In part, it read:

> The forces of the German army should be ready to smash the Soviet Union in a rapid operation even before the war against England ends . . . The preparations should be completed before May 15, 1941.

The preparations, although effectively camouflaged and shrouded in intensive diplomatic contacts, were readily perceptible on the ground. Concentrations of German forces in the eastern areas of occupied Poland grew to dimensions that no one could conceal. (On the day Hitler signed the Barbarossa order, 34 German divisions, representing about 23 percent of the Wehrmacht's entire strength, were positioned on the Russian front. This force was bolstered to about 65 divisions in March and 80 in early June.)[20]

The occupation of Yugoslavia, Greece, Romania, Bulgaria, and Hungary (over Soviet protests), the entrenchment of German forces there, and increasingly frequent "accidental" German aerial penetration of Soviet frontier airspace, were highly conspicuous indications that should have made the Russians more alert and suspicious.

Stalin, however, refused to read the writing on the wall. Instead he showered Hitler with gestures of understanding and conciliation, doing his best to demonstrate his fealty to the stipulations of the friendship agreement. To the very last moment he refused to believe that Hitler was out to attack the Soviet Union.[21]

Did the Soviet Union "Deserve It"?

Hundreds of books and studies have explored the reasons and motives that caused Stalin to behave as he did—to cling to his alliance with Hitler; to continue demonstrating his ostensible friendship toward the Germans; to ignore, reject, and dismiss roughly one hundred explicit intelligence warnings about an impending German invasion;[22] and to argue that it was all nothing but "Western provocation" meant solely to divert the major Wehrmacht thrust from England to the Soviet Union. Volumes have been written, too, on the psychological roots of the strategic surprise wrought by Operation Barbarossa. This is not the place rehash them.

All that matters in our context is that the German invasion struck the Soviet leadership and public like a bolt of out of the blue. It happened on Sunday, June 22, 1941.* At 3:15 a.m. German artillery began to rain fire on the Russian positions. At 3:40 the Luftwaffe began to assault the Soviet array of fortifications and airfields, wave after wave. At 4:15, German armored formations lurched forward. Then, too, the German ambassador reported to a stunned Molotov and read him the secret, urgent cable sent to his embassy from Berlin. It included the usual mixture of lies, distortions of facts, accusations, and name calling for which other German declarations had been noted.

The cable asserted that out of desire to dispel the contradictions between National Socialism and Bolshevism, and to reach understanding with the Soviet Union, the Reich Government had concluded agreements in September 1939, expecting this gesture to lead to stable relations characteristic of good neighbors. Shortly after signing the agreement, however, the Comintern embarked on anti-German subversion, sabotage, espionage, and terror. While Germany had loyally honored all stipulations of the agreement, the Soviets had begun to undermine the new European arrangement and

---

*Napoleon's invasion of Russia, too, began on June 22 (1812).

conspire with England against Germany. Furthermore, the concentrations of Russian forces along a front stretching from the Baltic to the Black Sea were clearly offensive in nature. Therefore the Soviet Government had violated its treaties with Germany and was plotting to attack her from the rear while she was fighting for her life. "Thus the Führer has ordered the German armed forces to resist this threat with all means at their disposal."[23]

Schulenburg finished reading the letter (which also marked the end of his career, built on his personal belief in improving relations with the Soviet Union). Molotov, shaken, recovered after a lengthy silence and responded like a devoted servant who has been unjustly fired:

This is war. . . . Do you think we deserved that?[24]

Molotov felt the Soviet Union did not "deserve" the surprise blow brought upon it because of Stalin's blindness. But this blindness, which cost the Soviet Union, its people, and its army dearly, persisted even after the German invasion had begun: incredible as it sounds (it is recorded in Khrushchev's memoirs), Moscow ordered the Russian formations not to return fire. Even when German artillery was thundering all along the front, Stalin was still convinced that it was nothing more than a provocation by some German field commander. Even then he believed that Hitler would not break his word by attacking the Soviet Union.

The Soviets' Munich

Addressing the nation apologetically on July 3, after the German invasion, a blustering Stalin claimed that the eighteen-month moratorium had permitted him to prepare the Red Army and enhance its might.[25]

The truth, however, is that his blindness had drugged him with respect to military, tactical, and logistical readiness as well. The German Chief of Staff, General Halder, noted after the fact, accurately, that the Red Army had been "tactically surprised along the entire front."[26]

The Red Army's deployment, too, had been guided by Stalin's erroneous conception. Based on the assumption that war would not break out, it positioned a total of 42 Russian divisions (not 119, as the Germans had assumed) against the 170 German divisions that blasted across the borders. Most of these, too, were not in a state of alert.[27] Khrushchev's memoirs give some indication of the magnitude of the Soviets' neglect and negligence, reporting that the Russians did not even have enough rifles.[28]

Thus the Soviets' own "Munich"—no less unethical than its forerunner, no less cowardly and obsequious, and much more cynical and blinded—reached its end.

The Soviet Munich led to the repartition of Poland and improved the Nazi war machine. It eased Hitler's occupation of Eastern Europe, and prolonged the war and its attendant agony. Churchill summarized Stalin's behavior incisively by saying that the wicked are not always clever, nor are dictators infallible.[29]

A New Era for Polish Diplomacy

Germany's invasion of the Soviet Union, driving the latter into the Allied camp, presented Polish diplomacy with new opportunities.

Taking to the BBC airwaves on June 23, 1941, the very morning following the invasion, Sikorski called for the normalization of Polish-Soviet relations, stressing that these must be based on the Riga Agreement of 1921.

On July 5, with Anthony Eden's mediation, talks began between Sikorski and Ivan Maisky, the Soviet ambassador to London.

Sikorski's demands included abolishment of the Soviet-German agreements of August and September 1939; restoration of the territorial *status quo ante;* clemency for the 1,500,000 Poles in detention or under arrest in the Soviet Union; the establishment of a Polish army on Soviet soil, subordinate to the commander-in-chief in London; and the exchange of ambassadors—with Poland's ambassador to the Soviet Union appointed by the government-in-exile in London.

Maisky replied that his Government wished to witness the resurrection of an independent Poland with an internal regime decided upon by the Poles themselves. As for borders, his Government believed that they should reflect ethnographic realities; hence certain territories would not be returned to Poland. With respect to Poles in detention, Maisky argued that they numbered no more than 20,000. As to the remaining stipulations, he had no objections of substance.[30]

Had the British taken action to influence and pressure the Soviet Government at the time—as Soviet defense lines collapsed against the German invasion—there can be little doubt that the Soviets would have had to accommodate the Polish demands. However, the British preferred to exert their influence on a weaker ally, one whose loyalty and friendship was secure in any case. Churchill subsequently explained that the British Government was in a quandary: it had the unpleasant duty of recommending that General Sikorski trust the Soviets to settle Russian-Polish relations, and refrain from demanding written guarantees at that time.[31]

Sikorski considered this "friendly persuasion" and contended with a hawkish opposition within his own Government (Foreign Minister Zaleski and General Sosnkowski, supported by President Raczkiewicz) that called for a firm position on the border question. With these in mind, he persisted in his talks with Maisky until the two reached an agreement that was signed on July 30, 1941.

The Sikorski-Maisky Agreement

The five-paragraph accord[32] established the following:

1. The Soviet Government acknowledges that its agreements with Germany from 1939 are null and void with respect to territorial changes in Poland.
2. Diplomatic relations will be established and ambassadors exchanged.
3. The two Governments will offer each other mutual aid in their war against Hitlerist Germany.
4. A Polish army will come into being on Soviet territory; its commander will be appointed by the Government of Poland with the consent of the Government of the Soviet Union. This army will be operationally subordinate to the high command of the Soviet Union, and will be represented in this command.
5. Clemency will be declared for all Polish citizens detained in Soviet territory.

The first provision was ambiguously phrased in the best diplomatic tradition, permitting each side to interpret it according to its understanding and aspirations. Each side believed that future developments, the actual balance of forces, and the international situation following the victory would tip the scales in its favor.

Thus the Poles interpreted the agreement as nullifying the Soviet annexation of the eastern territories. As future developments proved, this was so much wishful thinking. They gave the announcements and reactions of the British and American Governments a similarly optimistic reading.

On July 30, 1941, British Foreign Minister Anthony Eden proclaimed in Parliament that "His Majesty's Government do not recognize any territorial changes which have been effected in Poland since August, 1939."[33]

The next day, acting American Secretary of State Sumner Wells adopted much the same position:

> The position of the United States with regard to Poland was made clear immediately after the invasion of Poland. It was that this Government did not

recognize any change in the status of Poland as a free, sovereign and independent country. That position is maintained, is continued. It is my understanding . . . that the Soviet Union has abrogated the agreement of 1939 which the Soviet Union had entered into with Germany.[34]

So far, so good. However, these declarations were couched in a tone of cautious reservation. Thus, for example, Eden steered clear of explicit commitments and details on the border question. He confined himself to restating Churchill's cautious proposal of September 5, 1940, not to recognize border changes effected during the war, unless such changes were made with the consent and good will of the parties involved.

When two MPs presented him with direct parliamentary questions as to the continued validity of British guarantees of Poland's borders, Eden had to answer to the point: "No guarantees of frontiers in Eastern Europe will be undertaken by H. M. Government."[35]

The war was in full swing. The fate of the Soviet Union, Great Britain, and the entire war effort were still perilously unresolved. England wanted to be sure that the Soviet Union would continue fighting and not forge a separate peace with Hitler.[36]

In this state of affairs, the idea of considering the future borders of a Poland still under German occupation was a matter of putting the cart before the horse. Under the given circumstances, the British Government was not about to clash with Stalin on this issue. Appeasement of Stalin was the call of the hour; if it had to come at the expense of a smaller ally, so be it.

Thus the distance from not recognizing territorial changes to not providing border guarantees was a short one. Sumner Wells too, while lauding the Polish-Soviet agreement, added: "I want to make it very clear that I am not now discussing any details."[37]

Although it was clear that the "details" related to the eastern border, the Polish Government preferred to ignore, or at least underplay, the implicit contradiction. Sikorski hoped that once Germany had been vanquished, the Soviet Union would be forced under Western pressure to relinquish up the territories it had annexed. Then, on the basis of the new accord nullifying the Soviet-German deal (in principle at least), Poland's former border would be restored.

The Poles were further encouraged when Stalin, the "Father of Peoples," delivered himself of the following self-righteous remarks before the Supreme Soviet on November 6, 1941:

We have not, nor can we have, such war aims as the seizure of foreign territories or the conquest of other peoples . . . Our first aim is to liberate our territories and our people from the German Nazi yoke. We have not, nor can we have such war aims as the imposition of our will and our regime.[38]

However, the season of hopes and illusions passed quickly.

Sikorski and Stalin Meet

As agreed, Poland began organizing and mobilizing an armed force on Soviet soil, and appointed General Władysław Anders, an ambitious and pretentious man, as OC. (In many respects, Anders was a very bad choice. There is evidence that he took action to undermine Sikorski's position. Anders won the support of Rightist oppositionists in the government-in-exile—Raczkiewicz, Zaleski, Gen. Sosnkowski—who urged him on and toyed with the idea of making him Prime Minister in Sikorski's place.)[39] Anders quickly began to clash with both Sikorski and the Soviet authorities.

The mobilization lagged behind schedule, the Soviets dragged their feet in liberating Polish prisoners, and the arms and equipment sufficed for barely half the inductees. Any hopes of new mutual trust between the Soviets and the Poles were dashed by conflicting goals that immediately rose to the surface.

Solemn joint declarations aside, the Poles eyed the Russians with profound distrust. Russia's intent in agreeing to mobilize Polish units was to integrate them into the "patriotic war" of expelling the Nazi invader from Russian soil, while the Poles claimed that their army was not yet ready for the mission.

In fact, the Poles' strategy was to send a well-trained army into action in large-scale separate formations, in order to emphasize the political as well as the military effect. When the Soviets applied pressure by (for example) cutting supplies of food, clothing, and combat equipment, friction built up. Consequently, Polish generals began toying with the idea of transferring their forces from the Soviet Union to the Middle East. In principle, Sikorski and Anders shared this goal (in his memoirs, Anders contended that he had fathered the idea),[40] although they did not publicize it at first. Yet here, too, their views clashed. Anders hoped for a total or maximal pullout of Polish forces, while Sikorski believed it politically and militarily wise to leave part of the Polish corps in the Soviet Union.

Being more broad-minded than Anders, Sikorski considered it important to maintain coordination and cooperation with the Soviets, and to enable Polish units to participate in liberating their country and its eastern districts once the Soviet counteroffensive began.

As the tension and friction mounted, Sikorski attempted to clear the air by conferring directly with Stalin.

The talk, held in the Kremlin[41] on December 3, 1941, illustrates its participants' personalities and political aims. On the Soviet side were Stalin and Molotov; Sikorski, Anders, and Ambassador Kot represented Poland.

The Poles opened by raising the issue of clemency. "Many of our people," argued Sikorski, "some of them very prominent men, are still kept in labor camps and prisons." He added that this undermined the mutual trust and cooperation that both sides sought to strengthen. Anders (whose anti-Semitic propensities were an open secret) added that the first prisoners to be freed had been Jews, Ukrainians, and only after that some of the Poles—mainly the weak ones. Anyone still capable of work remained in captivity.

Impossible! retorted Stalin. He insisted that the clemency had applied to all the Poles, meaning that all of them had been released. Sikorski responded by mentioning a list in his possession of 4,000 officers still held in prisons and labor camps somewhere in the Soviet Union; every effort to locate and free them had been futile.

Stalin again rejected the claim forcefully and categorically. "That's impossible—they have escaped." When Anders asked where they could have gone, Stalin answered patly:

> Well, to Manchuria . . . They definitely escaped but they have not yet reached you . . . We have no interest in holding a single Pole. I even liberated Sosnkowski's agents, who attacked and murdered our men.

Sikorski then turned to the military issues, noting Poland's struggle against Germany in 1939 and its contribution to the protracted war effort—both in Poland proper by underground forces, and by Polish army units fighting alongside the Allies. Lauding the Polish fighting man and the nation's resolve to fight its enemy, Sikorski claimed that the units being organized in the Soviet Union would not be able to participate in the war due to harsh climate, poor living conditions, and inadequate equipment.

After this lengthy introduction, Sikorski arrived at the essence of his proposal:

> Therefore my proposal is for the transfer of the Polish Army, and of all those capable of military service, to Persia for example, where the climate and the assistance promised by the governments of USA and Great Britain will enable those men to recover and to turn into a strong army in a short time . . . It has been agreed with Churchill . . . and on my part I am ready to declare also, that all these forces then return to the Russian front . . . I am the kind of man [he continued self-importantly] that if I say yes, it's yes, and if I say no, it's no . . . We have full sovereignty in Great Britain. I can transfer a whole corps from Scotland here . . . or to attach our units stationed in Tobruk with our forces here . . .

Stalin, however, was impressed neither by Sikorski's theoretical ability to move forces nor by his promise (which probably reflected a tactical compromise between himself and Anders) to return the Polish force to the Russian front. On the contrary, Stalin was infuriated. Nor was he moved by Anders' dramatic accounts ("Where I am, the temperature has already fallen to 33° C. below zero . . . The people live in simple tents . . . They awaken in the morning with frostbitten ears and noses . . . Only two weeks ago they received shoes . . . They never received their due share of food . . .").

"I am a person of experience and of age," Stalin replied angrily. "I know that if you go to Persia, you will never return here . . . So, if the Poles do not want to fight, then let them go . . . They may go away . . . We shall liberate Poland and then turn it over to you . . . Then the whole world will laugh . . ."[42]

Now it was the Poles' turn to explode in rage at this insult to their soldiers. "Well, maybe I am a little harsh [*"grubiy"*]," said Stalin in a conciliatory tone. "But I want to know clearly: do you want to fight or not?"

The ice was broken, the conversation resumed, and the three gentlemen discovered at least one issue on which they were in full accord.

An Anti-Semitic Intermezzo

"I can have 150,000 soldiers; this is equivalent to eight divisions," said Anders. "Perhaps there are more (Polish citizens who could be mobilized—Y. C.), but many of them are Jews, who do not want to serve in the army."

Stalin: "Jews are poor warriors."

Sikorski: "Many of the Jews are speculators or smugglers. They will never make good soldiers. Those I don't need in the Polish army."

Anders: "Two hundred Jews deserted from Buzuluk when they heard a false rumor about the bombing of Kuibyshev. More than sixty deserted from the Fifth Division a day before the distribution of arms to the soldiers was made public."

Stalin: "Yes, Jews are bad warriors."[43]

Jews in the Polish and Soviet Forces

Parenthetically, Anders' army incorporated thousands of Jews and, in fact, was half-Jewish at the beginning of its formation. Anders found this situation displeasing, since the last thing he wanted was the "Judaization" of his army.

Thousands of Jewish volunteers were turned away on various pretexts, and those admitted became targets of their would-be comrades' anti-Semitism. Files in the Sikorski Historical Institute in London, especially minutes of the meetings of the Polish National Assembly in Exile, abound with examples of discrimination and anti-Semitism in Anders' army.

Anders displayed understanding of these anti-Semitic tendencies and tended to justify them. In his order for November 30, 1941, he addressed his men apologetically, explaining that outwardly he had to adopt a policy of equal rights and duties toward the Jewish inductees, because of "Jewish influence in England and the United States."

> Our defence of the Jews might seem incomprehensible or historically unjustified and even anomalous . . .

He concluded his order with a threat to "settle scores" with the Jews:

> . . . However, after the battle is over and we are again our own masters, we will settle the Jewish matter in a fashion that the exalted status and sovereignty of the homeland and simple human justice require.[44]

Many Jews who remained in the Soviet Union and were not admitted into Anders' army enlisted in the Kościuszko Polish Legion (see below), spending the duration of the war in its ranks.[45]

With respect to Soviet Jews in the Red Army, anti-Semitic jokes—fed by Russian tradition and Stalin's appraisal of Jewish soldiers as "poor warriors"—focused on Jews whose "fighting in Tashkent" had to do with victory in the black market, not the war. As for the facts, about half a million Jews fought in the Red Army, and some 200,000 fell in the line of duty. 160,772 of them were decorated, and 145 of them received the country's highest award, Hero of the Soviet Union. Many reached command positions; 186 attained the rank of general.[46]

The logic of anti-Semitism, of course, varies with time and place. Some hated the Jews because they were allegedly standoffish and separatist, while others argued that the Jews were assimilating and "Judaizing" pure Gentile culture. Some said they were capitalists sucking the proletariat's blood; others accused them of spreading the venom of the Bolshevik Revolution. Stalin and the Polish generals considered the Jews deserters and poor soldiers. Their successors stand united today in condemning the "racist," "militarist," and "aggressive" Zionists who "occupy Arab lands."

A Historical Opportunity is Missed

With the help of this anti–Semitic intermezzo and Stalin's racist pan-Slavic compliments ("The best and most daring pilots are the Slavs. They work fast, because they belong to a young race that has not yet worn out.") the two sides were able to soften their positions and arrive at a compromise. They decided to expedite the mobilization of 96,000 men, who would be equipped and transferred to Kazakhstan and Bukhara for a period of training. Sikorski also extracted a promise that if even more men enlisted, he would be permitted to transfer 25,000 of them to Persia.[47] (It should be assumed that Stalin had already concluded that he would do best to dispose of the political nuisance Anders' army represented, and to begin laying the foundations for a different Polish army, one politically and militarily more amenable.) On December 4, 1941, Stalin and Sikorski signed a "Declaration of Friendship and Cooperation," which solemnly reiterated general formulas in the manner conventional in proclamations of this kind. Because such events do not take place without festive banquets, this, too, was staged, and tremendous quantities of caviar and vodka played an essential role in it. Here Sikorski was given an opportunity, perhaps a historical one, to try to reach an arrangement on the border issue. During the dinner Stalin turned to him with a proposal which seemed natural and obvious to the omnipotent tyrant. He offered to arrange the border matter there and then, right at the dinner table. In exchange for the eastern territories, Stalin dangled a juicy tidbit: Eastern Prussia. Concurrently, Poland's western border would be relocated to the Oder River.[48]

Sikorski—either not wishing to assume the responsibility, or keeping faith with his position of rejecting any concession and modification of the former border, or, perhaps, reflecting his government's "Western orientation"—avoided any discussion of the matter. He told Stalin he was not authorized to act on the offer. Only Parliament could do so, he said. Stalin, unimpressed by the fine points of democracy, nevertheless tried to press the point a little, adding with a wink that "I'd like to have some alterations in those frontiers . . . some 'chut-chut' [very slight] alterations."[49]

Furthermore, as Sikorski himself informed the "London government" (January 12, 1942[50]), Stalin was willing to "help the Poles in their disputes with the Ukrainians about the Polish city of Lvov. . . ."

The truth is that by this time, the Poles' quarrel about Lvov was not with the Ukrainians but with Stalin's Government, and the latter's offer to volunteer as a friendly arbitrator could not be taken at face value. Nevertheless, the proposal provided a gateway to negotiations and perhaps should not have been rejected outright. Sikorski, by his own account, shot it down politely but firmly.

This was undoubtedly an example of a statesman's missing a historical opportunity which could not recur. There is no way, of course, of ascertaining how things would have developed had Sikorski reacted differently, and history abounds in "ifs." The incident might well have created a window of opportunity not necessarily for the future frontiers of Poland but, in any event, for a Polish-Soviet dialogue. What is clear is that Sikorski's categorical rejection of Stalin's proposal prevented any kind of inquiry or exploration of these or other possibilities.

Polish and Soviet Interests Clash

The Soviet-Polish "honeymoon," including the agreement in London, clemency for Polish citizens in the Soviet Union, and permission to organize a Polish army there, did not last long. Relations deteriorated steadily, and were officially severed in April 1943, less than a year and a half later. Polish historians, expressing the present-day official bias, argue that Poland's withdrawal of its forces from the Soviet Union was the fatal decision. This is groundless.

Admittedly, as the conversation quoted above proves, the Polish action angered Stalin. Its implementation, too, overshot the agreed-upon quota at first, mainly because of successful pressure and tactics adopted by Anders. In April 1942, 32,000 Polish soldiers and 12,000 civilians were transferred from the Soviet Union to the Middle East. In the second wave, In August 1942, 52,000 soldiers and approximately 19,000 civilians left.[51]

It was just then, too—the summer of 1942—that Germany's armies were mounting their assault on Stalingrad. The outcome of the war and the Soviet Union's future were hanging in the balance. Thus the Soviets had reason to view the Poles as betraying a shared interest and deserting the common front.

However, this episode did not lie at the root of the deepening rift. At its base were conflicting interests and goals, a genuine and profound clash that could not be resolved by solemn proclamations or banquets. The Polish army's withdrawal exacerbated and perhaps accelerated an inevitable process, but did not instigate it.

The Soviet Aims—A *Cordon Sanitaire* and "Friendly" Governments

The conflict of interest was evident. While the Poles were striving to resurrect an independent Poland within the August 1939 ("Riga Agreement") borders, Stalin wanted to provide the Soviet Union, after its victory over Hitler, with secure borders and strategic depth that would permit the Red Army to defend the centers of Soviet life and deny the Germans any possibility of mounting a future attack. To this end, Stalin aspired to annex a wide security belt from the Baltic countries in the north to the Balkans in the south, with Poland in the middle. Another way of securing the Soviets' "spheres of influence," Stalin believed, was by establishing "friendly" governments in all countries bordering the Soviet Union. In this context, a "friendly" government was one willing to comply with Soviet diktats in domestic and foreign affairs alike.

After his meeting with Stalin in December 1941, Anthony Eden was able to comment that the Soviet dictator's ideas were clearly defined, and changed but little in subsequent years.[52]

***

As early as 1918 and in 1919, as the smoke of World War I was dispersing and waves of insurrection (in the spirit of Trotsky's "permanent revolution") swept Europe, initial attempts were made to establish "friendly" governments in the Soviet Union's neighboring countries. These attempts (by Bela Kun in Hungary, Liebknecht in Germany, and Kuusinen in Finland) were swiftly put down.[53] The hard-core Communist cadres' revolutionary zeal failed to bring the "proletarian masses" in train, and the Soviet Union was not strong enough at the time to serve as a secure base and hinterland.

Under Comintern guidance, two attempts were made in Poland, too, to set up a revolutionary government. After the Red Army marched into Poland in the summer of 1920, "revolutionary committees" were organized here and there. The main one, seated in Bialystok, purported to function as the kernel of a Soviet Polish government. Its leaders were Julian Marchlewski, Feliks Dzerzhinsky (subsequently notorious as head of the Cheka—the secret police—and the father of the Soviet method of interrogation and confession extraction[54]), Feliks Kon, Edward Pruchniak, and Józef Unszlicht. Alongside them, as a source of inspiration, was a Commissar of the Russian Communist Party, Skworcow-Stiepanow. The "revolutionary committee" began to lay the organizational, administrative, and economic foundations for the new regime, and called on the populace to greet the Red Army with open arms. After all, it was fighting not the Polish people but the regime of the plutocrats, the landed gentry, and the capitalists.[55]

By counterattacking and repelling the Red Army, the Polish Army also put an end to the revolutionary committee in Bialystok.

The experience gained by the Comintern between the two wars, and, most importantly, the might of the Soviet Union, gave the business of "exporting revolution" a new lease on life in the 1940s. This time, however, the Comintern's major goal and beacon was not the export of revolution for its own sake and the mere triumph of Communism, but the strengthening and fortification of the "socialist homeland." For this reason the countries chosen as venues for such endeavors were not necessarily those where the social, economic, and industrial conditions for revolution were ripe, but rather the Soviet Union's neighbors, no matter how fledgling their industrial development, how weak their proletariat, and how shallow their class consciousness.

There was no overriding need for the existence of a strong local Communist Party in advance. It was enough to bring in from the Soviet Union a few "local leaders" fluent in the local vernacular, throw in a handful of "progressive" collaborators, and thereby create a "patriotic" front that purported to represent the nation's aspirations. In essence, all these measures were borne not on the winds of the Communist idea but rather on Soviet tanks. The establishment of the "progressive," "patriotic," "people's" governments in the 1940s was the result of Stalinist strategy in the service of Soviet Russia's defense and economic interests.

The first attempt in this series was made in the Baltic countries, which, as stipulated in the secret protocol of the Ribbentrop-Molotov Agreement of August 23, 1939, were to belong to the Soviet sphere of influence.[56]

What did these trends portend for Poland?

The Eastern Border Problem

The meeting on December 3, 1941, and Sikorski's refusal to discuss border changes, did induce Stalin to accede to transferring the Polish corps (part of it and, subsequently, most of it) out of the USSR, to Persia. However, it also strengthened his intent—if there were any further need to do so—to fix the Soviet Union's Western border on the Curzon Line, and to establish a "friendly" regime in renascent Poland.

His perception was clear and unequivocal, his intent resolute. In addition to the aforementioned strategic considerations, Stalin made sure to take weighty political considerations into account. Lvov is a case in point.

Although well aware that Lvov was a blatantly Polish city,[57] Stalin finally decided after his talk with Sikorski to incorporate it into the Ukrainian SSR. He hoped that by annexing this city, the capital and symbol of the "Western Ukraine," he would win over the forces of Ukrainian nationalism (millions of Ukrainians had provided the Nazi invader with massive support). He may once have been willing, in a moment of mercy or weakness, to introduce certain (*"chut-chut"*) modifications into his conception, but the opportunity had passed and did not recur.

The subsequent efforts of the Polish Government under Sikorski to change Stalin's mind on the territorial issue, or at least to plaster over the contradiction out of hope that the future would bring a change for the better, came to nothing. Only a few months after the Sikorski-Maisky agreement was signed, the first fissures already appeared. The first paragraph in the agreement, as stated, established that the German-Russian accords of 1939 were null and void where the Polish border issue was concerned. Thus the Polish Government had reason to assume that this meant Soviet agreement to restore the territorial *status quo ante*.

The Soviet Government read this stipulation differently. The content of the agreement had nothing to do with the "legitimate" fact, i.e., the establishment of the Ukrainian and Belorussian SSRs on the basis on the "free will" of the Slavic peoples.

The first official indication of trouble appeared on January 6, 1942, in a Soviet Foreign Ministry letter including Lvov in a list of Ukrainian cities. Poland's ambassador to Kuibyshev, Professor Stanisław Kot, felt duty bound to comment officially that there had surely been some mistake. "From the standpoint of history and international law," the ambassador claimed, "Lvov was and remains a Polish city." To this the Soviet Foreign Ministry replied on January 17, asserting forcefully that there was "no justification" for the ambassador's contention, and continuing:

> While finding it impossible to enter into discussion on the historical and legal bases on which the city of Lvov or any other town on the territories of the Ukrainian SSR belong to the USSR, the People's Commissar (for Foreign Affairs - Y. C.) deems it his duty to inform the Embassy that in the future he will not be able to accept for consideration Notes of the Embassy containing declarations of this kind.[58]

Despite the verdict-like "reprimand" in Molotov's reply, the Poles tried not to exacerbate and aggravate the disagreements. They preferred to adopt a conciliatory tone, hoping that the matter would "fix itself" and that the Western powers' growing strength and influence would tip the scales in Poland's favor. Almost a year after this exchange of letters (on December 18, 1942) Sikorski said at a press conference in Chicago:

> I can assure you that. . . . the partition of Poland between Germany and Russia is null and void under the treaty signed between Poland and Russia. The first paragraph of that agreement is quite explicit. It was on that basis that my Government decided to overlook past wrongs, to conclude this pact and to work for friendly relations with Russia.[59]

However, relations grew worse. Notes flew back and forth with increasing frequency, and their tone became more acerbic. The Soviet note of March 1, 1943, not only established the need to return to the Curzon Line (which the Soviet Government had previously spurned) but even accused the "London government," a helpless aggregate of exiles, of harboring imperialist intentions even more egregious than those of British imperialism. "Even Lord Curzon," the letter said, "despite his hostile attitude to the Soviet Union, acknowledged that Poland cannot claim a right to Ukrainian and Belorussian lands."

But an additional tone is evident in this letter: not only rebuke, polemics, and self-righteousness in the name of the Slavic peoples, but explicit exception to the government-in-exile:

> The declaration of the Polish Government bears witness to the fact that the present ruling circles do not reflect in this matter the genuine opinion of the Polish people, whose interest in the struggle for the liberation of their country and for the restoration of a strong and united Poland are indissolubly linked with the strengthening of the utmost of mutual confidence with brotherly peoples of the Ukraine and Byelorussia, as well as with the Russian people and other peoples of the USSR.[60]

This declaration contains the kernels of both long- and short-term political developments. The Soviet Union, with the Russians in the lead, defended and spoke for the Slavic peoples. These peoples, including the Poles, should come together under its leadership in order to throw off the German yoke. Only this leadership, in its manifest wisdom, would set the "ethnic" borders of all the Slavic peoples and secure their independence and well-being. The present Polish government neither represented (if only, for the meantime, "in this matter") nor faithfully expressed the genuine sentiments of the Polish people. The Polish "ruling circles" were estranged from the masses and the mainstream of history.

The conclusion that begged itself, of course, was the need to replace this government with a more "patriotic" and "democratic" one.

The Union of Polish Patriots (ZPP)

The first practical attempt to establish such a government (or at least to lay its foundations) was made long before the letter of March 1, 1943. On December 2, 1941, the day General Sikorski reached Moscow, *Izvestia* issued a "call to the Polish brethren." Did this manifesto include words of greeting to the Prime Minister of Poland, or a call for enlistment in Anders' army? Not at all. It did report, however, that "representatives of the Polish people," represented by Wanda Wasilewska (a Communist writer married to the Ukrainian author Alexander Korneychuk) had met in the city of Saratov on November 27, and laid the foundations for a "Union of Polish Patriots."

Sikorski, well aware of these patriots' conceptual attitude, considered the publication and timing of this article a transparent ploy to deter and pressure him. He boiled with rage, but preferred to ignore the matter during his talk with Stalin. The talk and its summations did not eliminate the "patriots"; the rabbit the Soviets had pulled out of their hat in honor of the Polish guest did not vanish when the visit ended. The Soviets had more in mind than toying with this particular guest at this particular time. Already then, it appears Stalin had decided to create a more convenient political "option" for himself in the event that Sikorski and his government did not kowtow. Indeed, the proclamation of March 1943, proved that the Union of Patriots was meant to be the core of an alternative government.

During 1942, as political relations deteriorated, the Soviets took all necessary steps to fortify the status of a "friendly" government that would express "genuine aspirations of the Polish people." The ZPP was transferred to Moscow, and once Anders' army had left the Soviet Union, efforts got under way toward establishing a new Polish Army, which would "fight should to shoulder" with the Red Army. Then, too, the Soviets began to hit the Polish government-in-exile below the belt, using brass knuckles. Soviet partisans terrorized the Poles in the eastern occupied territories, provoking reports to London of horrifying instances of looting, rape, and murder. They also refused to coordinate their military operations with the AK (which, under Sikorski's command since August 15, 1942, had become an all-inclusive, united organization subordinate to the "London government."[61])

The Kremlin then decided that it was also time to teach the Polish diaspora in the Soviet Union a lesson. Mass arrests were undertaken, and prominent figures were "eliminated." In December 1941, for example, two leaders of the Jewish Socialist Bund—Henryk Erlich and Viktor Adler— disappeared. Official sources had nothing to say as to their whereabouts, of course, and only more than a year later (February 23, 1943) did Litvinov report that the two had been shot for "collaborating with German intelligence."[62] The Soviet propaganda machine accompanied these operations with relentless venom aimed at undermining the London government in Polish, British and American public opinion. The standard theme was the tried-and-true one: accusing the "London government" of "imperialistic tendencies." Poland, the victim of German-Soviet aggression, was charged with robbing the Ukrainian and Belorussian peoples, and the Polish "bandits" (as the AK men were known) were alleged to have murdered Soviet partisans and aided the Germans.

If the Soviet Government lacked a final pretext for breaking off relations, it acquired one when the Katyń affair blew up.[63]

The Katyń Affair

On April 5, 1943, the Nazi newspaper *Völkischer Beobachter* ran an article claiming that the corpses of more than 10,000 Polish officers had been discovered in the forest of Katyń, about 20 kilometers from Smolensk. The report added that the victims had been POWs murdered by their Soviet captors. This was a cue for Goebbels' propaganda machine, which went into high gear. All German radio stations decried the murder of 14,500 Polish officers and demanded an international inquiry. The perpetrators of the "final solution," the knights of the annihilation of millions, experts at mass murder, and maestros of the crematoria suddenly displayed tremendous sensitivity toward the bitter fate of the Polish POWs, as befitting genuine humanists. The report was meant to besmirch the Soviets in Polish and world public opinion, and it indeed generated extraordinary shock and consternation throughout occupied Poland and among Polish emigrés. Previously, too, the Poles had been fearful and suspicious in the extreme, and the "London government" had often expressed an interest in the fate of the POWs, with no results.

Once Soviet-Polish relations were restored, the government-in-exile became aware that the number of Polish POWs in Soviet hands had reached 181,000, including some 10,000 officers. The "London government" also knew that most of the latter (about 8,700) were being detained in three large camps. It subsequently caught wind of rumors that in May 1940, the prisoners had been taken in small groups to unknown destinations. When the clemency and mobilization stipulated in the Sikorski-Maisky agreement were completed, the government-in-exile found that it was "missing" about 8,000 officers (it did know the names of about 4,000 of them). In their talks with Soviet officials (including Sikorski's talk with Stalin) Polish delegates often brought up the matter in an effort to ascertain the fate and whereabouts of the missing officers and effect their release. The evasive Soviet replies always boiled down to a solemn pronouncement that the clemency had been carried through to the end and that all the prisoners had been released. Stalin resolved the riddle with ease; he told Sikorski, as will be recalled, that his "missing" officers must have fled to Manchuria.

The fate of the missing men was shrouded in total darkness.

The Soviets had to respond to the dramatic report in the Nazi media, but it took them several days to phrase one. Finally, Tass accused the

"German-Fascist hangmen" of having murdered the POWs after having captured them during the Soviet retreat from the Smolensk area in the summer of 1941.

On April 16, the Polish Minister of Defense issued an announcement which, without accusing the Soviets of anything, nevertheless demanded that the despicable deed be investigated by an authorized international body, such as the Red Cross:

> We have become accustomed to the lies of German propaganda . . . Poland's enormous price in terms of victims and great suffering does not entitle the Germans to advance shameful pretences of being the defenders of Christian Europe and its culture against Russian "barbarism" . . . Whoever is guilty of these atrocities against the Polish nation should be punished.[64]

The Soviets could not let this transparent hint slip by without a reaction. On April 19, *Pravda* ran a fierce condemnation of the Polish government, auguring a total rift. The "London government" was accused of collaborating with the German hangmen and, by appealing to the Red Cross, helping them disseminate their lies. To Sikorski and his government it was clear that their action would not only infuriate Moscow but would eliminate any prospects of dialogue on the entire spectrum of problems. However, in view of the terrible discovery, whose findings and accuracy were almost unquestioned, the Poles felt they had no choice.

Their initiative did not come off well. Replying to the Polish inquiry, the Red Cross in Geneva announced that it could investigate Katyń only with both Soviet and German consent. Since the USSR refused to take part, the Red Cross backed away, and Germany set up an "international" committee of experts. This committee, almost fully staffed by citizens of the occupied countries,[65] confirmed all the German claims. The number of bodies found in the Katyń forests was 4,143, of whom 2,914 were identified beyond doubt. All had previously been in the Kozielsk camp. The fate of the other thousands of missing officers is still unknown.[66] The Soviets set up their own commission of inquiry after liberating the Smolensk area.[67] Its findings (January 1944), based on testimonies and studies, indicated that the executions had been carried out in the autumn of 1941 by a special German unit operating under false name "The 537th Engineering Battalion Command." The massacre at Katyń was also mentioned at Goering's trial in Nuremberg. However, Churchill subsequently attested that the victorious governments decided that the issue had to be avoided. The Soviet Government did not use this occasion to establish its innocence against the ghastly and widely invoked accusation, nor did it convincingly implicate the German Government. In its final judgement, the International Tribunal at Nuremberg omits Katyń from the section dealing with POWs in Nazi Germany.[68]

Cautious as this summation is, it leaves little doubt about whom Churchill held at fault. However, when Sikorski informed him of his defense minister's announcement, he was greeted not with the consolation and encouragement he expected, but with a splash of cold water and restrained anger: If they were dead, Churchill said, Sikorski could do nothing to bring them back.[69] This was a reflection of the conflict between an emotional response of a direct victim and the rational-pragmatic perception of a bystander. Churchill himself had been brought up on—and was a shaper of—the doctrine that bragged about how the sun never set on the British Empire. The entire Empire, it was asserted, would come to the aid of any British citizen, wherever he may be, who was threatened with the loss of a hair on his head. It is therefore reasonable to believe that had a disaster similar to that of Katyń befallen England—had a similar atrocity been carried out against 10,000 British officers—Churchill and his Government's placidity and lassitude would have given way to an outpouring of fury.

The Polish P. M. also reminded the British ambassador (accredited to the Polish government-in-exile) that when the Germans sentenced five Brit-

Churchill and Gen. Sikorski with Polish troops in Great Britain

ish officers to death, H. M. Government did not hesitate to ask for Red Cross intervention.[70]

As the circumstances added up, however, the direct victim representing agony and "particularist" interest, that of a nation being trampled by two giants and fighting for its freedom, was on the opposite side of the fence from Winston Churchill, who, with all his understanding and sympathy for the Polish cause, was mainly concerned with the "global" interest. His was the supreme task toward which he was leading his people and his allies— the eradication of Nazi Germany. This mission required the subordination of all other tasks, objectives, contradictions, and ambitions. It also required the unification of the anti-Nazi coalition, with Stalin within its contours. With this in mind, it was of secondary importance to Churchill who murdered the Polish officers, who could not be brought back to life in any case. Precisely because he must have suspected the presence of something real behind the German allegations, he believed it best to "bury" the matter; disinterring it might well cause a rift with Stalin. Therefore, in his talk with Ambassador Maisky, too, Churchill preferred to avoid any argument about the matter itself, stressing that they had to beat Hitler, and that this was not the time for quarrels and accusations.[71] Stalin, however, disregarded Churchill's advice and admonitions. On April 25, 1943, Molotov handed a letter to Romer, the Polish ambassador, informing him that relations had been broken off.

The Kościuszko Division

After Katyń, the Soviets took several measures intended to fortify the status of the alternative, "friendly" Polish government. In early May 1943, the ZPP convened in Moscow. Sixty-six delegates, most of whose names meant nothing in Polish public life, purported to represent the democratic and progressive parties. They adopted a resolution vigorously condemning the government-in-exile and calling for a shared war effort with the Red Army toward the constitution of a democratic, progressive Poland. On May 1, 1943, the Soviet Government announced its consent to the establishment of Polish Army formations under ZPP auspices.

Enlisted into these units were Polish POWs who had not been liberated (although clemency had been "fully" implemented in 1941) and others whom Anders and his officers did not permit to leave the Soviet Union in the ranks of his Army (nearly all of these were Jews).

In September 1943, the Soviet media announced officially that a Polish division named after Kościuszko had come into being. (This was something of a practical joke on Kościuszko and history. Kościuszko, who had led a

Polish uprising against Russian rule in the late 18th century—leading thousands of peasants armed only with scythes into battle—now became, by virtue of a Soviet propaganda trick, a symbol of "Slavic solidarity"). This time the Soviets made sure that military "cooperation" was very intimate and that the new Polish Army would be immune to anti-Soviet tendencies. General Zygmunt Berling was appointed as the new commander, subordinate to Soviet General Bevzink and subject to the political guidance of Colonel Zawadzki of the NKVD. Many field command positions were entrusted to Soviet officers in Polish uniforms. Senior command—from battalion commander and up—and, of course, the political commissars, were entrusted to regular Communists alone.[72]

In early February 1944, efforts commenced toward organizing another two divisions plus formations of artillery, paratroopers, armor, and airforce. On July 1, 1944, the "People's" Polish Army, according to official reports, had 54,598 soldiers.[73] The Kościuszko Division was integrated into the Red Army array; subsequently taking part in the battle for the liberation of Poland, it acquired a political and psychological value which Anders could never fathom.

As this went on, the Soviets sent their propaganda machine on a rampage in the international arena, with intent to destroy the government-in-exile's moral and political base. Under inspiration from Moscow, gatherings of people of Polish descent took place in London, various cities in the United States, Mexico, Buenos Aires, and Rio de Janeiro. These issued "spontaneous" appeals, variously phrased but with uniform intent, for the triumph of patriotism and democracy, abolishment of the recognized status of the "London government," for Polish and Russian solidarity and cooperation.

There was no longer any doubt that the Soviet regime and its Polish supporters were striving for a "friendly" postwar Polish government.

Churchill and Roosevelt in View of the Soviet-Polish Rift

Let us examine how Churchill and Roosevelt reacted to the contradictions that developed between the Polish and Soviet Governments before and after the rupture of their diplomatic relations. Did the leaders of the two great democracies stand by Poland, as Sikorski and his colleagues implored? Did they offer the Polish government all necessary moral and political aid so it could withstand Stalin's demands and continue functioning and leading its people as victory neared, and with it the constitution of a new, democratic Polish republic? Did Roosevelt and Churchill influence Stalin to retreat from his demands, or, at least, to moderate them? Did they call on him to stop trying to undermine the Polish government-in-exile and establish a Communist puppet regime? After all, as Churchill himself said, Britain had gone to war for its ally, Poland, when she had fallen victim to aggression. It was therefore the Polish "London government's" surmise that the two democratic powers would do their best to rectify the injustice Poland suffered when she was occupied and partitioned; that they would ensure that the 40 percent of Polish territory annexed by the Soviet Union in September 1939, in Russia's conspiracy with Nazi Germany, was restored to Polish sovereignty after the victory. One might have expected them to bolster the "London government," which represented a broad spectrum of Polish democratic political parties, and frustrate any attempt to turn Poland into a "People's Democracy" or a "Soviet Republic." After all, both Churchill and Roosevelt had frequently expressed their great appreciation and esteem for the valor of the Polish people and its love of freedom. Moreover, they had often and unequivocally reiterated their commitment to the resurrection of an independent and sovereign Poland.

The Western powers did not come through on any of the Polish government's expectations. Furthermore, the more serious the friction and clashes between the government-in-exile and the Soviet Government became, the more the fissures and breaches in the wall of Polish and English-American solidarity, in whose shade the "London government" resided, widened.

Chapter Nine

The Teheran Conference

In the Shadow of a Moral Debt and an Inferiority Complex

The trends reviewed in the previous chapter were reflected prominently, even decisively, during the summit conference at Teheran that began on November 28, 1943, seven months after Soviet-Polish ties were broken off. Although it is conventionally argued that Poland's fate was sealed at the Yalta conference, it was really in Teheran that the ground was prepared for setting Poland's eastern border as Stalin demanded.

To understand why the two Western leaders yielded to a Soviet *diktat* on this score, we should briefly survey the events unfolding on the battlefield.

The European theater was ablaze. True, the Western powers and their partners could already point proudly at their successful campaigns in North Africa and Italy, the growth in strength of their war machine, the massive military aid they were providing to the Soviet Union,* and the heroic exploits of their convoys. They could also take credit for the fact that their air forces were already busily bombing German cities and pinning down three-fourths of the Luftwaffe's strength.

---

*Only when the "second front" was opened in Western Europe did the Soviet Union admit publicly that it had received aid from the United States, Britain, and Canada. On June 11, 1944, Pravda published initial data as to the dimensions of aid provided under the Lend-Lease program.[1]

According to this source, the Soviet Union received (up to the date of publication) 8,782 aircraft, 3,734 tanks, 206,771 motor vehicles, and 2,199,000 tons of food. According to additional sources,[2] aid throughout the war approached 15,000 aircraft, 7,000 tanks, 6,000 self-propelled cannon and half-tracks, 300,000 motor vehicles, 2,000 locomotives, 11,000 railroad cars, 2,700,000 tons of oil, 912,000 tons of steel, and million of tons of food, ammunition, technical equipment, etc. Total supplies exceeded 17 million tons, of an estimated value of more than $12 billion (an enormous sum, representing 6.25 percent of the United States' 1943 GNP.[3])

Nevertheless, Roosevelt and Churchill displayed something of an inferiority complex toward the Russians, in view of their suffering and the war they were waging. The Red Army's success in throwing the Wehrmacht back by massive force left a tremendous impression on them, as did the Soviet victories in Stalingrad, Kursk, Orel, Kharkov, and Smolensk. Furthermore, the Red Army registered more triumphs just as the Teheran conference was about to open. By September the Germans were in retreat along the entire southern front, from Moscow to the Black Sea; Kiev, too, fell to the Russians three weeks before the conference opened. All this followed eighteen months of German occupation accompanied by horrifying mass murder, devastation, and repression. The impression left by the Red Army's successful victories was magnified all the more by the erroneous theories previously widely held in the West (based on the purges of the 1930s and inauspicious performance during the Finland war) about the Red Army's poor capabilities. All this flushed Roosevelt and Churchill with amazement and admiration.[4] Moreover, they were being pressed by Stalin to open a "second front." Before and during the conference, they repeatedly noted the need to meet the prerequisites for a Channel crossing. They pointed at their role in battering the Wehrmacht, thus making them indirect partners in the Red Army's victories, and, explained to Stalin that the landing would be doomed to failure without full and painstaking preparation.

Only by veiled hint did Churchill remind Stalin that the Soviet alliance with Hitler had facilitated the Nazi occupation of Western Europe. It was much easier, he remarked, to lose the once-staunch French front than to rebuild it.[5] Neither Roosevelt and Churchill saw any practical possibility of establishing a second front before the spring of 1944.[6] This fact, with the other factors we mentioned, discomfited them and imbued them with feelings of moral debt to the Soviet Union.

Thus, when the conference convened, the end of the war was still a long, hard, blood-drenched way off. However, the victories at El Alamein and Stalingrad marked the beginnings of a turnabout in Allied fortunes. For this reason, even as the conduct of the war was discussed, initial thoughts about the new, post-victory world order began to crystallize. Within this broad framework, the Polish question occupied an important, although not a pivotal, position.

The major problem that concerned Roosevelt and Churchill in the conduct and pursuit of the war to the final, total, and unconditional surrender of Nazi Germany was how to maintain, sustain, and solidify the fighting alliance between themselves and Stalin.

(The American President considered it vital to secure not only an anti-Nazi alliance but Soviet participation in the war against Japan).

The necessity of this alliance overshadowed past conflicts and enmities—the Ribbentrop-Molotov agreement; the misdeeds of the Comintern, the mutual hostility and contradictions of ideologies and regimes—and perhaps even consigned them to oblivion. In this matter Churchill was consistent, courageous, and generous. The day the Soviet Union was attacked, he broadcast to the British people one of his greatest speeches, in which he referred to the menace confronted by the Soviet Union as a threat to the British and the Americans as well, and to the Soviet struggle as that of all free persons the world over.[7]

Now, in Teheran, he told Stalin that they had to "remain friends" for the sake of well-being in both countries.[8]

Whether he was referring to true, long-lasting friendship, or a diplomatic and expedient device alone, his comments expressed a desire to appease and placate Stalin. Churchill and Roosevelt still feared that the Soviet strongman would again change his stripes and reach a separate arrangement with Hitler. This fear, of course, drew on memories of August 1939, and on rumors circulating widely in 1943 that a number of contacts were being held between Soviet and Nazi representatives with intent to sign a separate peace. One such account, for instance, spoke of a meeting between Edgar Klaus and Peter Kleist (one of Ribbentrop's aides); another even alluded to a meeting between Molotov and Ribbentrop. Even after denials by Berlin and Moscow, the allegations were of great concern to London and Washington.[9]

This fear, and the Western leaders' aforementioned sentiment of moral "debt," provoked Roosevelt and Churchill to make no few concessions at the Teheran conference in effort to placate Stalin. Moreover, in order to dispel Stalin's considerable apprehensions about a capitalist conspiracy, Roosevelt, when alone with Stalin, tossed in some innuendoes, barbs, and little wisecracks about Churchill.[10] Roosevelt—an angry Churchill later testified—even cautioned Stalin not to meet with Churchill alone.[11] (He did the same at the Yalta conference, cozying up to Stalin and joking at the expense of his British allies.)[12] All this was meant to hint to Stalin that the Anglo-American alliance had its little fissures, to say the least. Indeed, the fighting alliance, which Stalin needed no less, and perhaps more, than Roosevelt and Churchill, held together. However, the genuine and seeming nuances between the two Western leaders facilitated Stalin's efforts to extract far-reaching concessions from them.

Between Roosevelt and Churchill

In what ways were Roosevelt's and Churchill's outlooks, aspirations, and behavior different?

For Roosevelt, the dominant themes were victory in war; eradicating the might of the aggressive Axis powers—Germany, Italy, and Japan—and bringing them to their knees unconditionally; founding a world order on sound principles; and establishing an efficient international organization which would ensure such a new world order. Four "policemen" would safeguard it: The United States, the Soviet Union, Great Britain, and China. In all of these he sought a partnership embracing the Soviet Union and the Western allies.

In view of this background and Roosevelt's global perception, the problem of Poland, however important it was, played only a secondary role in his considerations. His aristocratic upbringing and his status as the President of the United States dictated an "on high" view of things. He was not prepared to let a "second-rate" country like Poland ruin his new world order and derail his alliance with Stalin. In a talk with British Foreign Secretary Anthony Eden, the democratic, idealistic Roosevelt (who detested the notion of world powers' "spheres of influence") asserted that the powers would decide what to give Poland and what not, and "Poland will have to agree."[13] All that really mattered was the contribution of the cause to world peace. He was not willing to bargain with Poland, or with any other little state, in a peace conference.[14] To him, the great, global interest was more important than and took preference over the particularistic interests of small countries; no trifling matter such as the future of a Poland that had not even been liberated yet should be permitted to disrupt the alliance with Stalin. Thus he set a principle: there would be no territorial changes while the war went on; final borders would not be set until the peace conference. This principle could have been interpreted as opposition to changes in Poland's prewar border. This was indeed the position Roosevelt presented in his talks with Polish Foreign Minister Raczynski in February 1942, and with Prime Minister Sikorski in December of that year.[15] Under this mantle of idealistic, lofty principles, however, Roosevelt also had pragmatic political motives and, to no less extent, domestic American electoral considerations—which at times clashed with those principles. For instance, although he did not explicitly support Stalin's demands on Poland at Teheran, his remarks in a *tête-à-tête* with Stalin on December 1, 1943[16] permitted no other interpretation with respect to the territorial changes demanded by Stalin. The excuse of "postponing the border issue" in fact served Roosevelt's electoral interest in not antagonizing millions of American voters of Polish extraction. He left the dirty work of negotiating with Stalin, and the thankless task of serving as lightning-rod for the Polish government-in-exile's furious reaction, to Churchill.

The latter, who knew how to stand up to a triumphant Hitler and lead his people and the Free World into war, was not daunted by the burden

Roosevelt had thrust upon him. He was hewn of seemingly sterner stuff other than his American colleague, and, unlike him, appeared to entertain fewer illusions. He was also more effective at sizing up Stalin. His admiration—as a born artist and as a historian—for Stalin's personality (the man had, after all, unified a mammoth nation and let it in a war of self-defense) was always adulterated with disgust, hate, and suspicion of the totalitarian dictator and his murky aims. Churchill also had his doubts about Roosevelt's international dream, and was more inclined to believe in a world order based on equilibrium and a demarcation of spheres of influence by the three Great Powers.[17] Victory over Hitler and the preservation of the British Empire's status were natural fixtures in this world view. Concepts that Roosevelt considered inadmissible and reactionary were nevertheless firmly entrenched in Churchill's *Weltanschauung*. He sought the resurrection of a free Europe organized under some 12 political entities, with Great Britain (and the United States) playing a senior and very weighty role relative to them.[18] He wanted to strengthen and solidify his alliance with Stalin in order to vanquish Hitler, not to hand Europe to him after the victory. The alliance was an instrument by which the war might be conducted and arrangements made that would secure the equilibrium of future Europe once the dust of the war settled.

Thus, while Roosevelt at least argued against territorial changes in Europe as long as the war continued, Churchill, who did not flinch from the notion of "spheres of influence," labored to reach arrangements with Stalin on this matter. As early as March 1942, for example, he had reached an understanding with Stalin about leaving the Baltic states annexed by the USSR in 1939 in the Soviet sphere of influence, explaining that while the Soviets were engaged in a life-and-death struggle for the "great cause," one should not thrust an unbearable burden upon them. In a telegram to Roosevelt (March 7, 1942), Churchill noted that the growing gravity of the war led him to feel that the tenets of the Atlantic Charter should be interpreted so as not to deny the USSR the borders it had had before the German attack.[19]

Churchill's view, based on the Soviets' war burden, led him into a trap of conscience and politics. On the one hand, he harbored a deep sympathy for the Polish people—"that noble race," he called them—and yearned to witness the resurrection of Poland as an independent, strong, and democratic state. In his world view, liberated Poland should be one of the major pillars of the new order and political equilibrium in Europe, because it was a medium-sized country alongside and in the shadow of the Soviet Union but nevertheless Western in state of mind, culture, and domestic regime. On the other hand, the principle of awarding the Soviet Union the borders it held in June 1941, also applied to the eastern territories taken from Poland in September 1939. True, in May 1942, Churchill still considered H. M. Government committed to the Polish-Soviet agreement of July 30, 1940, under which the Soviet Government acknowledged that its agreements with Germany in 1939 were no longer valid with respect to territorial changes in Poland. His position, however, was slowly but steadily crumbling.

The reasons for this process should be sought in the worsening, and, ultimately, the rupture of relations between the Polish and the Soviet governments; the government-in-exile's internal weakness and all-consuming internal rivalries; its inability to establish a military force of visible and direct impact in Poland's future liberation; and, in particular, the developments on the battlefield, which brought the Red Army closer and closer to Polish territory. Churchill did not want to let the Poland issue—however important and close to his heart it was—undermine the fighting alliance and unity between the West and the Soviet Union. From the "global" point of view, and with respect to the "great goal," Poland's eastern border as it stood in August 1939 was not ordained from on high. Thus Churchill, committed as he was to the cause of Poland's resurrection as an independent, democratic, and strong political entity, preferred to seek a compromise between the Soviet and the Poles' conflicting demands, satiating the wolf and leaving the sheep intact—almost—if possible.

The Principles of Churchill's Compromise

Such a compromise, he believed, had simultaneously to address itself to the rationale of Soviet defense interests and secure the rebirth of a strong, free and democratic Poland, with sovereign territorial powers conducive to security and existence worthy of being so called.

For him there was nothing sacred about the Riga Agreement, and the border proposed by his compatriot, Lord Curzon, was quite logical. He believed that moving the Polish state westward, exchanging territories and disentangling population groups (i.e., national minorities) would be a fair and useful arrangement. Thus he sent guidelines in this spirit to Anthony Eden, who was in Moscow at the time (October 1943) for a meeting of foreign ministers preceding the Teheran conference. Churchill was prepared to welcome any agreement between Poland and Russia which would afford the Soviets the security they needed for their western frontier while securing a strong and independent Poland.[20]

In view of this position, Churchill may have hoped for a quid-pro-quo from Stalin: re-recognition of the Polish government-in-exile. This, not as an end in itself, and not an expression of Churchill's affection for and appreciation of this government, but rather as a precursor of and basis for a democratic regime that would eventually come into being in liberated Poland. This, after all, was his intent: a democratic New Poland, linked to England by political perception, economics, and social policy, and clearly demarcating the Soviet and Western spheres of influence. By the time he realized that this was hopeless, it was already too late.

It may be assumed that had the two Western leaders, Roosevelt in particular, displayed greater unity and supported the Polish positions more firmly, they would have achieved better results. Stalin needed Western assistance no less than the West needed the Soviet Union's partnership and military might.

Even within Stalin's demands for border changes and a "friendly" Polish government, Poland could have been assured better conditions had the Americans displayed a more open and courageous stance, and had Churchill taken a more prudent approach.

The Mikołajczyk Government

The policies of the Polish government-in-exile, too, did not serve the cause of obtaining better terms. In view of Stalin's intentions and Churchill and Roosevelt's position, the "London government" took no political initiative that could have advanced its aspirations in any real way. Its posture was one of stubborn resistance. Instead of offering political alternatives, it vented its disappointment and bitterness. Paradoxically, the more this tone was voiced, and the more frequently and bitterly the Polish spokesmen repeated their claims, the more the attitude of the Polish government's Western friends deteriorated. They increasingly viewed the government-in-exile as a nuisance. Psychologically, an explanation proposed by Sovietologist Adam Ulam is undoubtedly correct: the grating Polish grievances, precisely because they were unanswerable, were bound to anger the West and cause it to hold Poland in contempt, in a manner often evoked by a bad conscience.[21]

One such expression of the Polish Government's position was provided in a memorandum presented by its Prime Minister to Roosevelt and Churchill just before the Teheran conference.

In July 1943, General Sikorski was killed in an aviation accident that is shrouded in mystery. Stanisław Mikołajczyk, a leader of the Farmers' Party, was chosen to replace him. Mikołajczyk sought an audience with Churchill and Roosevelt in the second half of November, and was turned down by each for various reasons. This was an indication of their part that he was not his predecessor's equal in personal prestige, and, in the main, that the Polish government had similarly slipped in esteem. Where it had once been a respected comrade-in-arms, it was now regarded as a junior partner, a troublemaker, a beggar at the door, dependent on the good will of its wealthy friends—but nevertheless audacious enough to remind them of troubling truths. When his request was rejected, Mikołajczyk drew up a memorandum and presented it to the two leaders.[22] It included a demand for assurances that the Polish government would be given the right to run the country from the moment it was liberated, and that Polish lives and property would be ensured from the moment the Red Army crossed into its territory.

Below the Polish government's refusal to enter into dispute about the border question is analyzed. The memorandum, couched in a mixture of dramatic and bitter formulations, stressed that Poland had never laid its guns down, had never produced a quisling, and did not deserve being treated like Italy; that the half of its territory that the Soviet Union was demanding for itself was essential for the country's future; that the very deliberation of this matter without effective British and American guarantees of Polish independence and security would by necessity lead to further

Polish PM, Mikołajczyk

Soviet demands. The memorandum went on to caution that were the Red Army to cross into Poland before relations between the two states were restored, the Government of Poland would have to take political action against "the affront to Poland's sovereignty." In such a case and if the Soviets used terror against Polish citizens, Mikołajczyk warned, the Polish administration and army would go underground and take defensive measures. Last of all was a plea for help, imploring the two Western leaders to intercede with Stalin for the resumption of Soviet-Polish ties. All of this merely repeated the Polish government's demands in principle, which were just and correct in themselves. Nevertheless, the memorandum epitomized Poland's blindness to events in the field and the political and military balance of forces. Mikołajczyk's warnings were a tragic reflection of the helplessness that characterized the "London government." They were tantamount to waving an unloaded handgun at an enemy while uttering battlecries that could not frighten a soul. There is no-record of the impression this memorandum left on the two leaders to whom it was addressed, but to judge by their attitude on the issue during the Teheran conference, its effect on them was nil.

How to Move a State

Against this background the summit conference opened on November 28, 1943, in Teheran.

The major concern of the Big Three, of course, was the conduct of the war in all its theaters. Although the matter of opening a second front in Western Europe was of particular importance, other issues came up during the deliberations as well. In this conference, as we have noted, the ground was prepared for setting Poland's eastern border as Stalin demanded. The two Western leaders found it preferable to play into Stalin's hands than to support their little ally. Stalin, in turn, adroitly exploited the discrepancies and differences in the Western leaders' attitudes, and their dread that the tripartite alliance would not hold together. Poland paid the price.

A "summit conference"—a concept that has long since become common coin in modern diplomacy—has an element of the surreal. The personal chemistry between rulers of peoples and of great powers, the human element, the setting, the surroundings, the banquets, the small talk, the jokes and hints, even an occasional toothache or headache—all serve as the background, and at times even a component, of deliberations in which the fate of peoples is decided. At Teheran, the formal sessions were interspersed with mealtime discussions between Roosevelt, Churchill, Stalin, and their aides, which were perhaps even more crucial. Here almost anything could be said and received with good humor.[23]

Such an opportunity arose on the very first evening in Teheran, when Roosevelt, tired, went to his quarters to rest. Churchill took Stalin by the arm, led him to a sofa in a corner of the hall, and suggested that they have a little chat "about what will happen after the victory." Stalin agreed to this, and the conversation described at the beginning of Chapter Five ensued. Then Churchill pulled out his three matches (representing the Soviet Union, Poland, and Germany) and demonstrated his ideas about moving Poland. Stalin, Churchill reports, was pleased.

We need not wonder why, of course.

There he sat, the nonpareil democrat and homophile, drawing contentedly on his pipe, smiling under his mustache, saying nothing. His counterparts were doing the talking. Poland's friends and patrons, who had gone to war for her sake, were proposing and contending that the major question was how to secure the Soviet Union's western border. They slid matches across the table of Europe; Stalin merely went along for the ride, noncommittal, still uncertain. Slightly puzzled and surprised, he asked if it were not necessary to "ask the lady." No, Churchill reassured him. Let the two of us reach an agreement first; then we shall advise the Poles to accept our proposals.

Thus, with three matches, Churchill demonstrated how a state, and a people which had lost millions of victims to aggression, can be moved.[24]

Some Comments on Churchill's "Deals"

Another two examples, one preceding and the other following these events, demonstrate Churchill's tendency to resolve complicated problems and determine peoples' fate with a few matches or strokes of the pen.

In March 1921, as Colonial Secretary in Lloyd George's Government, Churchill visited Palestine to clear up a few problems that were hindering the interests of the British Empire. One of these was the matter of Emir Abdullah, who, with the help of 1,200 Beduin, was threatening to upset the arrangements Britain and France had made in the area.

A stalwart friend of Zionism, Churchill had thus far insisted that Great Britain honor the Balfour Declaration and the commitments stemming from the Mandate for Palestine. In view of developments in the Middle East, however, he now regarded the sacrifice of Zionist interests as the only avenue to a solution. Thus he reached Jerusalem, sat down with Abdullah for a talk with the participation of Lawrence of Arabia, and agreed at its end to hand all of Transjordan to Abdullah. The accord also prohibited Jewish immigration to and settlement in that province.

This agreement, formally approved by the League of Nations on September 16, 1922, stood in stark contrast to the Balfour Declaration and the British Mandate. In one bold stroke it reduced the territory earmarked for the Jewish National Home from 40,000 square miles to 10,000.[25]

The second example puts the cart before the horse. Visiting Moscow about a year after the Teheran Conference, Churchill reached the Kremlin and, late in the evening of October 9, 1944, drew up the famous "Percentages Deal" with Stalin. On a half-sheet of paper, Churchill sketched out his formula for apportioning spheres of influence in the Balkans so as to prevent "friction":[26]

	Percent
Romania	
USSR	90
Others	10
Greece	
Britain (with American agreement)	90
USSR	10
Yugoslavia	50:50
Hungary	50:50
Bulgaria	
USSR	75
Others	25

Churchill pushed the scrap of paper at Stalin, who made a mark of approval on it with his blue pencil and handed it back. After a long silence, Churchill pondered aloud about the impression world opinion would acquire if it knew that problems so fateful to millions of people were solved so nonchalantly. Let's burn this paper, he suggested.

"No," said Stalin. "Keep it."

Churchill therefore seemed embarrassed, regretful, taken back by his own cynical audacity in rendering the fate of millions by jotting a few figures on a scrap of paper. Stalin was not agitated. Nor, perhaps, was he even willing to let Churchill retract the proposal. Two days later, Churchill sat down in Moscow to write a letter to Stalin "clarifying" the matter of the percentages. In this letter (which was never sent), and in another message to his "friends back home," he tried to play down the importance of the "percentages deal" by stressing that it was purely preliminary in nature, until such time as the Big Three would again convene at the victory table. Churchill considered his percentages nothing more than a method by which the participants might assess how close their positions had become and then decide upon the measures necessary to close the gap.[27]

In his memoirs, Churchill attempted to downplay the fateful implications of the deal, to stress his doubts about its ethical and political validity (neither should we underestimate the sincerity and intensity of these doubts), and even, perhaps, to retract the proposal.[28] These attempts do not conform with later findings. The personal documents of General Hastings Ismay, who accompanied Churchill and took notes during the fateful talk, atest that Churchill perceived and presented the provisional arrangements as "permanently provisional."[29] Ismay's records convey the clear impression that Churchill was striving for a permanent arrangement or understanding, not a temporary set of guidelines. He aspired to reach an arrangement which, during the transition period from war to peace, would prevent misunderstandings and friction among the three allies. During the talk, too, Churchill presented another line of reasoning for the same argument. It was better, he said, to express such matters in diplomatic terms, avoiding the phrase "dividing into spheres" because it might shock the Americans. However, as long as he and Marshal Stalin understood each other, Churchill added, he could explain matters to Roosevelt.[30]

Stalin understood and agreed.

Another fact to consider is that Churchill's proposed deal was discussed with full seriousness. The very next day, Molotov began to negotiate with Eden toward improving the percentages in the Soviets' favor, especially with respect to Hungary (from 50 percent to 80 percent). These talks were exhausting and frustrating, and only Churchill's proposals on Greece and Romania were reaffirmed.[31]

The Big Three Redraw Poland's Borders

Let us return to Teheran.

November 30, the day after the "match game," was devoted from beginning to end to discussion of Operation Overlord—the opening of the European second front. The very next day, however, the Polish question resurfaced as a major issue. The two Western leaders made Stalin's task much easier in their separate meetings with him by disclosing the nuances between them. Each tried separately to conclude some kind of deal with the Soviet dictator, who, poker-faced, advanced steadily toward his goals. Thus

Roosevelt invited Stalin that afternoon for "sincere" discussion of a matter that caused him no small concern: his intention to run for a fourth term as President in the winter of 1944—an unheard-of phenomenon in American history—and all this implied with respect to the agenda in Teheran. First of all, Roosevelt hastened to promise his support for Stalin's intention to establish a Polish state with its eastern border moved to the west and its western border shifted as far as the Oder River. However, Roosevelt added apologetically, Stalin had to understand that neither in Teheran nor the next winter could he be a party to this decision. Six to seven million ethnic Poles lived in the United States, the President explained; as a practical man, he did not wish to risk losing their votes.[32]

Stalin, undoubtedly quite amused by the President's electoral agonistes, pretended to commiserate. Now, he said, he could understand the President's attitude.

Roosevelt found this response greatly encouraging, and threw in a rather cynical comment just to make things even more intimate. The United States, he noted, was also home to quite a few Lithuanian, Latvian, and Estonian ethnics. When the Red Army captured these territories, however, he had no intention of embarking on war with the Soviet Union for that reason. At that time, Roosevelt continued, the American public neither knew nor understood the matter. But when it involved millions of Polish-American voters, not a few thousand Lithuanians and their like—and when elections were imminent—it was not so simple at all.

Here Roosevelt had the opportunity to hear friendly and professional advice from the kind of expert in public relations, conceptual-intellectual persuasion, and democratic elections that even cognoscenti would appreciate: "The public has to be given information," Stalin instructed Roosevelt. "You have to do propaganda work, too."

That very evening, December 1, 1943, the Big Three gathered to deliberate the Poland question, which seemed ripe for resolution.[33] A comment by Admiral Leahy, one of Roosevelt's confidants and a member of his entourage, may have been overly laconic when he asserted that the border question provoked little disputation in Teheran.[34] Basically, however, he was right.

Roosevelt opened the discussion, expressing hope that the Soviet Union and Poland would resume their relations. Stalin's reply appeared to leave room for this possibility. However, the Soviet dictator took pains to draw a clear distinction between the government-in-exile and the Polish people. He accused the "London government" of responsibility for the murder of partisans, anti-Soviet propaganda, and even connections with Nazi agents. Only a guarantee that this government would change its stripes would make negotiations possible. Then, however, he added that he was not sure this government could represent the Polish people. Poland's allies let these grave charges go unchallenged, and the discussion proceeded to the border issue.

Churchill reiterated his "three-match" proposal, noting again that it would result in the establishment of an independent and strong Poland, secure borders for Russia against German aggression from the west, and compensation for the Poles through the annexation of German territories. If the Soviet Union were prepared to accept this solution, Churchill said, and if a reasonable formulation were found, he would be willing to present the idea to the government-in-exile as the best deal it was going to get. He would tell the Poles that he just might talk the Russians into accepting his scheme, thus showing the government-in-exile that it was in good hands.[35]

If the Poles balked, the British would wipe their hands of them. Thus, Churchill not only presented and crystallized the idea of "moving" Poland to the west, but volunteered to promote it as well. In his readiness to ensure the Soviet Union "absolute security of its western border against a future surprise attack by Germany," Churchill disregarded the fact that Poland, too (as demonstrated by its history, including September 1939) needed secure borders in the west and the east alike. Paternalistically convinced that he knew the Poles' best interests better than they did, he was ready to give Stalin what he wanted without consulting them or considering the Polish government's position. It was his view that the Poles would be doing well for themselves if they swapped the Pripet marshes in the east for industrialized areas in the west.[36]

Thus the deliberations took a practical turn, as the Big Three and their aides bent over the maps and began to "move" Poland.

Now a considerable difference surfaced. Stalin was well-acquainted with the details of the map, the border issue, and the sites involved. By contrast, Roosevelt displayed little interest in the practical side of the matter, and Churchill preferred "not to go into detail" for reasons known only to him. (This certainly explains why his memoirs give the impression that he had not yet noticed at the time that the Western and Eastern Neisse are two different rivers.)[37]

Then a short argument developed as to the discrepancies between the Ribbentrop-Molotov Line and the Curzon line (the topic of the deliberations), which gave Poland more territory. Stalin, wishing to avoid this issue at that stage, demanded impatiently, "Call it what you will—we regard this line as just and correct."

A second bone of contention was whether or not to leave Vilna and Lvov in Poland or not. Eden tried to argue that the Curzon Line had not demarcated the southern part of the border, and that the intent at the time had been to leave Lvov within Poland. This Stalin dismissed categorically; the line of the British map, he ruled, had been misdrawn. Gesturing at the map, he asserted in no uncertain terms that Lvov was set in the heart of the Ukrainian area. But he would willingly relinquish the entire Polish-populated area. (With this, he seized a red pencil and, with a few energetic strokes, sketched the changes he had in mind. In the southern sector he marked the territory between the Ribbentrop-Molotov line and the Curzon Line to its east, including the city of Przemyśl. In the northern sector, the red pencil encircled a broad chunk of land stretching as far as the Curzon

MAP 3: Curzon Line and Ribbentrop-Molotov Line

Line in the area of Białystok.) Lvov and its vicinity, however, belonged to the Ukraine.[38] Now he made no mention of the hint he had broached, to no avail, to Sikorski.

Here Churchill declared himself unwilling to provoke a conflict because of Lvov, and this sealed the matter. The Prime Minister did insist, however, that Poland be offered suitable and equitable compensation in the form of the German territories she would annex.

Stalin neither rejected the idea nor made any explicit commitment. He did attach strings to his "generous" consent to abide by the Curzon Line: the USSR wished to annex the northern section of Eastern Prussia, including the city of Königsberg (subsequently renamed Kaliningrad).[39] While these deliberations were going on, Roosevelt, true to his tactics and the considerations he had previously explained to "Uncle Joe" (as Roosevelt and Churchill called Stalin) preferred to lend his implicit consent to the deal taking shape.

Indeed, although nothing was finalized officially,[40] all participants in the discussion understood that the principle had been accepted: there would be a new Polish state, with borders based on the Curzon Line in the east and the Oder River in the west, with the addition of the Oppeln area and Eastern Prussia ("as defined"[41]).*

Since Churchill had raised the possibility that border changes would also involve population transfer (he used a quasi-sociological term for this purpose—"disentanglement of population"), Roosevelt solicited Stalin's views on whether a population could be transferred from ethnically-mixed territories by its own volition. Stalin, who had found it possible to transfer millions of people to the Siberian wilderness and the Gulag Archipelago "by their volition," and whose expertise in shutting down whole republics (covering a territory of 60,000 square miles) and dispersing about a million and a quarter of their inhabitants (the Volga Germans, the Crimean Tatars, the Kalmyks, the Chechens, the Ingushi, and the Balkars[43]) would become widely known only years later, reassured the President: "Definitely."[44]

Thus the issue of Poland's future borders was resolved in principle. This solution, however, also contained the seeds of the Sovietization of postwar Poland.

---

*The all-inclusive and, at times, imprecise nature of these terms permitted Stalin to give them far-reaching interpretations. Thus, for example, the Oppeln area was extended west of the Oder River. It is also hard to understand Churchill's reference to Eastern Prussia "as defined" (who would define it, and how?). Stalin adroitly exploited inaccuracies of this kind. Some time later, Churchill panicked and attempted to backtrack in view of Stalin's behavior, but the damage had been done.[42]

Stalin and his Democratic Colleagues

With respect to Poland, there is no doubt that Stalin came away from Teheran with the upper hand. Both Western leaders were experienced statesmen of uncommon stature. One had saved the world from Nazi takeover by claiming the position of the first and only leader in the campaign; the other had carried the greatest of nations from isolationism to universalist responsibility. Yet both yielded to Stalin and his demands on Poland with stunning ease. Churchill was a proud, fighting statesman, imbued with the ideals of freedom and democracy. He was an audacious realist, and was friendly to Poland and its cause. However, things had come to such a pass that he was the man who gratuitously offered his ideas about moving Poland. It was he who volunteered to be the "bad boy" and to twist the Poles' arms. In fact, he assumed the dirty work himself, permitting Roosevelt to play the role of the "good guy," the onlooker.

The desire to appease and satiate the Soviet dictator, to blunt his criticism and impatience at the postponement of the "second front" campaign, to integrate him into the campaign against Japan, to make him a partner in the new world order—in view of all these "great" issues, Roosevelt and Churchill considered the topic of Poland's future borders, however important it was, a secondary concern.

It is worth noting how Roosevelt—a towering, experienced, tough statesman, and an expert in handling and manipulating politicians and people—fell victim either to his own naïvete or to the "spell" cast by Stalin. He was impressed by the Soviet dictator's personality, and was unable to fathom its shadowy recesses. Neither did he refrain from bragging to others—not only his closest confidants—that Stalin trusted him, not Churchill.[45]

Roosevelt's maneuverings were not lost on Stalin, of course. He followed the doings of his capitalist partners with cold curiosity, and became increasingly convinced that the capitalist world contained contradictions that would ultimately cause its total self-destruction. Indeed, even now it had fallen into a serious rift, with the Nazi-Fascist part fighting the Soviet Union and the other part, represented here at the conference, concurrently battling alongside her. His feeling of supremacy, based on the "scientific" Marxist world view and the determinism of historical processes, became stronger all the more when the Red Army began to register victories. Now Stalin was no longer afraid that his capitalist partners would join forces with Hitler; he knew they were even more eager than he to keep the anti-Nazi alliance alive.

Stalin attached very little importance to Roosevelt's lofty principles and Churchill's thundering rhetoric, and he treated the concepts of democracy they expressed with contempt.

This man—who had spent years of his life in the underground and under revolutionary conditions; building party bastions and waging domestic subversion; eliminating political rivals and masses of ordinary, "unreliable" people; implementing the principles of Bolshevism while enslaving peasants, presiding over mass expulsions and arrests, and filling forced labor camps with millions of "criminals"—was prepared to agree to formulations that would capture Roosevelt's heart.

However, he was not willing to forgo his goals.

These basic goals, at the Teheran stage, were to prod his two Western partners into promptly opening a second front, and to bring about a situation in which the Soviet Union would emerge from the war as the dominant power in Eastern Europe, from the Baltic to the Black Sea. The more confident he became in the Red Army's achievements, the stronger his aspirations grew.

Chapter Ten

Between Teheran and Yalta

The Teheran conference ended on December 1, 1943. The Yalta conference commenced more than a year later, on February 6, 1945.

Between the two dates, the Polish problem continued to occupy the three powers. The principles for its solution, as agreed upon in Teheran, began to take on substance as the powers acted to manipulate the diplomatic mechanism on the one hand and *faits accomplis* on the other.

The Polish government-in-exile, pressed by both sides of this vise, was left with little room to maneuver. Were this not enough, if failed to exploit even the little it had. Its responses were characterized by intransigent naysaying, failure to seek alternatives, and inability to be flexible at the right time. Its modest attempt in February, 1944 to present an alternative proposal was too little, too late.

The Tass Announcement of January 1944

The Red Army rode a crest of victories in 1944, driving the German invader out of Soviet territory along the entire front. The siege of Leningrad was lifted in January of that year, and the Soviet forces pressed rapidly toward the Baltic Sea.

Between January and March 1944, the Soviet forces continued to exploit their progress on the Western front, reaching the Bug and Dniestr Rivers after liberating Kiev. During the spring the Germans were driven out of Crimea, and in June the second front in France was opened, and Finland was removed from the circle of combatants. By July, Vitebsk and Minsk had been liberated, and the Red Army advanced to the Niemen and Vistula Rivers. During the autumn, the Germans were expelled from Romania, Bulgaria, Hungary, and southern Poland.

On January 4, 1944, the very beginning of a year of victories and bloodshed, Red Army troops crossed Poland's prewar border. The next day, the Polish government-in-exile issued a declaration congratulating the

Red Army on its progress, calling on the Polish underground to sustain and step up its war against the Germans, and, in the event that Polish-Soviet relations resumed, asking the underground to cooperate with the Soviet commanders.[1]

This gesture was not left without response.

Several days later, Tass issued a communiqué[2] including fierce criticism of the "London government" and contemptuously dismissing its nature and essence. It was "an émigré government," asserted the bulletin—estranged from its people, unable to establish friendly relations with the Soviet Union, and at the same time unable to organize an active struggle against the German invaders in Poland itself. But above and beyond this onslaught on the "London government"—which in itself contained nothing new—the Tass announcement took on a conspicuous tone that could be interpreted as an attempt to change the Soviet position.

The positive emphasis in the announcement was placed on the Soviet Union's interest in "establishing a strong and independent Poland, and in Polish-Soviet friendship."

Apart from the declarative sections of the announcement, however, the message also contained what sounded like relatively moderate and flexible formulations on the border issue. Addressing itself to Poland's eastern border, the announcement said that this frontier had been set "in accordance with the desire of the population of the Western Ukraine and Western Belorussia, as expressed in the plebiscite. . . ." This notwithstanding, the communiqué added, the border between Poland and the Soviet Union "can be demarcated by agreement. . . ." Furthermore, Tass felt it necessary to stress that "The Soviet Union does not consider the 1939 borders [those set in the Ribbentrop-Molotov agreement—Y.C.] as unchangeable. These borders can be adjusted to Poland's benefit on the basis of the rule by which all the districts in which the majority of the population is Polish will be transferred to Poland . . . approximately along the so-called Curzon Line. . . ."

In addition to these phrasings, which, although adhering to the Curzon Line were nevertheless encouraging in their tone at least, and were acceptable on the surface, the Tass announcement dangled before the Poles such things as their "historical rights" and "generous compensation" in the West.

"The western border of Poland," the announcement went on to say, "has to expand by the attachment of her ancient lands, which were taken from Poland by Germany . . . and by the attachment of an essential access route to the Baltic Sea."

With this, the "London government" faced a dilemma. The fact that Tass spoke of an "agreement" and presented various proposals indicated that the Soviets were willing to open a dialogue of some kind with the government-in-exile, even in the absence of formal relations between them. It was also positive to note the formulations that established, for the first time, that there was room to discuss rectifications of the border set in the Ribbentrop-Molotov agreement—in Poland's favor. As for "compensation" at Germany's expense, the Polish government needed no persuading.

These favorable hints made an impression on most members of the "London government," which, therefore, took care not to reject the Soviet announcement out of hand. Mikołajczyk, in particular, tended to move toward an accommodation with the Soviet Union. He believed at the time that within the framework of the East-West alliance it would also be possible to reach an understanding between Poland and the Soviet Union permitting his government to return from London to Warsaw and allowing Polish army formations to return from the West to Poland.[3] Even Mikołajczyk, however, was not ready to accept the Soviet demands as to the eastern territories; he was especially aware of the trends of thought within his government and in Polish public circles.

When Beneš returned from Moscow and brought Stalin's terms for a resolution of the conflict with Poland to his attention,[4] Mikołajczyk replied that he (Mikołajczyk):

> . . . knew the Poles. Even if they made matters still worse for Poland, nobody could get them to yield voluntarily about the Curzon Line. If only it were possible to shift the Polish-Soviet frontier to the east and to combine this with an exchange of population. If at least Lwów could be saved for Poland.[5]

Subsequent developments proved that Mikołajczyk indeed knew the soul of his government. While he had expressed an inclination to adopt some flexibility and readiness to present alternative proposals, most of his colleagues were not yet willing to hear of either of these. Those who opposed any concession of territorial integrity, insisting instead on the sanctity of the Riga Agreement, came away with the upper hand. Neither did Anthony Eden's intervention help. He tried to persuade the Poles not to spurn the Soviet proposal, which he viewed as a sign of major progress. "What will happen when Soviet troops advance inside Poland? Will you get a better frontier?"[6]

Eden's rhetorical question and his attempt to moderate the phrasing of the Polish response, combined with the intentions of Mikołajczyk and his supporters in the government, ultimately produced a compromise formula. The Polish government's announcement on January 14 preferred to refrain from entering into overt polemics.[7]

Although it rejected "unilateral decisions and *faits accomplis* on Polish territory," the announcement asked the Governments of the United

States and Great Britain to proffer their good offices toward the resumption, with their participation, of the negotiations between Poland and the Soviet Union. The talks would aim to resolve all the problems[8]* and establish friendly and durable cooperation between the two states.

The next day, however, the government-in-exile's representation (*delegatura*) in Warsaw "corrected" and unequivocally clarified that which the announcement had moderated and circumvented:

> The Polish nation categorically and firmly rejects Soviet aspirations to the eastern provinces of Poland, reaffirms the principle of inviolability of the frontiers established in the Treaty of Riga, and will never agree to new annexation of any part of Poland. The Polish nation is determined to defend by all possible means the integrity of the eastern territories of the Republic.[9]

This rigid phrasing, whether coordinated with the hawks in the "London government" or not, effectively closed off any possibility of negotiations between the Poles and the Soviets.

The Soviets reaction was swift, terse, and unequivocal. Gone were all the nice expressions such as "mutual respect," "agreement," and "rectifications." In their place was the assertion that the Polish government's failure to recognize the Curzon Line was tantamount to its rejection of this line. The new communiqué, according to the Soviets, also demonstrated the "London government's" unwillingness to establish good neighborly relations with the Soviet Union. In general, too, "The Soviet Union cannot enter into official negotiations with a government with whom diplomatic relations have been broken off."[10] By resorting to this formalistic, awkward rationale, the new Soviet announcement papered over the simple truth. The Soviet Government was willing to deliberate and negotiate with Poland only on condition that she accept its demands, chiefly the territorial ones, in advance. When its expectations in this regard were dashed, it decided to attain them without the benefit of negotiations.

Ugly as this truth undoubtedly was, the Poles should have treated it as a political fact. In principle, they may have been right from their point of view to refrain from mentioning, or even to explicitly reject, the Curzon Line as a basis for negotiations. By so doing, however, they disregarded military and political realities. The Tass announcement of January may have created room for a Polish-Soviet dialogue. Today we cannot assess where such negotiations might have led had they taken place. It is very likely that

---

*The Polish government empowered Anthony Eden to inform Soviet ambassador Gusev that "all the problems" included the border issue.

the Russians, as noted above, would not have yielded on any substantial territorial demand. It is also possible, however, that they would have conceded something at some stage. Practically speaking—principles aside— the Poles had nothing to lose in such negotiations; they could only have profited. Now, any chance for dialogue and coexistence between the democratic Polish leadership and the Soviet Union, if one still existed, had been wiped out for good. About a month later, the government-in-exile did try to soften its stance (see below) on the eastern border issue. This, however, no longer had any effect on Stalin's intention to eliminate the "London government" in favor of a "friendly" one.

Churchill's Pressure

After the modest attempt to re-establish Soviet-Polish contacts failed, Churchill applied himself to the task he had undertaken in Teheran.

On January 20, he met with Polish Prime Minister Mikołajczyk. Participating with them were their foreign ministers, Eden and Romer, and their ambassadors, Cadogan and Raczyński.[11]

True to the tactic he had proposed back in Teheran, Churchill now played his role. He had come with a proposal, he said. If the Polish government would be willing to accept it, he, Churchill, would immediately telegram Stalin and present it in his own name. Once the proposal was adopted, too, he would demand of Stalin to immediately restore full relations with the "London government" and refrain from any intervention in Poland's internal problems.

The major elements of his proposal:

A. The Polish government accepts the Curzon Line as a basis for negotiations.
B. Eastern Prussia, Danzig, and Upper Silesia as far as the Oder River, will be annexed to Poland.
C. All Poles east of the new Soviet frontier will be permitted to relocate to Poland, while all Germans within the confines of new Poland will be completely expelled.

Mikołajczyk's reaction was essentially negative, although it hinted that his government had softened its stance somewhat. While the Government of Poland, he said, was now ready, as it had not been in the past, to negotiate its frontiers with the Soviet Union, the Riga Agreement (not the Curzon Line) should serve as the basis and point of departure for any discussion. To accept the Curzon Line in this function was tantamount to accepting the major Soviet demand in advance. In such circumstances, one would expect to face subsequent further demands that would be even harder to reject. Churchill's proposal would cause a tremendous transfer of frontiers and population, which no nation could withstand. It would perhaps be better to resolve the matter through swapping population than by exchanging territory. What, then, of Lvov? Where would it be under the Churchill proposal? And would England and the United States guarantee the arrangement?

Churchill appeared to be losing his temper. He declared that he wanted the Polish government to accept the Curzon Line without Lvov as a basis for negotiations with the Soviets, considering this a just solution. The Poles, he said, had to accept it not only as a necessity but with enthusiasm, for it would resolve the Polish problem "on a grand scale."[12]

Mikołajczyk and his comrades refused to be "enthusiastic," but in view of the pressure of their friend and major patron, it was clear that an intransigent and uncompromising Polish stance would only undermine their status further. This time, after a month's delay, Mikołajczyk succeeded in tipping the scales in the direction of some measure of flexibility. Overcoming his more extreme colleagues, Mikołajczyk pushed through his government a resolution (on February 15, 1944) which, while rejecting the Soviet demands, nevertheless hinted at willingness to arrive at some kind of compromise. This resolution[13] said that the outcome of the frontier questions could take effect only after the end of the war. Even now, however, while the hostilities still continue, a demarcation line should be established east of Vilna and Lvov. Upon liberation, all territories west of this line would be handed over to the Polish authorities, while everything to its east would be entrusted to a Soviet military administration that would avail itself of the assistance of representatives of the Allies.

This proposal, regarded by its formulators as a serious concession and a means of opening a dialogue and negotiations with the Soviets, was categorically rejected by Stalin. Churchill, too, saw nothing new in it that would mandate a change in his position. Indeed, he brought the matter before Parliament in order to bring additional public pressure to bear on the government-in-exile. Addressing the house on February 22, 1944, he admittedly praised the Poles, "that noble race" whose national spirit had survived a bitter fate of centuries. At the same time, he saw fit to remind the MPs that H.M. Government had never agreed to guarantee the previous Polish borders. "We did not agree to the occupation of Vilna in 1920. In 1919, the British supported the Curzon Line . . ."

The intention, he said, was not to set the borders for keeps; that would wait until the end of the war. In view of the advance of the Russian Army, however, some sort of friendly working agreement had to be reached, permitting coordination and cooperation among all the forces fighting Hitler.

The Mikołajczyk-Roosevelt Meeting

In the meantime, Mikołajczyk attempted to assess Washington's stance and determine whether he had a chance of exploiting it in resisting Churchill's pressure. The Polish ambassador in the United States, Ciechanowski, presented Secretary of State Cordell Hull with a memorandum that included three questions:

> Whether the US Government considers it advisable to enter already now upon the final settlement of territorial problems of Europe. Would the US Government be prepared in principle to participate in bringing about such settlements and guarantee them. Does the US government regard it possible to lend its support to PM Churchill's plan and to its realization.[14]

Mikołajczyk presumably expected a clear-cut answer stressing President Roosevelt's opposition to setting borders before the end of the war. What he got was an evasive reply from the State Department.

The State Department's basic stance, as it had informed Mikołajczyk, was that discussing the demarcation of Europe's borders during the war would only sow general confusion and weaken the war effort. "However, this attitude does not prevent the possibility of the two states' reaching an arrangement between themselves by mutual agreement." The U.S. Government understood that the Polish Government might have an interest in reaching a solution with no delay. For caution's sake, however, the letter added: "As stated above, there can be no question of guarantees as far as the US is concerned."[15]

With the innocence of someone who confuses the elephant and the fly, the letter fostered the notion of a "mutual agreement" between the Soviet Union and the government-in-exile, as if the actual balance of forces would truly permit the Poles to arrive at such an agreement free of a steamroller of pressures, Churchill's included.

In view of this reply, Mikołajczyk tried to meet with Roosevelt, but was spurned each time for different reasons.

After more than four months passed, Mikołajczyk was granted an audience with the President on June 11, 1944. That very day, Roosevelt had received Stalin's telegram excitedly congratulating the American ally for its successful landing at Normandy (which had begun on June 6) and the opening of the second front. It is therefore no wonder that Roosevelt was in good spirits. He opened in a light-hearted tone:

> I have studied sixteen maps of Poland this morning. In only three hundred years, parts of White Russia have been Polish, and parts of Germany and

Czechoslovakia. . . . On the other hand, parts of Poland have at times been annexed to those countries.

Turning on his charming smile, Roosevelt concluded:

It is difficult to untangle the map of Poland.[16]

When Mikołajczyk reminded Roosevelt of his government's well-known demands, Roosevelt loyally promised him that the United States would not forsake its ally—if only, he added almost jocularly, because of the seven million Poles whose votes he did not want to lose. Despite his efforts to avoid real discussion of topics of substance, the differences in attitude between him and his counterpart surfaced promptly. Nor should we wonder that this was so. The one viewed the globe from the dizzying heights of his position as President of the United States, while the other was concerned "only" with his own nation's "parochial" interests.

Thus, for example, Roosevelt argued that he could not deal with the question of "whether this or that town would be on this or that side of the frontier line." For him, such matters were trivial, especially when the frontier was that of a distant nation. Roosevelt's discourse flowed, and he captured the visitor's heart by gracefully spicing it, as was his way, with anecdotes and recollections. As he retold the account of a bicycle tour he had taken in Europe as a young man, Roosevelt related that Stalin had impressed him in Teheran as a realist. His faith in Stalin was apparently unshaken. The President said that Stalin had impressed him "as a realist who was neither an imperialist nor a communist." He realized that he was "very deft," and said that he could not believe that Russia wanted to destroy Poland; moreover, he knew how difficult it would be to do so, "even for Russia."[17] Then, as if to make the ambience of the conversation even more intimate and friendly, Roosevelt took Mikołajczyk into his confidence on the state of affairs.

Stalin, he said, had much more faith in him than in Churchill. Mr. Roosevelt then switched to his talks on Poland with Stalin at Teheran, and pointed out that neither he nor Stalin had referred to the Curzon Line as a final frontier between Poland and Soviet Russia. It was Churchill who brought up this subject, and the President added that, naturally, Stalin took full advantage of the opening.[18] However, Roosevelt added, he would eventually function as a balance between the conflicting positions, and would help Poland retain Lvov, hold onto the oil and potash areas of Drohobycz and Tarnopol (in eastern Galicia), and annex Eastern Prussia (including Königsberg) and Silesia. The only thing he could not promise, he said, was to return Vilna.[19] Although everything was said in a tone so friendly as to verge on gaiety, including those delightful anecdotes, Mikołajczyk certainly had very good reason to be shocked. The news that Churchill—Poland's great friend—was the man who had initiated and proposed the Curzon Line at Teheran shocked him. Finally, by Mikołajczyk's request, Roosevelt promised to make an effort to persuade Stalin to receive the Prime Minister of the Polish government-in-exile. True to his word, he forwarded a letter on the topic to Moscow on June 19. For some reason, the President chose to adopt a conciliatory tone. He had found it necessary, he wrote, to receive Mikołajczyk, but could assure Marshal Stalin that the visit was not connected with any attempt on his part to interfere with the disagreements that existed between the Polish government-in-exile and the Soviet government.[20]

Stalin Demands a "Reorganization" of the Polish Government

Not wanting to turn Roosevelt down, Stalin replied on June 24 that he would be happy to meet with Mikołajczyk. There were, however, some strings attached. The Soviet Union would recognize the Government of Poland, Stalin cabled, if the latter recognized the Curzon Line and underwent a "reorganization" leading to the inclusion of democratic Polish statesmen presently in the United States, the Soviet Union, and Poland itself.

Accordingly, Mikołajczyk, after his return to London in a talk with Soviet ambassador Lebiedev, was presented with Moscow's demand that he dismiss President Raczkiewicz, Commander-in-Chief Sosnkowski, Defense Minister Kukiel, and Information Minister Kot from his government.[21] The fact that Stalin no longer settled for resolving the border issue as the only condition for resuming relations, rather presenting an additional demand—a reshuffling of the Polish government—brought a new political dimension into the affair. This autocrat now claimed to himself the right to determine who was and who was not a genuine democrat. According to rumor, he had already lined up candidates from the Polish emigré community in the United States, and the fact that they were politically anonymous attested to his intentions. One such candidate was one Orlemanski, a modest, little-known priest of Polish extraction from Springfield, Massachusetts, who set out for Moscow with an inner drive and a conviction that God had selected him as His instrument of reconciliation between the Kremlin and the Vatican, and between Russia and Poland. There is no reason to suspect Stalin, of course, of acting out of renascent religious and mystical feelings when he chose Orlemanski, of all people, as an ideal candidate for membership in the Government of Poland.

But Stalin did not settle for merely recording his recommendations and ideas. Once his Western allies opened the second front, he felt free to ignore their sensitivities and possible reactions, and began to consider the many new possibilities presently available to him.

He now had the power to carry out his plans, and he used it.

The Lublin Committee

While Mikołajczyk was making his way from London to Moscow, the "National Liberation Committee" (PKWN) was established on July 21, 1944, in Chełm, a town in the already-liberated part of Poland. Three days later the committee moved to nearby Lublin (and is therefore known as the "Lublin Committee"). Installed at its head was Bolesław Bierut. This body, like its previous metamorphosis, the ZPP (Union of Polish Patriots), comprised Communists and other leftist elements. The identity of its leadership was murky, and the names meant very little not only in Polish public circles but even among Polish Communists.

The period of Stalinist "purges" resulted in the liquidation of the Polish Communist Party and the physical elimination of its entire leading echelon, along with tens of thousands of other Poles who had resided in the Soviet Union.[22] Khrushchev testifies:

> It was easy for Stalin to destroy the leaders of the Polish Party because most of them lived and worked in the Comintern in Moscow. The only reason Bierut and Gomulka stayed alive was that they were relatively unknown in Party circles.[23]

These facts did not stop the Lublin Committee from behaving like a real government. On July 23, it issued a "manifesto to the Polish people," calling for "a Poland that never again will be threatened by German invasion." The document went on to demand the restoration to Poland of Pomerania, Eastern Prussia, and Silesia, and an eastern border based on the principle of "Polish land to Poland; [and] Ukrainian, Byelorussian and Lithuanian land to Soviet Ukraine, Soviet Byelorussia and Soviet Lithuania, respectively."[24]*

---

*The manifesto was issued after several days of deliberations that began in Moscow on July 5, 1944. Its general and declarative phrasing on the border issue expresses the differences of views that surfaced in talks between the Poles and Stalin. There is reason to believe that the particulars of the Committee's demands did not always conform with Stalin's positions, as in the annexation by Poland of all of Eastern

The establishment and activation of this committee therefore represented the Kremlin's way of greeting Mikołajczyk upon his arrival.

In legal and political terms, then, the situation was as follows: while relations between the Soviets and the "London government" had indeed been severed, Mikołajczyk had been invited to Moscow. The Kremlin also announced its willingness to recognize the "London government" if the two aforementioned conditions were met. On the other hand, a "National Liberation Committee" had been established with the Kremlin's encouragement. At the initial stage it was to function as a threat and a prod; if the Kremlin's demands were not met, it would become the kernel of an alternative government. What the Kremlin was really demanding was the government-in-exile's surrender, and the ground had already been prepared for its replacement with a "friendly" government in the event that it refused.

When Mikołajczyk reached Moscow, he was treated in accordance with these intentions. First Molotov informed him that Stalin was busy, and that he, Mikołajczyk, would do better to meet with the "Lublin people," who, too—certainly not by coincidence—had reached Moscow. The intent was transparent: to humiliate the guest, to lend the two "governments" equal status, and to portray Mikołajczyk's visit as meant to reach an arrangement not with Stalin but with the "Lublin people."

The Soviet press did its share, giving the "Lublin Committee" relatively extensive coverage and devoting only a few lines on the back pages to the visit of the Polish Prime Minister.

While Mikołajczyk was waiting in Moscow for his audience with Stalin, an event occurred that left a deep imprint on the future of Poland and the relations between the Polish and Soviet peoples.

The Warsaw Uprising

As stated, Red Army troops reached the eastern bank of the Vistula by July. On July 20, rumors about an attempt by German officers to assassinate Hitler began to circulate. On July 21, General Bor-Komorowski, Commander-in-Chief of the AK, sent London a highly optimistic appraisal of the strategic situation, claiming that "the three [German] armies holding the middle sector of the front have been crushed. . . . The Germans have not sufficient reserves . . . to stop the Soviet advance. . . . This may lead

Prussia, the Białowieza Forests east of the Curzon Line, and, in the west, territory extending as far as the Western Neisse.[25]

at any moment to their collapse." On July 22, the Poles detected a broadcast by the German Fourth Armored Corps indicating an intent to retreat from Warsaw.

The Poles assumed that before evacuating the city, the Germans would transport Poles capable of working into the Reich and subject the rest of the population to terrible abuse. The Germans disclosed their intent to destroy Warsaw as they left it by laying mines throughout the city.

In the opinion of the AK (underground army) leadership, this was the right and, in fact, the last opportunity to mount a rebellion that would liberate the city. This act would also permit the Poles to demonstrate their will to fight. After all, the AL (the "people's army") and the Soviets had often criticized the AK harshly for not fighting the Germans. Now another element was added: fear that inactivity at such a time would subsequently provide the NKVD with a pretext for accusing the Polish leadership of collaboration with the enemy, on which basis it would be "purged." For these reasons the AK was inclined to stage a rebellion that would symbolize and express the sovereign will of the Polish people, the resolution of its determination to liberate itself from the yoke of German occupation—and its independence from the Soviet command's decisions.

Thus it was both a political decision of the highest order and a dangerous gamble. Appraising the Polish-German balance of forces realistically, the Polish commanders should have reached the inescapable conclusion that the rebellion could succeed only if the Red Army crossed the Vistula and joined up with the Polish fighters. The Poles made their plans on the assumption that this would indeed transpire once their independent rebellion began.

They were encouraged in this line of thought by a broadcast picked up on the evening of July 29 on the "Kościuszko Station"—the radio station of the Polish National Liberation Committee: It was time for action, the announcer intoned. Direct struggle in the streets, homes, and factories of Warsaw would not only advance the liberation but even save their compatriots' lives!

The AK command viewed this broadcast as a green light.[26]

The issue was also discussed in advance, of course, by the "London government," to which the underground was operationally and politically subordinate. These deliberations were held just before Mikołajczyk set out for Moscow, but nothing was finalized. Disagreements and tense personal relations between Mikołajczyk and the Commander-in-Chief, General Sosnkowski, thwarted an unequivocal resolution. When several ministers expressed their opposition during the debate to launching the rebellion, no resolution was reached at all. Then, not for the last time, the "London government" took a step which proved its weakness and its reluctance to reach important decisions.

On July 28, it effectively "passed the buck" on the fateful matter by entrusting the final decision to the Commander of the AK, General Bor-Komorowski and to the government's delegate, Jankowski.[27] The rationale was that "only the commander on the site knows all the data":

> The Council of Ministers has decided to empower the Government Delegate to take every decision required by the speed of the Soviet offensive, in case of need, without prior consultation with the Government.

The "London government" thus failed to discharge its major duty—to govern and to reach decisions on the issue that would determine the nation's fate.

The rebellion broke out on August 1, 1944, at 5:00 p.m.

The Mikołajczyk-Stalin Talks

Stalin received Mikołajczyk on August 3, after keeping him waiting for several days. The Soviet dictator brought him neither good news nor consolation. He displayed no interest in Mikołajczyk's claims, and did not care how many parties he represented and how many would be represented in the Polish Government. For him, the main point was that all the "truly democratic" parties in Poland establish a single bloc as a basis for a new government.[28] Stalin took this opportunity to remind Mikołajczyk that the Soviet Union did not recognize his government, while it did maintain relations with the Lublin Committee. Thus, he advised, the Poles had to unite their ranks, and Mikołajczyk should meet with the Lublin people to this end.

On the border issue, too, Stalin had nothing new to say. Invoking Lenin's ideology, the Soviet dictator declared with pontifical solemnity that all that mattered to him was brotherhood and equality among peoples—large and small alike. Poles, Ukrainians, Lithuanians, and Belorussians should live in amity, declared the "father of peoples," and none should claim territory belonging to the other.

When Mikołajczyk, admitting all due respect for the high moral rectitude of Stalin's claims, tried to mention the historic importance of Lvov and Vilna to the Polish people, and the economic value of the oil fields and potash deposits in eastern Galicia, Stalin gave him a brief history lesson. The Curzon Line, he said, was the result of "objective scientific research," and had been conceived not by the Russians but by Lloyd George, Clemenceau, and Curzon, capitalists all.

Mikołajczyk now understood clearly that he had to seek new ways out of the crisis. For lack of choice, he overcame his feelings of rejection and disgust and met with members of the Lublin Committee. As he subsequently reported to Churchill,[29] he was ready to offer them full partnership and fourteen seats in his government.

The Lublin people had slightly different ideas. Bierut and Osóbka-Morawski informed Mikołajczyk that it was *they* who were willing to include *him* in *their* government—if he moved quickly, and if, first of all, he quit the anti-democratic gang seated in London.

In a second audience with Stalin (August 9), Mikołajczyk appealed for urgent help for the Warsaw rebels. Stalin appeared unaware that a rebellion was taking place at all.

"I give you my word of honor that a battle, a desperate battle, is taking place there," Mikołajczyk said. "I ask of you—as one who has the strategic ability—to help us." Stalin answered evasively.[30] On the other issues, too, Mikołajczyk got nowhere.

Thus the fruitless mission of the Polish Prime Minister came to an end. Stalin had clearly made up his mind. Neither was there any doubt that the Red Army and the NKVD were strengthening their toeholds in Poland with each passing day, and that Lublin Committee's political status was becoming increasingly entrenched.

The Rebellion Fails

In the meantime, a great drama was unfolding in Warsaw.

The Polish rebel forces numbered 40,000 men but only about half of them, or even fewer, were armed. There was enough ammunition and food for seven to ten days. The Poles faced five German divisions, fortified some time later by another three. Although they had not coordinated their operation with the Russians, the Poles believed that the Red Army would close in on the Germans from the rear.

As early as August 3, however, the very day Stalin received Mikołajczyk, the Red Army stopped in its tracks, virtually breaking off contact with the German forces besieging Warsaw.[31]

On August 4, the Germans launched an offensive, using the tactics and experience they had acquired in 1943 while annihilating the Warsaw Ghetto. Massive use of tanks and artillery, aerial bombardment, the total devastation by fire of streets and entire neighborhoods, shortly reduced the Polish capital to a smoldering ruin and a mass tomb.

On the first days of the rebellion, the Soviets looked on with puzzlement, disbelief, and contempt. Stalin fiercely criticized the action in his talk with Mikołajczyk, asserting that he had probably been misinformed about his Underground Army. What kind of army was it, he asked, without artillery, tanks, aircraft? They did not even have enough hand weapons. This was nothing in modern war, he ruled. He heard that the Polish Government had instructed these formations to drive the Germans out of Warsaw, but did not understand how they could do it.[32]

About two days later, in response to a telegram from Roosevelt, he wrote that the Poles' Home Army comprised a few detachments that they mistakenly called "divisions." They had neither artillery, aircraft, nor tanks. He (Stalin) could not imagine how such formations could take Warsaw, which was defended by four German tank divisions including one named for Hermann Goering.[33]

Behind these ostensibly objective and rational explanations lurked an intent to bring the AK to its knees and to teach the Poles, who had dared to act on their own counsel, a "lesson."

In the meantime, Warsaw had become a chamber of horrors. Fighting raged without letup. Reserves of ammunition and food dwindled; electricity, water, and sewage systems collapsed, together with houses, streets, and neighborhoods.

An American and English airlift of food, arms, ammunition, and other supplies was mounted. This, however, was a very hazardous proposition, and the quantity of aid delivered failed to reach any real proportion of the rebels' needs.

The Poles appealed to Stalin for Soviet help, at least with respect to equipment. Their supplications went virtually unanswered. Even the expression "virtually" is an overstatement, as Stalin's reply to Churchill on August 16 demonstrates. According to it, the Soviet leader ordered the Red Army command to drop arms "intensively" into the Warsaw sector, and alleged that one parachutist liaison officer had also been dropped, but was killed by the Germans.

In his memoirs Churchill added parenthetically that if Mikołajczyk's account was to be believed, the first paragraph of Stalin's telegram was mendacious.[34]

No less important, however, was the fact that the previous tone of puzzlement and contempt was absent in this telegram of August 16. The reader can sense Stalin's rage about this "hasty, criminal adventure," embarked upon by the Poles without advance disclosure to and coordination with Soviet headquarters. Now, Stalin announced, it was time for the Soviet command to distance itself from the Warsaw adventure.[35]

So absolute was this dissociation that the Soviet authorities refused, that very day, to permit American and British aircraft to land and park on Soviet territory after airlifting supplies into Warsaw.

The effect of this measure was to throttle the rebellion cruelly. Not only did Stalin refuse to deliver significant land or air relief when he was quite able to do so; he even decided to prevent the delivery of such relief by American and British planes, which had to approach their target via long, dangerous routes from Italy and England, entailing heavy losses.

Churchill was again called to the rescue. On August 20, Stalin received a telegram signed by him and Roosevelt expressing the hope that he would promptly drop supplies and ammunition to the patriot Poles in Warsaw. Alternatively, Churchill asked for Stalin's help in helping British and American planes do the job.[36]

Stalin did not approve. Sooner or later, he replied, everyone would know the truth about the criminal cell that had launched the Warsaw escapade in order to seize power.[37]

By the third week of August, terror had given way to atrocity. Tens of thousands of fighters and residents had already been killed or wounded, entire neighborhoods had been devastated and torched, and the fighting continued. The Soviet authorities responded on August 24 by ordering the troops to prevent any reinforcement of the AK and any movement of AK formations toward Warsaw from peripheral cities.[38]

In early October, after eight weeks of combat, the Warsaw rebellion came to an end with the surrender of the last of the rebels. Of the 40,000 Polish fighters, 15,000 had fallen. There were a quarter of a million civilian casualties. Most of the city had been razed to the ground. The Germans suffered 10,000 dead, 7,000 missing, and 9,000 wounded.[39]

Who's in Charge?

Apart from its being a national and human disaster, the rebellion in Warsaw and its failure were of far-reaching political significance in terms of Poland's independence. In late July, the government-in-exile relinquished its right and duty to decide, handing the historic decision of whether or not to launch a rebellion to the underground command. The "London government" (undoubtedly for political considerations), its representation in Poland, and General Bor-Komorowski, all preferred neither to announce the intent to revolt nor to coordinate the operation with the Red Army. Now, after the debacle, the "London government" found not only its capital city but its power base in ruins. The entire political and organizational structure that had been erected after great toil and danger during the war years, and the underground military force that could, upon liberation, have served as its major base of power, had been shattered. Thus Stalin had his way. This also explains the boundless forbearance of Marshal Rokossovsky's troops who, during those fateful months, sat across the Vistula without firing a single shot.

Now, over the smoking ruins of Warsaw, the way was paved for a new government. No longer was there any doubt about who was in charge.

Heading for Yalta

Four months from the day the Warsaw rebellion was put down for good, the Big Three reconvened at Yalta. During this interval the following trends surfaced with respect to the Polish question:

The Soviet military offensive continued, and additional Polish territories were liberated from Nazi occupation. The NKVD had taken over the foci of political and public life in liberated Poland. The "Lublin government" consolidated its position, even as the "London government's" political status weakened. Stalin's positions and demands grew stiffer, especially with respect to the nature and composition of Poland's future government, for which Churchill struggled while consistently attempting to convince the government-in-exile of the need to accept Stalin's territorial demands and proposals. The government-in-exile maintained its intransigence, a stance that stemmed more from weakness than from strength and valor.

Liberation, Repression, and Pressure

In September and October, as Rokossovsky's army looked on while Warsaw went up in flames, other Red Army formations drove the Germans out of Romania, Bulgaria, Hungary, Estonia, and Latvia.

Churchill reached the conclusion that it was time—while it was still possible—to strike a deal with Stalin that would preserve the status of Great Britain and the Western democracies on the European continent. The result was the famous "percentages deal" scribbled by Churchill on a scrap of paper during a meeting with Stalin in Moscow on October 9.[40]

This arrangement, however, determined the fate of the Balkan countries only. The Polish situation was still amorphous, despite the Teheran resolutions. Now Mikołajczyk was summoned to Moscow on the run, in order to add Poland to the roster of "percentage" countries.

Appreciating Poland's concession of the Pripet marshes in exchange for the industrialized territories of Silesia and access to the Baltic Sea as a fair compromise, Churchill considered it an urgent necessity, and perhaps a last opportunity, to persuade the Polish government-in-exile (which he regarded as an aggregate of decent but feeble individuals)[41] to conclude an agreement with both Stalin and the Lublin Committee. By all indications, the government-in-exile's bargaining power and endurance was ebbing with each passing week.

Reports from Poland indicated that wherever the Russians entered they immediately took draconian action against the Polish underground, which they accused of collaborating with the Germans. The reports spoke of the sudden disappearance of AK men, mass arrests of "hostile elements," and the infiltration of NKVD propagandists. Executions, too, accompanied the "liberation" campaign. In certain areas, a few attempts were made to establish military cooperation between the Red Army and the Polish formations for joint action against the Germans; these episodes usually ended with the arrest of the Polish commanders by the Soviets.

In January 1944, a radio broadcast from Moscow, instructing Soviet partisans to disarm the Polish troops and kill resistors as well as underground activists, was intercepted.[42] In July, the AK commanders reported the arrest of underground leaders in the Vilna and Nowogródek areas.[43]

In October, it was reported that Polish fighters in the Lublin area were being stripped of their arms and forcibly inducted into General Żymierski's units. Concurrently, two hundred AK commanders and thousands of their troops were exiled to the east. According to the report, arrests in the Lublin area reached 21,000. The situation in the areas of Lvov, Vilna, Białystok, Polesie, Volhynia (Wołyn), Tarnopol, and Stanislavov was much the same.[44] Danger of an armed clash between the Russians and the Poles was ever-present. The residue of the Katyń affair, too, had not dissipated. In the wake of the Soviet tanks, bayonets, and handcuffs, the "Lublin government" consolidated itself. At this late hour, the government-in-exile attempted to moderate its basic positions—or in any event to present them more moderately, and in a tone more amenable to Stalin. The Kremlin, however, brushed this endeavor aside, just as it had rejected the government-in-exile's response to the Tass announcement half a year previously (January 14) and its resolution of February 15.

In a memorandum issued by the "London government" on August 29, 1944[45]—as Warsaw burned and Rokossowsky's army camped across the Vistula—the founding principles and fundamentals of the liberated Polish state were sketched out, including details about the state's democratic and parliamentary structure. The future government would be based on representation of six parties (including the "Polish Workers' Party," the PPR); it would accommodate neither anti-democratic, fascist actors, nor those who had been responsible for the events preceding 1939 (members of the BBWR-Sanacja). The memorandum went on to spell out a plan for social and agricultural reform, and called for the establishment of "lasting Polish-

Soviet friendship," economic cooperation, and reinforcement of peace by 1) eradicating all German influence; 2) thwarting renewed German aggression; and 3) entering into alliances with all peace-loving nations. As for the eastern border, the Polish government repeated its compromise formula, which proposed "leaving the centers of cultural life and the sources of raw materials vital to the state's economy" within the confines of Poland. At hand, then, was a proposal which did yield on the principle of the Riga agreement borders, but also rejected the Curzon Line and proposed a frontier east of the Vilna-Lvov line.

Stalin ignored the memorandum altogether. The fundamentals of Polish democracy did not concern him, let alone excite him. Indeed, his main problem—now that the border issue had been resolved in principle in Teheran, and was materializing in the field as the Red Army advanced—was how to guarantee the establishment of a "truly friendly" government.

Churchill regarded this intent of Stalin's as the major danger to Poland itself—its future and independence—and, consequently, to the nature and future of free Europe.

Having been brought up on concepts such as "fair play," "give and take," and "negotiations between equals," Churchill was committed to a *quid pro quo* on the matter of Poland as well. He had not yet realized that Stalin's method was one of "Let's be friends: what's yours is mine and what's mine is . . . mine."

He believed that by meeting Stalin's territorial demands—while obtaining "appropriate compensation" in the west and the north—the resulting Polish state would be not only strong but independent and democratic.[46]

He sincerely believed that "moving" Poland would not only solve territorial, defense, and ethnic problems, but would also save Poland from total Sovietization. He assumed that in exchange for his support on the territorial issue, Stalin would be forthcoming on the composition of the Polish government. Although without excessive hopes, he believed it possible to arrive at a "fair compromise" with respect to the government's composition. He hoped for a politically "balanced" government which would prevent the Sovietization of Poland and facilitate the creation of a strong link in the twilight zone between West and East.

His ideas on this issue, expressed in his talks with Stalin and Mikołajczyk and his correspondence with Roosevelt, again crystallized into a set of "percentages" between Poland's "London" and "Lublin" governments, with the "London" Poles receiving at least 50-60%. As such, his conception complemented the "percentages deal" he had contrived for the Balkans. Moreover, the composition of this government was of cardinal importance to him. For it he was ready to struggle, support the "London government" to the hilt, and even risk a crisis with Stalin.

On November 2, 1944, British Deputy Foreign Minister Cadogan wrote to Polish Foreign Minister Romer that:

> The Polish Government would be in a much better position if negotiations broke down on this point (the composition of Government—Y.C.) on which they would have the support of His Majesty's Government and probably of the United States Government, than on the frontier question.[47]

Above all, Churchill believed, was the factor of urgency. He cautioned the "London people" in no uncertain terms that if they persisted in their indecision and refused to make the painful choices, they would find it too late to reach a compromise and an accord. Then Stalin would take over Poland altogether.

Although his sympathies for Poland were sincere, Churchill knew how to come across as an unyielding and even a brutal friend. When it was all over, Churchill wrote that he had pressed Mikołajczyk hard.[48] That was an understatement. As the government-in-exile stalled and balked, as it continued to re-emphasize the justice of its demands and the injustice being done to its cause, so did Churchill's patience ebb and his pressure mount. Slowly he and Roosevelt came to regard this government as a nuisance and a threat to the victorious alliance of the Big Three.

Mikołajczyk Goes to Moscow

Now Mikołajczyk was summoned to Moscow—not to present his objections and his government's proposals to Stalin and Churchill, but rather to "voluntarily" take the medicine that the Big Three had concocted for him.

Representatives of the three governments—Churchill and Eden, Stalin and Molotov, and Mikołajczyk and Romer convened on October 13, 1944. Churchill opened the proceedings by reminding Mikołajczyk that Great Britain, even though inadequately prepared, had gone to war to save Poland; as a result, she had found herself on the brink of defeat, with a guillotine poised over her neck. Thus Britain had the moral right to ask the Poles for a gesture on behalf of peace in Europe.

After thus appealing to his counterpart's conscience, Churchill presented two requests: 1) Poland's acquiescence to consider the Curzon Line as her *de facto* eastern border; the Poles would be entitled to bring up the matter for deliberation and final resolution at the peace conference; and 2) a friendly arrangement with the "National Liberation Committee" for the purpose of establishing a single Government of Poland.

Here Churchill was in for an embarrasing and disappointing surprise. The Soviet host, who had stood soundlessly as the others sat around the table, now pulled his pipe out of his mouth and said:

> In order that the whole matter may be quite clear . . . I want to state categorically that the Soviet Government cannot accept Premier Churchill's formula concerning the Curzon Line. I must add the following correction to the formula. The Curzon Line must be accepted as the future Polish-Soviet frontier. One cannot keep changing the frontier. . . . In its definite delimitation I agree, of course, to certain corrections . . . which may move the frontier 6 or 7 miles one way or the other.[49]

Concern for the peasant class, sympathy for the Ukrainians' national aspirations, and apprehension that people might suffer were not part of Stalin's character, as would subsequently be known. Yet he explained his opposition to setting a provisional border precisely on humanitarian and social grounds such as these. Frequent border changes, he said, would cause the population nothing but suffering. We have collective farms; the Poles have private farms. Let us spare this populace the misery that frequent changes of government would cause. When Mikołajczyk again tried to propose that Lvov be included in Poland, Stalin's moral indignation reached new heights: "We do not use Ukrainian soil as a bargaining chip," he proclaimed solemnly.

Mikołajczyk tried to protest vehemently:

> I cannot accept the Curzon Line. I have no authority to yield forty eight percent of our country, no authority to forsake millions of my countrymen and leave them to their fate. If I agreed, everyone would have the right to say: "It was for this that the Polish soldiers fought—a politicians' sellout."[50]

Stalin, the man who had rebuilt the Russian Empire, delivered a stinging answer to this representative of the occupied Polish nation: "You are an imperialist!"[51] With that, deliberation of the matter came to an end. Stalin was, however, willing to award Poland fair compensation at Germany's expense. We know that Churchill, too, regarded Poland as entitled to "equivalent compensation." Thus the two leaders had only to compete with each other to prove to the Poles, perhaps, that each placed Poland's well-being and strength in mind above all other concerns.

British Foreign Secretary Eden went first: "The formula in Teheran was that the new frontier of Poland in the west would go as far towards the Oder as the Poles would wish."

Churchill: "East Prussia, the territories earmarked for Poland extend to the west and south of Königsberg . . . Danzig is probably not worth less to Poland than Lvov. . . . "

Stalin: "I should like to declare that we Russians also speak of including in Poland not only Danzig but also Stettin."

Churchill: "Of course."

Stalin: "We have all the sympathy for this project."

Churchill: "So has the British Government."[52]

Mikołajczyk, staggering under this mass of generosity and broadheartedness, nevertheless tried to ask what this "Curzon Line," which everyone was talking about, really was. Laconically, Churchill promised him full assistance in procuring a map. Mikołajczyk persisted: was it equivalent to the 1939 partition line?

"No," Stalin said, "The Curzon Line gives you Białystok, Łomza, and Przemyśl." Thus he proved that he was making concessions on behalf of peace and friendship. It mattered not at all that the concession was just a small part of the booty.

Things began to get most difficult for Mikołajczyk, however, when Molotov entered the scene. If Mikołajczyk still thought that the third great leader, who had not taken part in the Moscow encounter, would serve as a final refuge, along came Molotov and dashed his hopes. Thus spake Molotov, as if parenthetically:

> I should like to add a few words about what was discussed in Teheran. . . . All those who took part are here today with the exception of President Roosevelt. I should like to repeat what he declared and if I am inexact I hope that the other witnesses will correct me.
>
> I can quite well remember that President Roosevelt said that he fully agreed to the Curzon Line and that he considered it to be a just frontier between Poland and the Soviet Union: he thought, however, that for the time being it would be advisable not to give publicity to his view. We can therefore draw the conclusion that the Curzon Line does not only correspond with the attitude of the Soviet Government but it has also the concurrence of the three powers. . . .[53]

No one denied or corrected Molotov's remark, and there stood Mikołajczyk, stunned, deceived, and disappointed.

It had been only four months previously that the President had told him, as if in effect disclosing a great secret, that only Stalin and Churchill had supported the Curzon Line; Roosevelt, by contrast, wished to delay the decision until after victory, then restoring Lvov and other territories to Poland.

Thus the encounter ended, but not the process of "breaking" Mikołajczyk. He later came under heavy pressure in Moscow. Churchill had reached the conclusion that time was working against Mikołajczyk and his colleagues, and that the way to prevent a total Sovietization of Poland and to save its independence required swift action toward a dialogue and agreements between the two "governments," with a decisive majority for the "London people."

Therefore he again assumed the thankless duty of applying "persuasion"—unpleasant persuasion at times. The very morning after the trilateral meeting, he had a talk with Mikołajczyk in the British Embassy. This "talk" was in fact a string of "terrible threats," as Churchill himself later admitted.[54] They were meant to exhaust his friend's ability to resist, and to "deliver the goods" to the mighty ally that was stalking him.

Unless Mikołajczyk accepted the Curzon Line as the border, Churchill thundered, Poland would have breathed its last. The Russians would sweep through his country and liquidate his people. Poland was on the verge of annihilation.[55]

When Mikołajczyk equivocated, trying again to explain that the Polish government lacked the authority to relinquish half the country's territory without consulting the people, Churchill exploded. The West would abandon the "London government" if it persisted in its indecision. The "London Poles" were a selfish, irresponsible, uncaring, and cowardly bunch, out to wreck Europe. Churchill would call on the "other" Poles; the Lublin government might perform very well. "We will be sick and tired of you if you go on arguing."[56]

Mikołajczyk, swallowing this dose of "friendly persuasion," still tried to cling to the American crutch, however rickety he knew it was after Molotov's comments. In a letter on October 16, he informed United States Ambassador Averell Harriman of his shock upon hearing from Molotov at the October 13 meeting that the representatives of all three Great Powers had definitely agreed at Teheran that the Curzon Line should be the Polish-Soviet frontier. In this connection, he reminded Harriman that during his conversations with the President in Washington in June 1944, he had been told that only Stalin and Churchill had agreed on the Curzon Line. Finally, he politely asked for the ambassador's help in resolving this misunderstanding on a subject of such crucial importance to Poland.[57]

This appeal earned him an evasive and, no doubt, disappointing American reply. Harriman preferred not to answer in writing. In a talk with Polish Foreign Minister Romer, the American ambassador claimed that Molotov had been "disloyal" toward the President and had misrepresented his comments. Again he explained the President's pre-election problems and difficulties, and advised the Poles not to overestimate the United States' ability to intervene in the territorial issues of Europe. "But Poland," he added, "can count on American defense if the Soviet Union will endanger Polish independence and freedom."

What kind of defense would this be, and on what scale? When would Poland's independence and freedom be considered "endangered," and who would adjudicate that matter? Would it not then be too late to come to Poland's rescue? These questions were not asked, and the American ambassador was vague and not explicit.

Finally, Harriman requested, advised, and implicitly warned Mikołajczyk not to repeat his comments before members of the Polish government-in-exile. "Repeating Molotov's statement regarding the President's position . . . would only raise further issue publicly which would lead to difficulties adverse to Polish interests."[58]

Before leaving Moscow, Mikołajczyk made a final attempt to melt Stalin's heart, but the layer of ice mantling this muscle was evidently too thick.

"Your name will be forever blessed by the Poles," he said with an obsequiousness that must have taken years off his life, "if you make some generous gesture. Even if only Vilna and Lvov remain ours—in addition to the territories promised us in the West—we shall be grateful."

As will be remembered, this was not the first time the topic of Lvov had come up, and everyone who had mentioned it met with a negative Soviet response. The historic opportunity missed by Sikorski was no longer attainable. Considering the choice of whom to anger less, the Poles or the Ukrainians, Stalin reached a clear-cut conclusion: Lvov would go to the latter.[59] In a talk with Molotov a few days earlier, Grabski (a minister in the "London government" and a veteran Russophile) invoked every rationale he knew for keeping Lvov and its surroundings in Poland. "Lvov is like a temple of the noblest of national traditions," he said.

The reply he received was to the point: "We cannot harm the Ukrainians."[60] On May 1, 1944, Prof. Oskar Lange interceded with Stalin, who appeared to seek the professor's esteem and had even mentioned him as a candidate for the future Government of Poland. Lange offered an interesting and unique line of reasoning:

> To the Ukrainians . . . Lvov means less than to the Poles. . . . In Poland there were five cultural centers: Warsaw; Krakow; Poznan; Lvov and Wilno. The loss of two of them would be very heavy, and acquisition of German cities without a Polish cultural heritage cannot be considered as compensation for the loss of old historical Polish cultural centers. If Poland must give up Lvov this will be a constant source of anti-Soviet feeling and agitation. . . . [61]

Stalin was not moved: "I cannot do it and will not do this."[62]

On the second issue too, Mikołajczyk's desperate attempt failed. He promised Stalin that the government under his leadership would be friendly to the Soviet Union. Very well, said Stalin, but the Lublin people had to have a majority there.[63] For some reason, Churchill assessed this difficult session, which lasted about an hour and a half, as "very friendly."[64] A statesman as experienced as Churchill could have arrived at this estimation only under the distortive influence of the kind of wishful thinking he expressed in a letter he sent afterwards to Roosevelt: "I am hopeful that even in the next fortnight we may get a settlement."[65]

***

The composition of the future Polish government was a very difficult bone of contention. True, Stalin would accept Mikołajczyk as a candidate for prime minister, but only if 75 percent of the government portfolios went to "Lublin people." Churchill considered this an absurdity that would strip the government *a priori* of real influence. He demanded 50 to 60 percent for Mikołajczyk and his colleagues.

Despite the disagreements, he felt that this matter, would not prove insurmountable if everything else were resolved.[66] As stated, he was still hopeful.

Under a Steamroller of Pressure

Mikołajczyk had not been graced with the stature of his predecessor, Sikorski, nor with the General's popularity. The tempest of the war and Sikorski's death elevated this former leader of the Peasants' Party to the position of head of a nation fighting for its independence and sovereignty.

His stance against Big Three pressure and his attempts to navigate his decrepit, floundering government entitle him to a place of honor in Polish national history. The talks in Moscow strengthened his feeling that it was high time to make difficult decisions, and that his leadership and his government's future would be judged by how adroitly and capably he did so.

Returning to London, he convened his government (October 24) to report on the failure of his efforts in Moscow and to recommend a move towards fateful compromises: "There are no chances of getting any land east of the Curzon Line,"[67] he said simply and sincerely. The session adjourned with no conclusions having been reached.

Churchill refused to tolerate any further procrastination. On November 2, Mikołajczyk was summoned for a talk[68] which would surely have been defined in an official communiqué as "an extremely frank exchange of views." Again Mikołajczyk tried to explain the hesitancies of his government, both as to the Curzon Line and its implications (the transfer of 5–6 million Poles and 7 million Germans) and with respect to future Poland's degree of independence and the composition of its government.

Churchill displayed an impatience that verged on anger. Unleashing the fury of his tongue ("I have had enough of it"), he castigated the Polish statesman and alerted him to some bitter facts. When leaving Moscow, Mikołajczyk had mentioned the possibility of the talks' resuming within 48 hours of his return to London. Now, two weeks later, no progress had been made. The Poles were stalling. Churchill said he did not go so far as to condemn Mikołajczyk, but called him a "confused man" who could not make up his mind: "You are playing delaying tactics, by posing to us still other new questions, . . . you care only about your *liberum veto*. . . . What did you accomplish in these two weeks? What did you return to London for?"

Then came another warning: the Soviet Government had informed him that it would not sit at the same table with the government-in-exile in any international forum. "Step after step you will be liquidated . . . Have the courage to say: No! I shall repeat it to Stalin." All this was only to "soften up" the target. Now Churchill trained his artillery directly at his counterpart:

"Are you ready to go to Moscow tomorrow evening?"

"No, I cannot. . . ."

"The day after tomorrow?"

"I'm not sure I can obtain the Polish Government's decision that quickly. You have to understand that it's a matter of Poland's independence, no trifling concern . . ."

Churchill had no further patience for Mikołajczyk's explanations, which sounded to him like a repetition of the previous evasion and delaying tactics. Now he issued an ultimatum: if no answer were forthcoming within 48 hours, he would cable Stalin and let the chips fall.

"The attitude of the British Government," Mikołajczyk commented, "does not make the decision any easier to reach."

At this, Churchill nonchalantly threatened to nullify the guarantees given him.

Mikołajczyk understood that he had reached the red line. He convened his government and recommended, not for the first time but more emphatically than before, that it agree to negotiate on the basis of willingness in principle to make concessions on the eastern border.

Describing the double pressure—the Soviets and Churchill's—Mikołajczyk warned his colleagues that a further delay would lead to a catastrophe, a Lublin coup, and the Sovietization of Poland. With a far-sighted realism that places national affairs in their proper perspective, he told his fellow ministers:

> Future generations will judge us not only by the frontiers which we may or may not secure, but also by the economic and political system which we may help establish in the new Poland.[69]

Mikołajczyk and his Foreign Minister nevertheless remained a minority.

***

It happens rather frequently that precisely those who are far from the arena, who are not personally involved in the struggle, and who are not directly affected by the pressure and constraints, are capable with greater "objectivity" and romantic courage, totally detached from the actual circumstances, to adopt the posture of heroes standing in the breach and defending the nation's honor.

This meeting of the "London government" was a case in point. A majority of its members, considering Churchill's attitude an insult to the Polish people, rejected Mikołajczyk's proposals. The objections of several ministers were rooted in political adventurism. They assumed that once Germany was defeated, the unnatural Western-Soviet alliance would crumble, and the tremendous power of the Western democracies would turn against the Soviet Union. Then Poland's true liberation would come—liberation from Russo-Soviet enslavement. This thinking was aided and abetted by memories of 1920, and its historical roots were further strengthened after the Ribbentrop-Molotov agreement, the Katyń affair, and Stalin's territorial demands. Even though it had been camouflaged in pompous official declarations about aspirations toward friendly Polish-Soviet relations and cooperation, it was not lost on the keen-eyed Allied leaders.

Stalin exploited the thinking of the Polish nationalist minority to attack, defame, and ultimately dismiss the entire "London government." At the same time, Roosevelt and Churchill frequently felt a duty and a need to warn Mikołajczyk in no uncertain terms to restrain his colleagues and explain to them the basic facts of political life.

The last thing these two leaders wanted him to provoke was a clash with the Soviet Union. During his talk with Mikołajczyk on June 7, 1944, Roosevelt cautioned:

> You Poles must find an understanding with Russia. On your own, you'd have no chance to beat Russia, and, let me tell you now, the British and Americans have no intention of fighting Russia.[70]

In the October 14 meeting in Moscow—of which we have quoted excerpts—Churchill had some very sharp comments for Mikołajczyk on this topic, too. Basing himself on something Anders had proclaimed ("After the Germans are defeated, the Poles will beat the Russians"), Churchill stormed at Mikołajczyk:

> You hate the Russians. . . . If you want to conquer Russia we shall leave you to do it. I feel like being in a lunatic asylum. I don't know whether the British Government will continue to recognize you.[71]

Mikołajczyk himself did not entertain any illusions on this matter. On January 26, 1944 he sent the following cable to the government-in-exile's representative in the underground:

> We must take into account the decision of England and America not to fight for Poland's eastern frontier. . . .[72]

In the October 24 government meeting, too—after returning from Moscow—Mikołajczyk warned the "hawks," who built their hopes on a new war by the West against the Communist world, that there was no such prospect.[73] However, as stated, his warnings and recommendations fell on deaf ears. On November 3, the "London government" proposed that the Three Powers reconsider the entire problem with the participation of the Polish Government.[74]

Roosevelt's Actions

One of the justifications for this unrealistic proposal was that the United States Government had not yet had the opportunity to take a position on the issue.[75]

In view of Molotov's statement at the Moscow meeting, which Mikołajczyk had undoubtedly reported to his colleagues, this formalistic explanation contained a healthy measure of disregard for reality, combined with the illusion that thus the door remained open to change in the American stance. This is what the authors of the "London government's" proposal were hoping for. If they still placed hope in Roosevelt—once re-elected, they ventured, he could act for Poland from a position of greater domestic strength—it is hard to understand why they confined themselves to sending notes and conducting diplomatic talks, without any calling for concrete action to help bring their hopes to fruition.

The "London government" possessed a weapon that it had never learned to use. There were six to seven million Americans of Polish extraction, and Roosevelt went to great pains not to anger them. They could have served the Polish cause as presented to them by the "London government" as an excellent fulcrum of public and political influence. Not only did Roosevelt pursue them; so did his rival, Governor Dewey. Handing out promises without coverage is a common ingredient of democracy when elections are around the corner. Thus Dewey, too, informed Ambassador Ciechanowski that if elected, he would side with the Poles against the ravenous Soviets.

However, when former President Herbert Hoover—a respected American citizen who undoubtedly knew the laws of his land—advised Ciechanowski to place the Polish issue before American public opinion, the Ambassador spurned his counsel. Trying to be more Catholic than the Pope and more American than the former President, he rejected in principle and practice the idea of such intervention in American domestic affairs.[76]

Lack of understanding of the pluralistic nature of the American nation; of the right of its constituent ethnic groups to express their special desires which do not clash with the interests of the American nation; fear of mobilizing the Polish lobby; reluctance to "intervene in domestic affairs"; the diplomatic approach in its narrow, distorted, and obsolete sense; reliance on promises given behind closed doors—these were some of the "London government's" worst blunders during its fateful struggle.

On November 7, 1944, Roosevelt was elected to an unprecedented fourth term as President of the United States.*

***

Although victory was on the horizon, difficult pitched battles were still raging on both the Russian and the "second" fronts. Between October and December the American forces met with stiff German resistance in the areas of Antwerp, Aachen, and the Saar, and tens of thousands of young Americans (29,000 in the Metz area alone[78]) paid with their lives for the victory.

In mid-December the Germans, under Field Marshal Rundstedt and General Hasso von Manteuffel, opened a massive counter-offensive in the Ardennes along a front some 80 miles long with twenty divisions, including seven armored. Chaos was sowed among the Allied forces when some German troops dressed as American soldiers. The Battle of the Bulge lasted ten

---

*He carried 36 states with 432 electoral votes, and Dewey 12 states with 99 electoral votes. Of 48,025,684 voters, 25,602,505 votes went to Roosevelt and 22,006,258 to Dewey.[77]

days and nights, and at one stage the Germans expected the American forces to surrender. Only on December 26 was the German offensive smashed.[79]

The Pacific front was ablaze at the time, too, as American forces under MacArthur and Nimitz fought hard to break the Japanese and retake the Philippines.

Roosevelt continued to view Stalin as an ally and partner in the establishment of the United Nations, and expected the Soviet Union to enter the war against Japan.

His health, which his personal physician, Admiral McIntyre, persistently defined as "excellent," progressively deteriorated. Even as indications of fatal illness could be seen in his face and behavior, the President and his physician preferred to ignore the symptoms.[80] Roosevelt wanted to complete the monumental task he had taken upon himself, even if it killed him.

Thus the Poland issue, the problem of its final borders and its list of claims—as important as he considered these—would have to wait until victory. Nothing would be allowed to undermine the alliance with Stalin. He was committed to avoiding any explicit undertakings on Poland's behalf, and nothing would budge him.

The former American ambassador to Poland, Arthur B. Lane, tried to change Roosevelt's mind. The United States, he said, was now the mightiest of all powers, with the world's strongest army, navy, and air force. She should therefore demand that Stalin accede to and respect a genuinely independent Poland. If the United States did not press this just demand, Lane argued, it would never be able to extract anything from Stalin in the future.

Roosevelt listened, emitted a little sigh, and asked: "Do you want me to go to war with Russia?"[81] Now, too, he dispensed with his fear of the Polish-American community—if he had ever in fact harbored any such fear. In another letter (October 26),[82] Mikołajczyk asked Roosevelt to make every effort to wrest at least one gesture from Stalin: cession of Lvov and the oilfields to Poland. "Such a policy," he wrote, "would do no offense to the principle of the Curzon Line, because it was never formally applied to Eastern Galicia."

Roosevelt's reply (November 17)[83] contained no real commitment. In his letter, Roosevelt repeated the routine declarative formula about the United States Government's abiding interest in the existence of a "strong, free, and independent" Polish state, and avoided any expression that might be interpreted as a binding declaration. If an agreement were attained—the President wrote—between the Governments of Poland, the Soviet Union, and Great Britain with respect to the future borders, including "compensation" in the west, the United States Government would not oppose it, although even then it would not guarantee any specific frontier. Neither would the United States Government oppose the transfer of national minorities from Poland—if the Poles desired this and if it were feasible.[84]

As can be seen from this formula, Roosevelt was noncommittal as to the nature of the United States' direct contribution and its position—in view of the fact that the concept of "if" does not exist in political reality; in the absence of a concrete agreement, and in light of the borders being created de facto by the Soviet Union day by day.

Thus Roosevelt indeed refrained at this stage from giving full backing to his promise to Mikołajczyk in June, to help Poland retain Lvov and its vicinity. However, he instructed his ambassador, Harriman, to ask Stalin to agree to leave Lvov and the oilfields in Polish territory.

It was clear to Harriman that this mission was doomed to fail. En route to Moscow, he met with Mikołajczyk in London on November 21, and admitted that he saw no chance for success.[85]

Three days later, Mikołajczyk resigned.

After Mikołajczyk's Resignation

Mikołajczyk was succeeded as Prime Minister by Tomasz Arciszewski, a veteran PPS (Socialist Party) leader. For five years Arciszewski had been operating in the underground, and reached London clandestinely. If this was meant to demonstrate the progressive character of the government-in-exile and to pretty it up for Stalin, the maneuver was misconceived.

Not only did Stalin consider every Social Democrat a "Menshevik," a "Social-Fascist," and a much greater evil than a capitalist agent, but he cared little if at all about the party structure of the "London government." By now, he wanted to eliminate it from the game altogether.

The Governments of Great Britain and the United States, too, had no further regard for the government-in-exile. Once Mikołajczyk left the scene, the two powers began in fact to ignore it altogether.

Chapter Eleven

The Yalta Conference

The State of the War

On February 6, 1945, the Big Three convened for their conference in Yalta, in the Crimea. The President, confined to a wheelchair in any case and now further disabled by his cardiovascular illness, was forced to fly 6,000 miles under war conditions—because Stalin insisted that the conference not take him out of the Soviet Union. He invoked reasons of health to justify this wish, and he got his way.

And not only on this issue.

Victory was in sight, but the job still had to be finished in both Europe and the Far East. The German offensive in the Ardennes, though halted and broken, undermined the optimism that had previously dominated the Allied camp. On the other hand, relations and mutual trust between Stalin and the Western leaders, Roosevelt and Churchill, reached a new pinnacle in the months preceding Yalta.

The opening of the "second front" considerably dispelled Stalin's suspicions, and he rewarded his allies with meaningful gestures.

When British forces put down a Communist uprising in Greece in early December 1944, Stalin did not lift a finger to help his comrades there, instead remaining loyal to his "percentage" arrangement with Churchill. When the Germans opened their offensive in the Ardennes and threatened to breach the Allied front, Eisenhower and Churchill asked Stalin to mount his own offensive so as to alleviate the German pressure on the west.[1] Stalin complied; Rokossovsky's army entered Warsaw three days later and thence began to advance rapidly toward the Oder River.

While the Western allies were still licking their wounds from the Battle of the Bulge, their progress arrested at the Appennine Mountains, the Soviets rolled westward—about 300 miles within a month. They flooded Poland, Eastern Prussia, Hungary, and eastern Czechoslovakia. By February 1945, the Red Army held almost all of Eastern Europe.

This was the background for Yalta. Because of the state of the war, as American Secretary of State Stettinius remarked, the question was not what Britain and the United States would allow Russia to do in Poland, but rather to what extent they would succeed in persuading her.[2] Again the Poland issue occupied the attentions of the Big Three to no small extent; indeed, Churchill felt it would be the most urgent question on the Yalta agenda.[3] Even before the conference opened, however, Roosevelt and Churchill were presented with a *fait accompli*.

The Lublin Committee Becomes a Provisional Government

On December 31, 1944, the Lublin Committee declared itself (certainly not without the Kremlin's blessing) "the Provisional Government of the Polish Democratic Republic." Bolesław Bierut was appointed as president. Osóbka Morawski took over as prime minister and foreign minister, Władisław Gomulka and Stanisław Janoś were named deputy prime ministers, and General Rola-Żymierski was appointed defense minister and commander-in-chief.

Roosevelt called on Stalin to postpone his recognition of the Bierut government for one month, so the Big Three might consult and reach a solution agreeable to all. The Soviet dictator replied with a brief lesson on the rules of democracy: one could not allow the Polish people to say that they were sacrificing Poland's interests in favor of those of a handful of Polish emigrés in London.[4]

In his letter of January 1, 1945, the omnipotent despot explained why his hands were totally tied:

> The fact is that on December 27 the Presidium of the Supreme Soviet of the USSR to an appropriate request of the Poles has already informed them that it intends to recognize the Provisional Government of Poland as soon as it is formed.[5]

Once the Supreme Soviet Presidium had made up its mind, what could Stalin do?

On January 5, the Soviet Union recognized the Bierut government, and Soviet cannon in Lublin fired rounds of honor.[6]

When the Red Army marched into Warsaw on January 17, 1945, the Bierut government followed in its tracks. The change was not only geographic but symbolic, psychological, and political: now it was no longer the "Lublin Committee" but the "Warsaw Government." The protest of the "London government" was a mere cry in the wilderness.

Poland on the Operating Table at Yalta

By the time the Big Three readied Poland for surgery at Yalta, the outcome had in fact already been decided. The diagnosis, the course of treatment, and the surgical tactics had already been determined in Teheran. The scalpels had been readied and sterilized in the Soviet crucible. The operating table had been leveled by Red Army tanks, and the duty nurse—the new "Warsaw Government"—was already waiting in the wings to provide post-operative care.

All this notwithstanding, the issue was so complicated and politically weighty that it was clearly one of the most controversial and difficult problems of all.[7]

The Big Three discussed Poland in no fewer than seven of their eight meetings.[8] The eastern border problem had already been resolved in principle in Teheran, but now, when it came time to put it into final form, several controversial points still remained.

Roosevelt, although committed in principle to the Curzon Line, appealed to Stalin's sense of generosity—personally this time—with a warm recommendation that he cede Lvov and the oilfields to the Poles as a gesture. He nevertheless stressed that he was just bringing up the idea for reconsideration ("I am not making a definite statement . . . but I hope that member states can make a gesture in this direction"[9]). This, of course, buried the issue.

Churchill could not take total exception from his colleague's remarks. Declaring that he was in favor of the Curzon Line—with Lvov in the Soviet sector—he added that he would be only too happy, of course, if a great power such as the Soviet Union displayed magnanimity toward the much weaker country and acceded to the President's appeal. The Soviet Union would be acclaimed and admired for this gesture.[10]

Stalin took his colleagues' exhortations in his stride, and ignored Roosevelt's appeal, especially when Roosevelt had watered it down with a remark that sounded disparaging: "Most Poles, like the Chinese, want to save face."[11] Stalin trundled out his previous and well-known lines of reasoning: "The Prime Minister said that for Britain the Polish question is one of honor. For Russia it is not a question of honor," he said with bitter sarcasm, "but one of life and death." Again, too, Stalin invoked the argument that it had been not the Russians but Curzon and Clemenceau who had proposed the now-objectionable border:

> Lenin had opposed giving Białystok Province to the Poles. But the Curzon Line gives it to Poland. We have already retreated from Lenin's position. . . .[12]

"Are we supposed to be less Russian than Curzon and Clemenceau?" he asked in a puzzled and injured tone of voice. However, he continued, he was prepared to maintain the war effort for some time—notwithstanding the price this would exact in Russian blood—in order to compensate the Poles at Germany's expense.

Then, by changing the subject from the eastern border of Poland to that country's western frontier, the disputation over the Lvov problem came to an end. A tepid attempt by Roosevelt to revive it died stillborn.

Stalin was clear and unequivocal on the issue of "compensation" in the west. He would give the Poles whatever they wanted, displaying the generosity of, well, a Czar:

> I asked Mikołajczyk what frontier he wanted. He was delighted to hear of a western frontier to the River Neisse. I must say that I will maintain this line and ask this conference to support it. There are two Neisse rivers, the east and the west. I favor the west.[13]

His laconic lesson in geography was not superfluous. Stalin and Molotov had mastered all the minutiae of the Poland issue, including, for example, Poland's prewar illiteracy rate.[14] By contrast, it was clear as far back as Teheran that geography was not one of the Western leaders' fortés. Stalin and Molotov found this fact highly encouraging.[15]

Churchill's memoirs on the Teheran conference give the impression that he was not yet aware at that time of the difference and the distance between the Eastern and the Western Neisse.[16] His attitude was general, to put it mildly: he had studied the Oder Line on a map, and "liked the picture."[17] He subsequently admitted that maps had not been used in the general discussions, and that the difference between the Eastern and Western Neisse was not as evident as it should have been.[18]

Now, in Yalta, Stalin apparently tried to conclude the debate on the Oder-Neisse line, laconically mentioning the two Neisse Rivers but not going into excessive detail as to the implications of the distinction. Between Teheran and Yalta, however, experts in the U.S. State Department and the British Foreign Office had managed to discover the two rivers and realize the ramifications of the difference. One of these was a population of no fewer than three million Germans between the two rivers.[19] It now dawned on them that the Soviet magnanimity might not necessarily be a reflection of love of the Poles but rather Machiavellian stratagems.

A memorandum drawn up by the State Department for Yalta read:

> By including a large section of German territory in Poland and the probable transfer of some eight to ten million Germans the future Polish state would

in all probability be forced to depend completely on Moscow for protection against German irredentists' demands and in fact might become a full-fledged Soviet satellite.[20]*

For this reason the State Department recommended a solution that would give Poland the southern part of Eastern Prussia, the Baltic coast west of the Danzig corridor, and Upper Silesia, whose population was mostly Polish. The Department also suggested that the Oder-Neisse line be opposed.

The British Foreign Office forwarded similar recommendations to Churchill. In a memorandum dated February 1, 1945, Eden informed Churchill that the points agreed upon between himself and Stettinius would involve the transfer of some 2.5 million Germans. If the western border was to be set at the Oder, another 2.25 million would be added to this figure. If the Western Neisse were chosen, with the cities of Stettin and Breslau included in the Polish zone, still another 3.25 million Germans—or a total of eight million—would be subject to transfer.[21]

Armed with these recommendations and data, Roosevelt and Churchill tried to make Stalin a little less "generous." Churchill reminded him that he had already sided with the idea of moving Poland's borders to the west and effecting a population transfer. He was not daunted by the problems of the latter operation, as long as it remained within the relative contours of the Poles' wishes and capabilities, and in accordance with number of Germans that the "fatherland" could absorb. It would be a pity to stuff the Polish goose so full of German food that it would get indigestion, he said. Even if Poland settled for Eastern Prussia and Silesia up to the Oder, he said, it would still be necessary to transfer six million Germans to Germany. Although this was perhaps feasible, he would nevertheless have to explain the ethical aspect to the British people.[22]

Stalin dismissed Churchill's concerns. There was no problem, he claimed, since all the Germans who had been living in those territories had already fled from the approaching Red Army.

In view of these disagreements, Molotov suggested that the final announcement did not have to be as specific on Poland's western border as it was on the eastern frontier. His proposal was accepted in the end. Then, however, Molotov sought to add a paragraph mentioning "the return to Po-

---

* See also a memorandum dated December 19, 1944, by Averell Harriman, U.S. Ambassador in Moscow, to Secretary of State Stettinius.

land of her ancient frontiers in East Prussia and on the Oder." Roosevelt, in an interrogative and slightly ironic tone, asked how long ago these lands had been Polish. This put an end to Molotov's rider.[23]

Thus the final Yalta communiqué on Poland's borders read as follows:

> The three heads of Government consider that the eastern frontier of Poland should follow the Curzon Line with digressions from it in some regions of five to eight kilometers in favor of Poland. They recognize that Poland must receive substantial accessions of territory in the North and West. They feel* that the opinion of the new Polish Provisional Government of National Unity should be sought in due course on the extent of these accessions and that the

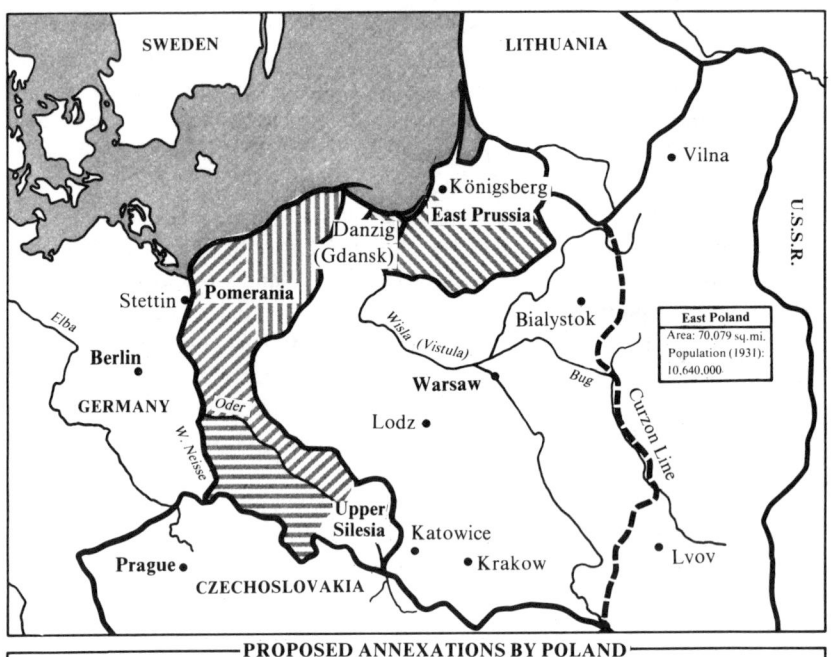

MAP 4: Poland — Territorial Changes

*As the final formulation was being drawn up, Roosevelt asked for certain amendments: replacement of the expression "the three powers" with "the three heads of Government," and the word "agree" with "feel."[25]

final delimitation of the western frontier of Poland should thereafter await the Peace Conference.[24]

Stalin's Spurious Concessions

We have separated the Polish border problem from the general Polish issue discussed at Yalta for reasons of methodology. The main theme of the debate on Poland was the nature and composition of the country's future government. Discussion of these issues was integrated and concurrent, and the government aspect now attracted more time and attention than the border question. The reasons for this are clear.

The eastern border had been deliberated and resolved in principle in Teheran, and all that remained at Yalta was to finalize it. The Red Army's advance into the Polish interior turned the Curzon Line debate into an academic issue. But the western border had yet to be resolved. The Western leaders, apprehensive of the traumatic demographic implications and suspicious of Stalin's intentions to turn Poland into a Soviet satellite, tried to delay the final decision and constrain his "generosity." Here too, however, they saw that the facts in the field, together with Polish support, gave the Soviet demands a substantial advantage.

For this reason, Roosevelt and Churchill turned the problem of the nature, composition, and political identity of Poland's future government into a "last bastion," from which they hoped to defend an independent and democratic Poland, and their influence in Eastern Europe.

Disputation on this question consumed a very long period of time; throughout the conference the sides, in various frameworks of discussions, prepared no fewer than ten draft resolutions.[26]

Here again, the democratic leaders faced *faits accomplis*, and Stalin had many more cards to play than his two colleagues. One of these was the "provisional government" seated in the Polish capital.

Yalta was Roosevelt's swan song. He was dying, though he refused to admit it, maybe even to himself. He did not want to step down before bringing the war to an end, but his illness was wearing him down. This may explain Stalin's success in outwitting him on several matters and deluding him that the Soviets were willing to make concessions. True, Stalin did agree to several concessions and gestures which Roosevelt viewed as achievements. Even so, as in Teheran, he adhered to his major demands tenaciously, and skillfully exploited Roosevelt's weakness and oversights. (For example, Roosevelt seriously undermined his bargaining position by declaring that the American forces would not remain in Europe more than two years after the war. He was undoubtedly expressing trends in American public opinion that sought to "bring the boys home." All he did, however, was strengthen Stalin's hand. Why give in to the Americans if they will vanish without a trace within two years?)[27]

We should mention that the "big" questions, too, were redeliberated in Yalta, especially with respect to the continuation of the war and its culmination in victory; the future of Germany, the punishment of war criminals and the adjudication of war reparations; the future of the states that had collaborated with the Germans; the status of France; the war against Japan; and, at the very end, the establishment of the United Nations Organization.

It was on the last two issues that Roosevelt came away with substantial accomplishments, and with what he considered concessions on Stalin's part.

Stalin agreed to enter the war against Japan about two or three months after the victory over Germany (though not before Roosevelt had accepted Stalin's own demands as to Outer Mongolia, the Sakhalin Islands, Port Arthur, Dairen, and the Kurile Islands).[28]

This agreement pleased Roosevelt, and the deal was finalized in a matter of minutes.[29] The second ostensible concession of Stalin's, also to Roosevelt's satisfaction, had to do with the U.N. After protracted and difficult argument, it was agreed that votes in the future Security Council, the U.N.'s executive body, would require unanimous agreement of all permanent members (the three allies, subsequently augmented by China and France). That is, every Security Council member state would have a veto. From the Soviets' standpoint, this was a concession to Roosevelt's positions.

As for membership in the U.N., serious disagreements again arose. Stalin demanded "additional votes," i.e., representation of each of the sixteen Soviet republics. Finally he settled for only three of them—the Ukraine, Belorussia, and Lithuania—because, as he put it, these had suffered the most in the war, and were as deserving as Turkey or Ecuador, which had contributed nothing to the war effort. Roosevelt, of course, did not regard any of the Soviet republics, sixteen or three, as being politically independent. But when Stalin made an additional "gesture" and yielded on Lithuania's candidacy, Roosevelt congratulated himself.[30]

This accumulation of facts, and the general atmosphere in the Livadia Palace (the American delegation's residence at Yalta), created the feeling that Stalin had made sweeping concessions, had been forthcoming toward the United States on many issues, and deserved a substantial measure of reciprocity. Harry Hopkins, Roosevelt's confidant and closest adviser, handed the President the following note:

The Russians have given in so much at this conference that I don't think we should let them down.[31]

Poland's future government was discussed against this psychological background. On this issue, more important to the Soviet Union than the additional votes in the U.N., Stalin stood his ground with respect to his share of the give-and-take (mainly "take").[32]

Deliberating the Make-up of the Polish Government

One of Stalin's bargaining chips in the debate on Poland's government, as stated, was the "provisional government" already seated in Warsaw. As far as he was concerned, Stalin argued, the government of Bierut and Osóbka Morawski was the Government of Poland. It enjoyed authority and popularity among the people of liberated Poland, unlike the "London emigrants" who had spent the war outside the country and had not shared their compatriots' suffering.* The entity they called an "underground" was nothing more than a collection of bandits and criminal gangs that had not fought the Germans at all. Indeed, the "London government's" agents in Poland had committed acts of sabotage and murder against the Red Army, slaughtering 212 Russian soldiers! The underground of the "Lublin people," by contrast, had been useful. For Russia, as he had already stated, the Poland issue was not one of honor alone; it was a question both of honor and security.

Now, as the Red Army was advancing into the heart of Germany, said Stalin, it had to know that its rear was secure. The men in the Red Army were indifferent to the type of government at hand, as long as it maintained order and kept them from being shot in the back. To achieve this, they needed the right kind of government in Warsaw.[33]

Then, aware of Roosevelt and Churchill's reservations about the personality of Charles de Gaulle, Stalin commended the "Warsaw government" as follows:

> Talk to them. . . . They are just as democratic as de Gaulle, and they can stop civil war and attacks on the Red Army.[34]

In contract to Stalin's clear-cut position and support of "his" Polish government, the two democratic leaders were quite reserved as to the government-in-exile in London, which had been their loyal ally throughout the war.

---

* It should be mentioned again that the prime minister of the "London government" at the time was Tomasz Arciszewski, who had spent five years operating in the underground within Poland.

They rejected Stalin's demand, of course, recognizing it as a transparent and undisguised augury of the establishment of a satellite government. Churchill, mustering all his eloquence and pathos, proclaimed Britain's sincere intent to establish the Poles as captains of their own ship and masters of their own fate.

Both he and Roosevelt dreaded the reaction of domestic public opinion, which would accuse them of having "sold out" Poland on both the border and the government issues. Churchill made it clear that to break altogether with the lawful Government of Poland which had been recognized during all the five years of the war would be an act subject to the most severe criticism in England:

> There is under our command a Polish army of 150,000 men. . . . This army has fought, and is still fighting very bravely. . . . Great Britain would be charged with forsaking the cause of Poland and I am bound to say that the debates in Parliament would be most painful and dangerous to Allied unity.[35]

Nevertheless, he saw fit to note that while his Government had at one time recognized the "London government," it "did not have intimate contact with it."[36]

Roosevelt bared his inner feelings even more liberally, announcing that he did not consider the problem of the legality or the continuity of the Polish government important at all. His feeling, he said, was that there had in fact been no Polish government for years![37] He suggested that a new government be set up, comprising representatives of the five major parties and recognized by the three powers. Churchill (who, on October 22, 1944, had spoken confidently of the imminent possibility of assembling a government with fifty percent or even sixty percent "London" representation, headed by Mikołajczyk)[38] now adopted a line similar to Roosevelt's, proposing that a provisional government be assembled at Yalta, to operate until general elections were held. As if tossing a lifesaver to the few survivors on a sinking ship, he proposed that the "qualifications" of Messrs. Mikołajczyk, Romer, and Grabski be put to use in this provisional government.[39]

This marked the end of the "London government," as a matter of political practice and general principle. Never again was it mentioned as the legal government of Poland, nor even as a basis for patching together a new regime. Now the argument centered on whether to fashion a government on the basis of the "Warsaw government" or to contrive a new body composed from both sides on more or less equal terms.[40]

Roosevelt's letter to Stalin (Feb. 6, 1944)[41] reflected the way the two democratic leaders' ideas had coalesced (Churchill attested that he had participated in phrasing it[42]). The letter proposed to invite Bierut and Osóbka

The Big Three in the patio of Livadia Palace, Yalta

Morawski from Poland to Yalta, together with two or three representatives of "other elements." The names mentioned in the letter were Archbishop Sapieha, the peasants' leader, Witos, Prof. Buyak, Prof. Kutrzeba, and Zurlowsky. Together with them it would be necessary to decide on the composition of a provisional government, which would also include several prominent Poles from abroad, such as Mikołajczyk, Romer, and Grabski. The provisional government to be assembled on this basis would be asked to hold free elections as quickly as possible.

It was now Roosevelt's position that significant progress had been made on the Polish issue, and that the whole matter was now only a matter of words and details.[43]

Molotov, Harriman, and British Ambassador Clark Kerr were entrusted with phrasing the final proposal. Again, in total disregard of the "London government," the argument focused on whether to bring members of "other circles" into the Warsaw government, or to assemble a "new government."[44]

Finally, on February 10, after exhausting deliberations, rephrasings, and many amendments, the following draft resolution was presented to the Big Three for approval:

> The Provisional Government which is now functioning in Poland should be reorganized on a broader democratic basis with the inclusion of democratic leaders from Poland itself and from Poles abroad. This new Government should then be called the Polish Provisional Government of National Unity. Mr. Molotov, Mr. Harriman and Sir A. Clark Kerr are authorized to consult in Moscow with members of the present Provisional Government, and with other Polish democratic leaders from within Poland and from abroad, with a view to the reorganization of the present Government along the above lines. This Polish Provisional Government of National Unity shall be pledged to the holding of free and unfettered elections as soon as possible on the basis of universal suffrage and secret ballot. In these elections all democratic and anti-Nazi parties shall have the right to take part. . . . When a Polish Provisional Government of National Unity has been properly formed in conformity with the above, the Governments of the USSR, the UK and the USA will establish diplomatic relations with this new Government. . . . [45]

As the Big Three approved this resolution, the deliberations came to a close. The government-in-exile's fate was sealed, and the foundations were laid for a new regime and order in Poland.

The Resolution and its Interpretations

At first, the resolution sounded like a compromise between the Soviet demand (full recognition of the provisional government in Warsaw) and the Western demand (a new government). Its deliberate vagueness and ambiguity left room for various interpretations and subsequent claims by each side that its was the correct one.

However, while the American and British governments stressed the element of "newness," as expressed and symbolized in the opening of the second sentence, the Soviets put the stress on the opening paragraph ("The Provisional Government which is now functioning in Poland should be reorganized . . . ") thus claiming upper hand. The agreement that had been attained was therefore temporary.

In any event, after the resolution was approved, Roosevelt and Churchill set to work to guarantee free elections. This, they hoped, might permit them to shape the democratic image and regime of Poland.

How soon could the elections be held? Roosevelt asked. Within a month, Stalin promised, barring a catastrophic reversal on the front—which was inconceivable.

But when Stettinius asked for a written commitment permitting the three ambassadors in Warsaw to monitor the elections and report that they were indeed free, Molotov objected categorically. Such a demand might, heaven forfend, impinge on the Poles' independence and pride, and this offended his democratic sensitivities. The Poles would feel they were not being trusted.[46]

American Admiral Leahy, a confidant and escort of Roosevelt's—although admittedly no expert on the ins and outs of diplomatic semantics—saw the future clearly. Studying the final communiqué, he told Roosevelt excitedly that it was so elastic that Russians could act almost at will without technically breaking it. The President acknowledged the truth of this, arguing only that it was the best he could do for Poland at the time.[47]

Churchill, in subsequent writings reflecting a mixture of apologetics, frustration, and helplessness, concurred.[48]

The End of the Conference . . . and Stalin's Zionism

For the Big Three and their alliance, Yalta was the summit of summits. Behind it had been five years of bloody, devastating war. Ahead, the light of victory was already blinking at the end of the tunnel. The days of fateful deliberations culminated in an evening banquet. The lives of the heads of state, the prime ministers, peace, and the peoples' victory were toasted. Spirits soared.

Churchill mentioned his upcoming elections, and Stalin assured him that the grateful British people could not possibly deny him another term in office. Churchill replied that this was not at all certain, and that there were two parties in Britain. Stalin found this rather puzzling: One party is much better, he asserted, profoundly convinced that he was right.[49]

When Roosevelt mentioned that he intended to head from Yalta to the Middle East and meet three kings there, Stalin complained about the existence of the Jewish problem: "[It is] very grave." He described the Soviet Union's futile attempt to establish a national home for the Jews in Birobidzhan. The Jews were tradesmen by nature, he judged; they stayed in Birobidzhan for a couple of years and then headed for the cities. Just the same, a few small groups in several agricultural areas had performed quite impressively. Roosevelt (who had not yet met with King Ibn Saud and still awaited the Arab chieftain's "instructive" lesson on Zionism) commented that he considered himself a Zionist. Did Marshal Stalin perceive himself as one, too? he asked. In principle, yes, answered the despot, to whom both Zionism and the Jews were anathema; but there were some practical difficulties.[50]

The ambiance of exultation and comradeship of arms began to fade shortly after Yalta.

Roosevelt's death a few months later (April 12, 1945) was the symbolic turning point. One of the reasons the tripartite alliance crumbled and the Cold War era opened was the Polish problem.[51]

The Government-in-Exile Rejects and Condemns the Yalta Resolution

The government-in-exile reacted to the Yalta resolution with helpless rage. It seemed from its point of view that after years of war and indescribable suffering, this resolution came along to herald the re-enslavement of Poland and its people. Emotionally and morally, the "London government" considered the Yalta resolution a greater historical injustice than the Ribbentrop-Molotov agreement, because this time her Western friends had participated in the sellout.

On February 13, 1945, the "London government" announced its rejection of the Yalta resolution, which "was adopted without consultation with and participation of the Polish government."

The resolution could not be binding on the Polish people, the communiqué continued. The government-in-exile condemned this "fifth partitioning of Poland, carried out this time by her allies," and the intent to expand the "Lublin committee, appointed by foreign actors," with people described in the vague formulation as "democratic leaders," and to turn it into a provisional government. This would only legitimize Soviet intervention in Poland's domestic affairs.

So long as the Soviet occupation of Poland persisted, such a government would not secure the Polish nation's right to free self-expression, even if English and American diplomats stayed in Warsaw.

Finally, the communiqué restated the government-in-exile's readiness to cooperate toward the establishment of a Polish government truly representative of the Polish people's will.[52]

Politically, this announcement was a feather in the wind.

Admittedly, the matter did not go over quietly in the British Parliament. Churchill and Eden were peppered with parliamentary questions in a debate on February 27, 1945, and they vehemently defended the resolution. "New Poland," said Eden, "will be as strong or stronger than Poland in 1939." When the resolution came up for a vote, 25 MPs voted against, and, more importantly, 11 cabinet ministers abstained.

In the end, the government's position won by a solid majority.[53]

Roosevelt, too, reported to Congress on March 1, 1945, that "The agreement on Poland, under the circumstances, is the most hopeful agreement possible for a free, independent and prosperous Polish state."[54]

Poland's fate was sealed.

The Provisional Government Pulls its Wagons Into a Circle

In the meantime, the provisional government in Warsaw, under Bierut and Osóbka Morawski, pulled its wagons into a circle.

Although officially this government was not Communist but rather "patriotic," "people's" and "democratic" (the Communist Party did not identify itself as such, going instead by the neutral title of PPR—the Polish Workers' Party), and several additional parties were permitted to exist within it, everyone knew a full Communist takeover was imminent. This was not because the Polish proletariat subscribed to the ideology and the principles of Marxism; not because the PPR and the provisional government were so popular—but rather thanks to Marshal Rokossovsky's tanks and the activities of NKVD agents (in Polish and Russian uniform) and their Polish disciples organized under the UB security services.

Alongside extensive propaganda, indoctrination, and the establishment of front organizations, a campaign of intimidation and terror was launched as well.

Thousands of AK men who had surfaced from the underground were arrested and exiled to the USSR. Activists in the democratic parties were murdered or "disappeared." Dozens of villages were torched. Factories and machines were dismantled and taken into the Soviet Union.[55]

Reports of these actions were silenced by censorship, and the shreds of information that filtered through were vehemently denied. Only one instance was publicized and officially confirmed by the Soviets.

At the end of February 1945, a proposal was communicated to the AK commanders to come out of the underground and negotiate with Marshal Zhukov toward relations. When sixteen underground leaders responded, they were captured and imprisoned. They included Deputy Prime Minister Jankowski and AK commander General Okulicki.[56]

The Soviets owned up to the deed in May, explaining that the detainees had been harassing the Red Army in its rear, caused the death of 100 Soviet officers and soldiers, and possessed unauthorized communications devices.[57]

Moscow's Message: Twenty-five Percent for "Other" Actors

Discussions of the Polish issue at Yalta did not detach this matter from the other great problems. As sometimes happens in conferences of this type, the interests of little states are dependent on and related to other, external, and alien interests. Compromises are cooked in the crucible of the negotiations conducted over their heads, and the bargaining occasionally takes place at the expense of them and their specific interests. These countries, and the powers negotiating for them, are usually guided by the objective of attaining a compromise the first purpose of which is to safeguard the interests that appear vital and important to the powers themselves.

In Yalta, Roosevelt sold his ideas and proposals on the U.N. to Stalin, and obtained Stalin's promise to enter the war against Japan, a matter of crucial importance to the Americans. In exchange, Roosevelt was willing to be lenient on Poland.

Although the maestros of formulation won the day at Yalta, the powers' conflicting intentions quickly resurfaced. The semantic ambiguity designed to bridge the contradictions was not long lived, and the sides developed their own, conflicting, interpretations.

Washington and London believed and hoped that the resolution would result in the establishment of a new government in which not only the "Lublin people" but representatives of the democratic forces—in London and in Poland—would participate under an arrangement of balance in terms of composition. Such a national unity government would be provisional, pending general, free, and secret elections to be held as quickly as possible.[58]

Moscow did not read the resolution this way. According to Stalin and Molotov, it required nothing but changes in the composition of the existing provisional government—the addition of a few people who would hold no more than 25 percent of the portfolios (which might as well be marginal ones). Molotov also reserved the right to approve or reject candidates according to his assessment of their democratic propensities, friendliness toward the Soviet Union, and willingness, as Stalin said, to be "honestly and sincerely prepared to cooperate with the Soviet state."[59]

By inserting an innocuous and seemingly obvious stipulation restricting participation in the elections to "anti-Nazi" parties, the Soviets reserved the right to reject democratic parties that did not meet their expectations and demands; to gradually eliminate what remained of Polish citizens' democratic rights; to prevent free movement for Western diplomatic representatives, and to stifle any criticism they might have about goings-on in Poland.[60] In his letter to Churchill Stalin stressed again that Poland and the USSR shared a common frontier. The Soviet Union had the right to work toward installing a friendly government in Poland, and would never approve one hostile to it. The prime attestation to this commitment was the Soviet blood profusely shed on the fields of Poland. Stalin did not know whether the Government of Belgium or that set up in Greece were truly democratic; the USSR was not consulted about them and did not insist on the right to interfere. This reflected Soviet understanding of the full significance of Belgium and Greece for the security of England.[61]

The message was unequivocal: Keep your nose out of my affairs, and I'll keep mine out of yours.

While Ambassadors Harriman and Clark Kerr were discussing how to interpret the Yalta resolutions with Molotov in Moscow, the Soviet Union established another fact.

On April 21, 1945, the Soviets signed a "agreement of friendship, cooperation, and mutual assistance" with the Bierut government. Thus the Warsaw government's political, international status was given further support.

(Incidentally, this was one of the steps that the Soviet Union took concurrently in several countries it had liberated. The Communist elements in the provisional governments of Yugoslavia, Romania, Bulgaria, Hungary and Czechoslovakia were substantially or massively strengthened.)

The Soviet action divested the Yalta resolutions of most of their content. American and British representatives were denied access to the Polish interior, and would thus be unable to monitor and report on events. Stalin brushed aside Truman and Churchill's protests as absolutely unjustified.

On May 5, he conveyed to Churchill his impression from the latter's message that he was not willing to treat the Polish Provisional Government as a basis for the future Government of National Unity, nor to accord the position it deserved in that Government. Such an attitude, Stalin asserted, precluded the possibility of an agreed solution of the Polish problem.[62]

Inter-bloc relations now exuded an atmosphere of crisis and stagnation. Churchill, who until Yalta had done his best to keep the great alliance together, and was willing to accommodate Stalin on many matters to this end, suddenly realized that an "Iron Curtain" was descending on half of Europe.

Hopkins' Mission

The new American President decided to treat the Russians forcefully but fairly. ("If the Russians did not wish to cooperate, they could go to hell."[63]) Neither was he inclined to encase his comments in a mantle of diplomatic semantics.

Molotov, visiting Truman on April 24, 1945, and describing all the virtues of the provisional Polish government, was informed by the new President that the United States was interested in Soviet friendship, but only on the basis of reciprocity in the implementation of agreements. Progress in this matter would not be a one-way street.

These remarks, which, even Admiral Leahy attested, were expressed in language that was not at all diplomatic,[64] enraged Molotov.

"I have never been talked to like that in my life." This left little impression on Truman. "Carry out your agreements and you won't get talked to like that,"⁶⁵ the President answered coldly.

Although this was a new style in White House etiquette, Truman, too, was interested in improving relations with the Soviet Union, not in worsening them.

To put matters aright—on Poland and other matters that had begun to arouse concern—Truman dispatched Harry Hopkins, the late FDR's confidant and close consultant, to Moscow.

Hopkins was poorly acquainted with Polish affairs. He knew very little about the major Polish actors and their background, and depended on information provided by Harriman, Bohlen, and State Department analysts. He viewed his mission primarily as one of effecting a reconciliation and renewing the "great alliance." As we have noted, too, he had felt at Yalta that the Russians conceded so much that they must not be let down.

In six talks with Stalin (beginning on May 26, 1945), he presented the Polish issue not necessarily as an important one in its own right but rather as a symbol of and prerequisite for continued United States-Soviet cooperation.⁶⁶

In words that left no doubt about his stance, Hopkins took exception to the "London government" and asserted that the United States had no interest in attaching anyone connected with it in the new Provisional Government of Poland.⁶⁷ All the United States wanted, he declared, was application of the Yalta resolutions and the establishment of a democratic government elected by the Polish people and friendly to the Soviet Union.

Stalin brushed aside Hopkins' weak attempt to cast some kind of aspersion on Soviet behavior. Then he launched a tirade against the West for having halted Lend-Lease activities and against the United States for engaging in "hostile propaganda" against the Soviet Union.

Speaking for "Soviet governmental circles," Stalin claimed that the Americans were behaving as if they had no further need of the Russians ever since Germany had been defeated. Posturing as the hapless victim of a mugging, he explained that:

> Despite the fact that they were simple people the Russians should not be regarded as fools, which was a mistake the west frequently made, nor were they blind. . . . It is true that the Russians are patient in the interest of a common cause but that their patience has its limits.⁶⁸

After thus shifting the burden of blame to the West, Stalin again recalled that Germany had twice used Poland as a corridor for invasion of Russia. "Neither the British nor American people had experienced German invasions, which were a horrible thing to endure and the results of which were not easily forgotten. . . . And talk of intention to Sovietize Poland was stupid. . . ."[69] The Soviet regime was not for export. He was sure that the Polish government would gladly promote "the well-known principles of democracy."[70] However, he added as a person very familiar with these principles, only in peacetime could they be applied in full. In wartime, certain restrictions were necessary, and, after all, Britain and France had imposed them as well. The possession in mid-war of communications devices with which people could broadcast reports to the enemy was an especially grave matter. True, the Soviets had acted unilaterally on a few occasions, but they had to establish a government in the territories liberated by the Red Army, which was advancing into the heart of Germany. Because it was not the Soviet way to impose a regime of its own on another people—that might be considered an act of repression and occupation, heaven forfend—the Soviet Union had recognized the provisional government, which had been helping the Red Army all along.

This tapestry of half-truths, feigned innocence, cunning, and pretense, was nothing but a preface to Stalin's real proposal.

Exploiting the fact that Hopkins' own proclamations had deviated from the Yalta resolutions, the Soviet dictator declared himself willing to discuss the expansion of the existing government. Of the 18–20 portfolios, four (he said five at first, but immediately corrected himself after Molotov whispered something into his ear) might be allocated into other Polish groups proposed by the United States and Great Britain. He apparently saw no contradiction in these remarks, proclaiming immediately afterward that Mikołajczyk, and perhaps even Professor Lange, might be acceptable to him.[71]

These were the only two prominent Poles Hopkins knew.[72] In effect, then, he endorsed Stalin's ideas and brought the matter to an end.

Thus the Soviet interpretation of the Yalta resolution was adopted, and the whole matter was finalized between Stalin and Hopkins—without the participation of the British, let alone the Poles.[73] Hopkins still tried to persuade Stalin that to improve the atmosphere he must free the sixteen Polish underground leaders. But the Soviet ruler made no commitment, merely promising (undoubtedly in the name of the "independent" Soviet legal system) that they would be leniently punished.

(Shortly thereafter, in June, the trials were held in Moscow. After all the AK men had been broken in interrogations in the Lubianka Prison and had "confessed," they were sentenced to one to ten years in prison.)

Churchill Persuades Mikołajczyk to Go to Moscow

Churchill considered the outcome of Hopkins' talks an initial breakthrough but not a genuine achievement. It augured only a few concessions, he wrote to Truman on June 4, through which the "outside" Poles might take part in preliminary discussions resulting—perhaps—in some improvement in the Lublin government.[74]

Despite this pessimistic, or, more precisely, realistic assessment, Churchill, too, believed in striking the iron while it was still hot. An opportunity to improve the state of affairs, even a little, should not be passed up. He believed that Mikołajczyk should be sent to Moscow. He considered him, and not the government-in-exile (which, formally, was still the political entity authorized and recognized by Britain), the only Polish actor who, by force of personality and political positions, could still improve the situation somewhat. Of all Poles, Churchill told Mikołajczyk, only he enjoyed the support of the Polish people.[75]

Even before Hopkins' mission, Churchill had gone to considerable lengths to make Mikołajczyk acceptable to Stalin and, through him, to save whatever could be saved of the Yalta resolutions. Thus, in mid-April 1945, Mikołajczyk, now free of the constraints of any official status, expressed his personal positions in public for the first time, marking a departure from the stances of the government-in-exile. Three of his assertions deserve special mention. The Polish statesman:

1. considered intimate and lasting friendship with Russia the major pillar of Poland's policy in the future;
2. declared that, in order to dispel any doubt as to his attitude, he accepted the Yalta Conference resolutions as to Poland's future, sovereignty, and independence, and the constitution of a provisional government of national unity;
3. supported the Yalta resolution calling for a conference of senior Polish personalities in order to establish the national unity government, which would represent the Polish people in the broadest and fairest manner possible.[76]

When the results of Hopkins' talks became known to Churchill, he summoned Mikołajczyk on June 9 and persuaded him go to Moscow.[77] This time, however, Churchill was not in his combative and optimistic mood. The Iron Curtain cast a heavy shadow over him, and he did not conceal his disappointment and anxiety.

He was more pessimistic than Mikołajczyk about the future of all of Europe, including Poland. The Germans were done for, but a new power had arisen in Europe. The Soviet Union would retreat only if threatened with war. The democracies, however, did not want war with Russia. Although they fought well, they preferred to finish the job and go to bed and rest. Thus there would be no war, and no one could predict the future of

Europe. As for Stalin, Churchill planned to tell him upon their next meeting that he did not believe a word he said.

Finally calming down, Churchill returned to the main topic for which he had invited Mikołajczyk. Here, of all places, he voiced a tone of optimism. Mikołajczyk should go to Moscow at once, he advised. Even if things did not turn out well, he should be a member of the future Polish Government. The Lublin Poles had no support in Poland, Churchill contended; the entire nation had lined up against its government. Of all Polish leaders, only Mikołajczyk commanded popular support, and should not pass up this last chance to force the door open. The Ambassadors of the United States and Great Britain, Churchill concluded, would back him to the hilt.[78]

Mikołajczyk expressed doubt as to the value of the ambassadors' support. Furthermore, the American Ambassador, he said, had tried to persuade him on several occasions that the Lublin Poles were decent people, who enjoyed total confidence of the people in Poland.[79]

The two of them, Churchill and Mikołajczyk, knew that the trip to Moscow entailed not only poor prospects for success, but also serious political and personal danger. A Polish Communist living in London, who maintained close ties with the Soviet Embassy, told Mikołajczyk: "You know, Mikołajczyk, you might have an aeroplane accident on the way to Moscow, or even be killed in a traffic accident after you get there. I'd suggest that you remain here."[80]

Churchill, however, did not yield. The British were responsible for his trip, he trumpeted; if anything happened to him, they would go to war. Although his voice recalled the great days, his words stood in stark contradiction to what he had previously said.

Mikołajczyk accepted the challenge.

As he parted from them, his host and Mrs. Churchill wept.[81] He set out for Moscow on June 16, 1945.

Establishment of the Provisional Government of National Unity

The Provisional Government of National Unity was established in Warsaw on June 28, 1945. Mikołajczyk was not installed as its head. Fourteen of the 21 ministers belonged to the Lublin group. Its character was determined not only by the number of portfolios but by their importance. All key positions (President, Prime Minister, First Deputy Prime Minister, Defense Minister, Interior Minister, and Finance Minister) were taken up by the Communists and their allies. Mikołajczyk was appointed as Second Deputy Prime Minister and Minister of Agriculture.

On July 5, after the new government had promised the United States and Great Britain to hold free elections promptly, it was officially recognized by the two democratic powers. With this, the government-in-exile was automatically stripped of the recognition it had enjoyed.

Thus the Soviet Union registered a political achievement of the highest magnitude, which it had consistently and systematically prepared, cultivated, and implemented for several years by exploiting opportunities and creating *faits accomplis*. Its efforts laid a solid foundation for the conversion of Poland into a Soviet satellite.

Hypothetical Questions

Could the government-in-exile have produced different results by behaving differently? Could the border have been improved, and—the major question—could Poland have been spared Sovietization? Could a more flexible policy have founded Poland's relations with the Soviet Union on a basis similar to those of post-war Finland with its mighty neighbor? Might acquiescence in principle to the Curzon Line during Sikorski's tenure have led to the establishment of a new Poland up to the Oder-Neisse line, strategically and politically connected with the Soviet Union, but enjoying considerable social, cultural, and economic domestic autonomy?

These are hypothetical questions, and we can only leave them unanswered.

Chapter Twelve

Potsdam and Its Implications

On July 16, 1945, the Big Three convened for the last time in Potsdam, next to vanquished, shattered Berlin.

How profoundly different this conference was from its precursors!

The terrible war had ended in the collapse and unconditional surrender of Nazi Germany. Hitler had taken his own life in his bunker. Plumbing the smoking ruins of Berlin, the Allies found reason not only to rejoice in revenge but to recoil in shock upon discovering the war crimes and the victims' fate.

Around the negotiating table, too, changes had occurred.

In place of the revered, charismatic President Roosevelt, now sat Harry S. Truman, whose personality, character, and policies were still a riddle to many. Churchill was no longer at his best, and Clement Attlee replaced him as Prime Minister by the time the gathering adjourned (August 1).

Of the Big Three, only Stalin was still in the saddle, and he cast his dominant personality over his surroundings.

However, something fundmental had changed in the internal balance of forces among this triumvirate. On the day the conference opened in Potsdam, the Americans carried out the first, and successful, detonation of a nuclear bomb in New Mexico. Now the West had a mighty weapon at its disposal, and would use it against Japan shortly thereafter. Truman, who had been in power only three months, could discuss all the unresolved questions with Stalin—Germany's future, reparations, war crimes, the future of the Far East, Russia's "traditional" demand for access to the Straits of Bosporus, etc.—from a new position of strength. The deliberations underscored the contrasts in approach and interests, and augured the end of the Great Alliance and the beginning of the Cold War.

In the meantime, the Sovietization process in liberated Eastern Europe gathered speed. To Stalin, it was natural and obvious that a country's conqueror imposed its social regime there.[1] The Soviet Union consolidated its presence wherever the Soviet soldier trod. The "provisional,"

Truman and Churchill at the Potsdam Conference

"democratic," "people's" governments of Bulgaria, Romania, Hungary, Yugoslavia, and Czechoslovakia placed ever-growing constraints on the role and influence of the non-Communists who had been incorporated into them at first. Parts of Romania and Czechoslovakia were "reunited" with Soviet territory. Properties, equipment, machinery, entire factories, and national resources were looted and transferred from the "liberated" and "friendly" countries into the Soviet interior in the guise of "war reparations." The Red Army entrenched itself wherever the winds of war had taken it.

The Problem of Poland's Western Border

As at previous conferences, Poland was an important issue at Potsdam. This time, however, the major problem was that country's western border.

As will be recalled, a decision had been taken to give Poland territorial compensation in the north and west, as determined with the consent of the Government of Poland. Now it was time to cash in the chips.

Stalin's objective was consistent and clear: to put the German menace at a greater distance from the Soviet border by moving Poland as far west as possible, specifically to the Oder-Western Neisse line. The transfer of the Polish and the German populations, too, was meant to enhance the USSR's sense of security and intensify Poland's dependence on the Soviet Union when, as expected, the German population would demand national unification.*

Truth to tell, the postponement of the final resolution at Yalta did not keep Stalin from establishing facts in the field. A Polish administration had been set up in occupied German territories as far west as the Oder and Western Neisse Rivers, including the cities of Stettin and Breslau.

As the Big Three convened in Potsdam, Truman and Churchill tried to turn the clock back, repeating arguments they had already voiced in Yalta. Truman was especially vehement, and his style was new to Stalin. On one occasion he proclaimed that he was not a diplomat, did not beat around the bush, and would act only on the basis of "yes" or "no."[3] On the western border issue Truman expressed resentment that facts were being established without consultation, and that the Poles had been handed a fifth zone of occupation—while the Yalta resolutions had spoken of only four. He also insisted on the need to postpone the final demarcation of the border until the peace conference, as stated in the Yalta resolutions. Stalin, though not conceding his basic position, again adopted tactics of reassurance; he declared that "The Western frontier question is open,"[4] even as he implored the President to understand the Russian conception. The Red Army was fighting, and its concern was victory. It needed a secure and friendly hinterland, which the Germans, obviously, could not guarantee. Fortunately, they had all fled: "No single German remained in the territory to be given

---

*Even as Stalin preferred to hand vast territories over to the Poles while expelling the German population, he did not think it possible to impose Communism on Germany. "Communism is as suited to Germany as a saddle is to a cow," he told Mikołajczyk on one occasion.[2] He had not yet imagined that the same blind sense of order and discipline that he had encountered as a young men in Leipzig would turn the Soviet sector of Germany into the very model of a disciplined satellite.

to Poland."[5] It was the Poles who had enthusiastically greeted the Red Army; it was the Poles who were now working the fields, operating the mines, and maintaining a friendly administration in the Red Army's rear. Thus there had been neither a *fait accompli* nor a pure and simple coup, but rather constructive, administrative activity meant to secure the Soviet rear.

Nine million Germans were a lot of people, Truman tried to protest. He found it hard to believe that every last one of them had fled. Stalin, however, solemnly assured him that this was precisely what had happened.

Churchill, whose initial enthusiam about "moving" Poland to the west and expelling the Germans had chilled since Yalta, commented that if Stalin's information was indeed accurate, an economic catastrophe was imminent. Those eight or nine million Germans who, according to Stalin, had fled into the German heartland would now afflict the country's shattered economy and ultimately become a burden on the occupation authorities. Setting the border as Stalin proposed would cut off one fourth of Germany's farmland (based on the 1937 borders), and the addition of eight to nine million mouths to feed portended conditions similar to those in the German concentration camps.[6] When one considered that another three to four million Poles living east of the Curzon Line were to be transferred to the west of that line, the combination of all these factors would horrify England. It was morally wrong, and it would do Poland no good, Churchill concluded.[7]*

This argument revealed the failure of the Western diplomacy with respect to Poland. After the leaders of England and the United States conceded the matter of Poland's eastern border, and after they accepted the principle of territorial compromise for Poland at Germany's expense—in order to preserve the unity of the Great Alliance and in hope of safeguarding future Poland's democratic nature—they suddenly found themselves clashing with Poland's interests and defending the Germans.

This was a grave distortion of historical truth and the Western leaders' genuine intentions, and Communist propaganda knew how to exploit it in a demagogic and most successful way. Moreover, Stalin was better informed than Churchill and Truman as to the Poles' anti-German sentiments, and an abyss gaped between them and Churchill's economic arguments and moral reservations.

It is therefore no wonder that Stalin casually tossed Churchill's explanations aside, especially the idea that some of the Germans who had fled their homes would return. Stalin expressed apprehension that the Poles

---

*A working paper drawn up by the U.S. State Department for the conference on June 30, 1945, included similar data.[8]

would hang them as soon as they showed up, adding that he himself understood their state of mind, i.e., a desire to avenge the Germans for the injuries they had caused them for centuries.[9]

If Stalin indeed correctly assessed the Poles' opinions and states of mind in this context, he proved himself to be historically shortsighted about and insensitive to the power and influence of the religious factor in Poland.

When Churchill posed the question of religious freedom and the Catholics' rights in Poland, Stalin pondered for a moment, stroked his mustache, and posed his famous sarcastic question:

How many divisions has the Pope got?[10]

After failure to reach agreement on the western border after protracted deliberations, it was decided to invite and consult representatives of the Polish Government (as required by the Yalta resolutions, too) and to "ask the lady."

The Polish delegation, comprising President Bierut, Foreign Minister Żymierski, and Deputy Prime Minister Mikołajczyk, met on July 24 with the three Allied foreign ministers and pressed for setting Poland's western border at the Oder and Western Neisse Rivers. There was nothing surprisingly new about this; nor did it reflect Soviet domination of Polish political thinking. On the topic of the western border—unlike the eastern border—all Poles had been united since the war broke out. All shades of Poland's political spectrum agreed that to be secure, an independent Poland required thorough-going change in the contours of its frontiers with Germany, as well as the "Polandization" of its western and northern sectors by means of a transfer of the German population from them.

The Polish representatives presented their demands for border changes and justified them on economic, demographic, and defense grounds. The fact that they presented a united front proved highly significant in substance and impact. The major points they presented were the following:[11]

> The border should run from the Baltic through Swinemünde including Stettin in Poland, along the Oder River and thence along the Neisse River to Czechoslovakia.
>
> This, for the following reasons:
>
> A. Poland was about to lose 180,000 sq.km. in the east.
> B. The territories to be transferred to its sovereignty in the west and north would be smaller in area than those it would lose in the east. Poland's territory would shrink from 338,000 sq.km. to about

309,000 sq.km., and its population would fall from 34 million to 26 million. However, this population would be more homogeneous. Poland would be a state without minorities.

C. There were about 1,000,000 to 1,500,000 Germans left in this area, but they would be willing to return to Germany.
D. From the point of security, this was the shortest possible frontier . . . and would be easy to defend.
E. These territories had served the German war industry and had been a bastion of German imperialism. The Germans had tried to destroy Poland and its culture. It would be an expression of historical justice that a Polish state be created that was powerful and which had the possibility to resist any German aggression. Poland had already ceded territory in the east for the sake of peace, and it was right that Germany should also cede territory for the sake of peace. . . .
F. Germany, defeated in the war, would lose less territory than Poland. If Poland's demands were accepted, Germany's territory would shrink by 18 percent, while Poland's would diminish by 20.
G. Poland needed the territory for its economy, industrialization efforts, urbanization of its excess rural population, and absorption of repatriates from the east.

The Polish delegation presented its demands forcefully and very persuasively. It held its ground even when Stalin, at a certain stage, was inclined to compromise in some manner with the Western position.*

We may readily appreciate that the Polish delegation's firm and united stance on a matter it considered vital to Poland's security and future made a great impression on the Allied leaders. Churchill, too, after a protracted talk with the Poles, seemed to have softened up. While reminding Bierut that he favored ample compensation for Poland, Churchill warned him that the Poles were making a mistake by asking for so much.[14]

One possible reason for Churchill's new moderation was the fact that the day he met with the Polish delegation was also his last day as Prime Minister of Great Britain.

The intensity and vitality of the democratic instinct, or perhaps the illogic and ingratitude of the electorate—depending on the point of view—

---

*(He tried to persuade Bierut that the border should be set not at the Western Neisse but at the Queiss River;[12] some associate this with a Soviet intention to link this concession to an American concession on the volume of German restitution due to the Soviet Union.)[13]

led to a rotation at the top even before the Potsdam Conference was over. The man who had fought audaciously and consistently against the appeasement policy, and who had led his people and the world from isolation, humiliation, and failure to war and victory by the might of his extraordinary personality, was replaced by drab, colorless Clement Attlee.

In his memoirs, Churchill wrote that he was relieved of all responsibility from that moment on, because had the British voter re-elected him and had he continued in Potsdam, he would never have recognized the Western Neisse line.[15]

One may legitimately doubt Churchill's resolve on this point. Furthermore, the Americans, after hearing out the Polish delegation, tired of the matter and proposed a "deal": provisional support in principle for the proposed line, in exchange for a Soviet concession on the matter of war reparations.

"If we made concessions, the Soviets should also," Secretary of State Byrnes argued.[16]

The Americans were now ready, if quite skeptically, to accept Bierut's promises that Poland would promptly hold unfettered elections, that freedom of press and religion would be assured, that foreign journalists would be allowed to move and cover events freely, that Polish soldiers and civilians returning to Poland from the West would not be harmed, and that the Red Army would evacuate Polish territory and retain only two traffic routes across the country—arteries linking their formations in occupied Germany with the Soviet Union.[17]

It often happens in international conferences that after protracted and exhausting deliberations, efforts are made to bridge gaps by means of an ambiguous "redeeming formula," which each side views and interprets as its own achievement. Thus it had been at Yalta, and thus it was at Potsdam; the deliberations on the Polish issue ended with what looked like a compromise resolution. Its voice was the voice of the United States, and its hands were the hands of the Soviet Union. That is, its phrasing was American, but its essence conformed with the demands of the Poles and the Russians.

An official communiqué issued on August 2 established that after the representatives of the Provisional Government of National Unity had been heard:

> The three heads of government agreed that, pending the *final determination* of Poland's western frontier, the *former German territories* east of a line running from the Baltic Sea immediately west of Swinemunde, and thence along the Oder River to the confluence of the western Neisse River and along the western Neisse to the Czechoslovak frontier, including that portion of

East Prussia not placed under the administration of the Union of Soviet Socialist Republics in accordance with the understanding reached at this conference and including the area of the former free City of Danzig, shall be under the administration of the Polish State and for such purposes should not be considered as part of the Soviet zone of occupation in Germany.[18]

As for implementing the population transfer, the Big Three ruled that "The transfer to Germany of German populations, or elements thereof, remaining in Poland, Czechoslovakia and Hungary, will have to be undertaken. They agree that any transfers that take place should be effected in an orderly and humane manner." The resolution also called on the Polish Government (and the Governments of Czechoslovakia and Hungary) to suspend temporarily further action concerning the expulsion of Germans until the Allied Control Council in Germany decided how these Germans were to be dispersed throughout the country.

In the pages to come we examine how the resolutions on Poland adopted at Teheran, Yalta, and Potsdam were in fact implemented. As will be recalled, the subjects finalized in the resolutions were Poland's eastern, western, and northern borders, the composition of the Polish government, and the population transfers.

The eastern border issue had been concluded in principle in Teheran and confirmed at Yalta. Its implementation was a consequence of the Red Army's advance, and the border was set, in keeping with the Yalta resolutions, along the Curzon Line with an adjustment to the east, with Vilna and Lvov left in Soviet territory.

The Polish Provisional Government of National Unity, of course, accepted this frontier without protest.

Communist Takeover

The aforementioned Yalta resolution on the composition of the Polish government became the topic of clashing Western and Soviet interpretations. In the meantime, the dispute did not prevent the establishment of a government which, in the Western leaders' assessment, was quite unlike that agreed upon. As previously noted, a decisive majority of the ministerial portfolios, and all the major ones, were handed to "Lublin people." Wasting no time, they started to turn Poland into a Soviet satellite.

In view of their actions, Bierut's remarks quoted below sound like a poor joke. At Potsdam on July 27, in a meeting with Churchill, Bierut promised his counterpart that Poland would be anything but a Communist state. If anyone attempted to force the Soviet system on Poland, he asserted, the Poles would probably resist; Poland would develop in accordance with the principles of Western democracy, and would be one of Europe's most democratic countries.[19]

Thus Bierut proved himself to be an assiduous disciple of Stalin, who had made similar proclamations to Roosevelt and Churchill. Bierut and his colleagues also proved themselves to be strong on the implementation side, though certainly not without the help of Soviet advisors, including NKVD agents.

It took no longer than two years to Communize Poland. Nor was this the result of Polish affection for and gratitude to the liberating Red Army. Feelings of that kind were negligible in the extreme, and confined to restricted circles.

Polish President, Bierut

Theoretically, reconstituted Poland had five political parties: the Polish Workers' Party (PPR) under full Communist control, and another three parties that were in fact Communist front organizations. Mikołajczyk's Polish Peasant Party was also permitted to exist. Behind this representative and parliamentary facade, the "people's democracy" method was applied at a quickening pace. Stalinist methods of administration were extensively used. According to Mikołajczyk,[20] the Soviet-organized and trained security police (UB) were 230,000 strong, and another 120,000 were organized under ORMO (armed civil guard units) for "defense of the people's democracy." Many security police personnel were Soviet nationals in Polish uniform, who did not even know Polish.

By various estimates, about 40 Soviet generals and 15,000 Soviet officers spent time in Polish army service in Polish uniform.[21] In addition— contrary to the Potsdam Conference resolutions[22]—about 300,000 Soviet troops under Marshal Rokossovsky remained on Polish soil (in the Lignica district of Silesia). This armed force was explained as necessary to help "uproot the remnants of capitalism and Fascism" and to consolidate the "people's democracy."

The last AK fighters had neither come out of the underground nor laid down their arms (especially the far-right and anti-Semitic elements, organized under the NSZ—"Armed National Forces"); they engaged in sabotage and guerrilla activities for some time after liberation, their targets including the authorities and Jewish Holocaust survivors (e.g., murder, throwing of Jews from moving railroad cars, a pogrom in the city of Kielce, etc.)

When the regime reacted, it did not stop at eradicating the extreme reactionary and violent groups. It also exploited the action taken against them to mount a broad campaign of repression against democratic elements, in order to strengthen the PPR's grip. The "coalition" government was in fact run by the Politburo of the Communist PPR. The functions and powers of Mikołajczyk and his colleagues were gradually constricted and effectively eviscerated. A year later, these men were no more than fig leaves. The authorities did not flinch from measures meant to destroy Mikołajczyk's party, which was a last stronghold of national and political independence. Especially brutal terror was invoked—particularly between November 1944, and May 1945—against Peasant Party members, local functionaries, and national leaders.

(The Stalinist Polish leaders, and activists who have since been removed from positions of power, now admit that the secret security services had applied ruthless terror to wipe out every trace of independent thinking and organization. In rather frank and sincere published interviews, they admit that masses of people were arrested and tens of thousands murdered, either through show trials or without trial.[23])

Finally, on January 19, 1947, after painstaking preparations under the watchful eyes of Soviet advisors and experts—including incarceration, repression of oppositionist expressions, total censorship, etc.—the "free and secret" general elections were held.*

The returns, as subsequently made public, granted the Government Bloc (the PPR and some PPS fellow-travellers) 394 seats in the Sejm (Parliament). The Christian Labor Party earned 12, the PSL (New Liberation Party) 7, the Catholic Progressive Party 3, and Mikołajczyk's Polish Peasant Party 28.[24] Those who dared to challenge and protest the conduct and results of the elections were imprisoned, beaten, and forced to retract their "slander."

Mikołajczyk's attempt to struggle for political equilibrium and save democracy in Poland came to an end when he found out in October 1947, that he was about to be arrested, court-martialled, and sentenced to death. Clandestinely, he fled Poland.

With this, the swift and vigorous Communist takeover of Poland was completed.

"Polandization" of the "Liberated Territories"

At the same time the Communists were taking over the Polish regime, the "liberated territories"** were being subjected to a swift "Polandization" process. Within several years, most remaining Germans were expelled from Silesia and Pomerania, and millions of Poles resettled there. Cities and villages changed their names, if not their form and character. Ancient Slavic names were exhumed from the tombs of ancient history. Beuten turned into Bytom, Görlitz into Gorlice, and Breslau into Wroclaw. In place of the swastika, red and white banners now fluttered from the

---

*How "secret" were the Polish elections? The following joke was current in Poland: a voter entered the polling room and went before the election committee with his ID card. After verifying his identity, the committee chairman handed him a sealed envelope with a voting slip inside. "Please put the envelope into the ballot box," he said. "But I can't see what the slip says," the voter tried to argue. "Don't you know the elections are secret?" asked the chairman.

***Ziemie odzyskane* in Polish, or, literally "lands redeemed anew."

Gothic-style buildings, and new residents settled into houses bursting with German porcelain and looted Jewish property. In the fields, factories, and mines, Poles replaced Germans, slave laborers, and concentration camp inmates.

The factor that lent this process its intensity and scope was the migration of Poles after the war. It became necessary to house, rehabilitate, and employ millions of Poles returning to the country from the Soviet Union, from territories annexed to the Soviet Union by force of the Yalta and Potsdam resolutions, from the forests, the partisan units, and the concentration camps. Most of them arrived destitute and could find no home, no person, and no means of subsistence in their places of origin. The Jews among them were greeted with hostility and the cruel suggestion that "Hitler didn't finish the job."

These masses could easily have become a source of domestic instability if an outlet for the pressure had not been found. They were directed to the liberated territories in the West. There they could start their lives afresh, under optimal conditions. Indeed, the Polish Government, encouraged by the Soviets of course, made every possible effort to divert this stream into the desired channel. Its obvious intent was to make Poland's foothold in these territories a permanent one; to forestall any possibility of reversing the new reality; to frustrate the resurrection of "provisional" resolutions; to fill the contours of the resolution speaking of "Polish administration" with the solid demographic, economic, national, and political substance that would turn "administration" into sovereignty; to implement Polish "historical rights" in the liberated territories; and to restore the Polish luster to territories, cities, and villages that had been German for centuries.

There was a national consensus in Poland as to the need to swiftly "Polandize" the liberated territories—a consensus drawing on both the demographic—economic situation and national emotions. Hatred of the Germans was a dominant element in this set of sensitivities.

This hatred was understandable and deeply entrenched. Nazi whips had slashed Poland mercilessly for almost six years, and the confines of this book prevent our describing the Nazis' demonic ways of repressing and trampling the civilian population, or the staggering dimensions of murder, devastation, and deliberate annihilation of millions of "subhumans" belonging to "inferior races"—Jews, Gypsies, Poles, and other Slavs; the silent consent of a decisive majority of the German people; the responsibility of the German citizenry, lovers of law and order, who neither heard nor saw, but nevertheless participated willfully in the plunder of the Jews' property, while expunging from consciousness all knowledge of the origin of these chattels and the fate of their former owners.

After the defeat came a now-familiar refrain: "We knew nothing, heard nothing, saw nothing. Not us. . . . After all, I was only a little cog, obeying orders." For years, however, the distinction between Nazi activists and party members with simple citizens, and the public at large was blurred.

In Pomerania, Upper and Lower Silesia, and the other areas that became Polish after the war, the German population was more than a staid, passive community obeying orders. The decisive majority of this population had identified with the Nazi Party even before the war, voting for it in Reichstag elections (68 percent in Eastern Prussia, 73 percent in the Stettin area, 57 percent in the Breslau area, 63 around Lignica, 50 in the Oppeln district, and an average of 64 throughout[25]). Thus the Poles considered the banishment of the Germans to Germany as an act of self-defense against the possible repetition of bloody actions by the fifth column.[26]

In view of this historical and psychological background, it is easy to understand that the process of "Polandizing" the liberated territories did not necessarily conform to the intent of the Potsdam resolutions. The endeavor was not "orderly and humane," and anyone who disregards the maelstrom of emotions and urges that dominated the period and accompanied the process—anyone who ignores the Poles' hate of Germans and wish to exact revenge on them—simply does not understand what actually, and by necessity, transpired.

Germans Out, Poles In

The Poles were not particular about the methods used to purge the liberated territories and resettle them at the Germans' expense.

How many Germans remained in these territories at the war's end? As will be recalled, Stalin had argued at Yalta that all the Germans had fled,[27] and ruled unequivocally at Potsdam that not a single German had remained.[28] True, many Germans had been killed in those areas during the war, and many others had indeed fled—either out of fear, personal initiative, or advice of the German commanders, when the rapid advance of the Red Army could no longer be concealed. Nevertheless, there were still no few Germans there. Stalin's blunt, all-inclusive formula was polished up by the Polish delegation that appeared before the foreign ministers: admittedly, "there were about 1,000,000 to 1,500,000 Germans left in this area, but they would be willing to return home. . . . ", i.e., to Germany.[29]

Of course, it is hard to ascertain what those Germans really wanted, but the fact is that within a very short time very few of them remained in their former places of residence. The Poles did not ask them to define their desires, and continued expelling them even when the Potsdam resolutions called for a moratorium. The Polish Government established a special ministry that dealt energetically with all the problems related to the expulsion of Germans, the resettlement of Poles, and the distribution of land and properties.

Thus, for example, about 4 million hectares (app. 1,600,000 acres) of agricultural land, and about half a million farmsteads (466,800, to be exact), were handed out to the Polish settlers between 1944 and 1949.[30] Comparison of these figures with additional Polish sources proves that almost all German-owned farmsteads were in fact expropriated (according to the data,[31] there had been 478,962 farms in those territories before the war). Compensation, was obviously not part of the bargain.

How many Germans were expelled?

German and Polish statistics, of course, clash on this point. The German sources speak of around 9,500,000 Germans and 250,000 Poles east of the Oder-Neisse line before the war. During the war, the German sources add, this number grew to over 10 million.[32] The Polish sources, by contrast, estimate the population of the territories at 7,300,000 Germans and 1,100,000 Poles.[33] Then again, each side had a different account of the number of persons expelled. The Germans, trying to emphasize the suffering imposed on them, speak of 9,000,000–10,000,000 refugees (half finding shelter in the Soviet sector, and half resorting to the English and American zones).[34]

The Poles dismiss these statistics categorically. First of all, they criticize the Germans', method of habitually and artificially inflating their statistics, blurring the distinction between refugees from the areas annexed by Poland and those from other areas (Czechoslovakia, Hungary, Bessarabia, the Baltic countries), and especially their disingenuous practice of including offspring born in new places of settlement in the calculation. Dr. Kokot, in a book packed with data and statistics, writes about this as follows:

> Children of resettlers born after their parents were transferred are also counted as resettlers. . . . With such statistical methods . . . the problem of resettlers will exist forever. Or at any rate until it appears that owing to the greater biological validity of the newcomers the whole population of Western Germany . . . is entirely composed of persons "expelled" from their fatherland (*Heimatvertriebene*). From the standpoint of statistical methods there are only two logically justified dates at which resettlement statistics can be closed: either on the day when the transference of population ends or when the whole population consists entirely of resettlers. The latter possibility is

obviously an absurdity, thus, only the former solution is acceptable and is applied to similar processes throughout the world.[35]*

What, then, do the Polish sources say about the number of German refugees? Kokot, relying on German sources, says that no more than 5,400,000 persons reached Germany from the territories east of the Oder-Neisse line.[36] About 4,000,000 of them had fled or were transferred by the Nazi authorities to Germany during the last period of fighting. Because some of them returned afterwards, a census taken on February 14, 1946, showed that 2,036,439 Germans were still present in the territories. Nearly 2,000,000 of them were transferred to Germany between 1946 and 1948.[37]**

Even though it is hard to arrive at the precise truth, and even if we accept the accuracy of the official Polish data, this was one of the greatest mass expulsions of all time—far exceeding the 1,000,000–1,500,000 cited by the Polish delegation at Potsdam.

The Potsdam resolutions also spoke of the need to carry out the transfer in an "orderly and humane" manner. In terms of efficiency of implementation, speed in transferring millions of Poles westward and resettling them in the territories, and, simultaneously, expelling the Germans into Germany, the affair was undoubtedly a smashing success. But was it "humane?" The assessments are widely divergent, and the differences are rooted in the two peoples' disparate scales of values and the sharp contrast between their aspirations and recollections.

After the war, the Germans published several thick volumes of testimonies and documentation, detailing the "brutal" manner in which the expulsion was carried out.

An official "black book," published by the Federal Ministry for Refugee Affairs, stresses the Poles' "abysmal hatred," "sadism," and "demonic inventiveness" in their atrocities against and humiliation of the German residents.[39] The book goes into detail and provides hundreds of accounts of atrocities committed during the expulsion—slave labor, abuse, kidnapping, incarceration, lynching, and mass death caused by starvation and infection. To believe these accounts, the expulsion was a brutal affair

---

*Judging by the last sentence, the author is apparently unaware that the Arabs, aided by the UN and the Communist bloc, use exactly the same absurd method. Thus the Arab "refugees," 630,000 in 1948, have exploded to some 3 million during the intervening years.

**This statistic, of course, bears the official Polish seal of approval. A scholar of Polish descent living in the United States offers different—though not very different—figures: 4,800,800 Germans having "emigrated" from the territories, and 2,500,000 expelled.[38]

indeed. The residents were given little advance notice, and were allowed to take nothing more than hand-held baggage.

The German sources, lamenting the German refugees' agonies and the Poles' brutality, seem to disregard the Nazi past of those who had been expelled. The reader is liable to come away with the misapprehension that the suffering had been inflicted on innocent victims, tranquil citizens, honest and upright peasants. . . . We said "disregard," because in one particular case the authors of this "black book" reached a pinnacle of impudence. Writing of the "atrocity" committed against German citizens in forcing them to uncover the mass graves of countless Jews and Poles killed by the Nazis, to disinter the remains, and to rebury them, the authors bemoan the "crude injustice" (*ein grobes Unrecht*) of their action, "even if one detainee or another had in fact been responsible for crimes against the Poles or the Jews."[40]

But this was not all.

This book, like others of its kind,[41] reiterates the claim that the expulsion had been carried out not only with hate and natural instances of death, but with mass murder as well, on a scale of 1.6 million Germans.[42]

The Polish sources reject these accusations with contempt. Their statistical computations led them to the conclusion that there had been 300,000 instances of natural death among the German population between 1946–1950.[43] In addition to this, the Polish sources[44] estimate that the German population also suffered additional losses as a consequence of hostilities, and the number of such casualties was assessed at 1,500,000 to 2,000,000.*

Even if we accept the Polish claim in full, it is worth bearing in mind that no few criminal elements, too, seized the moment. Alongside the historical blood reckoning of the Poles, Russians, and Jews, outlaws of various kinds were busily squaring other accounts. Their illicit operations blackened and marred the image of popular reaction that accompanied the population transfer. However the matter is assessed, three facts are clear: the popula-

---

*A. 400,000 as a result of aerial bombardment, both by the Western and the Soviet air forces;
B. 600,000 as a result of several cities' being changed into strongholds;
C. 400,000–450,000 as a result of combat in the field, frantic escape, and preventive action against Volkssturm and Wehrwolf units that continued to fight after Germany had surrendered;
D. 50,000–100,000 for "other reasons" and "post-war suffering";
E. 600,000 Wehrmacht soldiers who had fallen in these territories.

tion transfer was not suspended, it was not carried out "humanely," and it involved millions of Germans.

With these swift and absolute strokes, New Poland attained its national aims: expulsion of a national minority that had previously been and was henceforth liable to endanger its integrity and independence; reconstitution of Poland as an ethnically homogeneous state; conversion of the "provisional government" into a real government, and demarcation of secure borders without waiting for their "final determination" at the peace conference.

As they expelled the Germans, the Poles resettled the territories. The new Polish population of the "liberated territories" reached 2,000,000 within a few months (by the end of 1945) and climbed to about 5,100,000 by November, 1946. Of the 700,000 Germans remaining, another 100,000 were expelled in November.[45]

According to a 1962 census, the Polandization process gave the territories a population of 7,810,000 (out of 30,000,000 in Poland all told.)

These territories produced 28 percent of Poland's entire industrial output, and more than 4 million of the 13.5 million tons of Polish agricultural produce.[46]

Within ten years, the formerly German territories had become integral parts of the Polish state.[47]

The Powers' Position and Germany's Demand for "Restoration of Legitimate Rights"

The Soviet Union, of course, expressed unequivocal support for the Oder-Western Neisse line. When Stalin was asked by a journalist on October 23, 1946, whether Russia considered this line Poland's final border, he answered tersely: "Yes, she considers it as such."[48]

The Americans and the English still waged a rear guard action for some time, but this proved to be devoid of all operative political significance. The Western foreign ministers took various occasions to reassert that they did not accept the existing facts, and recalled that the Big Three had resolved in Potsdam to postpone the "final determination" of Poland's western frontier until the peace conference. At a meeting of the powers' foreign ministers in Moscow in April 1947, American Secretary of State Marshall and British Foreign Secretary Bevin took on Molotov in harsh disputation of this issue.

Returning from Moscow, Marshall issued a communiqué (April 21, 1947) stressing "total disagreement" on the controversial matter. In Potsdam, Marshall's announcement said, President Truman had confronted reality and accepted it as provisional only. The powers had to ensure good neighborly relations between postwar democratic Poland and democratic Germany. The United States proposed the establishment of a committee to set the borders, attended by the four powers (including France) and the states involved. Bevin, too, addressing the House of Commons on May 15, 1947, mentioned the Potsdam Resolution and the need to honor agreements.[49]

However, as stated, nothing positive was to come of the Western arguments and protestations. Instead, they allowed the Soviet Union and the Warsaw Government to open an anti-Western propaganda barrage, presenting the West to the Polish public as its enemy. On April 10, 1947, the Government of Poland announced that it considered the western border question as having been discussed and finalized in the Yalta and Potsdam resolutions. It categorically rejected Marshall's proposals, and added:

> All attempts at infringing this just and peaceful solution help only those elements who do not desire a stabilization of conditions in Europe, and above all, those German circles which already today are thinking of new aggression.[50]

True, no few Germans were already dreaming of obliterating the shame of defeat by means of an inter-bloc war. They hoped that the Cold War, whose manifestations were already evident, would escalate into an armed conflict between the Soviet Union and the West (including Germany), and that in its course the glory of the German Reich would be restored.

German circles interpreted the American and English protest against the Soviet and Polish reading of the Potsdam resolution as a green light for their own objections. They believed that the Cold War would expunge the crimes of Nazi Germany from memory, and rescind the punishment meted out to Germany at the war's end.

A crescendo of voices now inveighed against the "historical injustice," "plunder of the homeland," and "atrocities of the illegal expulsion," and demanded "the restoration of the German people's historical rights to its land." Their protestations then crystallized and acquired an academic-legalistic ring:

A. The Potsdam resolutions were contrary to every person's right to his homeland (*Recht auf die Heimat*).
B. The Potsdam resolutions were contrary to every people's sacred right to self-determination, and disregarded the wishes of those expelled.

C. The Potsdam resolutions admittedly established the need to expel Germans, but spoke only of "expelling Germans from Poland"[51] (and from Czechoslovakia and Hungary). Nowhere was it said that the expulsion would also apply to Germans domiciled in the territories placed under "Polish administration."[52]
D. The Potsdam resolutions spoke out not of annexation of the territories by Poland, but only of placing them under Polish administration, and this on a temporary basis alone.
E. Finally, millions of human beings had been expelled in a fashion other than the "humane" one called for in the Potsdam resolutions. Brutality and cruelty had been used, resulting in the deaths of 1,500,000 members of a peaceful civilian population.

The Arguments of the Polish Jurists

So as not to hand the German propagandists a victory in Western public opinion by default, the Polish propaganda mill cranked up to refute the German contentions. "The German circles which already today are thinking about a new aggression"—as described in a Polish communiqué on April 10, 1947—were then and thereafter called "revengistes," revenge seekers, warmongers who had not yet been weaned of their racist aggression and had not yet come to grips with the just punishment imposed upon them.

The Polish propaganda campaign continued for more than ten years. The best political and legal minds were recruited to present a set of principled arguments based on historical precedents and the views of the greatest Western and Soviet experts on international law. We may group these arguments as follows:

A. Border changes in view of international law.
B. Border changes and punishment of the aggressor.
C. The need for secure borders.
D. The advantages of ethnic-political homogeneity and the transfer of minorities.
E. The right to self-determination versus defense interests and the country's territorial integrity.
F. Historical rights.
G. The permanent nature of the new borders.
H. Existing facts.

Here, briefly, are the main contentions:

1. The existence of international borders is never truly static. The history of peoples shows many instances of such border changes, nearly always as the result of war. It had once been considered an accepted phenomenon and a norm—and was even recognized as such by international law[53]—that states expand and change their borders. One of the tenets of modern international law, however, is the territorial integrity of states and the inadmissibility of use of force toward changing a territorial status quo. Thus the United Nations charter (Paragraphs 2 and 4) prohibits the use of force or threat thereof by one state against another. Nevertheless, even this principle does not disregard conflicts of interest, the intrinsic dynamic of international relations, and the impossibility of maintaining a territorial status quo forever. Accordingly, international law leaves loopholes that permit the modification of existing borders, swaps of territory between states, the granting of sovereignty to an area seceding from the confines of an existing state, etc.

2. Basing themselves on a long list of experts on international law, both in Eastern Bloc countries[54] and the West,[55] the Polish jurists called special attention to two exceptions to the principle of "territorial integrity": 1) voluntary changes through mutual agreement, without the use of force, and 2) changes brought about in a war of self-defense, repulsion of an aggressor, and even punishment of the aggressor after his defeat.[56]

The postwar change of the Polish-German border was based on the principle of security and historical rights, and on another principle: the aggressor state's responsibility for the consequences of its aggression.[57]

Here the aggressor is punished not to satisfy a lust for revenge but to keep him from aggressing again and to avert the absurd situation in which the victim of aggression is forever bound by ethical rules and international laws, while the defeated aggressor is immune and protected by the same law.[58]

The victim of aggression, having defended himself and repelled the aggressor, is entitled to demand and receive territorial compensation for his agony and sacrifices—a compensation that would also deter the enemy from future aggression. Border modifications made during a war of self-defense are justified and accepted.[59]

Indeed, the Polish jurists argued, all the postwar border arrangements included an element of punishing the aggressor and undoing his conquests (territorial transfers from Hungary to Czechoslovakia, from Italy to Greece and Yugoslavia, from Japan to the Soviet Union, and, of course, from Germany to its neighbors).[60] Thus international law presents a solid foundation for border modifications to Poland's benefit, and any claim to the contrary "has no legal as well as moral basis."[61]

3. The previous borders had to be adjusted, too, in order to be secure and defensible. The old lengthy, winding Polish-German frontier in the

west, and the narrow "corridor" in the north—pressed from the east and west by two parts of Germany, with its narrow outlet to the Baltic Sea—and the dubious international status of the city of Danzig, all served as temptations for German aggression. One of the first and most important demands of Polish policy was therefore the alteration of this border, the Polish jurists noted. (One example is a declaration by the Polish National Council in London on December 2, 1942.[62]) The Big Three had unanimously recognized this demand; in Teheran, Yalta, and Potsdam, they had agreed that Poland should be compensated with German territories for the areas annexed by the Soviet Union, thereby arriving at more secure borders. A working paper drawn up by the State Department in July 1945, for President Truman in preparation for the conference had the following to say:

> Cession of this area to Poland . . . could reduce the Polish-German frontier to 250 miles and provide Poland with its most defensible frontier in the West.[63]

Indeed, comments by Roosevelt, Churchill, Stalin, Truman, and Attlee, quoted by the Polish jurists, bolstered this argument. Thus, for example, the Poles quote Churchill's explanation in Parliament of the need to hand German territories in the north and west to Poland.[64] Some time later (May 24, 1944), he referred to these territories as a "good, adequate, and reasonable homeland in which the Polish nation may safely dwell."[65]

An excerpt of a speech broadcast by Truman on August 9, 1945 was quoted with similar intent. In this speech, delivered after the Potsdam conference, Truman explains to the nation the compromise which, he argues, was obtained in the matter of Poland. Although the President stressed that the final demarcation of the borders would wait until the peace conference, the Polish jurists chose to emphasize the following sentences:

> The territory the Poles are to administer will enable Poland better to support its population. It will provide a short and more easily defensible frontier between Poland and Germany. Settled by Poles, it will provide a more homogenous nation.[66]

As viewed by the Polish jurists, these examples proved that the borders set and agreed upon by the Big Three had regarded the security element as one of the major factors.

4. The fourth Polish contention stressed the intrinsic relationship between shifting borders and relocating heterogeneous populations. The two operations were mutually supportive and shared one goal: strengthening Poland's security while creating, as Truman said, "a more homogeneous nation."

The idea of transferring national minorities and exchanging populations with intent to make a state nationally homogeneous had not been invented for the case of Poland. It had been tested in modern history.[67] In this context, the Polish arguments recall the population exchanges between Turkey and Greece (1919–1922), the relocation of the Karelian refugees to Finland, the transfer of millions of Muslims and Hindus between India and Pakistan, and the population exchanges in the Middle East resulting from the Arabs' war against Israel.

In view of Poland's (and its neighbors') bitter experience with the minorities problem in general and the German minority in particular, the recurrence of the deleterious phenomena accompanying the matter had to be prevented. The new Polish state had to be as ethnically homogeneous as possible, and the expulsion of the Germans, the Polish jurists said, was "an act of self-defense."[68] The Allies, too, reached the general conclusion during the war that the minorities problem, which had weighed so heavily on the states of Europe in the interwar period, had to be solved radically by means of population transfer.[69]

Churchill's blunt comments in Parliament on December 15, 1944, about the proposed shift in borders are often cited in this context. To disabuse his fellow MPs of any lurking doubts about the allusion he had used, Churchill added with emphasis that this would have to be accompanied by the disentanglement of populations in the east and in the north. Expulsion, Churchill reasoned, was the most satisfactory and lasting solution available. There would be no troublesome mixture of populations, as there had been in Alsace-Lorraine. Nor was Churchill worried by the prospect of the disentanglement of populations, even a large-scale one, for modern conditions made this an easier matter to attend to than it had been.[70]

Soviet spokesmen, too—obviously—supported the Polish arguments. A pertinent example was provided by Soviet Foreign Minister Andrei Vishinsky:

> The Soviet Government believes that one of the practicable ways of solving ethnic problems when a conflict of national interest is involved, is to free one country from persons allied by descent with another country and to settle these persons in favorable conditions in their fatherland.[71]

This combination, said the Polish jurists—security and ethnic/national arguments, the economic and demographic imperatives stemming from the need to resettle millions of Poles from the eastern territories, and Churchill's remark—made it clear that the matter discussed at Yalta and Potsdam was the expulsion of Germans from all Polish territories, including the liberated areas. The German revengistes' claim that the Big Three had decided in Potsdam to expel Germans from "Old Poland" alone, and not from the western territories, was conceptually, legally, and politically groundless. Describing the expulsion he envisioned, Churchill had used the word "total."

As for the scale and methods of effecting the transfer, the Polish spokesmen (basing themselves on German sources as well) argued that most of the German residents had in fact left every locale spontaneously, not necessarily as a result of the Potsdam resolutions or decisions of the Polish Government. Even according to West German sources, about half the German population formerly populating the lands east of the Oder and Western Neisse reached German soil in large-scale flight and evacuation ordered by the Nazis. The figure would undoubtedly have been higher still had it not been for the Red Army's rapid advance. These facts support the Soviet delegation's contention at Yalta and Potsdam that the German population was quitting the territories east of the Oder and Western Neisse by its own initiative.[72]

5. Modern history, the events concerning Poland, and the Yalta and Potsdam resolutions all led to the conclusion that what really mattered was the reinforcement of Poland's national homogeneity, political sovereignty, and territorial integrity, the Polish jurists said. In the current context, they defined the German demands as to "self-determination" and "every man's right to his homeland" as revengiste propaganda.

Of course, the Poles admitted, the right to self-determination was one of the fundamentals of contemporary international law. But so were sovereignty and political-territorial integrity. The right of individuals to settle and dwell where they choose is anchored in the principles of international law and the covenants governing human rights. It is a far cry, however, from this to the interpretation offered by the German revengistes. A national minority does not always and under any circumstances have the unrestricted right to secede from the political framework in which it has been cast, with intent to create an independent political framework in its place. Clearly, the individual's right to settle in a certain territory was one thing, while the right of an entire people to self-determination and the creation of an independent state was another.[73]

This confusion of concepts, the Polish jurists continued, was nothing but an extension of the Nazi arguments. These, even before the war, had rested on "the right to self-determination" for the German minorities in the neighboring countries—even as they rejected other peoples' right to self-determination and other states' right to independent existence. German minorities, riddled with hate and riding a tide of "self-determination," organized themselves into fifth column formations and served as springboards for German expansion and aggression. However, the right to self-determination, awarded today to all nations, cannot be exercised at the expense of others.[74] Now invoking Soviet doctrine, the Polish jurists went on to argue that the right to self-determination was admittedly recognized and important as a general norm, but not as the highest and most decisive norm of international law. Borders between states had to be set as peoples wished, taking account of factors such as ethnic composition, the history of the territory in question, and security concerns. Practical application of the right to national self-determination had to comply with the circumstances, needs, and historical peculiarities of neighboring states.[75] Not all irridentism was justified, and not every demand by a national minority to secede from an existing political framework had to be met. And if any contradiction arose between the right to self-determination and sovereign interest, "Socialist doctrine has raised territorial integrity to the rank of a fundamental principle of contemporary law."[76] Citing American jurists, too, the Poles stressed that self-determination was only one of the principles that had to be honored in international relations.[77] The preservation of peace and international stability were also ethical and political demands of the highest order, of which account had to be taken.

For this reason, the "plebiscites" (which should have expressed the desire for self-determination) were not accepted in theory or practice as an exclusive, recognized, and decisive instrument in the setting of international borders and the awarding of political independence to various ethnic groups. On the contrary. Apart from one instance (the transfer of a certain piece of land from Italy to France), all territorial changes after World War II were conceived and implemented without plebiscites.[78]

6. One might assume that pundits, statesmen, and jurists brought up on historical materialism would not base their reasoning on the exploits of feudal princes and Absolutist kings, who terrorized their environment for centuries. Here we are in for a surprise. The Polish jurists invoked historical reasoning, too, in claiming the right to re-inherit lands controlled by the 10th century Piast Dynasty—the cradle of the Polish nation, which had been overtaken by generations of German penetration and expansion.[79] They cited written accounts, history books, and the presence of Polish-Slavic ethnic groups that remained in the "liberated territories" (about a million strong) despite centuries of Germanization.[80]

They quoted from a Soviet declaration issued on January 11, 1944, which ruled unequivocally that "Poland must be reborn . . . through the restoration [to her] of lands which belonged to her from time immemorial and which were wrested from Poland by the Germans."[81] They made frequent use of remarks by Molotov on April 9, 1947: "In the west Poland has returned to her ancient lands which were once the cradle of the Polish state.

Her present territory corresponds to the historical areas Poland possessed under the Piast dynasty."[82] Neither did the Polish jurists refrain from mentioning the "historic" dialogue in Yalta (April 10, 1945). Already then, Molotov had tried to infuse the western border problem with a "historical dimension." Roosevelt, who must have regarded Molotov's proposal as a mere cynical diplomatic ruse meant to dress the territorial bartering in historical attire, had posed—as will be recalled—a question that was innocent in form but sarcastic in tone: "How long ago had these lands been Polish?"[83]

The Polish jurists, however, considered this question irrelevant. The fact that ancient parts of the homeland had been controlled, occupied and settled by Germans neither weakened nor undermined the Poles' historic attachment and right to return to them and restore their rule there. The principle of *Restitutio in integrum* had no statute of limitations, and "A document from the year 1200 has as much legal validity as evidence as a document from 1951,"[84] as proved in deliberations before the International Court of Justice in The Hague. Thus "historical rights" played an important role, or in any case had to be taken into account, in the Polish arguments.

7. The West's claims about the "temporary" nature of the western borders—with which the Germans, too, concurred—were categorically rejected by the Poles, with a certain measure of logic. The attempts of the German revengistes to turn the clock of history back, the Poles said, could neither negate the truth nor rewrite reality. The Big Three at Potsdam had accepted the conventional legal doctrine by which matters are deliberated according to the principle of *Uti possidetis*, i.e. a situation arising as a result of and following a war (*status post bellum*).[85]

True, the Potsdam resolutions stipulated that the final delimitation of the western border would have to wait until the general peace arrangement, but this, Polish Foreign Minister Modzelewski asserted, had been said "merely for formalistic reasons."

The Big Three had deliberately and explicitly agreed, after protracted and difficult deliberations, to set Poland's border at the Oder-Western Neisse line. The fine distinction between "final delimitation" and " final determination" was semantic alone, the Polish jurists argued. The emphasis on "finality" merely indicated a need to fine-tune a border whose details had already been determined.[86] After all, there was no disputing the fact that the border had been set at the Oder-Western Neisse line. As proof, two decisive processes incorporated into the Potsdam resolutions stressed that this border was for good:

a. Definition of the territories to be handed to Poland as "formerly German."[87] Had the formulators of the Potsdam resolution intended to set a different border in the future, they would not have used this term in description of these territories.

b. The resolution on transferring the German population from these territories into Germany. The creation of an *iunctim* (two-way linkage) between handing the territories east of the Oder-Western Neisse line to Poland and the expulsion of the Germans deliberately and preemptively obviated the possibility of turning the clock back and undoing the territorial changes.[88]

Surely no one in Potsdam had imagined, the Poles argued, one could temporarily transfer millions of people and subsequently re-transfer them back.

Thus the Polish Government summarized its viewpoint in a communiqué on April 10, 1947:

> The Polish Government considers the question of Poland's western frontiers as being decided and finally settled in accordance with the decision of the Yalta and Potsdam conferences, as well as in accordance with the agreements on the transfer of the German population, concluded with the Allied authorities on the basis of the Potsdam Agreement.[89]

8. If all these arguments were not enough, the Poles threw in the facts that had been created in the meantime. Important among them was a Polish population of close to eight million.

***

Thus the frontier was fashioned. It went through all the necessary stages: preliminary negotiations, crafting of instrumentalities for implementation, physical occupation, settlement and integration of the territory, and the installation of boundary markers along the line. Today it is part of Europe's physical, political, and economic reality. No one can reasonably content that there is any chance of its being changed. As Manfred Lachs says, it is backed by history and the realities of life. Thus anyone who describes it as a problem that is "pending" or that has to be "settled" is simply raising an artificial issue. There is no one with whom to settle it.[90]

Let us therefore summarize all the arguments as follows:

A. Border changes following a war of self-defense are justified, as are the aspirations of a state that has been attacked to adjust its borders so as to make them secure and defensible.
B. Ethnic homogeneity is a desirable objective, and population transfer is justifiable.

C. "Self-determination" is not a supreme value or norm in international law, especially when it jeopardizes a state's sovereignty and territorial integrity.
D. Historical rights, too, should be taken into account when setting frontiers.
E. The clock cannot be turned back, and facts created cannot be uncreated.

Everyone knows that legal principles do not create political reality, but rather the opposite.* We nevertheless considered it correct to present the arguments of the Polish jurists, which, from the moment they were made public, became part of the corpus of international and Polish legal doctrine. Even though they were conceived under a particular and defined set of circumstances, they do not necessarily become null and void when set in a different reality.

Border Agreements Between Poland and the Two Germanies

Any idea of trying to cast doubt on the "finality" of Poland's western border was delivered a stinging blow in 1950. On June 6 of that year, the Polish government and the provisional government of the Democratic Republic of Germany (DDR)—Poland's next-door neighbor—issued a joint communiqué recognizing the existing borders and viewing them as a permanent and "inviolable frontier of peace and friendship which does not divide but unites the two people."[92] The "thaw" processes and Chancellor Willy Brandt's *Ostpolitik* ultimately led to recognition of these borders by the Federal Republic of Germany.

Brandt's far-sighted policy led him to recognize not only the existing facts but also the historic responsibility of the German people, which had to pay for its crimes and acquiesce to the change that had occurred:

> We understand Poland's desire to live at last within guaranteed borders, and not to be a "state on wheels." A reconciliation with Poland is our moral and political duty. . . . Perhaps the declarations we have offered . . . can be formulated . . . in such a way that the present borders of Poland can be recognized . . ."[93]

---

*As expressed by Abba Eban, "It is more frequent for legal advisers in the Foreign Office to give judicial sanction to what their ministers want, than for ministers to change their policies as a result of legal advice."[91]

Indeed, West Germany signed a non-aggression treaty with the Soviet Union two years later, on August 12, 1970. On November 20 of the same year, it concluded an agreement for the establishment of diplomatic relations with Poland. The first paragraph of this agreement included German recognition of Poland's western border:

> The Federal Republic of Germany and the People's Republic of Poland state in mutual agreement that the existing boundary line . . . running from the Baltic Sea immediately west of Swinemünde, and thence along the Oder River and along the western Neisse to the Czechoslovak frontier, shall constitute the western state frontier of Poland.
>
> They reaffirm the inviolability of their existing frontiers . . . and declare that they have no territorial claims whatsoever against each other.[94]

The heads of State, convening in July, 1975 in Helsinki for the Conference on Security and Cooperation in Europe, lent full international support to the territorial status quo resulting from World War II.

The signatories to the conference's "Final act" established the principle by which the participating states recognized each other's borders as inviolable.[95]

Thus Poland's borders achieved full international recognition.

Poland Today

Thus the new State of Poland came into being. It was admittedly smaller than before, but was rather large and well endowed with natural resources. Its borders were shorter and more convenient than in the past, providing ample access to the sea. It was ethnically homogeneous, and was fully equipped and able to develop its indigenous culture. This Poland came into being by virtue of the struggle of its citizens and their aspiration to be free and independent. However, its contours, frontiers, and regime were in great part reflections of Stalin's will. Its domestic system of government, foreign and defense policy, economy and army, all remained linked to and even rather dependent on the decisions and requisites of Moscow.

***

Today, Poland is a respected and strong link in the Communist bloc. As domestic events there have proved, however, the past—with its memories and dreams, its grandeur and its disappointments—is not inclined to die easily. Under the thick layer of Communist internationalism and proletarian solidarity, the flame of national liberty still flickers.

PART THREE

***

Finland—The ''Winter War''

Chapter Thirteen

The Thunderhead Looms

On October 5, 1939, Foreign Affairs Commissar Vyacheslav Mikhailovich Molotov summoned the Finnish Minister in Moscow, Count Yrjö Koskinen, and asked him to forward an urgent missive to Helsinki. The note contained an official invitation for the Foreign Minister of Finland, Eljas Erkko, to come to Moscow for discussion of "certain concrete political questions."[1]

This rather uncommunicative invitation came with something that sounded like a command: the answer must arrive within 48 hours.

The government of Finland was in no rush to reply. Therefore, the Russian envoy in Helsinki, Vladimir Derevyanski, approached Erkko three days later and expressed "wonderment" that Finland was not behaving as were its Baltic neighbors.

Erkko, a huge, portly man and a Finnish presslord, was not agitated by the Russian diplomat's enquiry. "I do not know how the other Baltic states were invited to Moscow," he said. "Finland discusses the matter in the accepted manner and way." Erkko's tranquility and "business as usual" attitude were undoubtedly in keeping with typical Finnish stolidity and firmrootedness, and reflected the Foreign Minister's confidence in Finland's stability and durability. Had he studied the recent past and the present more painstakingly, he would perhaps have given the matter a different, more prudent reading—for any number of reasons.

The Finnish People's Right to Self-Determination

The Finnish people had not yet celebrated the twenty-second anniversary of their independence. Five hundred years of Swedish rule, followed by another century under the Russians, had neither obfuscated nor uprooted their distinctiveness. In its vast country, far from cultural centers and international events, abundant in forests, teeming with lakes, and subject to harsh climatic conditions, the Finnish people—although ruled by foreigners and technologically backward—had kept its culture intact, revived its language, developing its customs and democratic institutions, and in the end, on December 6, 1917, declared its independence.

On December 31, Lenin recognized Finland's independence, in keeping with his stance on "the right of peoples to self-determination" and a statement he had made in May of that year:

> It must be declared to the Finns that they are entitled to decide their destiny in their own way . . . We are for Finland receiving complete freedom, because then there will be greater trust in Russian democracy and the Finns will not separate.[2]

Those who wonder about the conceptual dichotomy of a Finland that lives in "complete freedom" and that "will not separate" must pave their own way through the intricacies of Marxist-Leninist dialectics and understand that even when two people say the same thing, it is not always the same thing. One person's idea of "the right of peoples to self-determination" is not necessarily the other's.

Lenin, as we know, consistently supported the "right of peoples to self-determination," including their right to break away from foreign nations and establish independent national states.[3] He perceived this right not only as a theoretical principle but also as an efficient vehicle for attaining practical political aims, and as an instrument of use in dismantling the Tsarist empire and building the Socialist revolution on its ruins.[4]

Lenin's doctrine—voiced at length in his speeches and writings, and expounded in harsh polemics with Karl Renner, Otto Bauer, Nikolai Ivanovich Bukharin, Rosa Luxembourg, Karl Radek, and other Marxist theoreticians—was obviously far from "bourgeois" political outlooks. He found Marxism to be inconsistent with simple nationalism, however "just," "pure," refined and cultured a given brand of nationalism might be, and sought to replace it with internationalism—the fusion of all nations into a higher unity.[5] He regarded national movements, particularly those in Central and Eastern Europe, as products of inequality resulting from imperialist repression and enslavement. This being the case, a people would exercise its right to self-determination in only one way: separation and liberation.

However, just as Marxism predicted the disappearance of the state upon the dissolution of class society, so did Lenin foresee an end to nations' need to self-segregate. Under the future Socialist regime, the sources of repression and inequality would be done away with, and so, de facto if not de jure, would nations' need to dissociate. Cession would become meaningless, contentless, and nonexistent.[6]

As J. Talmon puts it:

> If in the future, societies—let us call them nations—were to become so one-dimensioned, indeed merely sections of a homogeneous, one-dimensioned mankind, what would the right of self-determination signify? Surely, it would be of no relevance. Just as in a classless society no one would have reason to complain of being unfree and wish to assert his independence, so in a socialist world no nation would have any reason or possibility to oppress another, and thus none would have cause to complain of being oppressed.[7]

Thus, according to Bolshevik dialectic doctrine, the "right to self-determination" was only an indispensable stage in the progress of the proletariat and mankind—a progress that would reach its climax in the existence of the Soviet Union. Thus the seeming contradiction between a "completely free Finland" and one that would "not separate" did not stop Lenin from recognizing Finland's independence on the one hand, and expecting the eruption of a proletarian revolution in the selfsame country on the other hand. The latter development would certainly lead to Finland's voluntary reunification with Soviet Russia.[8] This expectation did not come to pass, and Soviet Russia was sorely disappointed.

The Soviet leadership's dissatisfaction with the "bourgeois" character of free Finland was expressed by Stalin, whom Lenin had instructed (in 1913) to specialize in the problems of nationalism.[9] Stalin came out against the Finnish Social-Democratic Party, and, in a speech delivered around the time of Finland's declaration of independence, said the following:

> In fact, the Council of People's Commissars against its will gave freedom not to the people, but to the bourgeoisie, of Finland, which by a strange confluence of circumstances has received its independence from the hands of Socialist Russia. The Finnish workers and Social-Democrats found themselves in the position of having to receive freedom not directly from the hands of socialists, but with the aid of the Finnish bourgeoisie.[10]

Bluntly and harshly Stalin attacked the Finnish Social-Democrats for their "hesitancy and cowardice." Everyone whose ears were attuned to this message understood it as a call for revolution and direct action toward an ascent to a "higher stage" of socialist internationalism. All this, "of course," would be undertaken in a spirit of peoples' right to self-determination and "free will."

The message was received in Finland, and the Finnish left, aided by Soviet soldiers stationed on Finnish soil, took up arms. In January 1918, a brutal, bloody civil war broke out in Finland between "Reds" and

"Whites," and was put down only in April of that year by Gen. Gustav Mannerheim with the help of German forces. The Finnish Civil War was noted not only for its revolutionary and class motives but by the depth of the combatants' hatred for each other, a hatred worse than any other—that between brethren. The magnitude of the eruption of violence loosed by the intrinsically taciturn, stiff, and chilly denizens of the north threatened to unravel the fabric of national existence. The thousands of casualties tallied as the battles died down, and especially the harsh fate reserved for the "Red" POWs, left deep wounds in the heart of the Finnish nation that took years to heal. (About 1,500 were murdered in the "red terror," close to

Marshal G.C. Mannerheim

7,000 fell in battle, 8,300 "Reds" were executed after the "White" victory, and 80,000 were taken prisoner, of whom 9,000 died.)[11]

The Treaty of Tartu and Finnish Neutrality

After the Finnish government regathered the reins, the Russian leadership recognized Finland's independence and sovereignty, and, on October 14, 1920, lent this recognition practical significance by signing a treaty at Tartu establishing the border between the two countries. Finland ceded the eastern portion of the Karelian Isthmus and two border districts, Porajärvi and Repola, to the Soviet Union for the defense imperatives of Leningrad and the region to its north, and agreed for the same purpose to demilitarize and neutralize several islands in the Gulf of Finland. The Soviet Union, in return, left Western Karelia and the Petsamo area in the north under Finnish sovereignty.

In 1932 Finland and the Soviet Union signed a mutual nonaggression pact (extended in 1934 to remain in effect until 1945), reaffirmed the Tartu treaty, and agreed to resolve any possible future conflicts through friendly negotiations.

Finland declared itself neutral like its Scandinavian neighbors, and believed that, through its agreements with the Soviet Union, its independence would be honored and preserved. A short-lived period of calm and hopeful independence ensued. But the traumas that swept the world during the 1930s—especially with respect to the Soviet Union's neighbors—did not spare Finland. Expecting war to break out and apprehensive of a German invasion, the Soviet Union began to apply pressure to the Finnish government.

Since April 1938, and for close to a year, the Soviets and the Finns had been conducting secret negotiations in Helsinki—a strange dialogue in the context of conventional diplomatic protocol. Moscow was represented by Boris Yartsev, a member of the secret service who nominally served as second secretary of the Soviet Legation (and who worked behind the back of his superior, the Ambassador). The Finnish were represented by Prime Minister Cajander, Foreign Minister Holsti, and Finance Minister Tanner.

This odd set of negotiators was better suited to a political spy novel than to serious talks.

An explanation for this unconventional method should perhaps be sought in the Russians' hostility toward and general suspicion of "bourgeois diplomacy." However, they were most suspicious of the Finns' intentions. They attributed no real value to the Finnish Government's declarations of intent to remain neutral, and did not rely on Finland's neutrality in the event that the Germans decided to attack Russia through or from Finnish territory. Furthermore, the Russians doubted that Finland could halt a German offensive if one were launched; the prevailing state of mind in Finland, too, was not altogether anti-German.

Indeed, wide and important public circles in Finland had been cultivating relations—culture, science, trade, and friendship—with Germany and Germans for many years. Recall, too, that the "Red" insurrection had been put down with the help of German army units, and that German influence in Finnish army ranks had been palpable during the 1920s and the 1930s. Thus, for example, the Army's supreme commander during the 1920s had been replaced, under pressure by the officer echelon, by one of the German-educated officers, who established the Finnish "hunter battalion" (*Jaeger*).[12]

Moreover, an attempt was made in independent Finland's early years to have Kaiser Wilhelm II install his son, Oskar, as King of Finland. When nothing came of this, the Eduskunta (parliament) decided in October 1918, to "settle" for Prince Frederik Karl of Hessen. Only Germany's defeat and capitulation in World War I ended these monarchist schemes.[13] The Finns were not excessively perturbed by the Nazis' ascent to power, and actually greeted the infamous Munich accord with a sigh of relief. (This, admittedly, did not necessarily reflect pro-German sympathies; it may have expressed an easing of fear, previously rife, of an outbreak of war between Germany and the West. Such a war, the Finns believed, would leave Finland totally at Soviet mercies.)[14]

For all these reasons—fear of German aggression, suspicions as to the Finns' philo-German tendencies, and lack of faith in Finland's ability to stand up to German intrigues—the Soviets now presented a number of demands. The "second secretary" of the Soviet Legation opened by demanding of the Finnish Prime Minister a Finnish undertaking to actively resist any German aggression and forcibly oppose German intentions to use its territory as a springboard for an attack on the Soviet Union. Furthermore, Moscow demanded the island of Suursaari in the Gulf of Finland as the future site of a naval and airforce base. The major thrust of the Soviet proposals as presented by Comrade Yartsev, however, was that Finland would have to appeal to the Soviet Union for aid if it found itself unable to honor these commitments. Deterred by this more than anything else, the Finnish government rejected Moscow's proposal, arguing that it "tends to violate Finland's sovereignty and is in conflict with the policy of neutrality which Finland follows in common with the nations of Scandinavia."[15]

To underscore its neutrality, Finland joined Sweden and Norway in rejecting Germany's offer of a non-aggression treaty on May 16, 1939. (Denmark broke ranks and signed; a year later, the Germans conquered Denmark anyway.)

The Ribbentrop-Molotov Agreement and its
Application in the Baltic Countries

Word that Ribbentrop and Molotov had signed an agreement (August 23, 1939) aroused no special concern in Helsinki. On the contrary: the prevailing assumption was that the agreement between the two mighty rivals augured for Finland, too, a period of peace and quiet. The Finns would obviously have taken a different view of the matter had they known the contents of the secret appendix to this agreement, establishing that Finland, Estonia, Latvia, Lithuania, and Bessarabia would belong to the Soviet "sphere of influence."[16] On September 25, Stalin notified German Ambassador Werner von Schulenburg that it was the Soviet Union's intent to "immediately take up the solution of the problem of the Baltic countries in accordance with the Protocol of August 23," and that it expected "the unstinting support of the German Government" in this matter.[17] That same day Molotov and Estonian Foreign Minister Selter, visiting Moscow for discussion of trade issues, met for talks. The latter quickly realized that the Foreign Affairs Commissar was hardly interested in export-import problems. Instead, Molotov expressed severe displeasure that a Polish submarine, the Orzeł, had managed to slip out of Tallinn port. This, Molotov ruled, proved that Estonia was incapable of assuming responsibility for defending and policing the Baltic Sea. Now Molotov opened his briefcase and pulled out a draft he had prepared of "a Soviet-Estonian treaty for mutual military aid," under which the Soviet Union would be permitted to establish military bases in Estonia and station an agreed-upon number of soldiers there. When Selter tried to protest, Molotov begged him not to force the Soviet government to invoke "more radical measures." He also advised Selter not to count on German assistance: "I am sure the German Government will support our proposal." Indeed, as the Estonian minister found out immediately, the German Government—a party to the conspiracy—began to evacuate its civilians and other ethnic Germans from Estonia.

Selter signed as demanded on September 28, and the Russians won the right to establish bases in Estonia. The next step, implemented immediately, was additional Soviet pressure on Estonia. To drive the point home, the Soviets moved an infantry division, an armored brigade, and aircraft into Estonia on October 18.[18]

Now it was Latvia's turn. The Latvian Foreign Minister was summoned to Moscow on September 30, reported on October 2, was received with all honors due a foreign minister, and, three days later, was presented with a document that he signed. Lithuania was next. On October 11, its Foreign Minister, too, signed an agreement calling for "mutual military aid." Each minister was promised, as recorded explicitly in the treaties, that the Soviet "proposals" were motivated by defense considerations alone, and that the Soviet Union had absolutely no intent to do even inadvertent harm to its neighbors' ideational posture, social order, or economic system.[19]

These assurances sound like crude jokes to us today, but the Baltic governments believed them and certainly wanted to believe them. They were quite relieved at the thought that by paying this price they had secured their continued independence. Shortly thereafter, all talk of Baltic sovereignty and independence became hollow rhetoric.

In any event, Russia had reason to believe that Finland, too, would fall into line, and that "friendly persuasion" would extract the concessions "required for the security of the Soviet Union" from this country, too.

The Finns, however, were made of different stuff.

After receiving the Soviet summons on October 5, the Government of Finland decided to send a delegation to Moscow headed by Juho K. Paasikivi, who was serving at the time as the Minister in Stockholm and who in 1920 had negotiated with the Soviets at Tartu. The Finnish Minister in Moscow, Yrjö Koskinen, a senior Foreign Ministry official, Johan Nykopp, and an Army officer, Colonel Aladar Paasonen, were appointed as his aides. The Finns refrained from including the Foreign Minister or anyone of ministerial rank in the delegation as a signal of their displeasure at the phrasing of the summons and their intent to reject attempts at diktat. The Government of Finland still did not know exactly what Moscow meant by "concrete political questions." However, since the general intent had been evident as far back as the Yartsev talks, and because reports of developments between the Soviet Union and Finland's Baltic neighbors had already begun filtering into Helsinki, Paasikivi was instructed to stress the following points:[20]

    A. The Tartu treaty, Finland's neutralist policy, and its being a small nation all prove that the sovereign existence of Finland presents no danger to the security of the Soviet Union.

    B. Finland, in the future as in the past, will resolutely defend its independence, safeguard its territorial integrity, and prevent any possible use of its territory for purposes of war.

    C. Finland opposes all territorial concessions and the establishment of Soviet bases on its soil. (Here, however, Paasikivi was given a small amount of leeway. If under extreme pressure, he might cede several little islands in the Gulf of Finland close to Leningrad, though not Suursaari Island. Any concession must be based on the principle of territorial compensation reasonable to Finnish and international public opinion).

D. Discussion of a "mutual military aid" treaty is out of the question, inasmuch as such a treaty constitutes a violation of Finland's neutrality.

Chapter Fourteen

Talks in the Kremlin

On the ninth of October—one of those overcast, gray autumn days typical of Helsinki, with the Baltic wind whipping in from the Gulf through the marketplace, the homes, and the streets to Senate Square—Paasikivi and his associates reached the Helsinki train station. The monumental structure, designed by Saarinen, an architect whose international renown reflected on the entire Finnish nation, bustled with people. They were not rushing for trains. Rather, they were citizens of all walks of life, who had learned of the delegation's departure and the purpose of its trip. The gravity of the historic moment could be sensed within the station confines.

The Finnish delegation leaving for talks in Moscow (Paasikivi second from the right)

Diplomat-author Max Jakobson described the events thus:

> They stood there quietly and solemnly, until someone started to sing and then the men took off their hats, and all joined in the national anthem and Luther's hymn, "God is My Castle." And all along the route, wherever the train stopped, there were more crowds to sing courage and faith into the hearts of the nation's representatives. Nor was this an empty gesture; it was a pledge that the people were prepared to redeem, with their blood and their lives if necessary. That was more than could be said of the diplomatic notes delivered in Moscow. The Kremlin knew exactly what those notes were worth. But apparently it failed to take into account the song of the Finnish people.[1]

The Finnish Government took several precautionary measures the next day, calling up several units of reservists (by years of birth) in numbers the Soviets would not interpret as a provocation, for "extra refresher courses." In fact, it was a partial and camouflaged mobilization meant to reinforce the existing deployment.[2]

Stalin's Demands

On October 12, the delegation was ordered to report to the Kremlin that afternoon. There it was greeted with a surprise; Stalin himself was waiting for them at the head of the Soviet delegation (which included Molotov, Potemkin, and Derevyanski).

Though no formal agenda had been set, there was no need for one because, as Jakobson remarks:

> There is a permanent Finnish-Russian agenda, and it has only one item: how to reconcile the stubborn Finnish will to independence with the Great Power ambitions of Russia?[3]

Stalin brought up several ruminations and demands, all of which violated the directives Paasikivi had received from his government.

"It is not the fault of either of us," he began, "that the geographic circumstances are as they are. We must be able to bar entrance to the Gulf of Finland. If the channel to Leningrad did not run along your coast, we would not have the slightest occasion to bring the matter up."[4] Several implicit conclusions suggested themselves: true, the border set during the reign of Peter the Great (1721) was optimal for Russia's security,[5] but the Soviet Union was prepared to settle for less. To secure Leningrad, the following were essential:

A. To bar entrance to the Finnish Gulf by artillery fire from the north and the south;

B. To adjust the border in the Karelian Isthmus area.

Therefore the Soviet Union asked Finland to lease it the Hanko area for 30 years. The Finns' arguments against any territorial concession were inconsistent with historical facts, Stalin claimed. Indeed, "Russia had sold Alaska to the United States and Spain ceded Gibraltar to England."[6] The Soviet Union intended to establish a naval and land base for 5,000 soldiers. From it, and from Paldiski on the Estonian coast (west of Tallinn), they could seal the opening to the Gulf with long-range artillery crossfire and prevent any possible attempt at naval incursion—English or German—in the direction of Leningrad. "We are on good terms with Germany now, but in this world anything may change." Finland was asked to contribute to Leningrad's defense by handing over several islands, including Suursaari, and to adjust the border on the Karelian Isthmus. The reason was simple: the border was too close. Russia already had cannon capable of firing 60 km., and if Finland were to acquire such cannon Leningrad would come into artillery range. Leningrad had a population of 3,500,000, roughly equal to all of Finland. "We can't move Leningrad, so the line has to move. We ask that the distance to the line should be seventy kilometers, not thirty-two as it is today. That is our minimum demand . . . " To underscore "delicately" how modest this was, Stalin mentioned something Ribbentrop had disclosed to him: Germany had gone to war against Poland because its border was too close to Berlin—only 200 km. away. "They had to move it." Indeed, it was now 300 km. farther away than before. Neither were these geographic "rectifications" restricted to the southern front alone. The Soviet demands, summarized in a detailed memorandum,[7] also called on the Finns to cede the western part of the Rybachi Peninsula, because of the danger facing the large Soviet naval base at Murmansk and the nickel deposits that the English and the Germans were ogling;[8] to destroy their border fortifications (the Soviets would reciprocate on their side) because they "prevented relations of peace"; and to bolster the bilateral non-aggression pact by adding a stipulation to the effect that neither side would participate in such groupings of alliances of powers as may be hostile to the Soviet Union or Finland.

Stalin hastened to emphasize how generous the Soviet Union's demands were: "We ask for 2,700 square kilometers and offer more than 5,500 (in the Karelian regions of Repola and Porajärvi) in exchange. Does any other great power do that?" he asked rhetorically, promptly replying in the tone of a Cossack who had been swindled, "No. We are the only ones that simple." The fact that they violated existing agreements and treaties, neighborly relations, and Finland's security interests and sovereignty, was of no particular concern to the Soviet leadership. "Of course we didn't have any legal or moral right for our actions against Finland . . . ," Khrushchev subsequently wrote with cynical frankness. "As far as morality is concerned, our desire to protect ourselves was ample justification in our own eyes."[9]

The Soviets' approach was therefore based not on right-makes-might but on a doctrine they perceived as natural and obvious: might makes right. Invoking this right, they demanded that the Finns, who certainly posed no threat to the Soviet Union, take the security interests of Leningrad into account.

The Finnish Government's Stance

The gaping abyss between the two sides, reflecting profound differences with respect not only to the actual demands but to the concepts as well, became apparent in the very first session. Both sides adhered to their declared positions; each ignored the other's point of view.

The Finns believed it their natural and legal right to preserve their independence, sovereignty, and territorial integrity. They wrapped themselves in the Tartu treaty, offered a series of legal rationalizations, and proffered strategic explanations designed to prove that if Leningrad faced any menace, it was not from the direction of the Gulf of Finland. Vehemently they argued that their neutralist policy prevented the exploitation of their territory by a third state for any purpose, let alone an attack on the Soviet Union, and that this neutrality was the best guarantee of regional peace. Acquiescence to the Soviet demands, they said, would result in Finland's being accused, either by the British or by the Germans, of offering one power its unilateral support and undermining peace and stability. Their neutrality, they argued heatedly, was not a paper tiger: the Finnish Army would forcibly resist any attempt to invade Finnish territory.

All this fell on deaf ears. The Russians disbelieved Finland's protestations of neutrality on two scores: suspicion that the Finnish leaders harbored anti-Russian, pro-German and pro-English tendencies and sentiments,[10] and doubt that an anti-Russian Finnish leadership would honor this declared neutrality, let alone defend it, if war broke out. Even if they sincerely tried, one could not conclude that such neutrality would indeed be respected (by Germany, for instance). I assure you that it's impossible. The powers will not permit it, said Stalin.[11]

Stalin's dread of a German or English invasion of the Soviet Union through Finland also pervaded his considerations (his pact with Hitler was still in its infancy, and his suspicion of Hitler was still keen). In such a case, he believed, the Finnish army, even if it did its best, would not be able to stop the invaders.

Thus while the Finns considered their neutrality sufficient guarantee not only of Finland's independence and security but even for the security of Leningrad, its value to the Russians was nil. To them, it was not even viable, let alone reliable. The Finns did not understand this.[12]

Neither did they appreciate the true gravity of the situation, especially when matters at the first session still progressed on calm waters. The Russians assumed that "friendly persuasion"—a little pressure here, a little temptation there—would make the Finns more malleable and compliant. The prevailing atmosphere in the talks was rather relaxed. Paasikivi, a man of rich political experience who knew the Russians, was actually impressed by Stalin's "charming" personality and sense of humor. Furthermore, the Russians behaved differently toward the Finns than toward their Baltic neighbors, and not a tone of threat emerged from their statements. The talks were businesslike, and Stalin did not doubt the logic of his proposals. When Paasikivi pointed out how very hard it would be for Finland to cede the territories demanded of her, Stalin sarcastically dismissed his arguments and asked him to compare the few kilometers being asked of Finland to the territories Germany had taken from Poland. When Paasikivi tried to explain to the Russians the "woes" of democracy—the need to bring the proposal up for discussion in the Eduskunta (parliament) and for ratification by a special five-sixths majority—Stalin showed no sign of concern. "You are sure to get 99 percent support," he said, being accustomed to this proportion of "national consensus." Molotov added confidently that "We'll sign the agreement on the twentieth and give you a dinner the next day."[13] Thus the first round of the talks ended, and Paasikivi returned to Helsinki to report to his government and receive its directives for the continuation.

A Majority in the Finnish Cabinet for a "Firm Stance"

Although it agreed to soften some of its positions and proposals somewhat, the Cabinet reaffirmed its opposition to the major Soviet demands. The Foreign Minister and others of like mind argued that if the government displayed consistency in its resistance, the Russians would back down. The senior Army commanders, who were summoned to the meeting for their professional opinion, also favored rejection of the Soviet demands. Handing over Hanko was especially out of the question, they said; this would leave a dangerous hole in Finland's defense posture and permit the Soviets to create a bridgehead that would threaten the vital areas of Finland. Border rectifications in the Karelia region, to the extent demanded by the Soviets, would deny Finland its natural defense zone, the Great Lakes area, and leveling the border fortifications ("the Mannerheim Line") would weaken Finland's military and political posture.[14] The chief of staff, Lt. Gen. Lennart Oesch,[15] noted that the existing border was Finland's shortest defense line, and that shifting it as required by the Russians would make it twice as long.[16] Armed with these guidelines, in which there was really nothing new, the delegation headed back for Moscow with a stronger composition. By Paasikivi's request, Finance Minister Väinö Tanner, a Socialist Party leader, joined the team. The Finns were greeted not only by representatives of the Soviet Foreign Ministry's protocol section but by thousands of red flags and posters all over Moscow in honor of the opening of an agricultural exposition. A gigantic poster carried a favorite slogan of the Party Secretary-General, Comrade Stalin:

"We do not want an inch of foreign territory, but neither do we want to cede an inch of our own territory to anyone."

En route to the Finnish Legation building, the delegation members pondered the extent to which this handsome dictum, especially its first half, reflected political realities. The two delegations met on October 23, and when the Finns gave Stalin their answer to his proposals he rejected it forthwith. The Soviet position, he said, was a bottom-line one over which there would be no bargaining. After about two hours of deliberations, the atmosphere no longer calm, Molotov asked a question that reeked of threat:

"Is it your intention to provoke a conflict?"

"We want no such thing," answered Paasikivi, "but you seem to."[17] Stalin said nothing, simply smiling in his usual enigmatic way.

Thus the session broke up, and the Finns returned to their quarters with intent to head back to Helsinki the next day. Only a short time passed when a special courier summoned them to return to the talks. Stalin greeted them with a broad smile, as if nothing of importance had just happened. He then produced some new, ostensibly generous proposals: fewer Soviet troops stationed in Hanko (4,000 instead of 5,000), less extensive territorial demands on the Karelian Isthmus, and acceptance of the Finnish stance as to a nonaggression pact. Because even these proposals violated the government's directives, this session, too, ended without results. The delegation returned to Helsinki and reported to the Cabinet for a penetrating, protracted debate (October 27–28). Although Marshal Mannerheim had warned that Finland was not ready for war (inadequate equipment, ammunition for only two weeks, etc.), and urged that a solution that would avoid war be sought, the majority rejected his contentions and dismissed the very possibility that war would break out. Foreign Minister Erkko stuck to his original reading of the situation: the Soviet Union would apply pressure and issue threats, but would not embark on war. As evidence, he pointed out: "Its chargé d'affaires here has called urgently today to inquire whether Finland planned to break off the negotiations, and he was gratified to hear that we intended to continue them."[18] Defense Minister Juho Niukkanen not only agreed with Erkko but went so far as to dispute Mannerheim's figures. If war nevertheless broke out, he asserted, Finland could hold out for half a year.

Influenced by these arguments and trends of thought, the Cabinet (and, the next day, the Parliament's Chairman and faction leaders) concluded that Finland would under no circumstances agree to the establishment of a Soviet base at Hanko, which would violate Finland's status as independent and neutral. However, Finland would be willing to arrive through negotiations at an agreement that would include some adjustment of the border on the Karelian Isthmus (much less than the Soviet demands), arrangements on Suursaari Island taking into account the security interests of both Finland and Leningrad, willingness to cede several small islands (Lavansaari, Tytarsaari, Seiskari, and Peninsaari) in the eastern part of the Gulf of Finland, and cession of the northwestern part of the Rybachi Peninsula. The Soviet demand for destruction of the border fortification was vehemently rejected. These, the Cabinet resolution asserted, were meant solely for defense and the preservation of Finland's neutrality. Composing his latest directives to the delegation, Erkko convinced himself to write the following:

> The Russians do not want a conflict. Nor will they risk a fiasco before the eyes of the whole world when they have waiting for them a ready-made agreement: the islands of the Gulf and a defense ring around Petersburg.[19]

The Russians, however, were of a different mind, and even expressed this in a way that left Finland flustered.

Molotov: "The military's turn"

While the delegation members were making their way again to Moscow and eating their fill in the restaurant at the Viipuri station, they received a phone call from the Foreign Minister in Helsinki. The previous evening, October 31, Molotov had disclosed the details of the negotiations in a public address before the Supreme Soviet.[20] The Cabinet and the delegation were stunned. "In Finland," Tanner writes, "we had constantly striven to preserve the strictest secrecy so that injured feelings might not affect the course of the matter. Even the Diet members had been sworn to silence. And now the opposing party had exposed the case to the whole world."[21] Indeed, the Soviets' tactic and their use of the communications media (unlike normal "quiet diplomacy") had brought an element of prestige into the picture. From now on, the Soviet Union would find it hard to trim its demands. In Helsinki, however, once the shock had ebbed a little, the matter was written off as mostly an exercise in fear-mongering. "This tactic worked against Estonia," Erkko informed the delegation by telegram, "but we are calm. The Russians must be shown a firm stance."[22] The delegation spent almost two weeks in Moscow. The negotiations broke off from time to time when deadlocks developed. Special events, too, such as the anniversary of the Revolution and deliberations of the Supreme Soviet, forced the Soviet leaders to absent themselves. The talks progressed at a frustrating pace. They were producing nothing, and the Finns were about to pack their bags on several occasions.

The Cabinet's rigid guidelines had tied the delegation's hands, and the envoys' diplomatic leeway was limited in the extreme. This was especially galling to Paasikivi, who, with Tanner listening in, accused Erkko of inflexibility and of attempting to shirk responsibility by threatening to resign. The Finns, he said, had been living for 20 years under the illusion that they could determine their own fate freely. Their Scandinavian orientation was erroneous, he added: "Our geographical position bound us to Russia."[23]

He knew that even the Marshal was not at ease with the course of events. Just before the delegation set out, Mannerheim had told him, "You absolutely must come to an agreement. The army cannot fight."[24] The orders from Helsinki, however, were unequivocal.

After days of difficult and frustrating deliberations, something like a threat was voiced again by Molotov, who headed the Soviet team: "We civilians can see no further in the matter; now it is the turn of the military to have their say."[25] But always, just as the negotiations appeared to be on the verge of collapse, Stalin would step in as the savior, throwing in an alternative proposal, ostensibly more flexible than its precursor. Not for the first time—and not for the last—the tactic of the "good guy" appearing after the "bad guy" was employed. Indeed, it cannot be said that this tactic didn't work. Even a seasoned politician like Tanner could not rid himself of the impression left by Stalin's ostensible "moderation." "From all we could see," Tanner writes, "we have received the impression that Stalin was ernestly for agreement.... Furthermore, he had sought compromises...."[26] At first he patiently and repeatedly explained his basic demands. Painstakingly he stressed to his guests that of all Russian regimes, only the Soviets, unlike the Tsars and Kerensky, had accepted the principle of Finland's independence. Now he demanded a modest gesture in exchange for his generosity: Hanko. Finland could choose the terms—sale, lease, territorial exchange, anything—so long as a Soviet base for the defense of Leningrad be established in Hanko. When the delegation rejected this demand again, Stalin produced alternative proposals that looked like concessions but demanded a Soviet foothold at the western entrance of the Gulf of Finland. "If not Hanko," he asked, pointing at a map, "perhaps the group of islands Hermansö-Koö-Hästo, Busö, near Hanko?" Then he tried a different tack: "Would you perhaps give up *this* island [pointing at Russarö]?" When the Finns spurned all these proposals, and since the Cabinet prohibited their suggesting the island of Jussarö, east of Hanko, as an alternative, their counterparts in the talks were visibly puzzled. By the same token, Stalin rejected the Finns' alternative proposals with respect to Suursaari and border adjustments in Karelia as insufficient. "On that patch of land you offer us we would sit as though on the point of a sharpened pencil," he summarized with a shrug.[27]

The Finnish position surprised Stalin but did not dislodge him from his intent. On the other hand, the Finnish Foreign Minister misread Stalin's apparent willingness to appease Finland as his (Erkko's) wishful thinking indicated: proof that the hard line was paying off. As evidence, Stalin had backed down. It actually looked that way. Even when the talks broke down, the delegation hoped they would resume. Such things were known to happen, and one never knew what Stalin still had up his sleeve. Stalin did bid the delegation a friendly farewell. Even Molotov's usually poker-face expressed an attitude of "till we meet again."

The delegation tarried another four days in Moscow in fruitless expectation of new instructions from Helsinki, boarding the train only on November 13. Two trains, one may say, began fateful voyages that day, ignoring the warning signals on the tracks leading to an inevitable collision.

Collision Course

Both sides misread each other's intentions and signals, and failed to treat the threat behind their designs as seriously as was warranted. As noted above, the "firm stance" position was represented in the Cabinet by Foreign Minister Erkko and Defense Minister Niukkanen, usually with the support of Prime Minister Cajander and President Kallio. Erkko was convinced that the Russians would retract their pressure and dangerous demands when faced with an unequivocal, proud, and consistent stance. The inverse was also valid: any Finnish concession would provoke further pressure. He considered every new alternative presented by Stalin during the talks as confirmation of his assumptions, and dismissed the possibility of war as so much hollow threat and bluff. Erkko was not alone in his assessments; in the later stages of the negotiations he had backing both in the Cabinet and in the Diet. The masses that bade the delegation bon voyage every time it set out from Moscow from Helsinki, and that lined the route, reflected both the nation's anxiety for independence and its desire to strengthen the negotiators' steadfastness against Soviet pressure.

The Finns had talked themselves into thinking that this Soviet pressure, which had persisted intermittently for a year and a half, would ultimately peter out if only met with consistent resistance. The Russians, in turn, thought they would encounter no difficulty in getting what they wanted out of Finland. They were prepared to tone down some of their demands as a matter of tactics, but there would be no retreat on the main points. The standard assumption of Stalin and his comrades, in Khrushchev's descriptive language, was that "All we had to do was raise our voice a little bit, and the Finns would obey. If that didn't work, we could fire one shot and the Finns would put up their hands and surrender. Or so we thought."[28]

Both sides were wrong, and the result was a collision.

It is proper at this point to examine not only why the Finns misread the situation but also how and why they dared resist the demands of the neighboring power, demands which, in the view of some observers, appeared over time as being "framed on a rational basis [and providing] greater security to Russian territory without serious detriment to the security of Finland.[29] A decisive majority in the Finnish leadership saw the matter differently. When the details of the demands became known, too, a decisive majority of Finnish public opinion concurred.

The factor that particularly concerned the Finns was not only, and not necessarily, the specific set of Russian territorial and military demands. Above everything else was the fear of undermining or even totally losing their independence. Thus we should understand their qualified willingness to approve certain territorial concessions and their resolute resistance to other territorial demands—especially in the Hanko area. The trauma of 1918 was still etched in the consciousness of many Finns. After this experience, and in view of events across the Gulf in the three Baltic countries, the Finns feared the Russians even when they offered generous territorial compensation; they wanted neither the Russians' sting nor their honey. They were afraid that the cession of Hanko and too extensive a retreat on the Karelian Isthmus would give the Soviets a foot in the door, leading to further Soviet demands for a deeper penetration and full takeover. The Russians, argued Defense Minister Niukkanen, would interpret any concession as a sign of weakness and would respond with further pressures.[30] A rare combination of attributes of the "national character," too, contributed to the Finns' vehemence.

What was Finnish about the Finns? A sense of ethno-cultural uniqueness, a will to go to any length to safeguard the freedom and independence they had won after hundreds of years of foreign rule; their adherence, as a nation of farmers, to every speck of land defined as Finnish; honesty (unsophisticated, perhaps); faith (naive, perhaps) in the values of ethics, religion, promises, agreements, the written word and the signed treaty; and a physical and spiritual toughness tempered in generations of struggle with unusually harsh climatic and natural conditions.

The Finns indeed proved that they were a tough people, as expressed by Soviet Foreign Trade Commissar Mikoyan[31] ("*tvyordyi narod*"), and they fortified their resistance to Soviet pressures with trust that Finland would not remain alone in its time of trial. The Finnish leadership thought that if matters indeed came to a crisis or even war, their nearby friend and neighbors, the Scandinavians, led by Sweden, would rush to their aid.

Their traditional sentiment for Germany encouraged them to believe that this country, too, despite the Ribbentrop-Molotov pact, would not let the Soviet Union rout Finland.[32] Ascribing great prestige to the Western powers, the Finns were convinced that even the great democracies would rally to the aid of this small, democratic state in its showdown with the totalitarian titan. Their morale was indeed boosted substantially upon word of Roosevelt's letter of October 10 to Soviet President Kalinin. The American President expressed deep concern about the deterioration in Soviet-Finnish relations; he would withhold recognition of relations based on the use of force, he wrote, and hoped that relations of friendship and peace would prevail between the two countries.[33]

Finland's optimism, nourished largely by innocent wishful thinking, was also based on rumors which floated in from foreign countries.

The noted Swedish scholar-explorer, Sven Hedin, conferring with Hitler in mid-October, was informed by the German dictator that Finland had no reason to fear a serious conflict with the Soviet Union. The Scandinavians and the British, too, voiced on various occasions the prevailing assessment in their countries that the Soviet-Finnish discord could be resolved through negotiation, and that war was not imminent.[34] The Italian attaché in Moscow reported to his government on November 23 that the Russians, so the diplomatic community in Moscow believed, would not resort to armed force.[35]

All these appraisals and communiqués, relayed to Helsinki or detected there, helped strengthen Finland's optimism and illusion of security with each passing day. The protracted and fruitless negotiations persuaded many that the Soviets, facing consistent Finnish resistance and steadfastness, would ultimately back down. All their maneuvers, this doctrine held, were scare tactics in a war of nerves.

Prime Minister Cajander said in a speech that Finland would not submit to becoming a satellite state of some kind, either by force of a war of nerves or attrition or by reasonable, fair promises. He believed the present situation could persist for a long time, and that the Finnish people had to get used to living and working under these changed circumstances—to plough while carrying a gun.[36]

***

The delegation returned to Helsinki to find an ambience of surrealistic calm. The fact that nothing had come of the talks was of no concern to the policy-makers. True, they said, there was no accord, but neither had there been a Russian ultimatum. The situation was conveniently interpreted as a moratorium; surely the talks would resume, and under better conditions. After all, the Soviets had spent the past 20 years talking about its commitment to peace and good neighborship. Why, if so, should anyone fear that the Soviet Union would want to twist its little neighbor's arm just because it stood up for its rights?[37]

This terrifyingly innocent trend of thought developed new momentum every day. People evacuated from the capital to the villages began to return to their homes. Reservists called to arms began a gradual demobilization. Strips of paper pasted over show windows to protect them from ricochets were torn down. The Government announced that schools would reopen on December 1. Life began to slip back in to routine. Foreign Minister Erkko expressed confidence that nothing would happen, at least, for sure, before spring: "They won't invade in mid-winter,"[38] he told Paasikivi, advising him to take a vacation.

Some were not swept away by this kind of thinking; however quiet things seemed, several prominent Finns were anxious. Paasikivi, who thought that anything, including peace and nothing at all, could transpire when the negotiations first began, now reached the conclusion that Finnish policy was wrong from the ground up. "We had lived 20 years in the lap of an illusion," he confessed to Tanner:

> Now we ought to fight, but we could not. Finland could not undertake a war. If it broke out, we would lose it, and in that case the result would be much worse than any we should reach through accommodation. The infection of Bolshevism would spread into Finland and it would lead us to final ruin.[39]

Incidentally, he spurned Erkko's generous offer and did not go on vacation.

Mannerheim, too—who knew the Russians even more than Paasikivi did, and who was highly regarded as a supreme military authority—warned against the optimism that had overtaken the Government and the public. As happens at times—against conventional wisdom—it was a man in uniform who took the rational, moderate, and sane point of view, while the civilians espoused extreme political assessments born in ideological preconceptions, speculation, and dilettantism.

Mannerheim believed the Soviet Union would not hesitate to resort to force to attain its aims. It had inherited the Tsars' pan-Slavic aspirations and dressed them in Communist ideology.[40] The Soviet Union could not yield to Finland on the main points of its demands for reasons of prestige, too. Build-ups of Soviet military forces in the Leningrad, Karelia, and Petsamo areas were surely cause for concern. All indications showed that the situation was grave, and that the Soviets might stage a provocation to justify an attack on Finland.

Relying on these assumptions, Mannerheim insisted on maximum caution and efforts to reach a compromise.[41] Finland had neither the ability or the will to cope militarily with a great power, he warned; its army was not properly equipped, and its ammunition would last only two weeks.[42]

He recommended several concessions which surpassed the Cabinet's proposals. Both he and Paasikivi advised the Cabinet to take an initiative that would lead to the resumption of negotiations. Their view was not accepted. Nothing would happen, they were told, if only Finland learned how to resist pressure.

It is worth noting here with appreciation, if not astonishment, the high level of democratic spirit in Finland during those difficult days. Paasikivi and Mannerheim, who did not conceal their ruminations and their dissent from the prevailing trend of thought, were not assailed by the majority, nor even by Government spokesmen, as "defeatists," "traitors," or "collaborators with the enemy." It also bears mention that both were affiliated with prominent right-wing circles—the former as representative of the conservative Farmers' Party, and the latter as a member of the officer aristocracy.

Neither were they forced out of their jobs. Indeed, the former was trusted with difficult, fateful negotiations, while the latter was subsequently handed the supreme command at the age of 72.

Their views were rejected but respected. They, too, knew how to respect and accept the verdicts of the majority, however ill-advised and disastrous they appeared to them.

***

The quiet that settled in after the collapse of the Moscow talks was just the calm before the storm. The facts that caused so many Finns to misread the situation and the Russians' intentions can also be attributed to a state of confusion that had temporarily overtaken the Kremlin. Thus the Finnish government's belief that the Soviet Union would back down if met by a Finnish "nyet" was fundamentally erroneous.

Judging by Khrushchev's comments quoted above, we may easily understand that the Russians were simply unprepared for the possibility that a small nation would dare disobey them; indeed, they had not imagined such a thing happening. Furthermore, Finland had been treated fairly, by Russian standards, throughout the negotiations. Stalin had honored the Finnish delegation by participating in person. The Soviet proposals were relatively moderate and included generous territorial compensation. And no attempt had been made, by explicit threat or bluster, to frighten the Finns during the talks.

And behold, the stunned Kremlin leaders said to themselves, how a little country rewards the mighty power for its generosity! Admittedly, the Russians were prepared to find the Finns tougher than the other Baltic peoples, but they had not imagined that they would be so stiff-necked as to issue an arrogant refusal. The only logical explanation the Kremlin leaders could accept was that the Finns were being egged on by the British and the Americans.[43]

Molotov, for example, hinted at such an assessment in a sarcastic response to Roosevelt's letter. In a speech on October 31, the Foreign Affairs Commissar said:

> Even the President of the United States considered it proper to intervene in these matters. . . . In a message to Comrade Kalinin, the Chairman of the Presidium of the Supreme Soviet, dated 12 October, Mr. Roosevelt expressed the hope that friendly and peaceful relations between the USSR and Finland would be preserved and developed. One might think that matters are in better shape between the United States and, let us say, the Philippines or Cuba, who have long been demanding freedom and independence from the U.S. and cannot get them, than between the Soviet Union and Finland, who long ago obtained from the Soviet Union both freedom and independence.[44]

Therefore Molotov saw fit to warn the Finnish leaders against " . . . yield[ing] to anti-Soviet pressure, or to incitement from any quarter."[45]

Because this warning was no more effective than the Russians' territorial temptations, and because the Finns did not "knuckle under" as expected,[46] the Kremlin was somewhat puzzled as to what its next step ought to be.

Admittedly, the Soviet General Staff had contingency plans for an offensive on Finland, but these had been drawn up in the event that a Western power threatened or continued to use Finnish territory for offensive anti-

Soviet purposes. No such plan covered the actual situation that had developed. It was clear by now that something more than "a single shot" was necessary.[47]

The Kremlin did not remain confused for long. There is support for the belief that the Kremlin decided to teach the Finns a lesson under the influence of the Party Secretary in Leningrad, Andrei A. Zhdanov. The issue, of course, came under his purview and responsibility, and he pressed for an immediate military resolution. His view, shared by the Army, was that the Finns could easily be brought to their knees, and that the forces under the Leningrad area command would suffice for the purpose.

This view was based not only on an estimate of the volume of military forces, but on a conceptual hypothesis as well. The Finnish proletariat, the thinking went, would lend its support to the Red Army, and the Finnish soldiers, the sons of laborers and farmers, would turn their weapons on their officers.

Similar appraisals, displaying ignorance of thought and developments in Finnish public affairs, began to surface in the Soviet press, confirmed and reinforced by "experts" sitting in Moscow. These pundits were a group of Finnish communist exiles led by Otto Kuusinen, who had resided in Moscow ever since the defeat of 1918 and had been out of touch with Finnish realities and developments ever since. Kuusinen, a Comintern Secretary who had been involved in planning the campaign against Finland, argued that once the Red Army invaded the country, a regime friendly toward the Soviet Union, led by the Finnish Communist Party, would come into being.[48]

Even leading members of the exiled Finnish Communist cell, however, resisted Kuusinen's designs. Finnish Communism, yes, but not the enslavement of Finland to the Soviet Union's intentions of takeover. The Secretary-General of the outlawed Finnish Communist Party, Arvo Tuominen, shared this view. On November 21, while in Stockholm, he was ordered to report to Moscow and assume the leadership of a new Finnish government which would take office once the "liberating" Red Army crossed the Finish border. Although a veteran, loyal Communist, he understood that the talk of liberating Finnish workers from the yoke of capitalism was fueled by resurgent Russian imperialism.[49] He rejected the demand and spurned further entreaties.

First Thunder

However, as stated, the momentary confusion passed, and the Kremlin decided that the time for verbal talk was over; artillery would henceforth do the talking. The first seven shells landed on November 26, less than one kilometer from the border on the Soviet side near the village of Mainila. Molotov summoned the Finnish Minister that evening and brandished a letter of protestation. The Finnish artillery attack, the letter read, had killed four Russian soldiers and wounded nine. The incident proved that the proximity of Finnish forces to Leningrad not only threatened the city but constituted an act of hostility in and of itself. Thus the Finnish forces were called upon to retreat 25 kilometers behind the border.

The "Mainila incident" has been a Soviet provocation. Not only had the shells not been fired by the Finns, but all their cannon, it was shown, were so far from the border as to be out of firing range.[50] The Finns' answer and their offer to conduct a joint investigation was not honored with any pertinent response.[51]

However, in another note dated November 29, Molotov informed them that due to "additional attacks" (fictitious, of course) by Finnish soldiers, the Soviet government was "forced" to break off relations with Finland.

Then, taking to the airwaves, Molotov announced that the present Finnish government, having become involved with imperialist powers hostile to the Soviet Union, was not interested in preserving normal relations with the Soviet Union. The only aim of the Soviet measures, he continued, was to guarantee the Soviet Union's safety, especially that of Leningrad. The USSR had no dispute with the "real" Finland, but in its relations to the Soviet Union, the Finnish government had to adopt not a hostile but a friendly attitude, so that a unanimous attitude could be brought to bear on the great problems of concern to both peoples.[52]

Now the Government of Finland opened its eyes to see its optimistic predictions going up in smoke. Urgently it formulated a new, conciliatory note, offering to reach an accord with the Russians for a pullback of its forces on the Karelian Isthmus to such a distance that no doubt about Leningrad's security would remain.[53]

The Soviets answered the next day.

Chapter Fifteen

War

In the morning of November 30, 1939, the streets of Helsinki filled with children and adults on their way to school and work, Soviet aircraft suddenly broke through the clouds, dove, and dropped their bombs on downtown. Only afterwards were the sirens and the barking of anti-aircraft cannon heard.

Thus the "Winter War" began.[1] (Radio Moscow called Helsinki's reports of the attack "provocations" and claimed that the planes had merely dropped bread for the starving Finnish proletariat. Thereafter the Finns called the Soviet bombardments "Molotov breadbaskets").

The Finnish Army

Can one speak of a "balance of forces" between David and Goliath? Can one compare the strength of 4,000,000 Finns (3,695,617 by official count in 1940)[2] with that of the Soviet Union's 190,000,000? The dry figures are nevertheless worth mentioning in order to understand the essence of the Winter War and the valor of the Finnish people.

The Finnish army comprised a small core of regular officers and NCOs, and conscript forces on one-year call-up. In peacetime this army was 33,000 strong, and could in emergencies be augmented by reserves (active reserve duty lasted 31 years).

The country was divided into nine territorial commands; in an emergency, each command was supposed to mobilize one division, equip it with its own emergency depot, and move it to its theater and positions within two weeks. In addition to this force of 127,800 (14,200 to a division), there was a supplementary reserve of 100,000 older men and a similar number in a civil guard. A women's corps (*Lovta Svärd*), also roughly 100,000 strong, handled nursing duties through the medical corps as well as clerical, cooking, laundering tasks, etc.[3] Thanks to the partial mobilization in October, the Finns had been able to retrain much of the army, deploy it, and even organize a 10th Division by November 30.[4] Inadequate equipment was the Achilles' heel. Mannerheim had taken no few occasions to warn of this, but the budget he had sought in 1938 (to outfit 13 divisions) was not approved.[5] Now he accused the Finnish politicians of having thwarted his attempts to strengthen the army and nurture its ability for many years, claiming that defense of the country had been made into a partisan issue from Finland's first year as an independent nation. The largest parties in Parliament had stubbornly opposed even small appropriations, and only when it was too late did they realize where such a policy led.[6]

Because of this and other blunders, the army's vital needs had long been unmet. Its equipment was scanty, the supply of arms from Sweden was not assured, and Finland's own military industry was of limited utility. Thus when the war broke out, no division had more than 250 submachine guns (of local manufacture), 116 machine guns, eighteen 81-mm. mortars, and 36 field cannon (all of pre-World War I vintage). The entire army had at its disposal another 174 cannons (even more obsolete) and 100 anti-tank guns, most positioned for the defense of cities. (With anti-tank guns in short supply, the Finns, with their ability to improvise, used bottles filled with inflammatory liquids—later known in the vernacular as "Molotov cocktails"—to stop tanks). Tanks were almost nonexistent, and there were no more than 100 aircraft (18 two-motor bombers, 48 fighters, and 34 reconnaissance planes). Rifle and machine-gun ammunition would last for two months by the Government's estimate, and two weeks by Mannerheim's.[7] There were artillery shells for twenty days, and aviation fuel for one month.[8] Communications relied on runners and field telephones. The small navy had nothing to do; the sea and the lakes were frozen over.

Soviet Forces on the Finnish Front

Facing these scanty forces was the Red Army, with the might of the Soviet Union behind it. The common assumption in the Kremlin, as stated, was that the affair would end easily and quickly (within three days, as Soviet diplomats in Berlin predicted).[9] Nevertheless (perhaps just to be sure), sizable forces were sent into action. At the initial stage the Soviet array included 26–28 divisions (17,500 men to a division, or close to half a million men), 2,200 artillery pieces, 1,200 tanks, and 800 aircraft.[10] The Russian quantitative edge was also reflected in the almost unlimited quantity of ammunition and firepower of their infantry. While the Finnish artillery came with 640 shells per gun at the beginning of the war, every Russian gun was provided with this quantity of ammunition every day of combat.[11] The Soviets' quantitative advantage was also evident in reserves: scanty on the Finns' side, relatively unlimited on the Soviets'.

Indeed, while the number of Soviet divisions in action hovered around 13 at any single stage of the war, the total number of Soviet divisions used during the war was 45, including 1,500 tanks and some 3,000 aircraft.[12]

Thus the Finns should have stood no chance. Just the same, they had several advantages that justified their willingness to dare to confront the Russians, and explained their ability to fight magnificently.

The first was motivation. The Finnish soldier was defending his land and freedom, and he knew it. All Finns, including members of the Communist Party—on whose support Kuusinen was building his plans—closed ranks to resist the Russian enemy. The Army's morale, like that of the nation, was high, and the Finnish soldier was fit to fight, durable, and full of initiative. From early childhood he was used to coping with difficulties of nature. He was brought up to undertake physical and athletic effort. His toughness and individualistic character prepared him for guerrilla warfare, audacious action in small units, and initiative. The skis he had used since childhood were his battle wagon. They permitted him to cover tremendous distances, take the enemy by surprise in the depths of the snow-covered forest, draw his blood, and vanish as quickly as he had appeared. All this was quite the opposite of the character, attributes, and combat tactics of the Russian soldier.

The Russians, Mannerheim believed, had two major weaknesses: ineptitude and inability to fight on skis. The Russians knew it, and began to train their men in these methods when the war broke out. That effected no real change, because such tactics are not learned in a few weeks.[13]

In addition, the Russian soldier, courageous and durable though he was, was trained primarily for combat in large formations and was unable to take his own initiatives. The Russians were prepared to attack the Finnish positions by wave-after-wave assault, to move against them in tight formations, and even to sing as they advanced—vaulting fences, crossing minefields, and progressing into enemy fire while shouting "hurrah" and paying no heed to the percentage of those falling. However, they were helpless, lethargic, and timid in situations especially typical of the Winter War: frequent clashes with *bielaja smert*—the "white death," small Finish commando units in white battle fatigues, gliding soundlessly on their skis in the snowy forest. The Russian soldier, of course, also lacked the strong motivation of people defending their homes. In general, the Russian soldier was poorly trained, and his officer was poorly equipped to command. The Russian airforce, too, was not adept at exploiting its numerical advantage, and its achievements were confined to bombarding cities and dropping supplies to cut-off Soviet units. Statlin's "great purge" of the Army during the 1930s had undoubtedly left its mark.

Terrain

The Finns made good use not only of the natural conditions but of topography. In their combat methods and operational planning, the Finnish generals displayed originality and adroitly exploited the character of the Finnish soldier, the natural conditions, and the terrain, refraining from blindly adopting combat methods used elsewhere.

One who studies the map of Finland is liable to draw the impression that the eastern border, more than 1,500 km long, could serve as an easy gateway for the Russian invader. The Finns were well aware of how wrong and misleading this was. The entire border was lined with swamps, lakes, and forests that no modern army could cross. The few poor roads traversing these natural obstacles precluded any deployment of the advancing units. They would have to progress in rear columns, exposing themselves to Finnish flanking raids.[14] The major danger, the Finnish command knew, came not from the long eastern border but from the narrow Karelian Isthmus. Mannerheim's decision to concentrate most of the forces there (six of out of ten divisions) was a daring and far-reaching strategic decision of which he had spoken in the 1920s. Then work had begun on establishing a line of firing positions and ground obstacles about 70 km. long between the Gulf of Finland to the west and Lake Ladoga to the east. The great advantage of this array (subsequently nicknamed the "Mannerheim Line") was that it sealed the Isthmus. The territory all around, carved by lakes and rivers, was crisscrossed with trenches, barbed wire fences, anti-tank obstacles, and minefields. Concrete fortifications—about 75 in number—had been erected in the 1920s at the points most critical for defense. However, they were effectively useless and obsolete by the time the war broke out, because new Soviet artillery could penetrate them. There were 44 new, effective bunkers that Soviet shells could not penetrate, but they did not come with effective anti-tank weapons[15] and, in fact, had no equipment heavier than machine guns. The flanks of the "Mannerheim Line"—at Koivisto in the west and near Lake Ladoga in the east—were fortified with banks of vintage heavy artillery.

Postwar Soviet propaganda described the Mannerheim Line as a mighty and impenetrable chain of fortifications, built under the supervision of foreign experts using the Maginot and Siegfried Lines as models.[16] This phrasing was undoubtedly meant to explain the failures of the Red Army after the fact. Mannerheim dismissed the Soviet exaggerations as "complete nonsense." "The 'Mannerheim Line,' he said, was the Finnish soldier stationed in the snow. It was not the strength of the position that made the line effective, the Marshal ruled. Rather, that it held was entirely due to the tenacity and courage of the Finnish soldiers.[18]

Be this as it may—and the truth is certainly in the middle—the Mannerheim Line was a serious obstacle to the Red Army's progress in the most important theater of battle.

If this account puts the cart before the horse, it does so to stress that when the few take on the many—as the Finns did against the Russians in the winter of 1939–1940, and as small nations have against their mighty enemies throughout history—they are not necessarily committing suicide after having taken leave of their senses. For the Finns, as in other cases, it was an act of courage and will, based on qualitative and natural advantages, which augured some prospects for success, albeit limited.

The Deployment of Forces

The major Finnish and Russian forces were deployed along the Karelian Isthmus front. On the Russian side was the 7th Army (later divided into the 7th and 13th) under Gen. Meretskov. It included 12 to 14 divisions (of which 7 saw front-line action), an armored corps with about 1,000 tanks, and several artillery brigades. Its task was to capture Viipuri and then move west. The Finns countered it with the "Karelian Army" under Lt. Gen. Österman, which included the 2nd Corps under Lt. Gen. Öhqvist and the 3rd Corps under Major General Heinrichs. West of the Viipuri was the reserve 6th Division under Major General Laatikkainen. All in all, seven divisions were stationed on the Finnish side, which, in part, deployed along the Mannerheim Line. The 8th Soviet Army (seven infantry divisions and two tank brigades) was deployed north of Lake Ladoga. Its major task was to breach the Finnish array and break through for an attack on the Mannerheim Line. The Finnish line was defended by the 4th Corps (2 infantry divisions and guard and auxiliary units), under Major General Hägglund.

Across from the vast, sparsely populated "waist" of central Finland (from Repola in the south to somewhere past Salla in the north) the Russians stationed the 9th Army. Its five divisions operated independently from one another along a broad front, plying the few and poorly maintained traffic arteries. Its major task was to bisect Finland. The 14th Soviet Army (three divisions), stationed in Murmansk, was responsible for the rest of the border north to the Arctic Ocean.

Against these eight divisions (comprising infantry, armor, and artillery), along a front roughly 1,000 kilometers (625 miles) long, from Suojärvi in the south to the Arctic Ocean in the north, the Finns were able to station only the "northern group" under Major General Tuompo. This was the name given to a thin line of strongholds, outposts, and positions held by platoons, companies, and battalions of a total strength not exceeding 13,000 soldiers. In the northernmost area, Petsamo, a Finnish infantry company and an artillery unit with cannon manufactured in 1887[19] faced a Soviet division. At the rear, around the city of Oulu (on the Gulf of Bothnia) stood the 9th Division, which, together with the 6th Division, served Mannerheim as a strategic reserve. Thus the forces stood as the war began.[20]

Soviet Expansionist Aspirations

To this day there is controversy in Finland as to the Soviets' long-term intentions and goals, and whether the war could have been prevented had the Government of Finland made more sweeping concessions. There is no absolute, unequivocal answer. Did the Soviets mean to extract only certain necessary territorial concessions for the defense of Leningrad, as Stalin claimed, or to gradually "Sovietize" Finland and draw it into the Soviet orbit, as the Finns suspected? Either way, it is clear that the Soviet's behavior toward Estonia, Lithuania, and Latvia sounded alarm bells in Helsinki and throughout Finland. So long as the Kremlin archives remain sealed and their documents classified, there is no chance of deciphering the issue thoroughly. What is evident, however, is that the secret appendix to the German-Soviet nonaggression treaty (the Ribbentrop-Molotov agreement) of August 23, 1939, placed Finland, together with the three Baltic countries, in the Soviet Union's "sphere of influence."[21]

Moreover, two events—the establishment of a puppet government under Kuusinen (see below), and remarks by Molotov in the Supreme Soviet on August 1, 1940—provide a clear hint as to the Soviet Union's expansionist aspirations and imperialist thinking. At that time, with the Soviet-Nazi pact still in its infancy and the war with Finland over, the Foreign Affairs Commissar permitted himself to speak with a measure of frankness. His comments clearly reflect the Soviet Union's wish to "recover" all the territories and populations that the imperialist Western powers had "stolen" from it during its military weakness after World War I. Molotov asserted with undisguised pride that the Soviet Union had augmented its population by 10,000,000 by annexing Lithuania, Latvia, Estonia, Bessarabia, and northern Bukovina, and had added another 13,000,000 by attaching western Ukraine and western Belorussia:

> Now they have been reunited with the Soviet Union . . . Their entry into the Soviet Union will . . . greatly enhance their security and at the same time still further increase the might of the great Soviet Union.[22]

Neither did Molotov conceal the fact that the Soviet Union meant to move its border to the shore of the Baltic Sea and its ice-free ports.

Because the facts are still debatable, the only possible answer from a historical standpoint should be sought in the realities of those days and the perspectives and states of mind that dominated public opinion, the Parliament, and the Cabinet.

Three of the leading figures—Mannerheim, Paasikivi, and Tanner—had been far more reserved than their colleagues, and counseled prudent action, moderation, and efforts to compromise with the Soviets. They remained in the minority, however, because the general mood in Finland at the time categorically rejected any concessions. In view of the neutralist and constitutional perceptions prevailing in Finnish political thinking, too, the Cabinet could not have behaved differently than it did. The Cabinet considered neutrality Finland's best defense, particularly when the international waters were stormy. Concessions to the Soviet Union, the Cabinet believed, would be interpreted in the friendly West as an abrogation of neutrality and an indication that Finland had joined the Nazi-Soviet alliance.

With respect to the Constitution, the Cabinet would have had to obtain a special 5/6 majority in parliament for any accession to Stalin's demands, had it wished to make any. Any such attempt was doomed to a stinging failure (despite Stalin's confidence that "99 percent support" would be forthcoming). The concessions the Cabinet was called upon to make—had it wanted to make them—would have forced it to prepare the psychological and political ground and wage a public struggle liable to last for months. It did not have this time at its disposal.

By contrast, the Cabinet's total support in the Parliament and public opinion for its "firm stance," and the response of the Finnish people to the war thrust upon it, proved that the Cabinet knew and correctly expressed its electorate's wishes and state of mind.[23]

The Kuusinen "Government" Affair

The Finnish people, which had not expected war to break out, greeted it with steadfast morale that could not be shaken by the "Molotov breadbaskets" that landed in the streets of Helsinki.

The spirit of volunteerism was high. The call-up proceeded according to plan. The public responded to the Government's summons, and within a short time more than 200 million Finnish marks and additional gifts flowed into the State treasury. Quite a few industrial plants and businesses not only paid half salaries to their mobilized workers as required, they began to give supplements based on the number of children.[24] Facing the Soviet Union's attempt to appropriate chunks of Finland's territory and independence, the ranks closed and a broad national consensus emerged.

The national consensus also reflected widespread recognition of the fact that it was time to reshuffle the Cabinet. Risto Ryti, Chairman of the Board of the Bank of Finland (Progressive Party), replaced Cajander as Prime Minister, and Tanner (Social-Democrat) replaced Erkko as Foreign Minister. Paasikivi, too, joined the Cabinet as a Minister without Portfolio.

These changes were supposed to signal to the Soviets that Finland meant to soften its stance, mainly by displaying willingness to resume the negotiations and avoid the continuation of war. The signal was left unanswered. The Soviet Union showed disinterest in the composition and intentions of the new Finnish Government. Now, in keeping with tactics used in other countries, the Soviets already had an alternative government ready for Finland. This practice was always explained, of course, along "ideological" lines. After all, it was inconceivable that the Soviet state would force itself on little countries as the capitalist states did. Its army too, the Red Army, would never wage wars of occupation and repression. It acted only to "liberate," as called upon by the repressed proletariat in a neighboring country. Thus the Russian Army had not fought against Poland in 1920; it had merely helped the Polish revolutionaries who were resisting Pilsudski's repressive regime. In September 1939, too, it rolled westward only when Poland had disintegrated and the Ukranian and Belorussian brethren needed protection.* Now it was necessary to defend the Finnish people against its capitalist, reactionary regime—especially when a new, truly democratic government had arisen in its place, a people's government, the Government of Comrade Kuusinen.

As stated, Moscow had spent several weeks organizing this government. On November 30, Radio Moscow broadcast the good news that a radio signal had been "detected" from "an unknown station, transmitting from somewhere in Finland," announcing the establishment of "a democratic Government of Finland" seated in the Finnish border town of Terijoki. The Kremlin recognized this government, including its Prime Minister, Kuusinen, the next day. "Diplomatic relations" were inaugurated, and the request of the "democratic" Government of Finland for mil-

---

*The Soviets would later behave in this fashion toward Hungary (1956), Czechoslovakia (1968), and Afghanistan (1980).

itary aid was approved. On December 2, the world was informed that Kuusinen had "reached Moscow" (even though by all appearances he had never bothered to leave the Russian capital)[25] in order to sign an "agreement" with Molotov.

Two days later, the Communist Party organ *Pravda* announced that:

> The Red Army approaches the frontier of Finland at the request of the People's Government. It will depart from Finnish territory as soon as the people's Government asks it to leave. The Red Army is going into Finland to the aid of the Finnish people. Only the Soviet Union which rejects in principle the violent seizure of territory and the enslavement of nations, could agree to placing its armed might at disposal, not for the purpose of attacking Finland or enslaving its people, but for securing Finland's independence and enlarging her territory at the expense of the Soviet Union.[26]

To wit, the whole issue was a rare and exceptional instance of altruism in international relations: one state had sent its armed forces into another for the sole purpose of stuffing a generous portion of independence and its own territory down the latter's protesting throat.

Not only was propaganda of this kind an insult to the intelligence of the Finnish people; it also displayed ignorance and lack of understanding of anything pertaining to that nation's state of mind. Kuusinen was sure that once the "People's Government" was set up, the "masses of starving laborers" would arise, flushed with revolutionary fervor, overthrow the capitalist "people's enemy" government and greet him with howls of jubilation and triumph as he passed through the gates of Helsinki as a victor after 20 years of exile. Leaflets by Kuusinen, dropped by Soviet aircraft over the cities of Finland, proved by their phrasing, style, and content, that the man had neither learned nor forgotten anything since 1918. The missives called on the "starving" Finnish proletariat to "free itself of its chains" and turn its weapons away from its brethren, the Soviet soldiers, to their "common enemy—the government of the Whites, the government of Tanner and Mannerheim." These obsolete, hackneyed phrases, drained of the power of their youth since 1918, provoked only guffaws among their readers.

To raise a flag to which the masses of Finnish workers and farmers would stream, Kuusinen installed the "First Corps" of his army in Terijoki. This formation, comprising 5,775 men, was supposed to "mount the flag of the Democratic Republic of Finland atop the Presidential Palace in Helsinki." This was not to pass. The "corps" saw almost no action, and was in effect a withered appendage throughout the war.

It did, however, make an impact on the other side, spurring the Finns to a greater cohesion and resistance. Even if the Soviets' long-term intentions were not totally clear and remain controversial to this day; even if we accept the assumption that the Soviet Union was not out to Sovietize Finland, as most Finnish leaders and citizens suspected; even if we assume that the Soviet demands originated in security imperatives alone, as Stalin and his comrades so often stressed, and reflected no intent to drag Finland into the sphere of total Soviet influence; even if the establishment of the Kuusinen Government was not part of a planned scheme, but rather germinated only after the negotiations collapsed—even if we accept all of this, it is a fact that Finland interpreted the establishment of this government as an imminent Soviet threat to its independence. If informed circles had previously debated the possibility of further concessions, the establishment of the Kuusinen Government was a watershed putting all doubts and confusion to rest.

The Finns, including members of the illegal Communist party, reacted with revulsion, derision, contempt, and will to go to war. Class, social, and party contradictions were pushed aside as the national ranks united against the menace. All strata of the people considered this Soviet action a transparent attempt to nullify Finland's right to independence, freedom, self-determination, and an autonomous way of life. The Finns were left with no choice but to fight.[27]

They met this imperative with supreme valor.

Chapter Sixteen

The Course of the Battles

Orders found on POWs from advance Red Army units included a warning: Do not mistakenly cross the Finnish-Swedish border while chasing the retreating Finns.[1]

Thus the Soviet command viewed this operation as a two- or three-week "outing." The level of planning was in keeping with these expectations, and ignored the precaution as old as the Bible—"Let not him that girds on his armour boast himself as he that puts it off" (1 Kings 20,11)—against underestimating the enemy. Optimistic predictions aside, the Soviet campaign bogged down from the very beginning in a quagmire of errors, blunders, failures . . . and snow. The Red Army hardly advanced on any front in December. "General Winter," Russia's friend in Napoleon's time and in 1941 during Hitler's offensive, sided with Finland this time. The winter of 1939 was unusually harsh in Finland, with temperatures from 40°C to 50°C below zero. With two exceptions, these were the coldest temperatures recorded in Finland since 1928.[2]

The Russian soldier, accustomed to cold though he was, fell victim to the winter of 1939. His clothing, equipment, and supplies were not up to this. The number of Russian soldiers frostbitten or even frozen to death was higher than estimated. Their corpses in the snow–blanketed forests undermined their comrades' morale.

The Finns left scorched earth wherever they retreated: roads and bridges sabotaged, houses burnt down or otherwise razed. The Russian soldiers found no shelter from the terror of snow and cold. Unfamiliar with the terrain and burdened with heavy equipment, the infantry found the going slow and difficult. Gen. Meretskov attested that Finnish minefields provoked panic among the Russian soldiers, who had not been adequately trained to deal with obstacles of this kind. Because the columns of Russian infantry and armor were confined to the few and narrow traffic arteries, the forces were packed together and vulnerable. There was no possibility of deploying armor and exploiting its maneuverability and mobility.

The Finnish Army adroitly took advantage of all these constraints. Its combat tactics were based primarily on a flexible holding defensive; drawing Russian columns into ambushes and raiding the Soviet flanks with highly effective surprise tactics; employing a high degree of mobility with rapid and soundless movement on skis; and use of a simple, ingenious trick: white camouflage uniforms.

The fact that he was up against a superior force did not deter the Finnish soldier. He learned to overcome his fear of the tank, and accustomed himself to storming it with a Molotov cocktail.

The motivation of a man defending his family, village, and country against the invader fortified the Finnish soldier's morale and will to fight. He certainly bested his Russian counterpart in this sense. His quick realization that he was superior to his opposite number, too, was based on personal experience, not national megalomania. "One Finn is worth ten Russians," it was commonly felt among the people and in the Army.[3]

Overconfidence about their "outing" boomeranged on the Russians, as one might imagine. Confident that the Finns would respond to their advance by retreating, the Russian command did not give sufficient thought to the problems of coordinating and centralizing the effort. Having failed to orient themselves and take field conditions into account, the Russians squandered their quantitative advantage and failed to use their armor efficiently.

As a consequence of these blunders and the Finns' courageous behavior under fire, the Russian advance on the Karelian Isthmus was arrested in mid-December. In the Lake Ladoga area, too, the campaign came to a halt. Neither did the Russians fare any better on the broad Eastern front. Not only did the surface conditions blunt the offensive, but the transport of forces to this front relied on a single railroad track, a westward spur of the Leningrad-Murmansk line. Thus the Russians' deployment possibilities were limited, and the divisions on this front had to operate independently and without coordination.

Two Russian attempts at penetration from this direction, designed to cut Finland's waist, ended in defeat. One offensive in the north, launched in mid-December by the 88th and 122nd Russian Divisions via Salla toward Kemijarvi (near the Arctic Circle), was met by several Finnish battalions that the command had "scraped up" from somewhere and thrown into the campaign.[4]

A second attempt to break through, also in mid-December, was made on the central front in the Suomussalmi area. Here the 9th Soviet Army, with massive air support, opened an offensive designed to bisect Finland from east to west. Leading the way were the 44th Armored Division (from the Moscow area) and the 163rd Division. Facing them was the 9th Brigade under Col. H. J. Siilasvuo.[5]

As soon as word of the new Soviet division reached General Headquarters, Mannerheim ordered the immediate dispatch of reinforcements to Suomussalmi. Colonel Siilasvuo received his first battery on December 16, a second on the 18th, and two anti-tank guns on the 20th. Five battalions reached him on Christmas day—an eleventh-hour arrival to be sure, because on Christmas Eve the reinforced 163rd Division renewed its attack while the 44th Division advanced from the east.[6]

The Russian offensive ended in a rout and retreat. The Finns cut the Russians' supply and retreat lines with deep flanking operations, waited until cold and starvation had worn the enemy down, and then attacked and destroyed the bulk of his forces. The Russians left 5,000 dead in the field. The Finns captured 500 POW's and dozens of tanks, artillery pieces, hundreds of machine guns, thousands of rifles, hundreds of trucks, tractors, horses and ammunition. Following through, Siilasvuo continued to tail the enemy for another week at 46 degrees below zero. Again he captured a large number of POW's, tanks, artillery pieces and light weapons. Mannerheim describes the special and brutal nature of this battle in his memoirs, noting that the enemy's losses could not be estimated because blizzards had covered both the dead in battle and the wounded who had subsequently frozen to death.

The Finns' losses came to 900 dead and 1,770 wounded.[7]

In the wake of these developments, unexpected by the Soviet command, the front stabilized and the Finns' morale soared at the end of 1939. The following example of morbid humor illustrates the mood in Helsinki: "They are so many and our country is so small—where shall we find the space to bury them all?"[8]

Chapter Seventeen

World Sympathy and its Expressions

The response of the outside world also boosted the small nation's morale. As previously noted, the Finns' resistance had from its inception drawn on the feeling that they would not be left alone in their time of travail. Now, every passing day seemed to reconfirm and fortify this feeling.

The Soviet Union's attack on its little neighbor kindled the rage of Western Europe and the United States,[1] while the stance and, especially, the success of the Finnish people generated waves of astonishment and admiration. Indeed, after months—years—of humiliation, surrender, appeasement, and self-mortification in the face of Fascism and Nazism; after the fall of Abyssinia, Republican Spain, Austria, Czechoslovakia, and Poland—at long last, a small, courageous nation had risen up and was fighting audaciously and successfully for its freedom against a mighty power. The western democracies, ridden by feelings of frustration, helplessness, and guilt, were still engaged in "phoney war" maneuverings rather than real war against the Nazi enemy. Now they watched in amazement as the tiny Finnish democracy pitted itself against the Communist titan, Hitler's ally. Reports of the Finnish Army's victories excited and enthused both the bourgeois right and the democratic left. The media extolled and glorified the Finnish soldier who took on the Soviet tank.

According to many accounts, the feedback that reached Finland had a massive, almost intoxicating effect on morale. A nation that had wallowed for generations in feelings of "provincial" inferiority suddenly became the center of world interest and sympathy. Hope abounded that "world sympathy" would translate into diplomatic and military action. Relying on these assumptions, the Finnish Government appealed to the League of Nations on December 3 for deliberations that would lead to a cessation of the war. The Soviet Union announced that it would not take part in such talks. Molotov, his expression innocent and dispassionate, claimed with a solemnity that oozed sincerity that, on the contrary: the Soviet Union was maintaining relations of friendship and cooperation with the Democratic Government of

Finland. All questions hitherto under dispute and unresolved in negotiations with the previous Government had now been settled by way of peace and understanding.[2]

The cynicism and feigned uprightness of Molotov's reply, delivered even as artillery boomed on the Finnish front and the fate of the other three Baltic countries was already a matter of public record, suddenly infused the dry bones of the League of Nations with fighting spirit. On December 14, 1939, the League decided to expel the Soviet Union and called on member states to offer Finland all possible help.[3]

Apart from its moral value, this resolution—the League's swan song—was of limited practical use to Finland. Expressions of sympathy and identification flowed in from all over—Abyssinia, Uruguay, Canada, Belgium. France shut down the Soviet Trade Delegation offices in Paris. In Rome there were mass demonstrations against the Soviet aggression; in their wake, Moscow recalled its Ambassador, and the Italian Ambassador was ordered in reaction to announce that he was going on vacation in Italy.[4] The Pope conducted a mass for Finland. Statesmen and politicians delivered fervent speeches advocating Finland's right to existence, independence, and security, while European and American newspapers vigorously expressed the position of world public opinion in support of the justice of Finland's cause.

Weapons and Volunteers from Abroad

Encouraged by the League of Nations resolution and its reverberations around the world, the Government of Finland tried to turn the world's sympathy as expressed in declarations and writings into something "tangible." Finland needed weapons, equipment, and men. In point of fact, the aid proffered to Finland was valuable, important, and—if we recall how poorly the country was armed at the beginning of the war—rather large in scale. It was nevertheless not enough to tip the scales and make a decisive impact on the progress of the war.

If Finland's needs met with little practical response at the outset of the war, its military successes prodded friendly governments to be more generous. The supply of military equipment took a marked turn for the better in January, and much of the Finnish General Staff's wish list met with a positive response, at least in principle. True, there were difficulties and delays. Exhausting, time-consuming deliberations preceded the transactions. Action limped behind the promises. There were also many real constraints stemming from genuine shortages of the Allies themselves. Logistic difficulties proliferated as well. Thus, for example, the ban on using English pilots to fly aircraft and equipment led to the crash of five aircraft flown by Finnish pilots who were not yet familiar with them. Bombers were shipped out without suitable communications systems and with bomb racks of the wrong size for the bombs used by the Finns.[5] Shipments from England took an average of one month to reach Finland;[6] the matériel was transported on Finnish ships from English and French ports to Norwegian ports, whence it was hauled by train across Sweden to the Finnish border and reloaded (because of the difference in gauge) for transport to the front. Thus none of this matériel reached the units until early February, and most of it arrived only in the final days of the war.

Nevertheless, the overall value of this aid should not be belittled. The British provided dozens of Gladiator fighter aircraft and Blenheim bombers, 64 pieces of field artillery, twenty-five 105mm. howitzers, twenty-four 76 mm. anti-aircraft guns, several anti-tank guns, large numbers of light weapons, thousands of hand grenades, 100 Wickers machine guns, communications equipment, uniforms, shoes, tents, etc.

The French delivered 30 Morane Saulnier fighters and several bombers, twelve 75 mm. field cannon, twelve 105 mm. howitzers, twenty-four 155 mm. howitzers, about 100 recoilless guns, 5,000 machine guns, tens of thousands of rifles, and a large quantity of ammunition and personal gear.[7]

Italy, Hungary, Belgium, Spain, the United States, Denmark, and Norway provided weapons as well. Sweden's contribution was 25 aircraft, 80,000 rifles, 500 machine guns, 85 anti-tank guns, more than 100 field artillery pieces, 100 anti-aircraft guns, and large quantities of ammunition, fuel, and winter clothing.[8]*

Although the many sources of weapons created difficulties in training, fighting, and ammunition supply, the shipments were quite important in both the practical and the moral senses.

Finland needed fighting men (30,000 in Mannerheim's estimate) no less than it did weapons, and was especially desperate for organized, trained military units. Here, apart from the participation of individual volunteers, Finland's friends turned her down.

The first address of Finland's appeal, of course, was its good friend and neighbor, Sweden. There the war had aroused a mighty wave of spontaneous public sympathy that included important groups that had organized to press the Stockholm Government for action.

---

*The statistics on foreign aid to Finland presented by Molotov to the Supreme Soviet at the end of the war[9]—350 aircraft, 1,500 cannon, 6,000 machine guns, 2,500,000 shells, etc.—were gross exaggerations meant to explain and cover the failures of the Red Army.

In this respect the Finns were in for a harsh, bitter surprise. The Swedish Government's position from the inception of the conflict until the end of the Winter War was consistent in the extreme. Before the war broke out, on October 18–19, the Nordic heads of state—including three kings and the President of Finland—convened in Stockholm. When Foreign Minister Erkko tried to find out if Finland could rely on Swedish help in the event of war, he was given an absolute "no."[10] Swedish Prime Minister Per Albin Hansson's stance was clear and unequivocal: with all due respect to Finland, Sweden would not abandon its neutral stance, anchored in Paragraph 7 of the Fifth Hague Convention.[11] Sweden was prepared to offer Finland any possible economic and diplomatic assistance that might bring the war to an end, as well as aid in the form of equipment and volunteers. It would even permit other countries to transport assistance of these types across its territory. But nothing more. No Swedish forces would be sent to Finland's aid, and, of course, no foreign forces would be allowed to pass through. In view of its duty to the Swedish nation, the Government would neither risk war, jeopardize its neutrality, nor enter into a war against one of the powers; it would prevent, insofar as it could, the involvement of an additional power in the war; and it would not risk a reaction on the part of Germany, the Soviet Union's ally.[12] However painful, that was Sweden's policy—even at the unfortunate price of Finland's demise.

(As is known, Sweden did not stick to this attitude under all circumstances. The principle of neutrality did not prevent Sweden's selling iron ore to Germany. Sweden also let the Germans ship war matériel across its territory after the conquest of Norway, and, in the summer of 1941, let a fully equipped German division advance to the Finnish-Russian front.[13]) The Governments of Denmark and Norway took a similar position. (In the vote on the Soviet Union's expulsion from the League of Nations, incidentally, all three had abstained; they had also voiced their objections to imposing sanctions on that country).

The Finnish Government's attempts during the war to persuade its neutral neighbors to reconsider were not successful. Thus the Finns learned the hard way about the gap that often exists between public sympathy and public opinion on the one hand, and government policy affected by additional, complex factors and considerations on the other. Just the same, the Finns did not topple from their high hopes into an abyss of disappointment and helplessness. Endowed with a healthy sense of realism, they knew how to make peace with reality and continue operating within its constraints. While persisting at its efforts to change its neighbors' minds, the Finnish Government made very sure to procure the little that had been proffered. Indeed, the flow of volunteers that reached Finland from the neighboring countries and elsewhere, though rather limited in number, was good for morale.

A total of 11,500 volunteers reached Finland from 26 countries, including 8,000 from Sweden, 725 from Norway, 800 from Denmark, 300 from the United States, and 225 from England (many more were ready to set out from other countries). Nearly all arrived during the final stages of the war, and only a few actually saw action.[14] Germany thwarted the arrival of many volunteers from Western Europe, Italy, and Hungary. Neither was there any shortage of volunteers and self-designated advisors among emigré groups from White Russia, the Ukraine, and anti-Communist circles. General Skoropadski suggested that Ukrainian volunteers be recruited in the United States. The son of former Prime Minister Kerensky expressed willingness to propagandize in Finland among the Russian POW's. Someone even suggested that Trotsky be brought to Finland to wage the propaganda war against Stalin from there and organize a provisional Russian Government. In rejecting this counsel and these proposals, the Finnish Government demonstrated no small measure of wisdom and responsibility.[15]

The Stance of Germany

Anyone in Finland who expected help from Germany, and who still hoped that now, as in 1918, German units would arrive to help fight the Bolsheviks, awaited a bitter disappointment.

Officially, Germany adopted a stance of "neutrality toward the Russian-Finnish conflict," as expressed in Ribbentrop's telegram of December 20, 1939. The continuation of his telegram, however, immediately reveals the unilateral nature of this neutrality:

> The basis for this attitude of ours . . . is our friendship with the Soviet Union.[16]

Indeed, Germany, bound to the Soviet Union by alliance, saw no reason to entangle itself. It was afraid that English-French intervention in the Scandinavian theater might disrupt its own schemes, and looked forward to a quick resolution of the Russian-Finnish conflict. The Nazi-Soviet "honeymoon" was in full swing, and Hitler, so long as his hands were full in the West, thwarted any move and intent that might provoke Soviet anger. True, the German Minister in Helsinki, Bluecher, bombarded the German Foreign ministry with telegrams in which he requested, begged, and demanded that Germany help Finland. He warned of the loss of German influence in Finland and the damage that would be done to German economic interests. All his appeals were turned down with unequivocal consistency, and he was asked to desist from any anti-Soviet expression.[17] His proposal that Germany mediate between Finland and Russia met a similar fate.[18] Secretary of State Weizsaecker informed him by telegram on December 5 that it was out of place,[19] repeating this view with greater emphasis in a telegram on January 18, adding that the decision had been "made by the highest authority (*massgebendster Stelle*) . . . in the light of the over-all situation.[20] Bluecher, disappointed and frustrated, poured his heart out to Tanner: "All my work in Finland to date is smashed to bits."[21]

In fact, Hitler, though having declared a policy of "non-interference," adhered to the letter of the Nazi-Soviet friendship treaty which, of course, abandoned Finland to the mercies of Soviet "influence." This was a highly selective "non-interference," of course. Thus, for example, Germany turned down Finland's request to allow the transport of military equipment across German territory,[22] and obstructed shipments of arms from Italy and Belgium. On the other hand, Hitler approved the refueling and reprovisioning of Russian submarines in the Baltic Sea by German ships.[23] In a circular dated December 7, Foreign Minister Ribbentrop called on German diplomats to prevent and refrain from any utterance that might offend the Soviet Union, and asked them to express support of the Soviet stance toward Finland.[24] To prevent any possible misunderstanding, Ribbentrop instructed his Ambassador in Moscow, Schulenburg, to inform Molotov that the German Government was consistently and persistently rejecting various requests, especially Scandinavian, for its mediation. In so doing, it was conforming with the Moscow agreements, "which placed us on the side of the Soviet Union in the Russo-Finnish conflict."[25]

The French-English Initiative

In view of Scandinavian neutrality and one-sided German "neutrality," France's and Great Britain's clear-cut support of Finland stood out. Public opinion in both countries was squarely on Finland's side from the day the war broke out, and the respective governments became increasingly involved as the conflict developed. There were several reasons for this.

As previously noted, Finland's war served as moral compensation for the frustrated Europeans. Little Finland, affiliated by lifestyle and democratic outlook with Western Europe, was heroically withstanding the aggression of a totalitarian power.

In addition to the emotional element that motivated public opinion, the two Western governments also had important political and strategic reasons of their own to come to Finland's aid. Unlike the Scandinavian states, they were not bound by the chains of neutrality, and, more importantly, were already in a state of war. Thus they were not only allowed to take a clear-cut stand, they even had to examine the strategic utility they could achieve by siding with Finland.

It is but natural that France, on the front line against Germany, was especially interested in the matter. Its Prime Minister, Daladier—one of the architects of the Munich accord—led the chorus of supporters of aid to Finland.[26] This democracy had to be rescued from the totalitarian aggression it faced, he said. Whereas at Munich he had sought to appease the Nazi dictatorship, he now took a combative approach to the Communist dictatorship.

Above and beyond slogans and conceptual considerations, however, Daladier was motivated by the thought that the longer the Russian-Finish conflict went on, certain scenarios would become more likely. Examples were the prospects of German entanglement, and perhaps even war between Germany and its Soviet ally; the chances of a diversion of some German pressure from the French to the northern front; the possibility that Germany would violate Norway's and Sweden's neutrality, causing these states to join the Allied camp; and the prospect of easing Soviet pressure on France's Balkan friends.

Thus, in December 1939, Daladier took the initiative. He suggested to the English Government that it and France offer Finland aid in the form of military equipment and units, and that the Scandinavian countries be assured support if they entered into confrontation with the Soviet Union.[27] To prove that his deed was as good as his word, the Prime Minister of France announced on December 14 that 30 modern combat aircraft were being delivered to Finland (see Chapter 17, p. 279).[28] In early January, he instructed a highly experienced and talented officer, Col. Antoine Béthouart, to organize an élite unit of regular forces based on high mobility and firepower. The force would be built on the Chasseurs Alpins battalion, with an artillery battalion annexed to it. Two Foreign Legion battalions and a company of armored vehicles were added in mid-February. This "Mountain Brigade" was given advanced training in expectation of a mission to Finland.[29] Daladier did not succeed in infecting his British colleague and partner to the Munich accord with his enthusiasm. Chamberlain did not consider the war in the north a threat to the Allies' interests, and asserted that France and Britain were unable to offer Finland any real assistance in any case. His view reflected the British Foreign Office's assessment of the Russian attack on Finland as no menace to the Allies and of the prospects of aid to Finland as nil.[30]

The most Chamberlain would do for the Finns was to ship military equipment—and even this only through private arms agents.[31] True, French and English shipments—in magnitudes that cannot be disparaged, although they were not large enough to tip the scales—did reach Finland in the end.

Chamberlain's objection to dispatching troops was unequivocal, especially in view of the stance of Sweden and Norway. Only volunteers in civilian dress may go, he ruled, laying down extremely restrictive conditions.[32]

At this point the French tabled a proposal which had several virtues and advantages from the British point of view. The Petsamo area in the Arctic north contained nickel deposits, and the Finns had awarded the concession to mine them to an English-Canadian company in which American capital, too, had been invested.[33] Assuming that the British therefore had direct interest and legitimate reason to establish a physical presence in the area, the French proposed that troops be sent to the Petsamo area to join up with and strengthen the Finnish force already there.

To prevent the possibility of a direct clash between the British or French forces and the Red Army, the French suggested that use be made of Polish forces under Gen. Sikorski's Government and Polish naval units anchored in British ports.

This scheme had two additional advantages. It would obviate the need to move forces through Norwegian and Swedish territory, thus requiring the consent of their governments; not only would this reinforce the Finnish foothold in the North, it would also permit the Allies to track and oversee the Murmansk area in the Soviet Union and monitor German naval movements in the Arctic Ocean.

Sikorski expressed willingness to dispatch the Polish destroyers and submarines presently anchored in British ports. The British, however, objected not only to this but to the departure of these ships from French bases.[34] This reflected their fear that the operation would lead to a clash with the Soviet Union, a clash they wished to avoid. In this, they undoubtedly displayed foresight.

In the meantime, reports were reaching Helsinki about the deliberations in London and Paris and the waves of public sympathy there. Thus, on December 22, the Government of Finland instructed its representatives in Paris and London to clarify to the Allied Governments that their military assistance was of supreme importance for Finland. At the same time, the heads of representations in Oslo and Stockholm were instructed to inform the respective Governments that Finland would welcome French and English units if and when they arrived.

The Finnish Minister in London, Gripenberg, recorded in his diary that Foreign Minister Tanner even called him the next day to stress that Finland was interested in the dispatch of British troops.[35]

The Finnish Foreign ministry's telegrams to its ministers, it is true, had a somewhat declarative and ambivalent tone, as if expressing more a wish than an official operational request. Nevertheless, the Finnish diplomats did as told, and Paris stepped up its pressure on London. Daladier brought forth another argument: the League of Nations resolution provided legal grounds both for military intervention and for an application to the governments of Sweden and Norway to permit the troops to cross their territory.

Under pressure of all these trends and factors, Chamberlain's resistance weakened, and his Government agreed, albeit with no particular enthusiasm, to discuss military aid to Finland under the aegis of the Allied Supreme War Council. The only decision taken in a debate on December 27, however, was to establish contacts with the Scandinavians and assess their willingness to permit the transit of equipment and "technicians." Norway and Sweden replied on January 4, 1940. The answer was favorable if reserved; it abided at least formally with the rules of Article 2 of the Fifth Hague Convention.[36] Sweden stressed that it agreed to the transit of equipment and war matériel if purchased commercially by Finland elsewhere. It would permit technical experts to accompany the shipments, provided that they were volunteers travelling as private citizens. The aid had to be provided secretly, and the entire operation must be carried out "so as not to create the impression that Sweden is taking part in the international activity." The Government of Norway sent a similar reply.[37]

On the basis of these reserved, restricted answers, the recruitment of volunteers and gathering of war matériel got underway in England and France. The matter of direct involvement of regular troops was left unresolved, but Army staffs began to develop a plan for an expeditionary force.

The French and British activity was obviously the product of more than public sympathy for the Finnish cause. It also reflected, to a considerable extent, strategic calculations involving their war against Nazi Germany. Having explored the French Government's considerations, we now devote a few words to another aspect of particular concern to the British. As soon as World War II broke out and the Allies imposed a naval embargo on Germany, the British strategists faced the question of how to keep iron ore, a raw material of supreme strategic importance, from being shipped to Germany by sea, when two thirds of it originated in Gällivare, Sweden. Germany's annual consumption of this substance approximated ten million tons.[38] During the summer, it was shipped from the port of Lulea on the Gulf of Bothnia. In the winter, when the Gulf was frozen over, the ore was hauled by rail to Narvik, Norway, where it was loaded onto ships sailing for Germany. The Industrial Intelligence Centre (IIC), a branch of the Ministry of Economic Warfare (MEW), estimated that by denying Germany this substance the Allies could paralyze the German steel industry within several months.[39] The first member of the British Government to display practical interest in the matter was the Minister of the Navy in Chamberlain's War

Cabinet, Winston Churchill. As early as September 19, 1939, Churchill suggested the mining of Norwegian waters.[40] Although the Government turned down his plan in order to safeguard the neutrality of the Scandinavian countries, the problem of how to deny Germany its Swedish iron ore began to cause the Government and the General Staff growing concern. It came to serve as one of the most important motives for considering some kind of operation on the Scandinavian front.

The man most instrumental in promoting this matter was the Chief of the Imperial General Staff, General William Edmund Ironside. He entertained the hope that the dispatch of relatively small forces to the northern theater with a declared intent of coming to Finland's aid might achieve several important aims "in one go." It would cut off the supply of iron ore to Germany, ease German pressure on France, wrest the war initiative from the Germans and disrupt their plans, and, perhaps, even change the direction of the entire war effort.[41]

In Ironside's initial scheme, the Allies would declare their intent to send an expeditionary force to Finland's aid in accordance with the League of Nations resolution of December 14. To this end, they had to ask Norway and Sweden for permission to cross their territory. They could not refuse, Ironside assumed. The expeditionary force, 3,000 strong according to his initial plan, would then land at Narvik, follow the railroad to Lulea, and establish its base there. Thence the force could send a unit into Finland. All this, resulting in the cessation of iron ore shipments to Germany, would by their very nature provoke a German reaction. Then the Allies could establish a second front in Scandinavia under conditions favorable to them, while turning the little expeditionary force into a base and a bridgehead that would absorb additional forces.[42]

This scheme was presented to the British Government in late December, and was turned down—though not fatally so. It was revamped and amended in various ways, so that its dimensions grew in the end. Ironside's adherence to his basic concept, the pressure of British public opinion, and Daladier's pressure, joined forces to melt away Chamberlain's last shred of opposition. He gave Ironside the go-ahead in mid-January.

H. M. Government reached the following binding conclusion: Finland should be saved as a matter of utmost importance; she could not hold out after the spring without reinforcements of 30,000–40,000 trained men; the current stream of heterogeneous volunteers was not enough; and Finland's downfall would be a major defeat for the Allies.[43]

In view of these guidelines, the Government lent the new scheme its consent on January 29, and the Allied Supreme War Council approved it on February 5. It resembled the idea presented by Ironside six weeks earlier in principle only.

According to the major contours of the plan, Finland would first have to make official application to the Allies for the help of an expeditionary force; on the basis of this request, the Allies would ask Sweden and Norway to permit it to cross their territories. The force, built ostensibly of "volunteers," would operate in northern Finland under Finnish command. To secure its supply lines, the expeditionary force would have to debark and consolidate itself in Narvik, and secure the railroad line from there to the Finnish border.

This expeditionary force would not only cut off Germany's supply of Swedish iron ore but take over the mines themselves. The expected German reaction would be forestalled by landing additional forces at ports further south along the Norwegian coast, i.e., Trondheim, Namsos, Bergen, and Stavanger.

To put this plan into action, the Allies would have to dispatch two brigades to Narvik, five battalions to the southern ports, and a reinforced brigade to Finland. At the second stage, when the Germans reacted, at least two divisions of reinforcements would be necessary. In sum, then, the planners estimated the manpower requirements not at 3,000 men but at 100,000 British soldiers and 50,000 French soldiers, not including naval and air units. Of all these, Finland would benefit directly from only one reinforced brigade. The forces were to sail on March 12 and land on March 20.

The scheme was grandiose and pretentious in the extreme, considering the relative military weakness of France and Britain at the time. It stood in inverse proportion not only to their actual strength but to their political will to act. True, it was in both France and England's strategic interest to strengthen Finland—and perhaps even to open a second front in the North—but the conflict of attitudes between Paris and London did much to throttle the chances of implementing any plan. The two allies were admittedly interested in having Finland continue to fight, so as to provide them with an opportunity to seize the mines or at least to prevent their falling into German hands, but they displayed no real will nor ability to put the plans into action. The grandiose schemes served as a smokescreen for inaction and hesitancy, and the political circumstances made them wholly unfeasible. Thus, for example, the first condition for the plan was Finland's consent to play its part. Admittedly, the Allies could assume that the hard-pressed Finns, in need of help, would eagerly seize the outstretched hand and officially ask for help as required by the plan. No account was taken of the possibility that the Finns, badly off as they were, would shun their role, correctly read the intentions behind the Expeditionary Force initiative, reach the correct assessment that the plan offered them no solution, and refuse to be anyone's fig-leaf. The British and French politicians and generals never imagined that the Finns would turn the tables and, instead of serving the Allies' interests, would use the Western "expeditionary force" idea for the imperatives of their negotiations with the Soviets.

The second weakness of the Western scheme was its assumption that Norway and Sweden would agree to let the expeditionary force through (to agree to be raped, so to speak). This was a gamble based on optimistic assumptions, not on solid political facts.

When the first reactions from Helsinki, Stockholm, and Oslo reached Paris and London, it indeed transpired that the plan as drawn up had neither a leg to stand on nor any prospects of fulfillment. The three Nordic nations refused to dance to the tune composed for them in London and Paris.

Thus January passed without any significant progress with respect to the expeditionary force; on the front, too, no indications of a resolution were evident. The battles went on, and the first diplomatic feelers for an end to the war were sent out.

Chapter Eighteen

Peace Feelers

The Russian attack on the Karelian Isthmus was arrested in January and did not meet the hopes of the Soviet command. On the eastern front, the Russians were suffering setbacks and heavy losses. Many Red Army units found themselves bogged down in the field, cut off from one another; they dug themselves into hedgehog positions (which the Finns called "mottis"), that included artillery and tanks ready to fire. These strongholds were subject to recurrent surprise attacks by the Finns, who materialized out of nowhere, ghostlike in their white camouflage uniforms. Airlifted supplies enabled the Russian soldiers to hold out in their positions and avoid starvation, but some of the supplies fell into Finnish hands. Attempts by several Russian mottis to breach the Finnish lines ended in their destruction; the invaders were not familiar with the terrain and were no match for the Finns in mobility in the snow.

Were it not for their shortage of artillery and aircraft, the Finns could have destroyed these mottis and moved much of their forces from the eastern front to the Karelian Isthmus. They continued to wage successful battles of attrition against pockets of Russian resistance until March, inflicting heavy losses on the enemy and providing themselves with a booty of light and automatic weapons, artillery pieces of various types, armored vehicles, tanks, and trucks. (A Russian officer recorded in his diary that his position had just been shelled by a battery of Russian 122 mm. cannon that had fallen into Finnish hands.[1]) The Finnish Army was now using weapons of Finnish, Swedish, English, French, Belgian, Spanish, American, and Soviet manufacture. Despite the difficulties this variety caused, the Finns made the most of what they had.

However, despite their achievements on the battlefield, the fighting spirit and valor of the Finnish soldier, the brilliance of the high command, and the entire nation's willingness to bear the burdens of the war, it was clear—at least to some of Finland's senior officials—that the achievements, however glittering, were not changing the strategic situation in any substantial way and could not last forever. True, the Russian attack had been blunted, but the Finnish Army, whose strength was withering and whose resources were limited, was not powerful enough to mount the counteroffensive that would throw the Russians back. On January 8, Paasikivi wrote in his diary:

> Our victories are considered tremendously great, and from our point of view they are magnificent, but they have no effect on the final result, since in view of the power of the huge Russian state, these defeats have no significance.[2]

Prime Minister Ryti, Foreign Minister Tanner, and, in particular, Marshal Mannerheim—who knew where matters stood in all senses—shared this sober assessment.

All four were also rather skeptical about the ideas and proposals concerning meaningful Allied military aid, especially with respect to notions of direct Allied involvement alongside Finland. Tanner, who had tried two or three weeks earlier to persuade the English and the French to become directly involved, apparently reacted to the reports from Paris and London by concluding that "there was no one to talk to." He now believed that the Western powers "had always been late to act. Before their aid reached us, all southern Finland might be occupied."[3]

Mannerheim, who had also hoped at first for substantial outside help, was increasingly convinced that it was a rickety crutch on which to lean. In the initial stages of the war, he pursued his contacts with the Allies along channels other than "official" ones such as the Foreign Ministry and its legations. Finland's envoy to Paris, Harri Holma, and the military attaché, Col. Aladar Passonen, were the ones who conducted the talks and reported directly to Mannerheim; at the same time, the French military attaché, Col. Ganeval, and the British attaché, Gen. Ling, energetically conveyed proposals from their Governments not to Helsinki but to Mannerheim's headquarters. There was neither coordination nor contact between the two government centers until Mannerheim felt a clear need to introduce them.

The "Peace Triumvirate"

This development indeed occurred gradually and with no advance planning. With neither the setting of official patterns or formal framework, and without a firm shared viewpoint among themselves, the three cabinet members—with the Commander-in-Chief's understanding and coordination from early February on—began to leave a decisive imprint on Finland's policy. Thus the activity of the three cabinet ministers, subsequently known as the

"Peace Triumvirate," was arguably quite unconstitutional. Often they acted without consulting with the President, who, under the Finnish Constitution, was responsible for shaping and setting foreign policy. They kept the rest of the cabinet in the dark about their deliberations and assessments, and launched fateful actions on no own counsel but their own. The "triumvirate" regarded this behavior, though inconsistent with Finland's nature and democratic tradition, as an inarguable necessity in view of the atmosphere in Finland and the hawkish positions of no few Cabinet ministers and members of Parliament. The decisions and initiatives first cooked up in their "kitchen" were brought to the cabinet and Parliament for ex post facto approval; the force of the facts created in the meantime—especially the strategic developments that the three ministers and Mannerheim had foreseen—secured the political establishment's support in the end.

On the basis of shared assessments and assumptions, the "triumvirate," with Mannerheim's tacit consent, reached the conclusion that Finland's actions should be based on three seemingly contradictory and nevertheless complementary elements:

A. All-out, unhesitant continuation of the war;
B. Continuation of the efforts to attain military aid—equipment and men—from the Allies.
C. Development of initiatives leading to negotiations with the Soviet Union toward an end to the war.

The first of these left no room for misunderstanding. The national consensus viewed the war as a matter of life or death, and the army was doing its best to attain the objectives that the national leadership set for it.

The second element was meant to complement and bolster the army's efforts. As mentioned, the "triumvirate" was skeptical about the possibility of obtaining substantial foreign aid; nevertheless it spared no effort, ignored no channel of communications, left no stone unturned to encourage outside powers to provide such aid and to promote trends favoring direct outside involvement—just in case something came of it after all.

The "triumvirate" was guided by four major trends (never given any programmatic formulation, they are presented schematically here):

A. Assistance in any shape and form—weapons, equipment, volunteers—would be welcome and viewed as a blessing and source of reinforcement.
B. Help in the form of equipment and volunteers, and rumors of direct Allied involvement, were useful for bolstering civilian and military morale.

C. It was nevertheless possible that the English and French positions might change, or their efforts on Finland's behalf intensify, as a result of pressure on Germany and Sweden concerning the right of transit. Therefore, Finland should maintain its contacts with the Allies in this regard.
D. Whatever the final outcome of these contacts might be, the very fact of such contacts, and of the rumors surrounding them, could produce all or some of the following results: deterring the Russians from continuing the war, generating of German pressure on Moscow to this end, the opening of talks toward ending of the war, and, perhaps, a moderation of the Soviet demands.[4]

At the same time, the "triumvirate" chose to cultivate the third of its avenues of action—striving to end the war through direct negotiations with the Soviet Union.

Mannerheim, whose military leadership was a source of inspiration for commanders and enlisted men alike, read the military map correctly. Firmly he carried on with Finland's audacious war. It was nevertheless clear to him that the struggle, heroic as it was, could not last long. A small, democratic nation's resources and endurance are limited. His opinion, which he communicated to the Prime Minister, was that Finland should aspire to obtain a peace treaty.[5] This view, of course, also had a decisive influence on Ryti's actions.

Political Sophistication and Unconventional Diplomacy

As we have seen, the "triumviriate" indeed took initiatives to resume the talks with Moscow, but this does not mean that the ministers had relinquished other options. Just as activity toward obtaining outside assistance was meant to spur peace negotiations, so the intent to reopen the talks, too, was not one-dimensional. The major avenue pursued did not totally rule out other, secondary, and seemingly contradictory directions.

In the "triumvirate's" sober assessment, it was in the Allies' strategic interest to keep the Russo-Finnish war going. The war presented the Allies with several previously discussed options. Therefore, the Finnish "kitchen cabinet" assumed that reports of peace feelers and the possibility of opening peace talks would prod the Allies to step up their shipments of weapons and equipment, and, perhaps, to become directly involved on a significant scale.

The result was therefore a sophisticated dialectic. It assumed that outside assistance, and even rumors about it, would augment not only Finnish fighting strength but also the prospects for negotiations with the Russians. Conversely, talks with the Russians—or rumors that such talks were in the offing—would either bring the war to and end or enlist the Allies on Finland's side.

Thus Finland, even while sticking to its guns, explored the prospects of peace negotiations. Just as their political and strategic presumptions were tortuous, superficially inconsistent, but actually quite sophisticated, so were the tactics adopted. The path to negotiations began to follow a cunning, exceptional route.

Hella Wuolijoki was a Finnish Bohemian, a playwright whose works conveyed a fiery revolutionary message (and, said the critics, were overwhelmingly shallow in the artistic sense). Her heroines were always tempestuous, "progressive," and strong-willed ladies who, with their revolutionary rhetoric, mowed down a cast of weak-willed, conceptually spineless men. Wuolijoki was on good terms with European and Finnish leftist circles. Her sister was married to a leading English Communist, and one of her friends was Alexandra Kollontai, the Soviet ambassador to Stockholm at the time.

Kollontai—then 68 years old—was an unusual character in her own right. Her rich and picturesque past had made her an actor in the myth of the October Revolution, in which she had played an active role (according to gossip, her feminine beauty, too, had much to do with her exploits). In any event, her grace had not fled her in 1940; neither had her individualistic inclinations weakened. She could get away with things that no other Soviet diplomat could even imagine.

Wuolijoki, who knew that Kollontai's friendship went beyond the personal level and included Finland, her birthplace, approached Tanner in early January with a strange proposal: she was willing to enter into peace talks with Kollontai. The proposal, like its sponsor, was rather eccentric. However, after giving it a second thought, and despite his many doubts, Tanner presented it to Ryti and Paasakivi. The three decided to allow Wuolijoki to set out for Stockholm to conduct the talks.

She did so on January 10.

Thus began an odd, fascinating episode, far from all conventions of diplomatic theory and practice—a unique chapter in negotiations toward ending wars between states. From the point of view of professional diplomacy, the two friends' negotiations, shrouded in heavy circumspection (although the Swedish Foreign minister was in on the secret) were catastrophic. The matrons took no notes, and, letting their understanding and inclinations take over, overstepped their governments' guidelines and instructions. They "improved" and "prettied up" anything they saw fit, and the personal comments and appraisals in their reports to their governments circumvented the facts in quantity and emphasis. In his memoirs, Tanner mentioned this tendency with wry irony: "Later events showed that it was necessary to deal cautiously with reports from both ladies."[6] Both yearned to succeed where conventional diplomacy had failed, and to bring their countries to the negotiating table.

The first indication of a breakthrough reached Stockholm (and thence Tanner) on January 29 in the form of a letter from Molotov announcing that "The USSR has no objection in principle to concluding an agreement with the Ryti-Tanner Government."[7] Thus, in principle at least, the Soviet Union had withdrawn its recognition of the Kuusinen puppet government and its "agreement" with it.

Two factors influenced the Soviets to change their minds. The Finnish army's victories and its success in withstanding the Soviet offensive for months had caused the Soviet leadership to rethink the matter, negating the immediate prospect of setting up a "Finnish SSR" and even strengthening the basis of Finnish sovereignty.

Hella Wuolijoki

The second factor inducing the Soviets to come to the table was the rising tide of rumors concerning the possibility of Anglo-French intervention and an Allied expeditionary force, sent either through Norway and Sweden or toward the Caucasus and the Soviet oil fields.[8]

On January 8, Molotov told Schulenburg that the Soviet Government was aware of the peril that would present itself if England and France were to use Sweden and Norway for their own ends.[9] But alongside this apparent accomplishment of the Finnish Government, Molotov's letter also included an explicit demand for further concessions and a warning that the demands the Soviets had presented in November would no longer do:

> Because since those negotiations blood had been shed on both sides, and that blood, which has been shed contrary to our hopes and through no fault of ours, calls for augmented guarantees to the security of the frontiers of the USSR.[10]

Thus a door had been opened for peace and border talks, and the "peace triumvirate"—without taking the rest of the Cabinet into its confidence—met to decide on the next steps.

Ryti and Tanner, relying on Mannerheim's military judgments, still believed that Finland should not yield on Hanko, but that Moscow should be offered a "compromise solution" and additional concessions as necessary for the defense of Leningrad. The Russian answer clarified beyond all doubt that the Hanko concession was a precondition to any negotiations. The "triumvirate" then decided to send Tanner to Stockholm for a meeting with Mme Kollontai. On February 4, under total secrecy, Tanner set out. In Stockholm, after a talk with his Swedish counterpart Günther (who expressed his wish and hope that the negotiations being held in the Swedish capital through its "good offices" would indeed lead to peace)—Tanner headed for the city's Grand Hotel,[11] again in total secrecy, for his meeting with Kollontai.

Acting on his own, Tanner presented an alternative proposal by which Finland would cede one of its islands along the Estonian coast in exchange for suitable territorial compensation. In his second talk, on February 6, the Soviet Ambassador communicated her Government's negative reply. The Soviets stood by their demand for Hanko and greater Finnish concessions on the Karelian Isthmus and the Gulf of Finland. Tanner returned to Helsinki empty-handed.

***

Thus far, the "triumvirate" had acted under conditions of virtual conspiracy, concealing its contacts from the President and the rest of the Cabinet. Tanner himself later justified this unconstitutional behavior as openly as could be, saying that when it came to peace-making he could not trust the Cabinet and Parliament, which were still in the grips of war fever and faith in victory. "These conversations were known only . . . to persons who aspired to bring about peace."[12]

On February 8, however, the "triumvirate"—with Gen. Walden standing in for Mannerheim—reached the conclusion that they could no longer bear exclusive responsibility for the negotiations, and decided to confide in President Kallio and the National Defense Council.

The Council, convening on February 10 in Mannerheim's headquarters, established a set of priorities and tactics for the negotiations. Three stages were decided on. First, the Finns would negotiate with the Russians, offering them further concessions on the Karelian Isthmus and the island of Jussarö as a base in the Gulf of Finland. These concessions would be made in exchange for suitable territorial compensation. If this move failed, Sweden would be asked to join the war. Only as a last alternative—in the event that Sweden refused—would an appeal be made to the Allies.

When these decisions were brought before the Ministerial Committee for Foreign Affairs two days later, the resolution was adopted by a majority of one vote, the President's. Kallio did in fact support the decisions, but with conspicuous reluctance. The votes of the six ministers were split.[13]

Ryti, Tanner, and Paasikivi supported the proposal, of course, but three ministers—Education Minister Hannula, Defense Minister Niukkanen, and Justice Minister Söderhjelm—came out vehemently against it. They thought it better to appeal to the Allies and keep the war going than to make any concession to the Russians. Finally, as a compromise, it was decided that Tanner would go to Stockholm to ask for Sweden's assistance. This, however, was not the end of the overt and covert inquiries. After the ministerial committee adjourned, the "triumvirate" again convened, joined this time by President Kallio, and decided that Tanner would indeed set out for Stockholm, but would adhere to the line he had previously fashioned.[14]

And while the Finnish leaders were agonizing in Helsinki over the desired diplomatic moves, a development took place on the Karelian Isthmus that changed the course of events.

Chapter Nineteen

The Front Collapses

Stalin was infuriated by the course of the war. A campaign which, according to the experts, should have been a "picnic" of two to three weeks' duration, had bogged down in blood and blunders. The Red Army was being made to look ridiculous. The beating it was taking from a little nation undermined its credibility and prestige, menaced the international status of the Soviet Union, and, as would subsequently be known, fomented Hitler's aggressive intentions.

In the Soviet Union itself, too, a public that usually knew to make its peace with the decrees of fate and the government, was starting to become restive. Rumors of how the war was going, especially with regard to the throngs of wounded and frostbitten soldiers who filled the hospitals in the outlying cities, created a gloomy atmosphere.[1]

Stalin, incensed, called on his military leaders to produce a quick victory. The front command and units were reorganized at the end of December. Marshal Timoshenko was installed as the Commander-in-Chief of all forces; even as he learned the lessons of the blunders, he began augmenting the forces, particularly armor and artillery. He resumed intensive retraining, stepped up ground and air patrols, and improved equipment. The final plan for the renewed offensive was finalized in consultations by Stalin with Molotov, Zhdanov on the political side and with Voroshilov, Voronow (the artillery expert), Timoshenko, and Meretskov.

Stalin instructed the two armies facing the Mannerheim line (the 7th and the 8th) to breach it at once. The 7th Army was ordered to capture Viipuri and the territory as far as Antrea. The 8th Army was ordered to reach the Antrea-Käkisalmi line, from which, if the war continued, it would advance into the heart of Finland.

Six Finnish divisions now held the Mannerheim line, and another two were stationed in the rear as a strategic reserve. The two Soviet armies included 11 infantry divisions and strong elements of armor, artillery, and airforce. Reserves included another three infantry divisions and a tank corps.[2]

Finnish soldiers on the Summa front

The Russians Break Through at Summa

The Soviets concentrated their main efforts on the western flank of the Mannerheim line in the Summa area, pitting five divisions against the Finns' two. The offensive began on February 1 with aerial bombardment and artillery fire meant to "soften" the opponent. With 400 cannon concentrated along an 80 km. section of the front, they systematically eradicated the Finnish positions. Overhead, some 500 bombers also joined the attack.

Protected by this murderous fire, Russian tank units and infantry units transported on snow vehicles raided and attacked the Finnish positions.[3] Paratroopers dropped behind the Finnish lines destroyed bunkers and machine-gun nests.

The battle of attrition lasted two weeks, inflicting heavy casualties on the defenders. On February 11, the Russian 123rd Division succeeded in overwhelming a Finnish battalion of fewer than 400 men in the area of Summa. Thus, on February 15, Mannerheim had to order a retreat.

Aware that political negotiations were in the offing, Mannerheim wanted to impede the Soviet advance as best he could, retain territory, and buy time so as to deflect the Soviets' political pressure and enable the Finnish politicians to attain the best terms possible. He therefore orchestrated a stubborn, sagacious retreat, fighting for every stronghold and line of positions. But Russian pressure mounted, while battle fatigue and casualties thinned the Finnish ranks. Also sapping the Finns' ability to hold out were the meager battle experience of the elderly reservists and young soldiers who now took the place of the decimated crack troops; the absence of shelter against the fire and cold on the retreat lines; the incompatibility of the weapons and ammunition that had begun to reach the front from various other countries; and a general shortage of ammunition and heavy weapons.

***

Thus, while fighting, the Finns continued to retreat. By March 1 they were 20–30 km. away from their opening position. It could still be said that the retreat was being staged successfully, and that the Finnish command was in control. This situation changed quickly in the first week of March, however, when the Russians threw seven fresh divisions (51, 53, 80, 84, 86, 100, 113) into the fray and began to encircle the Viipuri area from the east, south, and west. Exploiting the thick ice covering the Gulf of Finland, the Russians mounted a deep flanking operation using light tanks to cross the Gulf, protect attacking infantry, and function as firing posi-

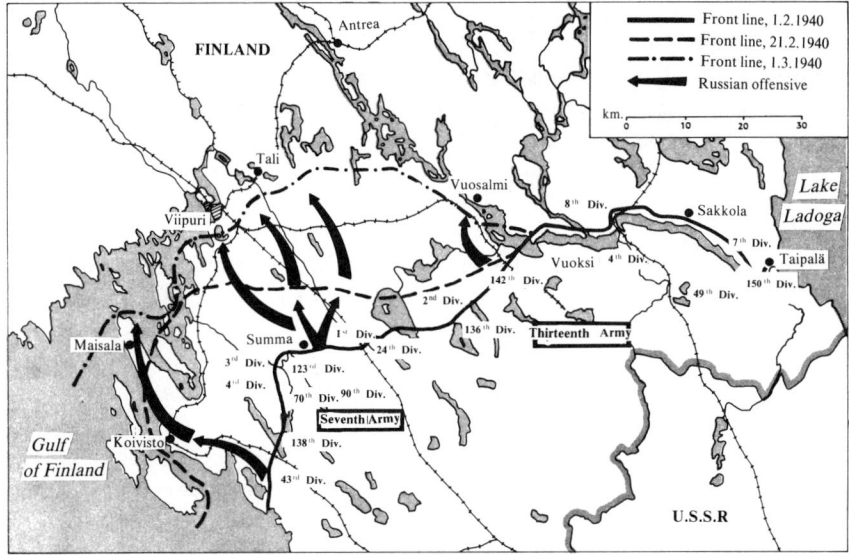

MAP 5: The Russian February Offensive

Finnish ski-troops on the move

tions. The two Finnish divisions deployed in the area (the 3rd and the 5th) held the enemy back, suffering heavy losses. But the Russians kept up the pressure, threatening to encircle Viipuri totally, cut off all access routes, and destroy most of the forces trapped there. Mannerheim tried to scrape reserve forces together and reinforce the defense positions as best he could. The results were of little use. The 23rd Division organized for defense in the Talli area east of Viipuri. This was a reserve division, hastily trained and readied for war, and its morale swiftly deteriorated under the relentless pressure of the Russian shelling and attacks. One of its battalions retreated frantically on March 8, marking the beginning of a general deterioration.

Russian advance units reached the center of Viipuri on March 12, although the Finns still held most parts of the city. On that day, in the sixth week of uninterrupted fighting, the general situation was as follows: the Russian offensive along the entire Karelian Isthmus was in full swing. The Finnish forces were not only in constant retreat but had begun to show clear signs of collapse. The Russians, with ample fresh manpower reserves at their disposal, did not let up, and they brought unprecedented artillery firepower to bear. By contrast, all the Finnish reserves—manpower and weapons alike—were dwindling.

The Finns, beginning the war with 150,000 soldiers, took 80,000 casualties (including killed, wounded, and disabled because of disease, combat fatigue, etc.) by mid-March. Even after the younger age groups and elderly reservists were mobilized, there was still a quantitative and qualitative shortfall. The Finnish Army was now fighting at no more, and perhaps less, than half its manning table in personnel, weapons, and firepower.[4] Now nothing serious stood in the way of a Russian advance to the Viipuri-Antrea-Käkisalmi line before the snow melted. From there they could mount a crushing offensive into the very heart of Finland.

The outcome of the war had in fact been decided.

The moment of truth had come. The few, however courageous, could not fight the many forever. The Finnish government had to decide how to end the war, in order to preserve the remnants of its army and its nation's life, not sacrificing them pointlessly.

Diplomatic Efforts and Harsh Ruminations

Let us backtrack a month, to February 12.

As will be recalled, it had been decided following deliberations of the Ministerial Committee on Defense Affairs that Tanner would go to Stockholm to communicate Finland's proposals to the Russians from there. This, however, was a lost cause from the outset. Even as he made his way by land and sea at night between Helsinki and Stockholm, events at the front took a decisive turn. The Mannerheim line had been breached in the Summa area. That very day, February 12, the Soviet Union gave the Government of Sweden its terms for ending the war. As Molotov had warned in his letter of January 29, the terms were harsher and included additional demands. The Soviet Union now demanded not only Hanko and several islands in the Gulf, but the entire Karelian Isthmus. Tanner's proposals were no longer relevant.

Enquiries with the Swedish government indicated that the latter was not about to change its own stance. Conferring on February 13 with the Swedish Prime Minister, Foreign Minister, and Defense Minister, Tanner was told in so many words that Sweden would continue helping as it had before, including volunteers, but under no circumstances would it permit its army to participate or be used in the war against Russia. The Germans would react to Sweden's detriment, the Swedish leaders explained.

Tanner recognized this as a groundless and blatant falsehood. He knew from reliable sources that the Germans had decided on a policy of nonaggression as long as Sweden helped Finland independently and did not permit the Allies to exploit its territory to establish bases for the crossing of troops.⁵ The Swedes, too, were undoubtedly aware of this, and their excuse was a fig leaf for cold calculation. True, they were prepared for reasons of Nordic-Scandinavian solidarity to continue helping Finland with supplies and volunteers. They wanted Finland to survive, wherever its new borders might lie, and were anxious to prevent its total defeat. Such a defeat would leave Sweden without a buffer between itself and the Soviet Union. For this very same reason, however, they were not willing to confront the Soviet Union themselves. At the same time, they were also ready to do everything possible to foster negotiations between the Finns and the Soviets. It was in their interest to see the war reach its end, as long as Finland was still alive and breathing, even if cruelly reduced in size. Better a smaller Finland than a Soviet Union, or a "People's democracy," as a direct neighbor.

The Swedes had another reason to further the negotiation process. They feared that if the war went on, the Allies would ultimately get involved, the Germans would react, and Scandinavia would become a war zone.⁶ Any illusions the Finnish Government may still have harbored about Sweden's rushing to its rescue with military aid were quashed for good now.

On February 21, in view of the Swedish reply and the Russian breakthrough at Summa, Tanner, speaking for the "triumvirate," cautiously informed the Parliament's Foreign Affairs Committee for the first time that there was a possibility of negotiating with the Russians. He also alerted the Committee members to the possibility (which, of course, had already become a fact) that the Russians' terms would be harsher than before. Only two Committee members who took part in the deliberations (one was Urho Kekkonen, subsequently President of Finland) expressed unequivocal opposition to the actions leading to the peace talks. Four days later, the government convened, chaired by the President, to examine the alternatives. The latest Soviet proposals, communicated to Helsinki by the Swedish Government on February 23, included demands that again exceeded the previous ones: cession of Hanko and the Karelian Isthmus, including Viipuri; cession of northeastern shore of Lake Ladoga as far as the border set by Peter the Great in 1721; and conclusion of a defense treaty between the Soviet Union, Finland, and Estonia concerning the Gulf of Finland. On the other hand, the Soviet Union was prepared to relinquish other territories, including Petsamo.⁷

***

Three months of fighting, the soldiers' valor, the casualties' blood—it all seemed like a cruel waste now. At this point the Government must have confronted the piercing question: had it all been for naught?

The second alternative—the possibility of Allied involvement—was amorphous and discouraging. The proposals communicated to Helsinki from Paris and London were riddled with contradictions and confusion. At first, the Government of Finland was informed of an intent to send about two and a half divisions, providing that Sweden and Norway let them cross.

Just before the Government met on the evening of February 23, the new British envoy, Gordon Vereker, reached Tanner's house with his military attaché, General Ling. The British minister brought the good news that a force of 20,000–22,000 soldiers, all equipped with automatic weapons (a very considerable improvement in those days) would reach Finland on April 16. In firepower, he said, "A battalion would be equal to a regiment."[8] To merit this beneficence, Finland had to put in an official request for this force, and obtain the consent of Norway and Sweden for its crossing. Tanner's reply—that such an operation was likely to drag Finland into a large European war—must have seemed rather strange to the British. After all, he said, Finland was not officially in a state of war with Russia, and neither would England be in such a case. As for Tanner's question about Great Britain's ability to guarantee Finland's borders and independence and finance a protracted war, the British envoy had no answer.[9]

It rapidly transpired that Vereker's information and numbers had no real backing. He had exceeded the boundaries of his instructions, apparently by his own initiative. He may have wanted to foster the expectations of the Finnish Government and secure its consent—thus permitting him to inform London of his dizzying and immediate success. Matters did not proceed as he had planned, and on February 27 the British Foreign Office directed him to let the Finns know where the facts truly stood:

The expeditionary force would have neither 20,000 troops nor 22,000, but rather 12,000–13,000, and its estimated date of arrival was the end of April.[10]

In any event, the cabinet ministers found themselves before a very difficult dilemma at that meeting. They had to choose between acceding to the harsh, uncompromising Soviet demands and an expectation of Western aid. The dimensions of this aid were not sufficiently clear, but there was no doubt that they were inadequate; furthermore, implementation was made conditional on the consent of Finland's Scandinavian neighbors. As they deliberated, as will be recalled, distressing reports continued to come in from the front.

Among the participants, only Ryti, Paasikivi, Tanner, and Finance Minister Mauno Pekkala favored peace talks with the Russians.[11] Five ministers vehemently objected to any negotiations, for the following reasons:

The army had not been routed. True, part of the front had been breached, but the Russians had not rendered a decisive blow. Esprit de corps was still evident, and if it were to become known that a Western expeditionary force was on the way, the valor of Finland's fighting men would grow all the more. The snow would soon melt, and the lakes, rivers and marshes, would slow the Soviets down. The Finns could again dig in and await the English-French expeditionary force. If the Finns had temporarily to retreat from Karelia, the British and French, by getting involved, would have to support the restoration of Finland's historical borders, once the time for peace came.[12]

Although President Kallio had supported talks with the Russians a few days earlier, he now seemed to decide with the naysayers.

As a way out of this agonizing dilemma, Tanner was again asked to set out for Stockholm and re-examine three alternatives: to obtain more amenable terms from the Russians, to procure more substantial aid from the Swedes; to secure Sweden's permission to let the Western expeditionary force cross.

Tanner's third journey to Stockholm produced nothing surprising and nothing new. Meeting with Alexandra Kollontai, he tried to assess the possibility of bargaining with the Soviet Government for peace terms. The Soviet ambassador, perceptibly agitated,[13] left no doubt in his mind that these were resolute demands, not bargaining cards. Swedish Prime Minister Hansson also left no room for misunderstanding. Sweden would continue helping for the moment; it would permit the recruitment of 16,000 volunteers, and would let foreign volunteers cross as long as they did so in small groups. However, under no circumstances would Sweden allow British and French military forces to march through. And if they tried to do so forcibly, Sweden would indeed enter the war—on Russia's side.[14]

Sharply and unequivocally, Hansson and his Foreign Minister, Günther, made it clear that Finland had to move quickly on peace with the Soviets, even at the price of difficult concessions, lest the window of opportunity slam shut. "Sweden," said Günther, "will not go to war for Viipuri and Sortavala. Even for Finland, the loss of these two cities does not mean the destruction of Finland." Then he added, nonchalantly, "At the appropriate moment you can take them back,"[15] as if it were a matter of passing a pack of cigarettes across a table. Günther gave clear indication that Sweden was now concerned for its fate ("Sweden is in a race against catastrophe"), and wanted Finland to sign a peace treaty quickly and at any price.[16] Sweden was willing to pay for peace; it would sponsor a defense alliance encompassing itself, Norway, and Finland, and would supervise the implementation of the Soviet-Finnish peace treaty. Sweden would also offer Finland economic aid for rehabilitation purposes. All this—but no more.

A Russian Ultimatum and a Finnish Decision

On February 28 at 3:00 p.m. the Government convened to hear a report from Tanner. It was pitch black outside, the only glimmer coming from the piles of snow that spilled onto the marble and wide steps leading to the entrance of the Bank of Finland building.

Prime Minister Ryti, a former Governor of the Bank, loved this building—its Neo-Classic beauty, the grandeur of its corridors, staircases, and halls. The meeting was called in the spacious Governor's office, whose wood-panelled walls were adorned with gold-framed, grave-faced portraits of Ryti's predecessors in this position. The electric lights were on, and six colorful candles around the table radiated their warm light as in bygone times. Cigarette smoke hung in the air, as did the palpable tension. The news from the front was bad. Now the ministers had to confront three facts: Tanner's report of his talks in Stockholm, which no longer left any room for illusions; the British envoy's corrected information on the size of the expeditionary force; and the Soviet Union's ultimatum, communicated via the Swedes, to which the Finnish Government had to give its final answer by 11:00 a.m. on March 1.

At this point most of those present saw no choice but to enter into immediate negotiations on the basis of the Soviet demands. It was a brutal decision to make. The Foreign Minister was of the view that "By cutting a limb from the body of our nation we could save the whole."[17]

In view of the minority's protestations, it was agreed, as proposed by President Kallio, to consult first with the Commander-in-Chief. Wasting no time, Prime Minister Ryti set out for Mannerheim's headquarters with four Cabinet colleagues: Minister of the Interior Baron Ernst von Born, Minister of Social Affairs Karl-August Fagerholm, Minister of Agriculture P. V. Heikkinen, and Minister of Justice Söderhjelm.

The marshal's stance was unequivocal:[18] a peace agreement must be attained without delay. If the Russians succeeded in breaking through, they would be very hard to stop, considering the quantity of tanks they had and the Finns' steadily dwindling supplies of ammunition. The men were living from hand to mouth.

When the delegation returned to Helsinki the next day, February 29, the Government met again. This time the debate was short. Only Ministers Hannula and, to some extent, Niukkanen maintained their resistance. The Parliament Foreign Relations Committee, too, approved the course of peacemaking, and only one of its members, Kekkonen of the Farmers' Party, maintained total opposition.[19]

That very night the Government adopted a resolution in which it viewed the terms presented by the Russians as "a point of departure for negotiations, and accept[ed] them in principle." This phrasing, certainly meant to satisfy the minority and preserve national unity, could not, of course, obfuscate the main point. The Government of Finland had decided to enter into talks with the Soviet Union, knowing full well that the Soviet terms were ultimative and harsh in the extreme.

Chapter Twenty

The Affair of the English-French Expeditionary Force

The stage appeared to be set for a new act. The deadline of the Soviet ultimatum was less than 12 hours off. Behind the scenes, however, a covert and dramatic race was under way. Word of the Government's resolution had leaked swiftly, reaching Paris and London within a few hours.

Promises and Clarifications

Dadadiėr reacted to the resolution with rage and hysteria, sensing that his political career was about to collapse. That very night, without consulting with the British, he summoned Finnish minister Holma and handed him a telegram for Helsinki. In it he promised that a force of 50,000 soldiers would reach Finland by the end of March. The Allies would assume responsibility for solving the problem of how to cross the Scandinavian countries. If Finland entered into talks with the Russians, however, all Western aid would become a dead letter. Thus the friendly promise came with a tone of threat.

The promises, issued without any real backing and vested ex post facto with hesitant, limited British support, upset the Finnish Government's equilibrium once again. Even though an aura of unreliability had shrouded the Allies since Munich, and notwithstanding the misgivings of many of the ministers, no one in the Cabinet was prepared to ignore so urgent and important a promise at this juncture.

Therefore, on the morning of March 1, the Cabinet decided for the meantime to refrain from sending the previous resolution and, instead, to gain time for a thorough and exhaustive inquiry with the Allies. A new formulation for Moscow, communicated through Stockholm, expressed Finland's intent to reach an agreement, but requested a "clarification" as to the proposed borders. A feverish race of consultations, telegrams, telephone calls, and pressures now ensued. Both the Allies and the Swedes called on Finland to make up its mind once and for all. The Soviets, concerned by the rumors of an English-French expeditionary force, preferred to bring the war to a speedy end, even at the expense of total victory, on terms relatively lenient to the Finns.[1] They, too, demanded an immediate response from Finland, and—to stress the element of urgency—intensified the military pressure on the front.

One communiqué followed another. New numbers sprouted every day, and instead of clarifications, the fog thickened as time passed.

In reply to the Finns' question, London answered that the figure cited by Daladièr—50,000—referred to the total scale of the expeditionary force in the operation's final stages; the first formation sent, however, would consist of 12,000–13,000 men and would land in Norway on March 20. One unit of this formation would be designated for Finland and reach the front no earlier than mid-April. This clarification, which substantially changed the content of the French Prime Minister's promise, had, of course, an immediate chilling effect on the Finnish Government. Nevertheless, the British added, the Allies were prepared to send fifty bombers at once (instead of the hundred Mannerheim had requested). Another detail in the British message: in order to embark according to the aforementioned schedule, the Finnish Government had to convey an official request to the Allies by March 5.

The offer was further "devalued" a little later. On March 3, the British envoy, Vereker, reported that the initial force would comprise 6,000 British soldiers and set out on March 11. Neither did this mark the end of the clarifications. Late the next evening, the French military attaché, Col. Ganeval, materialized with an upward lurch in the seesaw of numbers. Between April 10–15, he announced, a task force of 15,000 French soldiers (equal to one and a half Finnish divisions in terms of firepower) and 18,000 British troops would reach Finland. However—the attaché hastily added—this was only the start; the force would grow to whatever dimensions needed. He went on to assert that even before the first of these dates—within a few days, in fact—fifty British bombers and another twelve of French manufacture would reach Finland by order of Gen. Gamelin. Only because of the condition of the Finnish airfields was it not possible to bring in a larger number of aircraft. The British-commanded joint task force would be turned over to Marshal Mannerheim at once. The Allies, Col. Ganeval added, were also planning a naval action in the Petsamo area. Everything was ready to go; only a Finnish appeal for help was lacking. What a shame that time had already been wasted; the deadline for Finland's appeal was only a few hours away.[2]

This "clarification," which only added to the previous confusion and displayed additional contradictions in the details of the promised assistance, put the Finnish Government's agonized ponderings to an end.

Previously, too, the Finns were under no illusions. They knew that the Allied proposals originated not so much in sympathy and admiration of their blue eyes as in the strategic design of France and England already at war with Nazi Germany.

This, of course, did not stop the Finns from treating the generous offers favorably, provided that the promises be kept and Finland's war effort profited as a result. It now seemed that the grandiose promises were so much hot air. The frantic, jumbled "clarifications" proved that the task force—even if it arrived, even if it were permitted to cross Norwegian and Swedish territory, even if its landing did not provoke an immediate German reaction—would be, in Mannerheim's view, too little, too late.[3]*

Therefore—after further inquiries with Mannerheim (who espoused concurrent Finnish appeals to the Western powers and negotiations with Moscow), the Swedish Government, and members of the Foreign Affairs Committee—the Government (over Hannula's objections) decided to effectuate its previous resolution and enter into talks with the Soviets. Only if the latter refused to negotiate, the resolution stated, would Finland ask the French and the English to extend the deadline for the request for aid by one week, to March 12.

Another Round of Talks in Moscow

The delegation to the talks comprised Prime Minister Ryti, Paasikivi, Prof. Voionmaa of the Parliament Foreign Affairs Committee, and Gen. Walden. The four, bearing passports with false names, embarked on a nighttime flight via Stockholm and reached Moscow on March 7. There they were quickly disabused of hopes for real negotiations, diplomatic give-and-take, and prospects of extracting a Soviet concession on Viipuri and Sortavala—if they had ever harbored any such hopes.

It became clear in the very first meeting on March 8 that they had been invited not for negotiations but for a diktat. The Russians were represented by Molotov, Zhdanov, and Gen. Alexander M. Vasilevski. The ab-

---

*This assessment proved to be accurate; the Germans indeed speeded up their invasion plans in response to the reports of Allied intentions to land troops at Narvik. Denmark and Norway were occupied in April 1940. When England and France tried to put their troops ashore in Narvik in the second half of May, they were repelled by the Germans with heavy losses.[4]

sence of Stalin indicated by itself that there was no room for bargaining; the power to make concessions and soften positions was his alone. The atmosphere in the talks was harsh, and the Russians' tone intransigent. Ryti's appeal for moderate proposals that would create a basis for good neighborly relations in the future was cut short acridly by Molotov, who fixed his cold glare on the Finnish Prime Minister through his rimless spectacles and said gravely:

> We failed to appreciate adequately the intensity of Finland's enmity toward us. We did not believe the extent to which Finland became a dangerous tool of other powers. The war demonstrated this.

And when the Finns protested these remarks, arguing that there was no connection between their war of self-defense and the designs of foreign powers, Molotov yielded a little, saying that the Finns might perhaps have determined their own actions and policy, but had in fact supported the intentions of the most aggressive circles in England and France. Thus Finland had no right to Soviet generosity, and had proved herself unworthy of the degree of consideration the Soviets had displayed toward her in October.[5]

Then Molotov began to spell out the Soviet demands, which were now even harsher than those communicated through the Swedes on the previous occasion (February 3). The members of the Finnish delegation were deeply surprised, although they should have been used to Soviet diplomatic language by now and perceived that there was method to the madness, as Shakespeare said. Finland's delays and footdragging had cost her in casualties and now resulted in a stiffening of the Soviet demands. Finland was now asked to cede Hanko and its vicinity; the Karelian Isthmus; territories north, northwest, and northeast of Lake Ladoga (south of the Virolanti-Paatio line and as far as Salmijärvi) including Viipuri and Sortavala, and important industrial centers such as Enso and Värtsila. She would also have to accede to a border overlapping that set by Peter the Great, and cede a large area bordering the Murmansk railroad near the Arctic Circle, the cities of Kuusamo and Salla, and the entire Rybachi Peninsula. Furthermore, the Finns would have to build a railroad linking the Murmansk line with Tornio on the Swedish border and the Gulf of Bothnia. On the other hand, the Russians relinquished two demands of lesser importance to them: Petsamo and a "mutual assistance pact."

The Finnish delegation's protestations were useless. Molotov made it absolutely clear to them that these were the terms, period.

Thus the first meeting ended. The delegation retreated to its hotel to consider its next moves.

Government Deliberations

Upon receiving the delegation's report on the morning of March 9, the Government in Helsinki responded to the growing Russian appetite with an outburst of fury. Several ministers insisted that the talks be broken off.

The previous day, the Finnish military attaché in Paris provided new details from Daladiėr and Ironside on the promised Western aid. This time they spoke of an expeditionary force of 57,000 men. Its first formation, comprising 15,000 elite French and British troops, would set out for Narvik on March 15. A second formation of three British divisions (14,000 men apiece) would follow in its wake.[6]

At the sound of these new promises, the President and several ministers were infused with new hope, and their opposition to negotiations for surrender resurfaced.

Just then, however, Marshal Mannerheim's report came in. The Commander-in-Chief, who had waged a magnificent, heroic campaign for three months—and who always knew how to read situations realistically, in victory and in defeat—now sounded pessimistic. The situation on the front was grave. A battalion of the 23rd Division had retreated in panic that day. The noose around Viipuri was tightening. Manpower had fallen to an average of 250 men per battalion. Functioning weapons and ammunition were running out, and the battle fitness of the soldiers, many of whom were overage or raw recruits, was on the wane. The front could hold for no more than another week; continued fighting would lead only to further attrition and substantial loss of territory.

In his memoirs, Mannerheim wrote that in view of the uncertainty surrounding the expeditionary force, and with the firm belief that Finland did not have the strength to continue beyond the spring, he felt obliged to advise the Government categorically to conclude peace.[7]

This report tipped the scales. Over the objections of Hannula and Niukkanen ("If we give up these areas without a fight, we'll have lost them for good. But if we continue fighting, it will be possible to reclaim them when the final arrangement is made") it was decided to empower the delegation in Moscow to accept the verdict on the spot, on condition that it did so unanimously.[8]

The delegation spent another two days trying to chip away at the list of Soviet demands, but its every attempt and proposal was met with hostility and humiliation.

Molotov demanded Finland's surrender to his every last demand, and hinted that any further footdragging would induce him to take Kuusinen out of the "freezer" and bring him back to political life. Paasikivi's attempt to obtain compensation of some kind for the territorial concessions was shot down in much the same way. Neither did his claim that Peter the Great had acted thus in 1721 do any good. Molotov's answer was curt, sarcastic, and typical of the ambience of the talks: "Write a letter to Peter the Great; if he orders it, then we will pay."[9]

The delegation's report reached Helsinki on the morning of March 11. The Government convened again, and President Kallio announced that he was ready to lend his support to a continuation of the war, if the entire Government lined up behind him. Only the two consistent opponents of the talks, Hannula and Niukkanen, did so. Under the President's proposal, which still failed to come to terms with the Soviet diktat, it was agreed that before taking the final and decisive step the Government would do everything possible to persuade the people that there was no longer any choice. Otherwise its action would be misunderstood. The people, who still disregarded the army's grave circumstances and pinned hopes on its own ability and Allied help, would bring the Government down. Thus the President proposed an official Finnish appeal to the Governments of Sweden and Norway—at least for the sake of going through the motions—to let Allied forces cross their territory. If their answer was negative, as could be expected, would they be willing to sign a mutual defense agreement with Finland? Their answer would serve the Government as a response to public opinion.

The question was sent, and the Scandinavian foreign ministers promptly replied as expected: "no" to the first part of the question, and non-commitment to the second part—a promise to consider the matter of a defense agreement.

At last the Government had something to explain to the public. The people could be told the truth, presented with the difficult choice, and assured that Finland would remain independent despite the harsh peace terms.

London and Paris—Last-Minute Bustle

Finland's appeal to her neighbors did not remain secret. It spread on eagle's wings to Paris and London, where it was immediately interpreted as an inclination on Finland's part to spurn talks with the Russians and keep the war alive with Allied help. The hot-air saviors burst into action. Daladiėr and Chamberlain hastened to proclaim that their Governments had informed Finland of their willingness to help her as she requested. Daladiėr declared that a French formation of 50,000 men had been ready to move as of February 26. Finland had only to ask! Then he added a threat: if Finland did not ask the Allies for help now, the Allies, of course, would accept no responsibility for determining Finland's final borders at the end of the (world) war.[10] London, for its part, announced that the Allies' expeditionary force of 100,000 men was ready to jump at Finland's command.

"All this was indeed news to the Finnish people," Tanner remarked ironically in his memoirs.[11]

In addition to these sagacious proclamations, the Allies took several steps meant to stimulate the Finns' will to fight.

Chamberlain summoned the Finnish envoy and told him that Great Britain was prepared to send 12 bombers, followed shortly by another 42.

On March 12 H. M. Government, over the hesitations of several of its members, resolved to dispatch a military force even without the advance consent of Norway and Sweden. This novelty rested on the assumption that public opinion in the two Scandinavian countries would force their governments to make peace with the *fait accompli.*

The instructions given to Ironside as to possible complications with the Norwegians and the Swedes were a strange mixture of vague flexibility and flexible vagueness: H. M. Government intended his force to land, if it could do so without serious fighting. It was not the Government's intention to have the force fight its way through Norway or Sweden. The troops should fire on Norwegian or Swedish forces only as a last resort. At one and the same time, however, the commanders were to receive instructions not to be deterred by a show of resistance.[12]

The plan finally decided on called for a limited operation: a landing in Narvik and securing of the railroad to the Swedish border. As for debarkations in ports farther south, it was agreed to wait for Germany's reaction. Finally, as for the operation's subsequent stages—and, in fact, its declared objective, the transfer of the force to the Finnish-Russian front—time alone would tell.

Chapter Twenty-One

The Fateful Decision

In the center of Senate Square stood the large monument created by sculptor Walter Runeberg. It was erected at the end of the 19th century by the Finnish people in memory of Czar Alexander II, who had bestowed favors and rights on them. Now, however—the morning of Tuesday, March 12, 1940, after three months of war between Finland and Russia—the Czar's likeness was appropriately blanketed with thick snow and had become a mass of white.

Indeed, the entire vast quadrangle, designed and laid out about a hundred years earlier by Austrian Carl Engel in impressive neo-classical symmetry, was hibernating under piles of snow that had not been removed. Its northern side was dominated by the white cathedral that loomed over the houses, streets, marketplace, and bay. Yellow government and university buildings enclosed the square's remaining three sides, and an overcast sky capped the snow-covered rooftops.

This sight, blanketed in the gloom of morning, appeared through the frosted, foggy windows of the government conference room. Ministers were seated around a huge, heavy walnut table at whose head, on a chair with a high backrest, sat the president. The air was infused with tension and a definite feeling that a moment of truth had come.

That morning, Russian advance troops had nearly reached the center of Viipuri, and the delegation's cable arrived from Moscow. There would be no Soviet concessions, it read. The delegation requested official permission to sign the agreement.

A decision had to be made, and it was not an easy one. The two dissenters, Hannula and Niukkanen, pressed for continued fighting while requesting aid from the Allies—that is, no surrender under the humiliating conditions. The others believed this was the last chance to sign an agreement, which, however harsh its terms, would avert disaster and destruction and permit Finland to maintain its independent existence.

Additional questions worked their way into the heated debate. What of the people dwelling in the territories about to be severed from Finland?

What of the immovable property left behind—factories, machines, buildings, farms? The atmosphere was gloomy. Both the proponents and the opponents of the treaty, as well as those more hesitant, contemplated visions of the war: the brave fighters on the front, the civilians' intrepid stand, the men, the women, the wounded filling the hospitals, houses bombed into rubble, three months of suffering and valor. . . .

They had to decide.

The Foreign Minister presented a draft of the cable which, once sent to the delegation in Moscow, would authorize the signature of an agreement that would lead to "the termination of hostilities between the two countries."

President Kallio studied the paper and said: "This is the most disgraceful document I have ever signed." Then he added:

> This is a distressing situation. We know nothing of the fate of half a million of our fellow citizens whose homes will be on the other side of the new line . . . I should be ready to go on with the war if I had the support of the Diet and the Cabinet, but we have come to this pass . . .

Finally, he picked up the pen, hesitated a moment, and said:

> May the hand wither that is forced to sign such a paper as this.[1]

He signed. Hannula and Niukkanen submitted their resignations on the spot; they were and remained men of principle.

The meeting was over.

Some months later, President Kallio suffered a stroke that paralyzed his right arm. A second stroke killed him in mid-December.[2]

The peace treaty and its terms

The peace treaty was signed in the Kremlin on March 13, 1940, early in the morning. Its purpose, as stated in the preamble, was to "put an end to the hostilities and to create lasting peaceful relations between the two countries."[3] It was also stated in the agreement that it was meant to secure Leningrad, Murmansk, and the Murmansk railway.

According to the treaty's terms, Finland ceded to the Soviet Union several islands in the Gulf of Finland; the entire Karelian Isthmus up to the borderline set by Peter the Great, including the cities of Viipuri, Käkisalmi, and Sortavala; the Kuusamo-Salla area; and the Finnish part of the Rybachi Peninsula, excluding Petsamo, which remained in Finnish

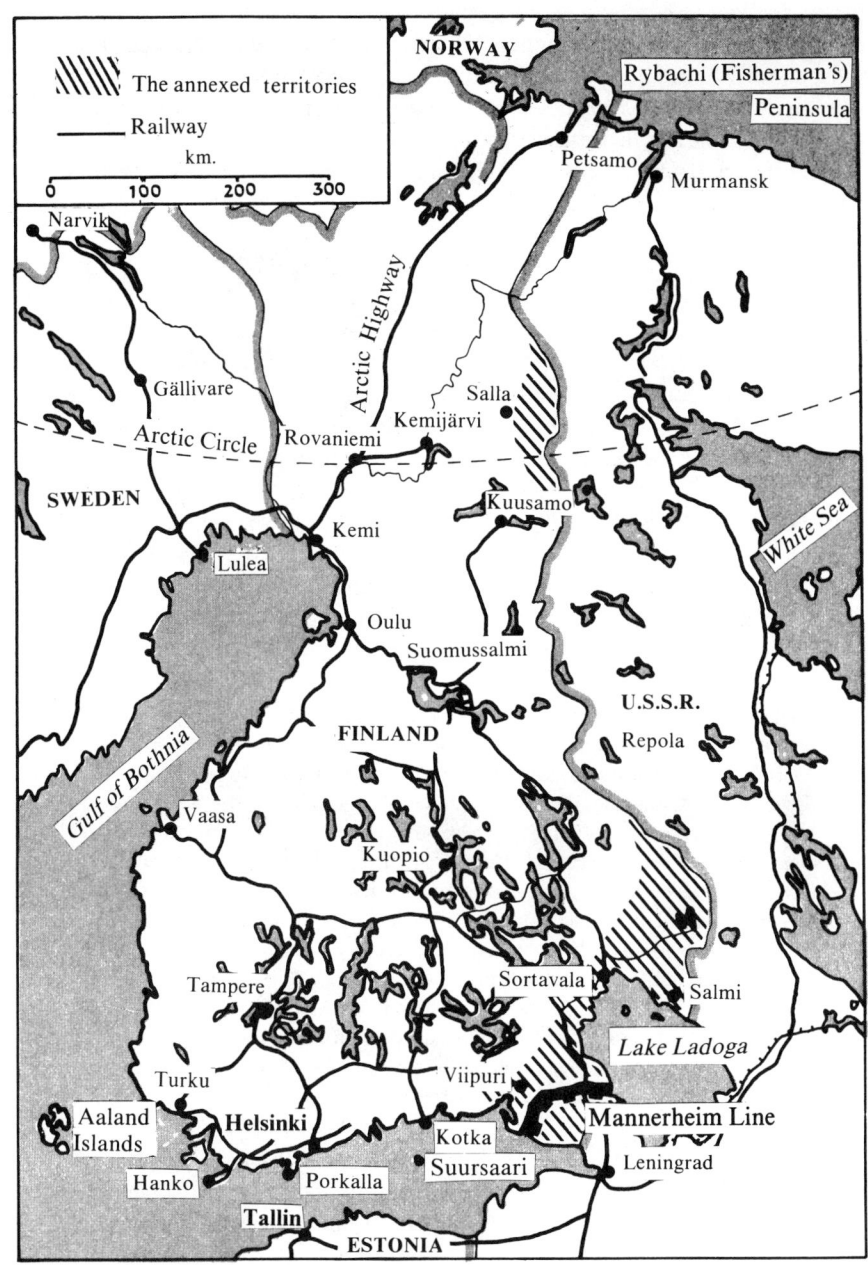

MAP 6: Finnish Territory annexed by the Soviet Union in 1940

hands. Finland also agreed to lease Hanko Cape and the surrounding waters and islands to the Soviet Union for 30 years, and to evacuate its forces from those areas within ten days. The treaty went on to prohibit attacks by either side on the other, and forbade either country's entering into alliances with a third party to attack the other.

That very day, the guns fell silent and the 105-day Winter War came to an end.

***

The legislature building was completed in 1931. It was a massive, magnificent structure. The forty steps climbing to the wide, impressive front; giant columns supporting the roof; stone walls rising into the sky; lavish use of marble on the floors, the interior stairs, the ranks of columns, and the walls of the halls; the sculptures symbolizing "future," "faith," and "toil" stationed in niches in the assembly hall—all these expressed and symbolized Finland: freedom-loving, proud, hard-working, democratic, as firm as the granite stones and as polished as the marble. On March 15, 1939, the delegates to the Eduskunta (Parliament) convened to ratify or reject the peace treaty presented to them by the Cabinet. Prime Minister Ryti reviewed the course of the war:

> We had trusted in the justice of our cause and had been confident that Russia would not attack us lawlessly. We had had no promises of aid from any quarter. Contrary to what was said, no one had incited us to oppose the Soviet Union's demands during the phase of negotiations. The whole world had at first considered Finland's cause to be hopeless. Of sympathy we received an abundance, but not effective aid from any quarter. Only when it turned out that Finland was capable of effective defense was humanitarian and material aid furnished in ample measure. . . . In contradistinction, no aid worth mentioning had come in the form of manpower. . . . Consequently, with respect to manpower we had fought the war virtually alone. When it proved beyond our power to go on, the Cabinet had after serious deliberations come to the conclusion that, despite the burdensome nature of the peace terms, we must pull out of the war while it was still possible. The future would show whether we had acted rightly and wisely.[4]

Delegates of the IKL (the essentially Fascist "Patriotic Movement") and several other MPs attacked the Cabinet for the way it conducted the talks and for its unconstitutional behavior. Reject the treaty and keep the war going, they demanded.

Kekkonen of the Agrarian Party, previously an opponent of the negotiations and the peace terms, had not really changed his mind but saw no way to turn down the proposed treaty under the circumstances that had arisen. Hannula, another consistent opponent of talks with the Russians, who had resigned three days earlier from his post as Education Minister, acknowledged that his struggle had ended:

> We must grit our teeth and go forward, and show the world that Finland lives and intends to go on living.[5]

Whereas Prof. Voionmaa, Chairman of the Foreign Affairs Committee and a participant in the Moscow talks, said:

> Much though we have lost, we still retain what is more important and valuable to our country than all the territories of which it is shorn—the independence of our nation and the freedom of our people . . . Was it in vain that Finland's army has fought, and our fearless young soldiers have reddened with their blood the wintry drifts at our borders? No; for they have fought victoriously for indestructible values.[6]

Once put to a vote, the treaty was ratified by a majority of 145. Three MPs voted against, nine abstained, and forty-nine preferred to absent themselves from the hall.[7]

The Toll in Blood and the Soul Reckoning

The Finns' losses in the Winter War were 24,923 dead and missing, and 43,557 wounded (10,000 seriously)[8]—a high and exceedingly painful proportion for a nation of 3,700,000, whose armed forces numbered no more than 300,000 throughout the hostilities. The Russians officially reported 48,745 dead and 158,863 wounded;[9] Mannerheim, however, estimates the number of Russian dead alone at 200,000.[10]

To explain the magnitude of the losses and failures, and to minimize the blow to the Red Army's prestige, Molotov concocted the "imperialist conspiracy" version of events. Appearing before the Supreme Soviet to summarize the war's progress and results, the Soviet Foreign Minister said that it had become apparent during the war that enemies of the Soviet Union—imperialist circles, "third powers" and their allies in Finland, and all those "Attlees, Blums, Citrines, and Jouhaux, Tranmaels and Hoegeunas, all those 'prostituted socialists' from the Second International"—conspired even before the war to turn Finland into a springboard for an attack on the Soviet Union, Leningrad in particular. The proof, Molotov told the Supreme Soviet, was "the Mannerheim Line," built in imitation of the

Maginot Line and Siegfried Line; the copious volume of arms injected into Finland from other countries; and armed forces from various countries in the guise of "volunteers."

> What was going on in Finland was not merely our collision with Finnish troops. It was a collision with the combined forces of a number of imperialist states, most hostile towards the Soviet Union. By smashing these combined forces of our enemies, the Red Army and the Red Fleet have added another glorious page to their history.[11]

When news of the signing of the treaty spread across Finland, the people, psychologically unprepared for the dramatic turnabout, reacted with sorrow, indignation, and a general feeling that a gross injustice had been inflicted upon them.

They had been attacked by a powerful enemy and had held their ground. Courageously, fearlessly, and firmly they remained united and prepared to sacrifice their lives. World opinion was on their side, but they had fought alone. Now, all this notwithstanding, they had to surrender, lay down their arms, and retreat from their lands.

Finnish newspapers framed articles about the treaty in black. Flags were lowered to half-staff. Women, children, and the elderly closed themselves in their homes, grinding their teeth in wrath and concealing their wounded pride. And the soldiers—weary, bloodied, but not routed—began to retreat to the new lines.

Following the army came the population of Karelia[12] in an evacuation that had to be completed within twelve days. Of the area's population of 450,000, a mere handful chose to remain; everyone else preferred to abandon homes, possessions, birthplaces, and way of life, and to migrate as war refugees into the heart of Finland—anything but to come under Russian rule. Although the Finns mobilized all private and public transport for the operation, most property and livestock could not be saved. Homeless and destitute, the refugees of Karelia reached Finland to start over. The Finnish people, though buckling under the expenses of the war, made yet another tremendous effort to enable the refugees, who represented 12 percent of the total population, to reintegrate themselves economically, productively, and socially.

The leaders, headed by Mannerheim, mounted a drive to sustain national morale. The Finns, they claimed time and time again, had done everything humanly possible to defend their freedom. The entire world gaped in astonishment at Finland's valor. Though Finland was finally forced to yield to a superior force, its war effort had saved its independence. Yes, an important part of her territory had been torn away, but the nation remained intact and united. On this basis, and on the basis of the peace treaty, the nation could embark on its rehabilitation and reconstruction.

The coming generations, declared Mannerheim, can with pride look back on the Winter War, on the valiant defense performed by the Finnish army, and on the devotion and greatness of the Finnish people. Such a nation, said Mannerheim, has earned the right to live.[13]

These words of Mannerheim's reached an attentive Finnish people, thirsty for encouragement, and infused the nation with new hope.

Chapter Twenty-Two

The Winter War Saved Finland's Independence

The Winter War can be viewed as one of many historical episodes; as a dramatic account of a small nation's war against a mighty neighbor attempting to thrust itself upon her and rip chunks out of her hide; as a war that ended—as could have been foreseen—with the victory of the strong side and with subjugation of the small nation to its demands. It can be described as pointless bloodletting; a war that could have been prevented had the Finns taken a more "realistic" approach and yielded to the Russians in advance—had they paid in October 1939 the price they were forced to pay "with interest" in March 1940.

The Winter War can also be assessed differently, not only out of esteem for the Finns' heroic stance against the mighty enemy, but also by a different reading of the outcome. This reflects the unmistakable and perhaps puzzling fact that of all the countries bordering the mighty Soviet Union—from the Baltic Sea to the shore of Turkey—only Finland has remained politically independent, free, and democratic. We should not belittle this fact. It would be simplistic to say that the Finns' war effort, and it alone, brought this about. There were additional factors, which we mentioned while describing the events. But had the Finns not fought as they had, their fate today would not have been much different from the Lithuanians' or the Czechs'. By the same token, had they not succeeded in extricating themselves from the war by means of negotiations and with the help of an international constellation, the Soviets would ultimately have defeated them soundly and overrun their territory.

Johan Nykopp, a senior Finnish diplomat and a member of the negotiating team sent to Moscow in November 1939 asserted that: "The Winter War and the peace treaty saved Finland from disappearing completely from the map of Europe."[1] We accept this testimony.

Despite the territorial losses, this seems to us the decisive value and the most conspicuous result of the Winter War. We conclude this chapter with an excerpt from Michael Walzer's analysis of just and unjust wars:

The new borders established in March 1940 were far worse than those that had been offered to Finland four months earlier; thousands of Finnish soldiers (and a greater number of Russians) were dead; hundreds of thousands of Finnish civilians were driven from their homes. But against all this must be set the vindication of Finnish independence. I don't know how one strikes the balance, still less how one might have done so in 1939 when vindication seemed an unlikely or at best a chancy prospect. Nor can its value be measured even now; it involves national pride and self-respect as much as freedom in policy making (which no state possesses absolutely and Finland, since 1940, to a lesser degree than many). If the Finnish war is commonly thought to have been worthwhile, it is because independence is not a value that can easily be traded off.[2]

Final Remarks and Reflections

Final Remarks and Reflections

Can We, Should We, Derive Lessons from History?

We have told the story of three small nations, and traced their political, diplomatic, and military behavior in one of the most dramatic periods of their history and the world's.

One often hears about the need to derive historical lessons. Is this truly possible? Can one draw tangents from the events described here to the present and future, applying the past to occurrences in today's world? Can one learn lessons and draw conclusions about all small nations on the basis of a sample of three in Europe? The answer to these questions is "no."

As we study the annals of Czechoslovakia, Poland, and Finland, each of us undoubtedly encounters phenomena and situations that hint at current events, recall analogies, and dredge up associations with other contexts. Nevertheless, we should beware of rushing into hasty conclusions. "World affairs"—observes Hans J. Morgenthau—"have surprises in store for whoever tries to read the future from his knowledge of the past and from the signs of the present."[1]

Only the intellectually shallow would foster an inclination to obfuscate the differences between "similar" and "identical" and to reach the superficial conclusion that "history repeats itself." Just as no two people in the world are identical, neither are two situations in international relations. The circumstances in which Czechoslovakia, Poland, and Finland found themselves were not identical, nor were their responses. Their different responses and actions were the outcomes of both the different conditions each of the three nations faced, and the decisions taken by each nation's political leadership.

There are no uniform rules that bind nations and dictate their actions when time, place, circumstances, and the actors within them are all different. Every situation—especially one of confrontation between two forces, two nations—has to find its own solution, particular to it and its specific factors.

Furthermore, even if each of these three nations faced identical conditions and situations, it does not stand to reason that they would react identically.

Every nation—like every individual—can apply more than one solution to any given problem, situation, and dilemma. There is no predetermined prescription for the optimal action; there are always alternative solutions, and the eternal problem is how to make the correct choice and decision.

Everything is foreseen from On High, but we are nevertheless given freedom to choose and act, the Talmudic sages say. "Foreseen" are the external, objective conditions, such as geography and natural resources. However, freedom to act, too, does not exist in a void. It depends first and foremost on the nation's moral, economic, social, and military strength; its aspirations; its historical tradition (the "national fiber"); its prevalent trends of thought; the national leadership's ways of thinking and conceptual motives; and the extent of popular support it enjoys. Thus every situation, with all its material and human components, requires fresh, unprejudiced thought, and paths toward solution attuned to the circumstances of the setting, time, and nature of the players involved. The worst tendency in historical and political action is to treat precedents like interchangeable parts. Today's problems have to be solved along today's routes, not yesterday's. For this reason, the annals of Finland's "Winter War," or the Beneš Government's behavior during the Munich period, should not be made a "guide for the perplexed," a political and operative handbook for small nations confronted with superior forces. These historical events should not be turned into "lessons," or worse still, historiosophic doctrine.

This is all the more so considering that today's world is fundamentally different from that of pre-World War II history. The great powers of the earlier era dominated continents and oceans; now they are large, respectable states, but no more. The number of UN member states has grown from 51 in the founding stage to 157 in our time. The "third world" was under the colonialist heel before World War II; it is now an international factor, and superpowers compete for its support and votes in the UN. Yesterday's "basket cases" flex their muscles and nascent abilities. The two superpowers determine the fate of the world, and, perhaps, future events in outer space. However, other candidates for world power status are already preparing their debuts and primping for the big time. The superpowers' nuclear "closed shop" is menaced by several medium-sized and even small states that aspire to master the secrets of the atom. Japan, defeated in war, now threatens the economic stability of the mightiest of powers. "Local" wars in which American and Soviet troops clashed with local forces—in Vietnam and Afghanistan—tarred the two superpowers with failure. In short, today's world is no longer that of 50 years ago.

Hence, the contents of this book are nothing but history.

Nevertheless, after having put safe distance between ourselves and the exaggerated tendency to "derive lessons," and having clarified the constraints of this thinking, we must point out how serious an error it would be for decision makers and people who seal nations' fate to disregard the historical experience that has accumulated in the "collective memory" of nations—theirs and others'.

To ignore the common trends and elements in the history of peoples, the dilemmas and principles that surface in human annals, the behavioral rules derived from the essence of political action, and the moral ideals and tenets that guide people, is to admit to intellectual blindness. Anyone who aims to understand the progression of history would do well to identify shared elements in the history of peoples. Anyone interested in influencing political affairs should explore the principles which hold true even when circumstances, time, and setting change. True, one cannot draw tangents from one realm to another. However, one should and even must study other peoples' history to find out if their situation is not similar to ours, if their actions are worthy of imitation under our circumstances, and if we can refrain from repeating their mistakes.

"When people speak of learning lessons of history"—historian Barbara Tuchman writes:

> They have in mind, I think, two ways of applying past experience: One is to enable us to avoid past mistakes and to manage better in similar circumstances next time; the other is to enable us to anticipate a future course of events. . . . To manage better next time is within our means; to anticipate does not seem to be.[2]

In this final chapter, then, we are not out to anticipate the future course of events nor to derive "lessons," "proposals for action," or "operative conclusions." The conditions and circumstances in Europe of the 1930s and the 1940s no longer exist, and the behavior of Czechoslovakia, Poland and Finland is not a subject for imitation. Something about how they behaved may well arouse sentiments of identification, agreement or rejection, admiration or criticism. These feelings, however, must not be allowed to overwhelm reasoned thinking about the situation in which we find ourselves in the current time and place. Our judgment and conclusions have to be firmly rooted in the setting actually at hand.

Nevertheless, the study of these and other nations' experience and the fundamental factors which most of them shared and which sealed their fate can serve us as a message, helping us understand a small nation's situation and illuminating the path along which it would do well to march.

Without venturing into excessive detail, let us try to summarize and explore four such factors:

    A. The occasional threat against small nations' existence and independence by their mighty neighbors through no direct fault of their own.

B. The right and duty of small nations to defend themselves against aggressors.
C. The role of both the military and diplomacy in the integrated system that the small nation must invoke in its struggle for existence.
D. The ways in which small nations can foster friendly relations with a great power while developing their own ability to endure.

In the Shadow of Threatening Night

We selected Czechoslovakia, Poland and Finland as our case studies mainly because they shared several similar circumstances. Each found itself in a confrontation rooted in constant crisis and geopolitical friction between itself—a relatively small, young nation—and a mighty neighbor. They had the misfortune of being situated alongside two powers whose leaders were infused with a sense of mission and motivated by fierce ambition to change the existing world order—alongside the might of Nazism, the most inhuman regime of modern times, the most demonic in its aspirations, and the most ruthless in its methods of implementation, and Russian imperialism guided by Communist ideological motives under the uninhibited leadership of Stalin and his spear-carriers.

This was an essentially existential confrontation. Its theme: a small nation's right to survive and exist independently. It was the asymmetry in the balance of power that made it dramatic. The three nations, each in its own way, tried to prevent the confrontation in the years preceding it and strived to cope with it once it arrived. All three failed. Was this their fault?

A small nation's independent existence, sovereignty within its territorial confines, right to unhindered spiritual and material development within recognized, defensible and inviolable borders—rights considered inalienable according to the UN charter and the solemn pronouncements of world leaders—all are in fact subject to potential threats. These are generally latent, but at times they flare into activity.

Mighty powers, especially when the latter are led by factors that espouse aggressive, expansionist policies are the major actors menacing small nations. The might of such a neighbor is something like a great river, which keeps within its banks when skies are clear but may flood fields, orchards, and villages when storms strike.

The small nation's major concern and supreme task must therefore be to create relations, conditions, and tools that will permit it to continue existing and developing under conditions of peace and security. Peaceful, amicable relations with powerful neighbors are in its vital interest. Insofar as this depends on the small nation, its policymakers must exhaust all possibilities and all political and diplomatic avenues that might further this supreme goal, as long as its life-and-death concern—its independence and sovereignty—are not harmed thereby. Nevertheless, it must be acknowledged that a small nation's efforts to arrive at peaceful coexistence, however sincere and manifest they may be, are no guarantee of reciprocity. Even if the Finns erred in underestimating the Russians' resolve to rip Karelia from them, should they be blamed for the Winter War?

It was not the liberal Czechoslovak Government's attitude towards the Sudeten Germans that led to Czechoslovakia's dismemberment at the hands of Germany, but rather Hitler's *Drang nach Osten*.

It was not Stalin's concern for the Ukrainians' and Belorussians' national independence that induced him to forge an alliance with Hitler and to partition Poland, but rather Stalin's own intention to distance the German menace from Soviet Russia.

The initiative for the confrontation is always taken by the powerful state, even if it wears sheep's clothing, and bleats pitifully, accusing the little state of wolfish propensities and castigating it for "oppression," "expansionist aims," and "imperialism."

True, the governments of Czechoslovakia, Poland, and Finland made mistakes and thereby worsened their situation, as we have seen at length. However, there is one thing of which they cannot be accused: fanning the flames of conflict and provoking confrontation. This distinction, similarly apt with respect to other nations, must always be borne prominently in mind. This is because the mighty neighbor always attaches propaganda to its aggression with the intent to obfuscate the truth, turn white into black, undermine the small nation's international status, and delegitimize it in international public opinion. At times third-party states not directly involved in the conflict join the propaganda campaign. These calls are voiced not only by hired propagandists in the service of an aggressor state, but also by innocent "peace mongers" who apparently believe that the best and shortest road to peace crosses the small nation's back. They generally preach "noble principles" and call on the small nation to get back into line. Toward the aggressor, by contrast, they usually behave with restrained politeness and take care to "understand" its problems and demands. The notorious London *Times* editorial of September 7, 1938 on the Sudeten Germans was a good example of this pattern, and there have been no few others since then.

In a situation such as this—when all its leadership's endeavors to prevent by peaceful means confrontation have been exhausted; when its survival is at stake; its independence, national character and territorial integrity threatened by force of its enemy—a small nation has no choice but rise up in self-defense.

On the Complexity of "Simple" Concepts

These three nations were not the instigators of confrontation. On the contrary: all of them, each in its own way, tried to prevent it and, when this proved impossible, to cope with it. We noted that they failed, and that it was the imbalance of forces that made the confrontation and its outcome so dramatic. True as these assertions are, however, they are generalized, and their content is more complex than one would suspect.

"Balance of forces," for example, is a rather complex concept expressed not only in the number of divisions, tanks and aircraft, but also in the small nation's cohesion, its leadership's wisdom and determination, its army's combative moral, preparedness and technological standard, which reflects the caliber of the entire national society and the international constellation.

"In a conflict"—an experienced senior Finnish diplomat said—"between a great power with wide and varied interests and commitments and a small nation with the single objective of survival, the balance of forces does not always yield to simple arithmetic calculations."[3]

Examining each case, each defeat separately, we find, for example, that the pre-confrontation balance of forces between Czechoslovakia and Germany was not altogether negative, and that one of the reasons for Czechoslovakia's demise was that it refrained from using its defense capabilities.

In Poland's case, the failure was rooted not only in the disparity of numbers, but also in conceptual and technological backwardness, misguided political action, and unrealistic assessments of the balance of forces.

David and Goliath

Peoples schooled on the Bible recall the account of David and Goliath as a symbol of the spirit of valor, the victory of the seemingly weak over the strong. This is a correct reading. A more painstaking analysis of the Biblical account, however, will alert us to further details. Let us therefore return to I Samuel 17.

It happened in the Elah Valley, where the Israelite and Philistine camps had squared off. On one side was Goliath, a giant "six cubits and a span tall" (more than nine feet, the commentators say), a "warrior from his youth." His equipment was ample and sophisticated ("bronze helmet on his head . . . a breastplate of scale armor . . . bronze greaves on his legs . . . a bronze javelin [slung] from his shoulders"), and a heavy spear ("the iron head of his spear weighed six hundred shekels . . . "—about 220 pounds, say the commentators).

Even if we treat these weights and measures with a degree of skepticism and consider them propagandistic exaggerations of ancient Hebrew historians, the well-reasoned impression still remains that this was a large, powerful man, properly armed, whose mere appearance and arrogance terrified the Israelite camp.

And who was his opponent in the campaign? A shepherd boy, whose combat experience was limited to killing a bear and a lion that had attacked his sheep. David turned down King Saul's offer of armor and a sword to wear on his belt: "I cannot walk in these, for I am not used to them." Instead he armed himself with the light "weapons" to which he was accustomed: a stick, a sling, and five smooth stones from the brook.

The "balance of forces" seemed irretrievably lopsided, and Goliath was actually insulted when he eyed his opponent: "Am I a dog that you come against me with sticks?"

Eliab (David's older brother) and Saul tried to talk him out of joining the hopeless battle. "You cannot go to that Philistine and fight him," the King protested. But David was not deterred. He knew no fear—whether because of his youth and inexperience, or because of his faith in God: "The Lord who saved me from lion and bear will also save me from that Philistine." His motivation, too, was strong. It was conceptual, religious in nature ("For he has defied the ranks of the living God . . . "). Perhaps, too, he was tempted by the King's promise to reward the Israelite victor "with great riches . . . his daughter in marriage and . . . exemption to his father's house in Israel."

David honed his alertness and all his senses as he approached the haughty, contemptuous Philistine. Armed with motivation he faced the Philistine giant, and—wonder of wonders—the battle was decided by this factor . . . and his light arms.

Goliath's overwhelming advantage was neutralized not by imitation and use of similar weapons, but precisely by the use of different tactics, by maneuverability, and by arms suited to the attributes and habits of a shepherd. While the armored Philistine giant advanced methodically toward David to cut him down with his spear, his would-be victim exploited his agility and arms, which he could also use from a distance: "David quickly ran up to the battle line to face the Philistine. David put his hand into the bag; he took out a stone and slung it. It struck the Philistine in the forehead." We know the outcome.

The conclusion to be drawn is that "balance of forces" is not a simple arithmetical concept. Stripping the Biblical account of its religious and miraculous mantle, David's victory, the triumph of quality over quantity, was based on spiritual and personal motivation, physical fitness, speed and skill, combat techniques and equipment suited to the fighter's ability, and exploitation of tactical surprise, getting the most out of the combatant's force and maneuverability. These turned relative weakness into an advantage, and quantitative advantage into a cause of failure.

Indeed, the annals of mankind abound with instances in which the fate of nations was decided by factors other than quantities alone, and collisions with quantitatively superior forces ended in something other than defeat. In no few cases, "barefoot soldiers" have outfought armored knights, highly mobile and maneuverable forces with light weapons outperformed heavily armored units, and guerrilla formations bested regular armies.

We may say therefore, that a small nation does stand a chance of surviving a clash with a mighty neighbor, in times of both crisis and confrontation (and this is so insofar as the confrontation is military, not only political, and as long as it is waged with "conventional" tools of war, assuming that the small nation has them in reasonable quantities). All this, if—and this "if" is an integral part of the problem—it knows how to implement its strength and maneuverability resolutely, wisely, and competently.

"A chance of surviving a clash" does not mean the small nation can register a "victory," let alone a sure victory. It suffices for a small nation to frustrate and disrupt the enemy's intent, to repel his offensive, and to moderate his demands and pressures. The small nation's willingness to embark on military self-defense against the aggressor and to contend with his attack on its independence and existence strengthens its right to exist and, in the final reckoning, its independent existence—even if it pays a heavy price for this.

One can, of course, arrive at different assessments and reactions, and this question—identifying the best course of action with respect to national interests—may well provoke disagreement that cannot yield to a totally objective and dispassionate resolution. In this context we can only concur with Michael Walzer (*Just and Unjust Wars*), who writes:

> The "Munich principle" would concede the loss or erosion of independence for the sake of survival of individual men and women. It points toward a certain sort of international society, founded not on the defense of rights but on the adjustment to power. No doubt there is realism in this view. But the Finnish example suggests that there is also realism in the alternative view, and in twofold sense. First, the rights are real, even to the people who must die to defend them; and second, the defense is (sometimes) possible. I don't want to argue that appeasement can never be justified, only to point to the great importance we collectively attach to the values the aggressor attacks. These values are summed up in the existence of states like Finland—indeed,

of many such states. . . . The Finnish war is a paradigmatic example of the necessary defense. That is why, for all the complexity of the diplomatic maneuvering that preceded the war, the actual fighting has about it a great moral simplicity.[4]

Diplomacy

A small nation has the right and duty to defend its right to exist with all means at its disposal, fully exploiting its latent capabilities to this end. Nevertheless, it must not consider its army, however superb, the only or even the major response to its most acute political problem. When armed conflict breaks out, a small nation's armed forces are capable at the utmost of repelling the enemy's offensive, inflicting heavy losses and grave damage, and proving to him that his aggression will cost him dearly in blood. A small nation does not have the ability to bring the aggressor—whose human and material resources are several times greater, its territory vast, and its ability to "take a punch"—to his knees. A small nation's army cannot dictate terms to the enemy and ensure a protracted period of stable peace and security thereby. A small nation's army can further, but not replace, policy. Just as David in his struggle with Goliath summoned not only his physical strength but his maneuverability, so must a small nation, while cultivating its military prowess, develop diplomatic agility.

It needs diplomacy to surmount crises in its foreign relations, to prevent potential confrontation with a mighty neighbor, and to bring the confrontation, once begun, to an end. Its diplomacy must be more active and competent than that of a large, strong nation, which needs only raise its voice, apply economic pressure, or rattle its sabers when its interests are threatened. When a small nation is under pressure or in a situation of conflict, these are not enough. It has to use political imagination, agility of thought, and negotiating skill. Its status in such situations also has much to do with the personal ability of its representatives. We find no few examples of competent diplomats representing small nations who, by virtue of their personalities, furthered their national interests in a manner far exceeding their countries' true weight.

Negotiations

Political negotiations are the quintessence of diplomacy. The negotiating table is the diplomat's major battlefield, and his ability to maneuver on it has frequently been known to produce impressive achievements.[5]

In the absence of negotiations, an international conflict is liable to escalate into a confrontation that would undoubtedly do great damage to the small nation's human, spiritual, and material resources. In such a situation, too, outside parties may intervene alongside the protagonists or as an alternative to them, imposing their will and often disregarding the small nation's considerations and positions.

With these alternatives at hand, it is in the small country's interest to exploit any opportunity to enter into a dialogue and negotiations with its neighbor. It is the national leadership's interest and duty to take the initiative—before and during the confrontation in advancing toward dialogue and improved relations. Constant initiative—not only reaction to proposals, pressures, and temptations of outside factors—and a positive diplomatic dynamic that strives for good neighborly relations, coexistence, and peace, are the measures that bolster a small nation's status. Even if these measures do not attain their major, declared goal; even if not everyone acknowledges that the powerful state was the culprit, these measures can strengthen and improve the small nation's status and international image, and—no less important—strengthen the awareness of its own populace, especially the young, that the national leadership is doing its best to avert the menace of war, or bring it to an end.

Negotiations, when conducted by nations in a state of confrontation, are a difficult, complex, nerve-racking process that demands maneuverability and endurance at one and the same time, as each side struggles to obtain more and more important achievements from its point of view. It is a process involving struggle, pretense, use of pressure of various kinds, doorslamming, and difficult decisions.

The decisions are not always simple choices between good and bad proposals. Edmund Burke (1729–1797) found that "Most political decisions are a choice between the disagreeable and the intolerable."

We can well understand reluctance to reach decisions such as these. For one thing, any concession comes with an element of psychological difficulty. For another, our protagonists have to contend with negative public opinion at home, including accusations of "folding," "frittering away the military achievements," and "selling us out for a scrap of paper." Public opinion, after all, usually prefers what Sir Harold Nicolson calls "the heroic conception of diplomacy" rather than the "shop-keeper conception."[6] The "heroic" style certainly comes with a great deal of charm, albeit tragic charm. With respect to results, however, its achievements are usually dubious. The Polish government-in-exile practiced this kind of diplomacy with its "steadfast stance," inflexibility, and hollow adherence to principles that it could neither attain nor fulfill. This style was an outgrowth more of unwillingness to grapple with the need to reach difficult decisions than of genuine power. It did muster some popularity on the folk level, but its results spelled political failure.

By contrast, Finnish diplomacy, although unbending and backed with stubborn military struggle, produced an agreement which, despite its serious blow at Finland's territorial integrity, secured its future as an independent nation. This was undoubtedly a difficult, painful decision for the Finnish leaders, but without such decisions, without the courage to yield on less important points to secure what really matters ("By cutting a limb from the body of our nation we could save the whole")[7], negotiations do not stand a chance. And just as there is no war without human casualties, there is no peace without concessions and compromise.

Concessions and compromises are not dirty words from which diplomacy should flinch. At times they are political necessities, as when (in Abba Eban's words) leadership reaches the conclusion that "making a concession will be more useful or less harmful than refusing it."[8] The lurking pair of alternatives is either war or a solution imposed by one of the outside powers, including harsher, farther-reaching concessions handed down from a "global," not necessarily a "local," overview.

The only way to negotiate one's way to an agreement is by finding a golden path between the conflicting positions. Obviously, in serious negotiations no one runs to that path in an outpouring of glee. No one kisses its asphalt, and no one plots its course with precision as the deliberations begin. It is not drawn with a ruler; it does not necessarily bisect a piece of territory—if the issue is territorial—but it certainly stays away from its fringes, too. It is paved, perhaps even hewn, with bargaining and hard deliberation about every landmark and every paragraph in the agreement. It is not a predesigned conceptual model but the outcome of a process, a collision of all forces in the field and positions of strength. It is a political necessity and a laudable one, as long as it secures the main point, even at the expense of the inessential; as long as it guarantees the nation's durable security, dignity, sound neighborly relations, and peace.

Might and Maneuver

After speaking in praise of diplomacy, let us clarify that it alone should not be considered the only avenue to the resolution of international conflicts. Diplomatic negotiations irrespective of the other components of national policy cannot attain the goal. When the diplomatic negotiating process lacks the backing of force and the national leadership's will to use it as a last resort, the initiation of negotiations is liable to be interpreted as an sign of weakness and an invitation to pressure.

In this context, the unforgettable words of John F. Kennedy, president of the strongest of nations, are worth mentioning. They are valid for small nations, too:

> Let us never negotiate out of fear. But let us never fear to negotiate.

The small nation must resort to pragmatic diplomacy in times of peace and crisis, as surely as it needs a heroic stance by its army in wartime. Both approaches and styles are crucial to the nation's existence, each in its own time and way. The more efficient and sophisticated a small nation's diplomacy is, the greater its prospects of keeping its army in their barracks. The more capable the army is of withstanding the enemy's pressure, the more readily the diplomats will attain positive compromises and better results during the negotiations.

A Political Staff to Lean On

A small nation needs a political staff to lean on, and a great power can provide one. As true as this was in the past, it is even more valid today. A small nation requires political, military, and in many cases even economic support, and when thrust into crisis and confrontation, it must summon the deterrent strength and even the help of the friendly power. The more successfully it formalizes these relations in a written alliance and implements them by developing extensive relations, the more it can assume that it is thereby strengthening its security and reducing the threat it faces.

We shall not explore these truths at greater length. Rather, we shall confine ourselves to the other side of the coin—the problematic nature of the complex tapestry of small-nation–friendly superpower relations.

Who Will Guarantee the Guarantor?

We have noted that a great power's support has the effect of deterring a small nation's potential enemies. A caveat is in order, however: the efficacy of this deterrent is relative, transitory, and different from one case to another. Much depends on the friendly superpower's resolve to honor its commitment, and the question of "who blinks first"—the friendly superpower (at times far away) or the belligerent (and neighboring) state.

The historical examples in this book prove that at the moment of trial, when the friendly superpower is supposed to meet its commitment—not only to warn and deter, but to come to the small nation's aid—reluctance often outweighs commitment. In such cases, guarantees recall an umbrella that, though elegant and impressive so long as the sun is out and folded up against its owner's forearm, falls into tatters and flies into the wind once rain begins to fall.

A study on this topic[9] proves (statistically, in any case) that of 115 guarantee agreements signed since 1815, only 45 (48 percent) were clearly both reliable and adequate, and this also in those cases when the Great Power had a strong presence or strategic interest in the territory being guaranteed.

Rationales explaining that unreliability are not lacking.

Rebus Sic Stantibus

In our section on Czechoslovakia, we explored the development and substance of this legal principle. Here we shall only say that over the years it has become the fig leaf of those who wish to avoid their duties and casually abrogate signed agreements.

This is how Stalin behaved when he informed a Finnish delegation during the negotiations in Moscow that the Tartu Treaties of 1921 had no more practical value, because "they were made under totally different circumstances."[10] All the arrangements made after World War I, Foreign Minister Molotov claimed later, "had been forcibly imposed by the Western imperialist powers when Soviet Russia was militarily weak."[11] Now, however, circumstances and times have changed, and so should the agreement be modified—by "mutual agreement" if possible, and by force if the other side balked.

"Different circumstances" applies not only to objective conditions or changes in the balance of forces; a guarantor can invoke the idea when the beneficiary refuses to heed his "advice." He can also wrap himself in this mantle when his country's public opinion, or its national interest as he perceives it, clashes with the commitment.* In 1938, neither changed objective

---

*Israel, too, experienced the practical meaning of "different circumstances." For example, in May 1967 President De Gaulle told Foreign Minister Eban that France's commitment to freedom of shipping in the Gulf of Aqaba was no longer valid, because the circumstances had changed: "1967 is not 1957," he asserted.[12] And because Israel failed to heed his counsel, he rushed (even before the fighting broke out) to embargo aircraft Israel had purchased from France.

In the United States, too, circumstances changed at the same time because of the ambience produced by the Vietnam War and external constraints. Thus President

circumstances nor weakness deterred France and its ally England from firmly aligning themselves with Czechoslovakia. The change that did occur between the days of the Locarno Pact and 1938 was the rapid slackening of the will to fight for democratic values; a spread of naive pacifism, aided actively by the Comintern; a deepening fear of Hitler and a desire to appease him; and cultivation of the illusion that every concession was "the last" and "final." All these resulted in weakened military preparedness. Not the circumstances but the will had changed.

As long as the "changed circumstances" argument serves as cover for self-serving expediency—"realpolitik"—the gambit is logical, if unfair. If the rationale for an appeasement policy is the enemy's military supremacy, economic strength, abundant energy, and natural resources, this policy may still be understood, whether one accepts or rejects its premises. However, when such a policy wraps itself in a mantle of "morality," it compounds betrayal with hypocrisy.

The Psychological Gap

There is also a psychological element which may explain the world view of superpower leaders, and the gap between it and that of leaders of small nations. The first deal with "global interests" and "world peace" while eyeing a globe in a conference room, while the others ponder their own "provincial" problems while studying a 1:20,000 map. Against the Czechs' "selfishness" and "provincialism," then, stood the weighty "global" doctrine of the Great Powers' leaders, with their terrible responsibilities.

Just as the Absolutist kings identified the state with themselves, thus the leaders of Great Powers identify their countries' interests, as perceived by themselves, with "the well-being of mankind," "world peace," and "global interests." Small nations defending their rights and vital imperatives puzzle their great friends, the heads of world powers, inducing in them an anxiety tempered first by disgust and finally by anger. After all, they know best what is good for humanity, the world, and even their obsti-

---

Johnson was in no hurry to implement President Eisenhower's commitment concerning freedom of shipping in the Gulf of Aqaba. In his memoirs, Johnson writes with characteristic frankness: "I am fully aware of what three past Presidents have said . . . but that is not worth five cents if the people and the Congress do not support the President."[13]

nate, inflexible ally.* The ally's protracted and pointed insistence on its need for a certain piece of territory make them uncomfortable and short-tempered. How can a country argue endlessly about several square kilometers, this or that hill, or some miserable little town, when "world peace"— or at least "regional peace"—hinges on immediately forgoing such trivialities?

Thus Chamberlain and Daladièr behaved with regard to Czechoslovakia. Neither did Churchill spare the Polish government-in-exile his anger and pressure when he felt Stalin's demands had to be met.

In the name of "world peace" and "global interests," the leaders of Great Powers frequently make far-reaching concessions, compromises, and arrangements with aggressive actors—especially when the bone of contention is a "local interest" and when the concessions are made at the expense and out of the hide of the small ally. These leaders, fighting for the "great" goals, often call upon small nations to subjugate their "regional interest" to the "shared ideals." The small nation, however, must not only ensure the long-term victory of these ideals, but must have the strength to survive long enough to witness that victory. The government of a small state, says Annette Baker Fox, has to "concentrate on short-run possibilities."[15]

Friendship, Ltd.

The third point to mention in this context is that the friendly relations between a small nation and a world power are usually not exclusive. This is not a one and only true love; a world power has a range of interests and many other friends. Not all the enemies of a small nation are enemies of the world power, and vice-versa. Thus the leaders of the small nation have to draw clear distinction between their own nation's benefit and the interests of the friendly superpower. When the two clash, it is their duty—however unpleasant and difficult it may be—to insist on safeguarding their own nation's vital interests.

Fourth, friendly relations of this kind should not be considered "timeless values." A realistic analysis of historical events underscores the fact that bilateral and multilateral agreements and treaties earn their strength and validity not from the festive signatures they bear. They remain in effect as long as this is in their signatories' political, strategic, and economic interest, and as long as the balance of forces and the international constellation that brought the arrangements into existence continue to prevail.

---

*Typical of that kind of paternalism is the title of an article published in the 1970s by a senior American diplomat: "How to Save Israel in Spite of Herself."[14]

The aforesaid should not lead us to the hasty and overgeneralized conclusions that—paraphrasing the Proverb—alliances are deceptive and agreements are illusory; that the conventional and familiar norm in international relations is the constant violation of treaties; and that the value and importance of such pacts in ensuring international stability and the reciprocal benefit of the signatory states is as durable as the skin on one's teeth. Indeed, the complicated nature of international relations mandates and underscores all countries' vital need to cling to agreements that fortify the element of stability, and to implement them with care and in full. Small nations, more than any others, should be interested in strengthening and formalizing friendly international relations in agreements and alliances. Nevertheless, it is the duty of a small nation's leaders to refrain from over-reliance on external guarantees, and to recall that the glue of alliances does not hold forever. Alliances should be treated with all due respect . . . and with a measure of skepticism.

A Staff—Not a Crutch

If a small nation's friendly relations with a world power are to reflect the nature of an agreement and not of "protection"; of partnership, rather than dependence; of a durable connection, not a passing flirt—the small nation should rely first and foremost on itself, go to greater lengths to strengthen itself, and at the same time maintain its sense of proportion (i.e., to acknowledge the limitations of its own strength), and nevertheless not to snivel like a pauper at the door; not to issue a torrent of heated, boastful declarations; and not to "flex muscles" with pointless demonstrations. Rather, it should keep its reach within its grasp, and, at the same time, cling to aspirations that would make it a small but great nation.

Insofar as friendship and alliances with great powers are based on shared values, political coordination, ceaseless efforts by the small nation to improve its strength (in the broadest sense of this term), its positive image in world opinion, its respected position in the community of nations, and its leaders' and citizens' resolute will to exist as an independent and free nation—the friendship will rest on firm foundations. Conversely, the weaker these elements become, the stronger the small nation's one-sided dependence will be. Its dignity and value will diminish grievously; its staff will become a crutch; its will-power will degenerate; its ability to maneuver and grow will wither; and its desire to exist will diminish into paralysis. Agreements will be reduced to meaningless words on paper; commitments will be violated, and the small nation's justified bitterness concerning all these will be greeted with a shrug of the shoulders.

A world power's support for a small nation depends largely on historical ties and cultural values. At the same time, much also has to do with the great power's self-interest and its leaders' will to uphold commitments, however daunting and formidable the task may be. A major power's interest in supporting a small nation and keeping its word will intensify insofar as the small nation displays vitality, independence, self-defense capabilities and performance, and international political activity—i.e., insofar as it proves itself an ally and not merely a nuisance and a burden.

A Small Nation's Fate—In Its Own Hands

The fate of nations is decided by many factors, alternately labelled "historical laws," "the hand of God," or the outcome of economic processes or the decisions of charismatic leaders. Determinists believe that history repeats itself, and that there is nothing new under the sun. Others point at the wane of empires and the ascent to greatness of young nations as proof of history's changing character.

Whatever the nature of history and the factors determining its progression may be, one of the major facts in that progression is the struggle of small nations for their existence.

These nations and their leaders are not always the epitome of perfection, just as mighty powers do not always fulfill the finest of the vision of man. This does not detract from the right of small nations to live in peace alongside other nations, including mighty ones. This right is undoubtedly related to and emphasized by the richness of their historical experience and cultural creativity, by their contribution to human civilization, and by their achievements. Their right, however, to existence, independence, and sovereignty within recognized and defensible borders should be acknowledged as inalienable in and of itself, not to be attached to or conditioned by any particular qualities.

Unfortunately, however, this lofty principle is not always self-fulfilling. From time immemorial it has been accompanied by struggle. Quite often in the annals of history, small nations had to rise in self defense against mighty neighbors, who—in Hitler's words about Czechoslovakia—"could not tolerate an inimical thorn in their flesh."

The outcome of such a struggle and the small nation's fate are largely dependent on, and determined by, the nation's own endeavors, its peoples sagacity and audacity; their will and ability to maintain an enlightened, productive society; their pride in their national heritage; and their ability and resolve to defend the nation's existence, peace, liberty, and values.

A small nation's fate is largely dependent on, and determined by, its own endeavors, its people's sagacity and audacity; their will and ability to maintain an enlightened, productive society; their pride in their national heritage; and their ability and resolve to defend the nation's existence, peace, liberty, and values.

Notes

Chapter One: An Obstacle on the Road to Lebensraum

1. *Trials of Major War Criminals—Nuremberg* (TMWC), Vol. X, p. 259.

2. *Documents on British Foreign Policy 1919–1939* (eds. E. L. Woodward and R. Butler), third series, Vol. I, p. 302, HMSO, London, 1949.

3. The population censuses undertaken in Czechoslovakia overlooked the distinction between the two peoples, and the count was inclusive. Thus 8,760,937 Czechoslovaks were counted (of whom an estimated 2,000,000 were Slovaks) in the 1921 census, and 9,668,770 in the 1933 census. In 1940, "independent" Slovakia had a population of 2,653,564 Slovaks. As for the total population of Czechoslovakia, a census taken on December 1, 1930, found 14,729,536 (thereof: 3,231,688 Germans), including 10,674,486 in Bohemia-Moravia. The data are taken from H. Seton-Watson: *Eastern Europe Between the Wars, 1918–1941* p. 414; J. W. Bruegel: *Czechoslovakia Before Munich*, p. 41; R. Luža: *The Transfer of the Sudeten Germans*, p. 1; and L. Thompson: *The Greatest Treason*, p. 15.

4. Elizabeth Wiskeman: *Germany's Eastern Neighbours*, p. 52; Hubert Ripka: *Munich—Before and After*, p. 413.

5. *Documents on German Foreign Policy* (DGFP), series D, Vol. II, p. 198.

6. E. Wiskeman, p. 50.

7. Ibid., pp. 236, 240; Erwin Wickert: *Dramatische Tage in Hitler's Reich*, pp. 174–175, 221–222.

8. E. Wiskeman: *Czechs and Germans*, p. 266.

9. Nevile Henderson: *Failure of a Mission*, p. 150.

10. Paul Schmidt: *Hitler's Interpreter*, p. 60.

11. Tom Jones: *A Diary with Letters*.

12. Eduard Beneš: *Memoirs*, p. 20.

13. H. Seton-Watson, p. 282.

14. Victor S. Mamatey: *The US and East Central Europe 1914–1918*, p. 213.

15. Ibid., p. 174.

16. Robert Lansing: *The Peace Negotiations*, pp. 97–98, 102.

17. William L. Shirer: *The Rise and Fall of the Third Reich*, p. 447.

18. N. Henderson, pp. 130–131.

Chapter Two: In the Crucible of Appeasement

1. Adam Ulam: *Expansion and Coexistence*, p. 229.

2. Ibid., p. 231.

3. Ibid., p. 228.

4. Ibid., p. 323.

5. L. Thompson, p. 53.

6. Thierry Moulnier: "Combat," Novembre 1938, as cited by J. Wheeler-Bennett: *Munich*, p. 301.

7. Haffner, p. 70.

8. E. Beneš, p. 39.

9. Winston S. Churchill: *The Second World War*, Vol. I, pp. 208–210.

10. J. Wheeler-Bennett, p. 29.

11. E. Beneš, p. 8.

12. H. J. Morgenthau, pp. 420–421.

13. J. Wheeler-Bennett, p. 38.

14. Ibid., p. 32.

15. Churchill, Vol. I, p. 242.

16. J. Wheeler-Bennett, p. 61.

17. J. W. Bruegel, pp. 133–134.

18. N. Henderson, p. 139.

19. L. Thompson, p. 80.

20. J. Wheeler-Bennett, p. 91.

21. N. Henderson, p. 139.

22. H. Ripka, p. 22.

23. J. Wheeler-Bennett, p. 91.

24. Ibid., p. 46.

25. Albert Speer: *Inside the Third Reich*, p. 110.

26. *Parliamentary Debates (Hansard)*—fifth series, House of Lords, March 29, 1938, Deb. 461.

27. L. Thompson, p. 113.

28. W. Churchill, Vol. I, p. 248.

29. J. Wheeler-Bennett, p. 184.

30. N. Henderson, p. 149.

31. P. Schmidt, p. 93.

32. L. Thompson, p. 156–157.

33. P. Schmidt, p. 93.

34. Ibid., p. 126.

35. E. Beneš, p. 43.

36. W. Shirer, p. 478.

37. L. Thompson, p. 89; A. Ulam, p. 256; SDFP-Degras, III, p. 303.

38. W. Shirer, p. 476.

39. "Es tut mich furchtbar leid, aber das geht nicht mehr"—N. Henderson, p. 155.

40. Ibid., p. 157.

41. Ibid.

42. L. Thompson, p. 181–182.

43. Ibid., p. 211.

44. DGFP, Series D, Vol. II, pp. 976.

45. L. Thompson, pp. 219–221.

46. W. Churchill, Vol. I, p. 261.

47. L. Thompson, p. 229.

48. DGFP, Series D, Vol. II, pp. 960–962.

49. S. Hoffman: *Duties Beyond Borders*, p. 20.

Chapter Three: Munich

1. L. Thompson, p. 248.

2. H. Ripka, p. 232.

3. TMWC, Vol. XII, p. 531.

4. *Documents and Materials Relating to the Eve of the Second World War* (Dirksen Papers), p. 51.

5. W. Shirer, p. 513; L. Thompson, p. 258.

6. W. Churchill, Vol. I, p. 269, 271.

7. J. Wheeler-Bennett, p. 185.

8. Ibid., p. 195; H. Ripka, p. 492.

9. W. Shirer, p. 522.

10. J. Wheeler-Bennett, p. 195.

11. W. Churchill, p. 282.

Chapter Four: Surrender

1. H. Ripka, p. 232.

2. Ibid., p. 299.

3. Beneš, p. 29.

4. Gen. M. Gamelin: *Servir*, Vol. II, p. 374.

5. D. Vital, pp. 25–31.

6. Robert Leurguin: "The Czech Army," The *Times*, 27 September 1938.

7. Brig. H. T. C. Stronge: "The Czechoslovak Army and the Munich Crisis," *War and Society*, London, 1975, pp. 162–178.

8. H. Ripka, p. 135.

9. R. Leurguin, The *Times*, 27 September 1938.

10. R. Leurguin, The *Times*, 24 March 1939.

11. R. Leurguin, The *Times*, 28 September 1939; D. Vital, pp. 28–30; Brig. H. T. C. Stronge, p. 172.

12. A. Speer: *Inside the Third Reich*, p. 111.

13. Williamson Murray: *Munich 1938, The Military Confrontation*, pp. 283–284.

14. Gen. M. Gamelin, p. 347.

15. Williamson Murray: *German Air Power and the Munich Crisis*, p. 112.

16. D. Vital, pp. 28–30.

17. Williamson Murray: *Munich 1938, The Military Confrontation*, p. 288; TMWC, Vol. XII, p. 374; W. Shirer, p. 462.

18. Brig. H. T. C. Stronge, p. 168; Williamson Murray, *Munich 1938*, p. 286; D. Vital, p. 33; A. Speer, p. 111.

19. L. Thompson, p. 101.

20. W. Murray: *Munich 1938*, p. 288–289.

21. Haffner, p. 71.

22. TMWC, Vol. X, p. 584.

23. TMWC, Vol. X, p. 509.

24. TMWC, Vol. XX, p. 606.

25. TMWC, Vol. XV, p. 361; NCA, p. 364.

26. W. Churchill, Vol. I, p. 264.

27. Williamson Murray: *Munich 1938*, p. 288–289.

28. Josef Korbel: *Twentieth Century Czechoslovakia*, p. 149.

29. Ibid., pp. 140–143.

30. H. Ripka, p. 134.

31. L. Thompson, pp. 179, 180.

32. Otakar Odlozilik: "E. Beneš on Munich Days," *Journal of Central European Affairs*, Vol. XVI, p. 392.

33. J. Korbel, p. 139; D. Vital, p. 49.

34. O. Odlozilik, p. 393.

35. E. Beneš, p. 8.

36. Ibid., p. 9.

37. Oppenheim-Lauterpacht, Vol. I, p. 966.

38. H. Lauterpacht, *International Law*, pp. 576–577.

39. Marion Mushkat: *Halakha ve-ma'ase be-yahasim bein-leumi'im*, Vol. I, pp. 22–27.

40. E. Beneš, p. 36.

41. T. Schelling: *The Strategy of Conflict*, p. 20.

Chapter Five: Poland Between the Two Wars

1. Winston S. Churchill: *The Second World War*, Vol. V., pp. 283–285; Anthony Eden: *Memoirs—The Reckoning* (Cassell, London—Boston, 1965), p. 427; *Foreign Relations of the US—the Conferences at Cairo and Tehran*, (Washington, 1961), pp. 510–512.

2. These data are taken mainly from the official Polish publication: Jerzy Topolski (red.): *Dzieje Polski* (Panstwowe Wydawnictwo Naukowe-Warszawa, 1976), p. 845.

3. Oskar Halecki (ed.): *Poland* (Fr. A. Praeger, New York, 1957), pp. 46, 50.

4. According to German sources, 2,167,000. See *Dokumentation der Vertreibung der Deutschen aus Ost-Mittel Europa*, Band I/1 s. 159 E. According to Polish statistics, 1,900,000. See Jozef Kokot: *The Logic of the Oder-Neisse Frontier* (Poznan, 1959), p. 14, Table 6.

5. Ibid. (J. Kokot), Table 11.

6. From a Polish Government communiqué of January 27, 1947. See Marjorie M. Whiteman: *Digest of International Law* (Dept. of State, Washington, 1964), Vol. III, p. 363.

7. According to Halecki, the population of Poland in 1939 was 35,100,000, including 7.7 million Ukrainians and Belorussians, 3.35 million Jews, 0.741 million Germans, and 0.83 million Lithuanians. Including other ethnic groups, the total minority population reached 12 million. Halecki, pp. 44–45.

8. L. Grosfeld, H. Zielinski (red.): *Historia Polski*, tom IV (Polska Akademia Nauk, Warszawa, 1969), p. 120.

9. Ibid.; *Foreign Relations of the US: Paris Peace Conference 1919* (Vol. XIII), p. 794; *Historia Polski*, tom IV, pp. 374–77; E. H. Carr, Vol. III, p. 212; Edward J. Rozek: *Allied Wartime Diplomacy*, pp. 12–15.

10. J. Topolski, p. 646; E. Rozek, p. 17.

11. *Concise Statistical Yearbook of Poland*, 1935, p. 6.

12. *Rocznik Statystyczny* (publ. Glowny Urzad Statystyczny, Warszawa, 1939), p. 5; H. Seton-Watson: *Europe Between the Wars*, p. 413; E. Kozłowski, p. 325, n. 6; Commission Statistique de la République Polonaise, 1925–6, p. 26.

13. DGFP, Series D., Vol. VI, p. 1053.

14. W. Shirer, p. 261; A. Ulam, p. 205; W. Pobog-Malinowski, Vol. II, pp. 738–739; Jozef Lipski: *Diplomat in Berlin 1933–1939* (Columbia University Press, New York, 1968), pp. 92–93.

15. J. Lipski, pp. 252–254.

16. W. Pobog-Malinowski, p. 857.

17. Ibid., pp. 778–837.

18. DGFP, Series D., Vol. V., p. 38.

19. Robert Conquest: *The Great Terror* (Macmillan, New York, 1968), pp. 525–535; A. Solzhenitsyn: *The Gulag Archipelago*, Vol. II, p. 191; R. Medvedev, p. 239; R. Conquest, p. 485.

20. R. Medvedev, pp. 209–214.

21. W. Shirer, pp. 649–650.

22. Eugeniusz Kozłowski: *Wojsko Polskie* (Wyd. Min. Obrony Narodowej, Warszawa, 1974), pp. 345–346.

23. DGFP, Vol. VI, p. 1042.

24. W. Pobog-Malinowski: *Najnowsza Historia Polityczna Polski*, t. II, pp. 793, 802–805; H. Seton-Watson, pp. 166–168.

25. Salo W. Baron: *European Jewry Before And After Hitler* (The Catastrophe of European Jewry—Yad Vashem, 1976), p. 223.

26. J. Lipski, p. 411.

27. PGPSR, p. 27.

28. Ibid., p. 334, PGPSR, p. 43.

29. Weizsaecker to Moltke, DGFP, Vol. V, p. 40.

30. Ibid., p. 39.

31. Ibid., p. 44.

32. DGFP, Series D., Vol. V., pp. 104–107; J. Lipski, pp. 453–458; DEPOW, p. 200.

33. DGFP, Series D., Vol. V., pp. 152–158; Paul Schmidt: *Hitler's Interpreter* (Heinemann, London, 1951), p. 121; DEPOW, pp. 205–207.

34. W. Shirer, p. 554.

35. Ibid., p. 570–571; TMWC, Vol. VII, p. 223.

36. Adolf Hitler: *Mein Kampf* (Houghton Mifflin Co., Boston, 1943), p. 326.

37. NSR, pp. 50-52.

38. DGFP, Series D., Vol. VII, pp. 156-157.

39. Ibid., p. 168.

40. Nikita Khrushchev, *Khrushchev Remembers* (Little, Brown, Boston, 1970), pp. 129-130.

41. NSR, pp. 76-77.

42. Ibid., p. 78.

43. W. Shirer, pp. 645-662.

44. Ibid., p. 709.

45. P. Schmidt, p. 151.

46. DGFP, Series D., Vol. VIII, pp. 477-479.

Chapter Six: The War

1. Eugeniusz Duraczynski: *Wojna i Okupacja 1939-1943* (Warszawa, 1974), p. 17.

2. NSR, p. 96.

3. SDFP-Degras, p. 374.

4. Eduard Rozek: *Allied Wartime Diplomacy* (John Wiley & Sons, New York, 1958), p. 38.

5. B. H. Liddell Hart: *History of the Second World War* (Pan Books, London, 1977), p. 33.

6. SDFP-Degras, p. 389.

7. M. Whiteman, Vol. 3, pp. 182-183.

8. Nikita Khrushchev: *Khrushchev Remembers* (Little, Brown, Boston, 1970), p. 147.

9. Ibid., p. 146.

10. E. Rozek, pp. 39, 40, 46; Adam B. Ulam: *Expansion and Coexistence* (Praeger, New York, 1969), p. 320.

11. E. Rozek, p. 43.

12. M. Whiteman, Vol. 3, p. 227.

13. J. Topolski, p. 765.

14. E. Duraczynski, p. 29.

15. DEPOW, p. 219; DGFP, Series D, Vol. VI, pp. 1035–1043.

16. Lewis B. Namier: *Diplomatic Prelude 1938–1939* (Macmillan, London, 1948), p. 295.

17. Winston S. Churchill: *The Second World War* (Reprint Society, London, 1956), Vol. I, p. 324.

18. B. H. Liddell Hart, p. 18; *Polskie Sily Zbrojne*, Kampanja wrzesniowa, 1939 (Instytut Historyczny Gen. Sikorskiego, London, 1951), Tom I, czesc druga, p. 440.

19. B. H. Liddell Hart, pp. 17–19; Eugeniusz Kozłowski, *Wojsko Polskie* (Wyd. Min. Obrony Narodowej, Warszawa, 1974), p. 119.

20. B. H. Liddell Hart, p. 18.

21. L. B. Namier, p. 350.

22. E. Kozłowski, p. 119.

23. B. H. Liddell Hart, p. 20.

24. E. Duraczynski, pp. 14–15; W. Pobog-Malinowski: *Najnowsza Historia Polityczna Polski* (London, Tom III, 1981), p. 37; E. Kozłowski, pp. 20, 335.

25. E. Duraczynski, p. 19; *Polskie Sily Zbrojne*, Tom I, Czesc druga, p. 14; W. Churchill, Vol. I, p. 356.

26. B. H. Liddell Hart, p. 21–22.

27. DGFP, Series D, Vol. VI, p. 1039.

28. L. B. Namier, pp. 457.

29. Gen. M. G. Gamelin: *Servir—le Prologue du Drame* (Paris 1946), pp. 416–417.

30. L. B. Namier, pp. 455–463.

31. Gamelin, pp. 416–417.

32. L. B. Namier, p. 296.

33. W. Churchill, Vol. I, p. 327.

34. Alan Dowty: *The Role of Great Power Guarantees in International Peace Agreements* (Hebrew University, Jerusalem, 1974), p. 20.

35. W. Shirer, p. 762.

36. SDFP-Degras, p. 388–389.

37. NSR, p. 98.

38. Ibid., p. 88.

40. Ibid., pp. 105–107.

41. E. Duracznski, p. 92.

42. A. Ulam, p. 284; Roy A. Medvedev: *Let History Judge* (Alfred Knopf, New York, 1972), p. 222.

43. NSR, p. 107–108.

44. DGFP, Vol. VIII, p. 942.

45. E. Duraczynski, pp. 23–32.

Chapter Seven: Under the Yoke of Occupation

1. Robert Conquest: *The Great Terror* (Macmillan, New York, 1968), p. 482; Eduard Rozek: *Allied Wartime Diplomacy* (John Wiley & Sons, New York, 1958), p. 46.

2. R. Conquest, p. 532.

3. TMWC, Vol. VII, pp. 224–226.

4. Jerzy Topolski: *Dzieje Polski* (Panstwowe Wyd. Naukowe, Warszawa, 1977), p. 844.

5. Ibid.

6. Lucy Dawidowicz: *The War Against the Jews 1933–1945* (Penquin Books, 1977), p. 479.

7. Norman H. Baynes: *The Speeches of Adolf Hitler* (New York, 1942); Gerald Reitlinger: *The Final Solution* (Barnes & Co., New York, 1961), p. 22; Gideon Hausner: *Justice in Jerusalem*, p. 48.

8. E. Duraczynski, pp. 269–273; Winston S. Churchill: *The Second World War* (Reprint Society, London, 1956), Vol. II, p. 168; Vol. III, pp. 179, 657; Vol. IV, pp. 366, 602, 659, 737; Vol. V, p. 203; Vol. VI, pp. 301, 519; W. Pobog-Malinowski: *Najnowsza Historia Polityczna Polski*, t. III, p. 844.

9. S. Mikołajczyk: *The Pattern of Soviet Domination*, p. 75; W. Pobog-Malinowski, III, p. 664; other sources also affirm that a much smaller quantity of arms was found in AK's possession—see Jan Ciechanowski: *The Warsaw Rising of 1944* (Cambridge University Press, 1974), p. 225.

10. Jan Karski: *Story of a Secret State*, p. 131.

11. E. Duraczynski, p. 376.

12. S. Mikołajczyk, p. 137; W. Pobog-Malinowski, III, p. 364.

13. For example: Jan Ciechanowski: *Powstanie Warszawskie*, p. 58; Jranek Osnicki: *Zarys rozwoju AK*, p. 8; Władyslaw Anders: *Bez Ostatniego Rozdzialu* (Gryf Publishing, London, 1959), p. 250.

14. Dowodztwo Głowne GL i AL, pp. 306–307; J. Ciechanowski: *The Warsaw Rising*, p. 114.

15. Emmanuel Ringelblum: *Polish-Jewish Relations during the Second World War;* J. Kermish: *Relations Between the Poles and the Jews during the War and the Holocaust* (from *Massuah*, no. 7, April, 1979) (Hebrew); Yisrael Gutman: *The Jews of Warsaw 1939–1943* (Hebrew); Gideon Hausner: *Justice in Jerusalem*, pp. 195–220; CEJ, pp. 723–734.

16. L. Dawidowicz, pp. 384–386.

17. Y. Gutman, p. 425.

Chapter Eight: The "London Government"

1. Edward Raczyński: *In Allied London* (Weidenfeld & Nicolson, London, 1962), pp. 55–56.

2. Jan Karski: *Story of a Secret State*, p. 120.

3. Eugeniusz Duraczynski: *Wojna i Okupacja 1939–1943* (Warszawa, 1974), p. 118.

4. SDFP-Degras, Vol. III, p. 492.

5. NSR, pp. 108–109.

6. Ibid., pp. 131–134.

7. Ibid., p. 319.

8. Ibid., pp. 339–341.

9. Nikita Khrushchev: *Khrushchev Remembers* (Little, Brown, Boston, 1970), p. 131.

10. William L. Shirer: *The Rise and the Fall of the Third Reich* (Pan Books, London, 1976), p. 955.

11. NSR, p. 132.

12. Ibid., p. 133.

13. Max Jakobson: *The Diplomacy of the Winter War* (Harvard University Press, 1961), p. 111; Gustav Hilger & Alfred Meyer: *The Incompatible Allies. 1918–1941* (Macmillan, New York, 1973), p. 311; W. Shirer, p. 835; Winston S. Churchill: *The Second World War* (Reprint Society, London, 1956), Vol. I, p. 437.

14. George F. Kennan: *Russia and the West under Lenin and Stalin* (Little, Brown, & Co., Boston, 1961) pp. 343–344.

15. SDFP-Degras, p. 389.

16. Roy A. Medvedev: *Let History Judge* (Alfred Knopf, New York, 1972), p. 443.

17. V. Mastny: *Russia's Road to the Cold War* (Columbia University Press, 1979), p. 26.

18. Adam B. Ulam: *Expansion and Coexistence* (Praeger, New York, 1969), p. 228.

19. NSR, p. 88.

20. Barton Whaley: *Codeword Barbarossa* (MIT Press, Cambridge, Mass., 1973), p. 26.

21. W. Laquer: *Russia and Germany* (Weidenfeld & Nicolson, 1965), p. 261; Hilger & Meyer, pp. 331–332.

22. B. Whaley, pp. 23–129; DGFP, Series D, Vol. XII, p. 195: NSR, pp. 330, 341, 345–346; Winston S. Churchill: *The Second World War* (Reprint Society, London, 1956), Vol. III, pp. 289–290; N. Khrushchev, p. 588; Harrison Salisbury: *900 Days;* John Barron: *KGB;* Deakin and Storry: *The Case of Richard Sorge:* C. L. Sulzberger: "Espionage and Dissent," *International Herald Tribune,* 18 July 1977; ibid., 24 April 1979.

23. NSR, pp. 347–349.

24. W. Churchill, Vol. III, p. 297.

25. SDFP-Degras, Vol. III, p. 491–492.

26. W. Shirer, p. 1018.

27. A. Ulam, p. 311.

28. N. Khrushchev, p. 589.

29. W. Churchill, Vol. III, p. 297.

30. Eduard Rozek: *Allied Wartime Diplomacy* (John Wiley & Sons, New York, 1958), pp. 52–54; E. Duraczynski, p. 255–256.

31. W. Churchill, Vol. III, pp. 315–316.

32. DPSR-GSHI, Vol. I, pp. 141–142.

33. M. Whiteman, p. 197.

34. Ibid., p. 198.

35. Ibid.

36. Jan Ciechanowski: *Defeat in Victory* (Doubleday, New York, 1947), pp. 91, 156.

37. M. Whiteman, p. 197.

38. Ibid., p. 206.

39. E. Rozek, p. 130.

40. Władyslaw Anders: *Bez Ostatniego Rozdzialu* (London, 1959), p. 87.

41. DPSR-GSHI, Vol. I, pp. 237–246; W. Anders, pp. 87–105, E. Rozek, pp. 82–94.

42. W. Anders, p. 96; E. Duraczynski, p. 263, J. Ciechanowski, pp. 65–75.

43. DPSR-GSHI, Vol. I, p. 241; W. Anders, p. 99.

44. W. Anders, p. 82; Y. Gutman: *Jews in Anders' Army.*

45. Alexander Zvieli: "Jews of Koltubianka," *Jerusalem Post Magazine,* August 18, 1978; Leopold Cohen, "Yehudim be-sherut ha-tzava ha-polani ba-ma'arav," in M. Mushkat, ed., *Lohamim yehudim ba-milhama neged ha-nazim,* pp. 113–151.

46. Dov Levin, "Ha-'amida ha-yehudit be-tekufat ha-shoah," Yad Vashem, Jerusalem, 1968; Y. Guri (Podriaczyk): "Yehudei brit ha-mo'atzot ba-milhama neged germania ha-nazit," in Y. Mushkat, ed., *Lohamim yehudim ba-milhama neged ha-nazim;* N. Blumenthal and J. Kermish, "Iddisher anteil in der 2 veltmilhomeh," Volk Und Zion, April 1965; Dov Levin, "'Uvdot ve-ha' arakhot 'al hayehudim ba-tzava ha-adom," *Massuah,* Annual Collection, Vol. 10, 1982, pp. 79–105; Yehoshua A. Gilboa, "Ba'al ha-brit ha-nishkah," *Massuah,* Vol. 10, 1982, pp. 106–111.

47. E. Duraczynski, p. 263; DSPR-GSHI, Vol. I, p. 246.

48. E. Duraczynski, p. 263.

49. Mikołajczyk, p. 23; E. Rozek, p. 94, J. Ciechanowski, pp. 78, 79.

50. DSPR-GSHI, Vol. I, pp. 264–265.

51. E. Duraczynski, pp. 270, 273.

52. A. Eden: *Memoirs—The Reckoning,* p. 289.

53. E. Carr, Vol. III, pp. 114–115, 135–136.

54. "When confronted with evidence, criminals in almost every case confess; and what argument can have greater weight than a criminal's own confession?"— *Novaya Zhizn,* June 8, 1918, quoted by R. Conquest, *The Great Terror,* p. 147.

55. *Historia Polski,* tom IV, pp. 396–404.

56. NSR, p. 78; M. Jakobson: *The Diplomacy of the Winter War,* pp. 166–172.

57. W. Anders, p. 102.

58. M. Whiteman, p. 207.

59. Ibid., p. 208.

60. Ibid., p. 214.

61. E. Duraczynski, p. 364.

62. Yehoshua A. Gilboa, *Ha-shanim ha-shehorot*, p. 38.

63. Wiktor Sukiennicki: *Report on the Massacre of Polish Officers in Katyn Woods*, London 1946; J. K. Zawodny: *Death in the Forest*, 1962; W. Anders: *Bez Ostatniego Rozdzialu*, pp. 160–162; Michael Charlton: "The Eagle and the Small Birds," *Encounter*, June 1983.

64. E. Rozek, p. 126; DPSR-GSHI, Vol. I, p. 525.

65. Ibid., p. 179.

66. R. Conquest, p. 483.

67. E. Rozek, pp. 463–464.

68. W. Churchill, Vol. IV, pp. 611–612.

69. W. Churchill, Vol. IV, p. 610.

70. S. Mikołajczyk, p. 61.

71. W. Churchill, Vol. IV, p. 611.

72. M. Mushkat (ed.), *Lohamim yehudim ba-milhama neged ha-nazim*, pp. 93, 97.

73. Ibid., p. 90.

Chapter Nine: The Teheran Conference

1. A. Ulam, p. 329; V. Mastny, p. 162.

2. *Encyclopaedia Britannica*, 1965, Vol. 23, p. 348.

3. *Economic Report of the US President, 1983*, Table B-1, p. 163, Table B-3, p. 167.

4. W. Churchill, Vol. V, p. 107.

5. Ibid.

6. Ibid., pp. 229–231.

7. W. Churchill, Vol. III, p. 301.

8. W. Churchill, Vol. V, p. 284.

9. V. Mastny, pp. 74, 80, 84.

10. A. Ulam, pp. 354, 369.

11. W. Churchill, Vol. V., p. 295.

12. FRUS—Malta and Yalta, p. 572.

13. A. Eden, *Memoirs—The Reckoning,* p. 372.

14. R. Sherwood: *Roosevelt and Hopkins,* p. 710.

15. E. Rozek, p. 109, J. Ciechanowski, p. 132.

16. M. Whiteman, p. 221.

17. W. Churchill, Vol. V, p. 284.

18. W. Churchill, Vol. IV, p. 645.

19. W. Churchill, Vol. IV, p. 272.

20. W. Churchill, Vol. V, p. 228.

21. A. Ulam, p. 342.

22. E. Rozek, pp. 157–159.

23. W. Churchill, Vol. V, p. 283.

24. W. Churchill, Vol. V, pp. 283–285; A. Eden: *Memoirs—The Reckoning,* p. 427; FRUS—The Conferences at Cairo and Teheran, p. 512.

25. *Palestine—A Study of Jewish, Arab and British Policies* (ESCO), Vol. I, pp. 266–269.

26. W. Churchill, Vol. VI, p. 194.

27. Ibid., p. 198.

28. Ibid., pp. 199, 200.

29. Daniel Yergin: *Shattered Peace,* pp. 59–60.

30. Ibid., p. 60.

31. V. Mastny, pp. 208–209.

32. M. Whiteman, pp. 222–225 (Bohlen minutes); A. Eden: *The Reckoning,* p. 427.

33. M. Whiteman, pp. 222–225; W. Churchill, Vol. V, pp. 309–312.

34. Leahy: *I Was There,* p. 210.

35. W. Churchill, Vol. V, p. 317.

36. Ibid., p. 311.

37. E. Wiskeman: *Germany's Eastern Neighbours,* p. 76.

38. W. Churchill, Vol. V, pp. 311–312; FRUS—Cairo and Teheran, p. 601.

39. M. Whiteman, p. 224.

40. Ibid.: "Although nothing definitively was stated . . . " (Bohlen's protocol).

41. W. Churchill, Vol. V, p. 317.

42. E. Wiskeman: *Germany's Eastern Neighbours,* p. 76.

43. R. Conquest: *The Soviet Deportation of Nationalities,* pp. 51–54, 201; A. Fisher: *The Crimean Tatars,* pp. 165–183.

44. E. Wiskeman, p. 224.

45. Mikołajczyk, p. 65.

Chapter Ten: Between Teheran and Yalta

1. DPSR-GSHI, Vol. II, pp. 123–124.

2. Ibid., pp. 132–134.

3. Raczynski, pp. 154, 155.

4. V. Mastny, p. 135.

5. Beneš, *Memoirs,* pp. 264–268.

6. DPSR-GSHI, Vol. II, pp. 134–136.

7. Ibid., pp. 138–139.

8. A. Eden: *Memoirs—The Reckoning,* p. 436.

9. DPSR-GSHI, Vol. II, p. 139.

10. M. Whiteman, p. 229.

11. DPSR-GSHI, Vol. II, pp. 144–152.

12. E. Rozek, p. 195.

13. DPSR-GSHI, Vol. II, pp. 176, 249.

14. M. Whiteman, p. 232.

15. Ibid.

16. J. Bishop: *FDR's Last Year,* pp. 102–103.

17. Mikołajczyk, pp. 65, 66; J. Ciechanowski, pp. 292, 294.

18. E. Rozek, p. 221; J. Ciechanowski, p. 293.

19. Mikołajczyk, pp. 65, 66; J. Ciechanowski, p. 305.

20. A. Ulam, p. 359.

21. Mikołajczyk, p. 72.

22. R. Conquest, pp. 433–434.

23. Khrushchev, p. 107.

24. M. Whiteman, p. 286.

25. V. Mastny, p. 178.

26. W. Churchill, Vol. VI, pp. 116–129; E. Rozek, p. 235; A. Ulam, p. 362; W. Anders, p. 283.

27. W. Anders, p. 253; Pobòg-Malinowski, III, pp. 578–582; J. Ciechanowski: *The Warsaw Rising,* p. 231.

28. E. Rozek, p. 238.

29. W. Churchill, Vol. VI, p. 125.

30. Mikołajczyk, p. 86.

31. W. Churchill, Vol. VI, p. 119.

32. E. Rozek, p. 239.

33. W. Churchill, Vol. VI, p. 118.

34. Ibid., p. 120.

35. Ibid.

36. Ibid., p. 121.

37. Ibid., p. 122.

38. Bor Komorowski: *The Secret Army,* p. 294; V. Mastny, p. 185.

39. Mikołajczyk, p. 86; W. Churchill, Vol. VI, p. 129.

40. W. Churchill, Vol. VI, p. 194.

41. Ibid., p. 204.

42. DPSR-GSHI, Vol. II, p. 143.

43. Ibid., pp. 288–291.

44. GSHI, A 12 49/WB/SOW. 44.

45. DPSR-GSHI, Vol. II, pp. 372–375.
46. W. Churchill, Vol. VI, pp. 205, 398.
47. M. Whiteman, p. 287.
48. W. Churchill, Vol. VI, p. 200.
49. M. Whiteman, pp. 235–237.
50. Mikołajczyk, p. 107.
51. Ibid.
52. M. Whiteman, p. 237.
53. Ibid., p. 236.
54. W. Churchill, Vol. VI, p. 197.
55. M. Whiteman, p. 241.
56. Ibid; E. Rozek, p. 283.
57. E. Rozek, p. 286.
58. M. Whiteman, p. 240.
59. A. Eden: *Memoirs—The Reckoning*, p. 487.
60. DPSR-GSHI, Vol. II, pp. 426–427.
61. Ibid., p. 239.
62. Mikołajczyk, p. 111.
63. W. Churchill, Vol. VI, p. 205.
64. Ibid.
65. Ibid.
66. Ibid.; DPSR-GSHI, Vol. II, pp. 419, 439.
67. E. Rozek, p. 294.
68. M. Whiteman, pp. 290–293.
69. E. Rozek, p. 294; DPSR-GSHI, Vol. II, p. 442.
70. Mikołajczyk, p. 66.
71. Ibid., p. 110; E. Rozek, p. 283.
72. DPSR-GSHI, Vol. II, p. 154.
73. E. Rozek, p. 294.
74. Ibid., p. 312.

75. Ibid.

76. Ibid., p. 300; J. Ciechanowski, pp. 313, 347.

77. Samuel E. Morison: *The Oxford History of the American People*, p. 1037.

78. Ibid., p. 1038.

79. B. H. Liddell Hart, pp. 669–690.

80. J. Bishop, *FDR's Last Year*, pp. 268, 269.

81. Ibid., p. 272.

82. FRUS—Malta and Yalta, p. 209.

83. Ibid.

84. Ibid., pp. 209–210.

85. E. Rozek, p. 313.

Chapter Eleven: The Yalta Conference

1. W. Churchill, Vol. VI, p. 232.

2. Edward R. Stettinius, Jr.: *Roosevelt and the Russians—The Yalta Conference*, p. 301.

3. W. Churchill, Vol. VI, p. 302.

4. W. Churchill, Vol. VI, p. 276.

5. FRUS—Malta and Yalta, pp. 225–226.

6. Mikołajczyk, p. 121.

7. E. Stettinius, p. 300.

8. W. Churchill, Vol. VI, p. 301.

9. E. Stettinius, p. 151; FRUS—Malta and Yalta, p. 677.

10. M. Whiteman, p. 260; FRUS—Malta and Yalta, p. 668.

11. FRUS—Malta and Yalta, p. 677.

12. Frus—Malta and Yalta, p. 669.

13. M. Whiteman, p. 297; FRUS—Malta and Yalta, p. 680; W. Churchill, Vol. VI, p. 305.

14. A. Ulam, p. 375.

15. E. Wiskeman: *Germany's Eastern Neighbours*, p. 76.

16. W. Churchill, Vol. V, p. 317.

17. Ibid., p. 311.

18. W. Churchill, Vol. VI, p. 308.

19. FRUS-Malta and Yalta, pp. 230–234; FRUS—POTSDAM, Vol. I, p. 748.

20. FRUS—Malta and Yalta, p. 232; Whiteman, p. 256.

21. FRUS—Malta and Yalta, p. 509, Whiteman, p. 296.

22. FRUS—Malta and Yalta, p. 717; M. Whiteman, p. 261; W. Churchill, Vol. VI, p. 308.

23. FRUS—Malta and Yalta, pp. 905–906.

24. FRUS—Malta and Yalta, pp. 905, 980.

25. Ibid., pp. 905, 911; E. Stettinius, pp. 269–271.

26. FRUS—Malta and Yalta, pp. 568, 667–669, 716, 792–793, 803–807, 816, 867–871, 882–884, 897–898, 938, 973–974.

27. Ibid., p. 617; A. Ulam, p. 370.

28. W. Churchill, Vol. VI, p. 320.

29. J. Bishop, p. 501.

30. E. Stettinius, pp. 191–196.

31. R. Sherwood: *Roosevelt and Hopkins,* p. 860.

32. V. Mastny, p. 246.

33. W. Churchill, Vol. VI, p. 304–305; FRUS—Malta and Yalta, pp. 669–670.

34. Ibid.

35. FRUS—Malta and Yalta, p. 779; Churchill, Vol. VI., p. 311.

36. FRUS—Malta and Yalta, p. 668.

37. E. Stettinius, p. 168.

38. W. Churchill, Vol. VI, p. 205; DPSR-GSHI, Vol. II, pp. 419, 439.

39. FRUS—Malta and Yalta, p. 668.

40. W. Churchill, Vol. VI, pp. 311–314; DPSR-GSHI, Vol. II, p. 561.

41. E. Stettinius, pp. 157–159.

42. W. Churchill, Vol. VI, p. 306.

43. FRUS—Malta and Yalta, p. 846.

44. E. Stettinius, pp. 224-229.

45. FRUS—Malta and Yalta, p. 898. The final formulation, included in the Polish section of the Conference summaries, is almost identical to the principles and phrasing of the draft resolution quoted here. See FRUS—Malta and Yalta, p. 980.

46. W. Churchill, Vol. VI, pp. 313-316.

47. Leahy, pp. 315, 316.

48. W. Churchill, Vol. VI, p. 316.

49. Ibid., p. 322.

50. FRUS—Malta and Yalta, p. 924; E. Stettinius, p. 278; A. Ulam, p. 377.

51. W. Churchill, Vol. VI, p. 302.

52. M. Whiteman, pp. 264-265.

53. W. Churchill, Vol. VI, p. 329; M. Whiteman, p. 269.

54. M. Whiteman, p. 270.

55. W. Churchill, Vol. VI, p. 465; Mikołajczyk, p. 117; J. Zurawski: *Poland— The Captive State*, p. 25; Torańska: *Oni*, pp. 116, 117, 286.

56. E. Rozek, p. 370.

57. W. Churchill, Vol. VI, pp. 401-402.

58. Ibid., pp. 328, 580, 581; DPSR-GSHI, Vol. II, pp. 551-553, 555-556.

59. W. Churchill, Vol. VI, pp. 395, 401; DPSR-GSHI, Vol. II, pp. 561-563.

60. W. Churchill, Vol. VI, p. 465.

61. Ibid., p. 396.

62. Ibid., p. 402.

63. Margaret Truman: *Harry S. Truman*, p. 236.

64. Leahy, p. 532.

65. Harry S. Truman: *Memoirs—Years of Decisions*, p. 82.

66. R. Sherwood: *Roosevelt and Hopkins*, p. 898.

67. Ibid., pp. 907, 910.

68. FRUS—Conference of Berlin (Potsdam), Vol. I, p. 32.

69. Sherwood, p. 900.

70. Ibid., p. 906.

71. Ibid., p. 901.

72. Ibid., p. 908.
73. Ibid., pp. 898–910.
74. W. Churchill, Vol. VI, p. 465.
75. Mikołajczyk, p. 131.
76. W. Churchill, Vol. VI, p. 393.
77. Ibid. p. 465.
78. Mikołajczyk, pp. 131–132.
79. E. Rozek, p. 388.
80. Mikołajczyk, p. 135.
81. E. Rozek. p. 390.

Chapter Twelve: Potsdam and Its Implications

1. M. Djilas: *Conversations with Stalin*, p. 114.
2. Mikołajczyk, p. 87.
3. FRUS—Potsdam, Vol. II, p. 1584.
4. M. Whiteman, p. 318.
5. Ibid., p. 320.
6. Ibid.; W. Churchill, Vol. VI, pp. 522–526.
7. M. Whiteman, p. 323.
8. FRUS—Potsdam, Vol. I, pp. 748–752.
9. M. Whiteman, p. 331.
10. Leahy, p. 408.
11. FRUS—Potsdam, Vol. II, pp. 332–336.
12. Ibid., p. 1539.
13. V. Mastny, pp. 299, 300.
14. W. Churchill, Vol. VI, p. 529.
15. Ibid., p. 535.
16. FRUS—Potsdam, Vol. II, p. 489.
17. M. Whiteman, p. 341.

18. The resolution, together with its last drafts and final formulation, appears in FRUS—Potsdam, Vol. II, pp. 1457, 1459, 1490–1491, 1945, 1508–1509, 1511; Whiteman, p. 347.

19. W. Churchill, Vol. VI, pp. 529, 530.

20. Mikołajczyk, p. 259.

21. R. Staar: *Poland 1944–1962*, p. 130.

22. FRUS—Potsdam, Vol. II, pp. 1540–1541.

23. S. Mikołajczyk: *The Pattern of Soviet Domination;* J. Reynolds: *Lublin Versus London,* pp. 637, 644; Torańska: *Oni,* pp. 117, 126, 268–271, 286, 293.

24. Mikołajczyk, p. 222; E. Rozek, pp. 432–433.

25. J. Kokot: *The Logic of the Oder-Neisse Frontier,* pp. 133–134.

26. Ibid. p. 135.

27. W. Churchill, Vol. VI, p. 308.

28. W. Churchill, Vol. VI, p. 523.

29. FRUS—Potsdam, Vol. II, p. 335.

30. J. Topolski, p. 846.

31. J. Kokot, Table 28.

32. *Deutschland-Jahrbuch 1953;* Johannes Kaps, p. 41; *Dokumentation der Vertreibung,* Band I/1, pp. 138E, 158E.

33. J. Kokot, Table 11.

34. Kaps, p. 87.

35. J. Kokot, pp. 104, 105.

36. Ibid., pp. 137, 138, Tables 11, 12.

37. Ibid., p. 138.

38. Halecki, p. 50.

39. Vertreibung, p. 111E.

40. Vertreibung, p. 112E.

41. Kaps, p. 88.

42. Kaps, p. 88; Vertreibung, pp. 158E, 159E.

43. J. Kokot, Table 11 n.3.

44. J. Kokot, pp. 99, 101, 103; Tables 6, 9, 11.

45. J. Kokot, Table 28; M. Whiteman, p. 363.

46. Manfred Lachs: *The Polish-German Frontier*, pp. 7, 8.

47. M. Lachs, p. 7.

48. M. Whiteman, p. 362.

49. M. Whiteman, pp. 375–378.

50. Ibid.

51. FRUS—Potsdam, Vol. II, pp. 1495, 1511.

52. Vertreibung, p. 143E.

53. B. Wiewiora: *The Polish-German Frontier in the Light of International Law*, p. 34.

54. Barsegov, E. M. Fabrikov, Y. A. Korovin, F. I. Kozhevnikov, S. B. Krylov, G. Tunkin.

55. R. Binschedler, I. L. Claude, Ch. Fenwick. W. L. Gould, Oppenheim-Lauterpacht, Ch. Rousseau, E. de Vattel.

56. B. Wiewiora: *Frontier*, p. 653.

57. B. Wiewiora: *Frontier*, p. 62.

58. B. Wiewiora: *Uznanie nabytkow terytorialnych*, p. 69.

59. Ibid., p. 67.

60. B. Wiewiora: *Frontier*, pp. 45, 46.

61. M. Lachs, p. 49.

62. M. Whiteman, p. 285.

63. FRUS—Potsdam, Vol. I, p. 754.

64. Parliamentary Debates (Hansard), Official Record, 22nd February 1944, Vol. 397, c. 698.

65. M. Whiteman, p. 234.

66. Ibid., pp. 348–349.

67. Joseph B. Schechtman: *The Refugee in the World*.

68. J. Kokot, p. 135.

69. B. Wiewiora: *Frontier*, p. 136.

70. Parliamentary Debates (Hansard), Official Report, Fifth Series–Vol. 406, No. 1, p. 1484.

71. B. Wiewiora: *Frontier*, p. 139.

72. Ibid., p. 132; J. Kokot, pp. 137–138.

73. M. Lachs, pp. 52–53.

74. Ibid.

75. B. Wiewiora: *Frontier*, p. 42.

76. Ibid., p. 48.

77. Ibid., p. 45.

78. Ibid., p. 46; B. Wiewiora: *Uznanie*, p. 144.

79. G. Labuda: *Ekspansja Wschodnia Niemcow*.

80. B. Wiewiora: *Frontier*, p. 61.

81. DPSR-GSHI, Vol. II, p. 133.

82. B. Wiewiora: *Frontier*, p. 61.

83. M. Whiteman, p. 298.

84. A. Klafkowski: *Granica Polsko-Niemiecka*, p. 106.

85. Ibid., p. 39.

86. Ibid., p. 40.

87. Ibid., 40, n. 24; FRUS—Potsdam, Vol. II, p. 1509.

88. B. Wiewiora: *Uznanie*, p. 212.

89. M. Whiteman, p. 375.

90. M. Lachs, p. 61.

91. Abba Eban: *Autobiography*, p. 235.

92. M. Whiteman, p. 380.

93. Willy Brandt: "German Policy Toward the East," *Foreign Affairs*, April 1968.

94. *Keesing's Contemporary Archives*, Vol. XVII, pp. 243–246.

95. Conference on Security and Cooperation in Europe—Final Act, Helsinki, 175, 1aIII, p. 79.

Chapter Thirteen: The Thunderhead Looms

1. *The Development of Finnish-Soviet Relations*, Ministry of Foreign Affairs, Helsinki, 1940.

2. V. I. Lenin: Selected works in three volumes, vol. 2, Moscow, 1967, pp. 108–109.

3. V. I. Lenin: *The Right of Nations to Self-Determination,* selected works in two volumes, London: Lawrence & Wishart, vol. 1, p. 553; Edward Hallet Carr: *The Bolshevik Revolution,* vol. I, p. 421.

4. Lee C. Buchheit: *Secession—the Legitimacy of Self-Determination,* p. 121; E. H. Carr, Vol. I, p. 265.

5. E. H. Carr, Vol. I, p. 432.

6. Ibid., p. 280.

7. J. L. Talmon: *The Myth of Nation and the Vision of Revolution,* p. 425.

8. Tuomo Polvinen: "Lenin's Nationality Policy and Finland," *1977 Yearbook of Finnish Foreign Policy,* Helsinki, p. 7; Joe Brady: "Finland—30 Years after Soviet Treaty," *International Herald Tribune,* 2 May 1978.

9. E. H. Carr, Vol. I, p. 425.

10. Ibid., p. 294.

11. D. G. Kirby: *Finland in the Twentieth Century,* London, 1979, p. 64; E. Jutikkala and K. Pirinen: *A History of Finland,* p. 259.

12. D. G. Kirby, p. 70.

13. E. Jutikkala and K. Pirinen, pp. 261–264.

14. Max Jakobson: *The Diplomacy of the Winter War,* p. 48; Vaino Tanner: *The Winter War,* pp. 19–20.

15. V. Tanner, p. 10.

16. R. J. Sontag and James S. Beddie (eds.): *Nazi-Soviet Relations* (NSR), p. 107.

17. *Documents on German Foreign Policy* (DGFP), series D, Vol. VIII, p. 130.

18. C. G. Mannerheim: *Memoirs,* p. 308.

19. Ibid., pp. 307–308.

20. Ibid., p. 310.

Chapter Fourteen: Talks in the Kremlin

1. M. Jakobson, p. 114.

2. C. G. Mannerheim, p. 309; V. Tanner, p. 23.

3. M. Jakobson, p. 115.

4. V. Tanner, p. 27.

5. C. G. Mannerheim, p. 312.

6. V. Tanner, pp. 26–30.

7. J. Degras (ed.): *Soviet Documents on Foreign Policy* (SDFP), Vol. III, pp. 382–84.

8. C. G. Mannerheim, p. 312.

9. N. Khrushchev: *Khrushchev Remembers*, p. 152.

10. DGFP, series D, Vol. VIII, pp. 151–154.

11. C. G. Mannerheim, p. 313.

12. Osmo Apunen: "Geographical and Political Factors in Finland's Relations with the Soviet Union," *1977 Yearbook of Finnish Foreign Policy*, p. 21.

13. V. Tanner, p. 30.

14. C. G. Mannerheim, p. 314.

15. In the Finnish military hierarchy, the Chief of Staff was the third in rank, following Marshal Mannerheim and the Commander in Chief, General Österman.

16. V. Tanner, p. 32.

17. Ibid., p. 42.

18. Ibid., p. 55.

19. Ibid., p. 57.

20. SDFP, ed. Degras, vol. III, pp. 396–397.

21. V. Tanner, p. 59.

22. Ibid., p. 62.

23. Ibid., p. 43.

24. Ibid., p. 74.

25. Ibid., pp. 66–67.

26. Ibid., p. 77.

27. Ibid., p. 76.

28. *Khrushchev Remembers*, p. 152.

29. B. H. Liddell Hart: *History of the Second World War*, p. 48.

30. Anthony Upton: *Finland 1939–1940*, p. 32.

31. V. Tanner, p. 72.

32. D. Vital, p. 104.

33. V. Tanner, p. 83.

34. Ibid., pp. 82, 83.

35. A. Upton, p. 43.

36. Ibid., p. 42.

37. V. Tanner, p. 84.

38. A. Upton, p. 43.

39. V. Tanner, p. 43.

40. C. G. Mannerheim, p. 315.

41. Ibid., p. 314.

42. V. Tanner, p. 51.

43. DGFP, series D, Vol. VII, p. 427.

44. SDFP, ed. Degras, Vol. III, p. 397.

45. Ibid.

46. *Khrushchev Remembers,* p. 152.

47. Ibid.

48. A. Upton, pp. 45, 46; M. Jakobson, pp. 144–148.

49. M. Jakobson, p. 146.

50. C. G. Mannerheim, p. 320.

51. It should be noted here, perhaps, that in May, 1967, the Soviets accused Israel of an aggressive amassing of forces on the Syrian border. When the Soviet ambassador brought Israeli Prime Minister Levi Eshkol a message including grave accusations and threats in the middle of the night, Eshkol suggested, then and there, that they set out together to the Syrian border and verify that none of it was true. The ambassador, as is known, turned down the offer; he was not willing to let his thinking be confused by the facts.

52. A. Upton, pp. 49–50.

53. C. G. Mannerheim, p. 321.

Chapter Fifteen: War

1. C. G. Mannerheim, p. 322.

2. *Finland—Facts and Figures,* p. 196.

3. A. Upton, pp. 51-60; Richard Condon: *The Winter War,* pp. 29-36.

4. A. Upton, p. 61.

5. D. G. Kirby, p. 108.

6. C. G. Mannerheim, p. 373.

7. V. Tanner, p. 51.

8. R. Condon, p. 30; A. Upton, pp. 52-53.

9. M. Jakobson, p. 168.

10. C. G. Mannerheim, p. 330; R. Condon, p. 30.

11. A. Upton, p. 54.

12. A. Upton, p. 56; C. G. Mannerheim, p. 365.

13. C. G. Mannerheim, pp. 367-369.

14. B. H. Liddell Hart, p. 49; A. Upton, p. 60.

15. A. Upton, p. 55; R. Condon, p. 32.

16. SDFP, ed. Degras, Vol. III, p. 440.

17. C. G. Mannerheim, p. 371.

18. Ibid.

19. R. Condon, p. 103.

20. C. G. Mannerheim, p. 330; A. Upton, pp. 61-63; R. Condon, pp. 32-36.

21. NSR, p. 78.

22. SDFP, ed. Degras, vol. III, p. 465-466.

23. L. A. Puntila: *The Political History of Finland,* p. 164-165.

24. V. Tanner, p. 35.

25. M. Jakobson, p. 166.

26. Ibid., p. 168.

27. C. G. Mannerheim, p. 346.

Chapter Sixteen: The Course of the Battles

1. M. Jakobson, p. 168.

2. C. G. Mannerheim, p. 329.

3. M. Jakobson, p. 173.

4. B. H. Liddell Hart, p. 48; R. Condon, pp. 101–103.

5. His son, Ensio—a captain at the time—subsequently served as commander of the UN forces in the Middle East.

6. C. G. Mannerheim, p. 339.

7. C. G. Mannerheim, pp. 330, 339, 340; R. Condon, pp. 86–94; B. H. Liddell Hart, p. 48.

8. M. Jakobson, p. 173.

Chapter Seventeen: World Sympathy and Its Expressions

1. W. Churchill, Vol. I, p. 433.

2. L. Oppenheim—ed. by H. Lauterpacht, *International Law,* Vol. II, Sixth Edition, p. 153, n. 4, p. 236.

3. Ibid., pp. 143, 507, 564.

4. DGFP, series D, Vol. VIII, p. 583.

5. Jukka Nevakivi: *The Appeal That Was Never Made,* p. 80.

6. C. G. Mannerheim, pp. 376–377.

7. J. Nevakivi, pp. 81, 140; V. Tanner, p. 132.

8. C. G. Mannerheim, p. 377.

9. SDFP, ed. Degras, Vol. III, p. 442.

10. V. Tanner, pp. 32, 33.

11. L. Oppenheim, ed. Lauterpacht, vol. II, p. 552.

12. W. M. Carlgren: *Swedish Foreign Policy during the Second World War,* pp. 28, 49.

13. Roderick Ogley: *The Theory and Practice of Neutrality in the Twentieth Century,* p. 165.

14. C. G. Mannerheim, pp. 358–359; J. Nevakivi, p. 174.

15. J. Nevakivi, p. 174; Anatole G. Mazour: *Finland between East and West,* p. 117.

16. DGFP, series D, Vol. VIII, p. 559.

17. Ibid., pp. 251, 252, 253, 267, 496, 555, 559.

18. Ibid, pp. 486, 555, 650, 785.

19. Ibid., p. 486.

20. Ibid., p. 682.

21. V. Tanner, p. 123.

22. DGFP, series D, Vol. VIII, p. 614.

23. Ibid. p. 511.

24. Ibid.

25. Ibid., p. 869.

26. J. Nevakivi, p. 67.

27. Ibid.

28. Ibid.

29. Ibid., pp. 67, 94.

30. L. Woodward: *British Foreign Policy in the Second World War*, Vol. I, p. 38.

31. J. Nevakivi, p. 68.

32. Ibid., p. 175.

33. Hans Peter Krosby: *Finland, Germany and the Soviet Union*, p. 10.

34. C. G. Mannerheim, p. 378.

35. J. Nevakivi, pp. 68, 69.

36. L. Oppenheim, ed. Lauterpacht, Vol. II, pp. 550, 552.

37. J. Nevakivi, p. 72.

38. W. M. Carlgren, p. 32.

39. D. Salmon: *The Problem of Swedish Iron-Ore*, p. 53.

40. W. Churchill, vol. I, p. 428.

41. R. Macleod and D. Kelly (ed.): *Ironside Diaries* pp. 184, 185.

42. Ibid., pp. 185, 191.

43. W. Churchill, Vol. I, p. 449.

Chapter Eighteen: Peace Feelers

1. A. Upton, p. 81.

2. Ibid., p. 91.

3. V. Tanner, p. 172.
4. C. G. Mannerheim, p. 376.
5. J. Nevakivi, p. 103.
6. V. Tanner, p. 127.
7. Ibid., p. 125.
8. Adam B. Ulam: *Expansion and Coexistence*, p. 293.
9. DGFP, series D, Vol. VIII, p. 630.
10. V. Tanner, p. 125.
11. Ibid., pp. 145–148.
12. Ibid., p. 151; M. Jakobson, p. 222.
13. V. Tanner, pp. 154–157.
14. A. Upton, p. 107.

Chapter Nineteen: The Front Collapses

1. DGFP, Series D, Vol. VIII, p. 630.
2. A. Upton, p. 110; R. Condon, pp. 106–107.
3. B. H. Liddell Hart, p. 50.
4. A. Upton, p. 122.
5. V. Tanner, pp. 158–160; DGFP, series D, Vol. VIII, pp. 761–762.
6. W. M. Carlgren, pp. 38–53.
7. V. Tanner, p. 172.
8. J. Nevakivi, p. 123.
9. V. Tanner, pp. 177–178.
10. Ibid., p. 187.
11. Ibid., p. 179.
12. M. Jakobson, p. 247.
13. V. Tanner, p. 185.
14. Ibid., p. 183.
15. M. Jakobson, p. 246.

16. W. M. Carlgren, pp. 45, 48.

17. V. Tanner, p. 188.

18. C. G. Mannerheim, p. 384; A. Upton, p. 130.

19. V. Tanner, p. 191.

Chapter Twenty: The Affair of the English-French Expeditionary Force

1. George F. Kennan: *Russia and the West under Lenin and Stalin*, p. 338; H. P. Krosby, p. 10.

2. A. Upton, pp. 130–132; V. Tanner, pp. 196–199, 200, 202, 205, 208.

3. V. Tanner, p. 211.

4. W. Churchill, Vol. I, pp. 484–524.

5. A. Upton, p. 137.

6. V. Tanner, p. 219; C. G. Mannerheim, pp. 385–386.

7. C. G. Mannerheim, p. 387.

8. V. Tanner, p. 230.

9. A. Upton, p. 140.

10. J. Nevakivi, p. 140.

11. V. Tanner, p. 249.

12. *Ironside Diaries*, pp. 226–228.

Chapter Twenty-One: The Fateful Decision

1. V. Tanner, pp. 242–244.

2. A. G. Mazour, p. 126.

3. V. Tanner, pp. 263–267.

4. Ibid., p. 255.

5. Ibid., p. 257.

6. Ibid.

7. L. A. Puntila, p. 169.

8. R. Condon, pp. 153, 154; A. Upton, p. 152; C. G. Mannerheim, p. 370.

9. SDFP, ed. Degras, Vol. III, p. 442.

10. C. G. Mannerheim, p. 370.

11. SDFP, ed. Degras, Vol. III, pp. 439–442.

12. M. Jakobson, p. 254.

13. C. G. Mannerheim, p. 373.

Chapter Twenty-Two: The Winter War Saved Finland's Independence

1. Uusi Suomi, 20.4.1979.

2. Michael Walzer: *Just and Unjust Wars*, p. 71.

Final Remarks and Reflections

1. H. J. Morgenthau: *Politics Among Nations*, p. 22.

2. B. Tuchman: *Practicing History*, p. 249.

3. M. Jakobson: "Substance and Appearance," *Foreign Affairs*, Summer 1980, p. 1037.

4. M. Walzer: *Just and Unjust Wars*, p. 72.

5. A. B. Fox: *The Power of Small States*, p. 2; H. J. Morgenthau, pp. 147, 148.

6. H. Nicolson, *Diplomacy*, p. 144.

7. V. Tanner, *Winter War*, p. 188.

8. A. Eban: *The New Diplomacy*, p. 378.

9. A. Dowty: *The Role of Great Power Guarantees*, pp. 15–21.

10. V. Tanner: *Winter War*, p. 41.

11. SDFP-Degras, p. 466.

12. A. Eban: *Autobiography*, p. 343.

13. L. B. Johnson: *The Vantage Point*, p. 293.

14. George Ball, *Foreign Affairs*, April 1977.

15. A. B. Fox, p. 181.

Select Bibliography
(Abbreviations in Capital Letters)

Published Documentary Material

Concise Statistical Yearbook of Poland, 1935, Warsaw, 1935.

The Development of Finnish-Soviet Relations Finnish Government Publication, Helsinki, 1940.

Digest of International Law, Marjorie M. Whiteman (ed.) Department of State, Washington, 1964 (WHITEMAN).

Documents and Materials Relating to the Eve of the Second World War 1937–1939 (Dirksen papers), 2 vols. Foreign Language Publishing House, Moscow, 1948 (DIRKSEN).

Documents on the Events Preceding the Outbreak of the War published by the German Foreign Office, Berlin, 1939, New York, 1940 (DEPOW).

Documents on British Foreign Policy, Third Series, 1919–1939, E. L. Woodward and R. Butler (eds.), HMSO, London, 1949 (DBFP).

Documents on the Foreign Policy of the U.S.S.R., Vol. III. Moscow, 1959, (DFPSU).

Documents on German Foreign Policy, Series D, 1937–1945, Vols. II, V, VI, VIII, Department of State, Washington, 1957 (DGFP).

Documents on Polish-Soviet Relations 1939–1945, 2 Vols. Instytut Historyczny Gen. Sikorskiego, London, 1961, 1969 (DPSR-GSHI).

Dokumentation der Vertreibung der Deutschen aus Ost-Mittel Europa—Band I/1, Bonn, 1953 (VERTREIBUNG).

Dowodztwo Główne GL i AL-Zbiór Dokumentow, Ministerstwo Obrony Narodowej, Warszawa, 1967 (GL/AL).

Economic Report of the President, transmitted to the Congress, February, 1983, Washington, D.C., 1983.

Foreign Relations of the U.S. The Paris Peace Conference, 1919, vol. XIII, Department of State, Washington, 1947 (FRUS-PARIS).

Foreign Relations of the U.S., The Conferences at Malta and Yalta, 1945, Department of States, Washington, 1955 (FRUS—MALTA and YALTA).

Foreign Relations of the U.S., The Conferences of Cairo and Teheran, 1943, Department of State, Washington, 1961 (FRUS—CAIRO & TEHERAN).

Foreign Relations of the U.S. The Conference of Berlin (Potsdam), 1945, Department of State, Washington (FRUS—POTSDAM).

Official Documents Concerning the Polish-German and Polish-Soviet Relations, 1933-1939, New York, 1940 (PGPSR).

Nazi-Soviet Relations 1939-1941, Raymond J. Sontag and James S. Beddie (eds.), Department of State, Washington, D.C., 1948 (NSR).

Nazi Conspiracy and Aggression, Washington, D.C., 1946 (NCA).

Parliamentary Debates Hansard, Fifth Series—London, 1944.

Polskie Sily Zbrojne, Kampanja wrzesniowa, 1939, Instytut Historyczny Gen. Sikorskiego, London, 1951.

Rocznik Statystyczny, Publ. Glowny Urzad Statystyczny, Warszawa, 1929.

Soviet Documents on Foreign Policy, Vol. III, 1933-1941, Jane Degras (ed.) Oxford University Press, 1953 (SDFP-DEGRAS).

Trials of the Major War Criminals Before the International Military Tribunal, Nuremburg, 1948, 42 vols. (TMWC).

General Works

Alexander, Yonah, and Friedlander, Robert (eds.). *Self-Determination,* Boulder, Colorado, Westview Press, 1980.

Anders, Władyslaw. *Bez Ostatniego Rozdzału,* London, Gryf Publishing, 1959.

Balfour, Michael. *Propaganda in War 1939-1945,* London, Routledge & Kegan, 1979.

Baynes, Norman H. *The Speeches of Adolf Hitler,* 2 vols., New York, 1942.

Beck, Józef. *Pamietniki,* Warszawa, Czytelnik, 1955.

Beneš, Eduard. *Memoirs—From Munich to New War,* London, Allen & Unwin, 1954 (BENEŠ).

Bishop, Jim. *FDR's Last Year,* New York, Pocket Books, 1975.

Bruegel, J. W. *Czechoslovakia before Munich*, Cambridge University Press, 1973.

Buchheit, Lee C. *Secession—The Legitimacy of Self-Determination*, Yale University Press, 1978.

Carlgren, W. M. *Swedish Foreign Policy during the Second World War*, London, Ernest Benn, 1977.

Carr, Edward Hallet. *The Bolshevik Revolution 1917–1923*, 3 vols., Penguin Books, 1973, 1977. (CARR).

Churchill, Winston S. *The Second World War*, 6 volumes London, The Reprint Society, 1956. (CHURCHILL).

Ciechanowski, Jan. *Defeat in Victory*, New York, Doubleday Publ. & Co., 1947.

Ciechanowski, Jan. *The Warsaw Rising of 1944*, Cambridge Univ. Press, 1974.

Cobban, Alfred. *National Self-Determination*, Oxford Univ. Press, 1945.

Condon, Richard W. *The Winter War*, New York, Ballantine Books, 1972.

Conquest, Robert. *The Great Terror*, New York, Macmillan, 1968.

Conquest, Robert. *The Soviet Deportation of Nationalities*, London, Macmillan, 1960.

Dallin, Alexander. *German Rule in Russia 1941–1945*, London, Macmillan, 1957.

Dawidowicz, Lucy. *The War against the Jews, 1935–1945*, Penguin Books, 1977.

Djilas, Milovan. *Conversations with Stalin* New York, Harcourt, Brace & World, Inc., 1962.

Dowty, Alan. *The Role of Great Power Guarantees in International Peace Agreements*, Jerusalem, Hebrew Univ., 1974.

Duraczynski, Eugeniusz. *Wojna i Okupacja 1939–1943*, Warszawa, 1974.

Dziewanowski, *Poland in the Twentieth Century*, N.Y., Columbia Press, 1977.

Eban, Abba. *An Autobiography*, New York, Random House, 1977.

Eban, Abba. *The New Diplomacy*, London, Weidenfeld & Nicolson, 1983.

Eden, Anthony. *Full Circle—Memoirs*, London, Cassell, 1960.

Eden, Anthony. *The Reckoning*, London, Cassell, Boston, 1965.

Fisher, Alan. *The Crimean Tatars*, Stanford Univ. Press, 1978.

Fox, Annette Baker. *The Power of Small States*, Chicago Univ. Press, 1959.

Gamelin, Maurice. *Servir—le Prologue du Drame*, Paris, 1946.

Garlinski, Józef. *Poland in the Second World War*, London, Macmillan Press, 1985.

Grosfeld, Leon & Zielinski Henryk. (red.) *Historia Polski*, tom IV, Warszawa, Panstwove Wyd. Naukowe, 1969. (HISTORIA POLSKI).

Gutman, Israel and Rothkirchen Livia. (ed), *The Catastrophe of the European Jewry*, Jerusalem, Yad Vashem, 1976.

Gutman, Israel. *Jehudey Warsha 1939–1943*, [Hebrew], Tel Aviv, Sifriyath Hapoalim, 1977.

Haffner, Sebastian. *The Meaning of Hitler*, New York, Macmillan Publ. Co., 1979.

Halecki, Oscar. *Poland*, New York, Praeger, 1957. (HALECKI).

Hausner, Gideon. *Justice in Jerusalem*, New York, Harper & Row, 1966.

Henderson, Neville. *Failure of a Mission*, London, Hodder & Stoughton, 1940. (HENDERSON)

Herring, George Jr. *Aid to Russia*, Columbia Univ. Press, 1973.

Hilger, Gustav and Meyer Alfred. *The Incompatible Allies. 1918–1941*, New York, Macmillan, 1973.

Hitler, Adolf. *Mein Kampf* [English], Boston, Houghton Mifflin, 1943.

Hoffman, Stanley. *Duties beyond Borders*, Syracuse Univ. Press, 1981.

Horowitz, Dan. *Israel's Concept of Defensible Borders*, Jerusalem, Hebrew Univ., 1975.

Ironside, *—Diaries 1937–1940*. Edited by Roderick Macleod and Dennis, Kelly, London, Constable, 1962.

Jakobson, Max. *The Diplomacy of the Winter War*, Harvard Univ. Press, 1961. (JAKOBSON).

Johnson, Lyndon Baines. *The Vantage Point*, New York, Holt, Rinehard and Winston, 1971.

Jutikkala, Eino and Pirinen Kauko. *A History of Finland*, New York, Praeger, 1974. (JUTIKKALA-PIRINEN).

Kaps, Johannes. *Die Tragödie Schlesiens*—Dokumenten, München 1945–46, Verlag "Christ Unterwegs", 1952/53.

Karski, Jan. *Story of a Secret State*, Boston, Houghton Mifflin, 1944.

Kennan, George F. *Russia and the West under Lenin and Stalin*, Boston, Little, Brown & Co., 1961.

Khrushchev, Nikita. *Khrushchev Remembers*, Boston, Little, Brown, 1970. (KHRUSHCHEV).

Kirchmayer, Jerzy. *Kampania Wrześniowa*, Warszawa, Czytelnik, 1946.

Kirby, D. G. *Finland in the Twentieth Century*, London, Hurst, 1979.

Klafkowski, Alfons. *Granica Polsko-Niemiecka a Konkordaty*, Warszawa, Pax, 1958.

Kokot, Jozef. *The Logic of the Oder-Neisse Frontier*, Poznan, Publ. Wydawnictwo Zachodnie, 1959.

Korbel, Joseph. *XXth Century Czechoslovakia*, Columbia Univ. Press, 1977.

Kozłowski, Eugeniusz, *Wojsko Polskie*, Warszawa, Wyd. Min. Obrony Narodowej, 1974.

Krosby, Hans Peter. *Finland, Germany and the Soviet Union*, Wisconsin Univ. Press, 1968.

Labuda, G. *Ekspansja Wschodnia Niemiec*, Poznan, 1963. (LABUDA).

Lachs, Manfred. *The Polish-German Frontier*, PWN, Warszawa, 1964. (LACHS).

Langer, Robert. *Seizure of Territory*, Princeton Univ. Press, 1947.

Lansing, Robert. *The Peace Negotiations*, N.Y., Kennikat Press, 1969.

Laun, R. *Das Recht auf die Heimat*, Hannover, 1951.

Lauterpacht, Hersch. *International Law*—edited by Elihu Lauterpacht, Cambridge Univ. Press, 1977. (LAUTERPACHT).

Leahy, William. *I Was There*, London, Whittlesey House, 1950.

Lenin, V. I. *The Right of Nations to Self-Determination*, London, 1947.

Leskinen, Jyrki. (ed), *Finland, Facts and Figures*, Helsinki, Otava Publ. Co. 1976.

Liddell Hart, B. H. *History of the Second World War*, London, Pan Books, 1977. (LIDDELL HART).

Lipski, Jozef. *Diplomat in Berlin 1933–1939*, Columbia Univ. Press, 1968.

Luža, Radomir. *The Transfer of the Sudeten Germans*, New York University Press, 1964.

Mackiewicz, Stanisław. *Polityka Becka*, Paryż, 1964.

Mamatey, Victor S. *The United States and East Central Europe 1914–1918*, Princeton Univ. Press, 1957. (MAMATEY).

Mannerheim, C. G. *The Memoirs of Mannerheim*, London, Cassell, 1953. (MANNERHEIM).

Mastny, Vojtech. *Russia's Road to the Cold War*, Columbia Univ. Press, 1979. (MASTNY).

Mazour, Anatole G. *Finland Between East and West*, Princeton, N.J., 1956.

McKenzie, Compton. *Dr. Beneš*, London, George Harrap, 1964.

Medvedev, Roy A. *Let History Judge*, New York, Alfred Knopf., 1972.

Mikołajczyk, Stanisław. *The Pattern of Soviet Domination*, London, Sampson Lou, Marston, 1948. (MIKOŁAJCZYK).

Morgenthau, Hans J. *Alliances in Theory and Practice*, John Hopkins Press, 1959. (MORGENTHAU, ALLIANCES).

Morgenthau, Hans J. *Politics Among Nations*, Fifth edition, New York, Alfred Knopf, 1978. (MORGENTHAU, POLITICS).

Morison, Samuel Eliot. *The Oxford History of the American People*, New York, Oxford Univ. Press, 1965.

Namier, Lewis B. *Diplomatic Prelude 1938–1939*, London, Macmillan, 1948. (NAMIER).

Nevakivi, Jukka. *The Appeal That Was Never Made* London, Hurst & Co., 1978. (NEVAKIVI).

Nicholson, Harold. *Curzon: The Last Phase*, London, Constable & Co., 1937.

Nicholson, Harold. *Diplomacy*, Oxford Univ. Press, 1963.

Ogley, Roderick. *The Theory and Practice of Neutrality in the XXth Century*, New York, Barnes & Noble Inc. 1970. (OGLEY).

Oppenheim, L. (edited by Lauterpacht H.) *International Law*, vol. II, sixth ed. London 1955. (OPPENHEIM—LAUTERPACHT).

Pipes, Richard. *The Formation of the Soviet Union 1917–1923*, Cambridge, 1954.

Pobog-Malinowski, W. *Najnowsza Historia Polityczna Polski*, London, tom II 1967, tom III 1981.

Pomerance, Michla. *Self Determination in Law and Practice*, The Hague, Martinus Nijhoff Publ. 1982.

Preston, Adrian. (ed.) *General Staffs and Diplomacy Before the II World War*, London, Croom Helm, 1978.

Puntila, L. A. *The Political History of Finland*, Helsinki, Otava Publ., 1974.

Raczyński, Edward. *In Allied London*, London, Weidenfeld & Nicolson, 1962.

Rafael, Gideon. *Destination Peace*, New York, Stein and Day Publ., 1981.

Reitlinger, Gerald. *The Final Solution*, New York, A Perpetua Books—Barnes & Co., 1961.

Ringelblum, Emmanuel. *Polish-Jewish Relations during the Second World War*, Jerusalem, Yad Vashem, 1974.

Ripka, H. *Munich—Before and After*, London, Victor Gollancz, 1939.

Rozek, Eduard. *Allied Wartime Diplomacy*, New York, John Wiley & Sons, 1958. (ROZEK).

Ronen, Dov. *The Quest for Self-Determination*, Yale Univ. Press, 1979.

Schelling, Thomas C. *The Strategy of Conflict*, Galaxy, Harvard Univ. Press, 1965.

Schmidt, Paul. *Hitler's Interpreter*, London, Heinemann, 1951.

Seton-Watson, Hugh. *Eastern Europe Between the Wars, 1918–1941*, Archon Books, 1962, (SETON-WATSON).

Shechtman, Joseph B. *The Refugee in the World*, New York, Barnes & Co., 1963.

Sherwood, Robert E. *Roosevelt and Hopkins*, New York, Harper & Brothers, 1948. (SHERWOOD).

Shirer, William L. *The Rise and the Fall of the Third Reich*, London, Pan Books, 1964. (SHIRER).

Speer, Albert. *Inside the Third Reich*, New York, Macmillan Co., 1970.

Staar, Richard F. *Poland 1944–1962*, Louisiana State Univ. Press, 1962.

Stettinius, Edward R., Jr. *Lend Lease*, New York, Macmillan, 1944.

Stettinius, Edward R., Jr. *Roosevelt and the Russians—The Yalta Conference*, New York, 1949.

Sukiennicki, Viktor. *Report on the Massacre of Polish Officers in Katyn Woods*, London, 1946.

Talmon, J. L. *The Myth of the Nation and the Vision of Revolution*, London, Secker & Warburg Ltd., 1981.

Tanner, Väinö. *The Winter War*, Stanford Univ. Press, 1957. (TANNER).

Taylor, A. J. P. *The Origins of the Second World War*, London, Hamish Hamilton, 1961.

Thompson, Laurence. *The Greatest Treason*, New York, William Morrow, 1968.

Topolski, Jerzy. *Dzieje Polski*, Warszawa, Państwowe Wyd. Naukowe, 1977. (TOPOLSKI).

Torańska, Teresa. *Oni*, London, Annex Publishers, 1985.

Triska, Jan & Slusser, Robert. *The Theory, Law and Policy of Soviet Treaties*, Stanford Univ. Press, 1963.

Truman, Harry S. *Memoirs—Years of Decisions*, Doubleday, 1955.

Truman, Margaret. *Harry S. Truman*, New York, Morrow & Co., 1973.

Tuchman, Barbara W. *Practicing History*, New York, Ballantine Books, 1982.

Ulam, Adam B. *Expansion & Coexistence*, New York, Praeger, 1969 (ULAM).

Upton, Anthony F. *Finland 1939–1940*, London, Davis—Poynter, 1974.

Vital, David. *The Survival of Small States*, London, Oxford University Press, 1971.

Walzer, Michael. *Just and Unjust Wars*, New York, Basic Books, 1977.

Whaley, Barton. *Codeword Barbarossa*, Cambridge, Mass., The MIT Press, 1973.

Wheeler-Bennett, John W. *Munich*, London, Macmillan, 1948. (WHEELER-BENNETT).

Wickert, Erwin. *Dramatische Tage in Hitler's Reich*, Stuttgart, 1952.

Wiewióra, B. *Uznanie Nabytków Terytorialnych w Prawie Miedzynarodowym*, Poznan, 1961. (WIEWIORA : UZNANIE).

Wiewióra, B. *The Polish-German Frontier in the Light of International Law*, Poznan, Instytut Zachodni, 1964. (WIEWIORA : FRONTIER).

Wiskeman, Elizabeth. *Czechs and Germans*, Oxford Univ. Press, 1938. (WISKEMAN).

Wiskeman, Elizabeth. *Germany's Eastern Neighbours*, Oxford Univ. Press, 1956. (WISKEMAN: NEIGHBOURS).

Woodward, Llewellyn. *British Foreign Policy in the Second World War*, Vol. I, London, 1970.

Yergin, Daniel. *Shattered Peace*, Boston, Houghton Mifflin, 1977.

Zawodny, J. K. *Death in the Forest*, 1962.

Zurawski, Joseph. *Poland—the Captive State*, Detroit, 1962.

Periodicals

Apunen, Osmo. "Geographical and Political Factors in Finland's Relations with the Soviet Union," *Yearbook of Finnish Foreign Policy* (Helsinki, 1977).

Brady, Joe. "Finland—30 years after Soviet Treaty," *International Herald Tribune* (May 2, 1978).

Charlton, Michael. "The Eagle and the Small Birds," *Encounter* (June, 1983).

Gutman, Yisrael. *Jews in Gen. Anders' Army in the Soviet Union* (Yad Vashem, Jerusalem, 1977).

Jakobson, Max. "Substance and Appearance: Finland," *Foreign Affairs* (New York, Summer, 1980).

Kermish, Joseph, "The Warsaw Ghetto Uprising," *The Catastrophe of European Jewry* (1976).

Odlozilik, Otakar. "Edward Beneš on Munich Days," *Journal of Central European Affairs*, (Vol. XVI, University of Colorado, Boulder Co. 1957).

Pipes, Richard. "Some Operational Principles of Soviet Foreign Policy," *The USSR and the Middle East* (Israel Universities Press, Tel Aviv, 1973).

Plaut, Steven. "Czechoslovakia 1938—Israel 1980," *Commentary* (New York, August, 1980).

Polvinen, Tuomo. "Lenin's Nationality Policy and Finland," *Yearbook of Finnish Foreign Policy* (Helsinki, 1977).

Reynolds, Jaime. "Lublin versus London," *Journal of Contemporary History* (Vol. 16, Sage publications, London, October, 1981).

Salmon, Patrick. "The Problem of Swedish Iron Ore," *Journal of Contemporary History* (Sage publications, London, January, 1981).

Seaton, Albert. "Stalin and the Red Army General Staff," *General Staffs and Diplomacy before the Second World War* (Croom Helm, London, 1978).

Stronge, H. T. C. "The Czech Army and the Munich Crisis," *War and Society* (Vol. I, Croom Helm Publ., London, 1976).

Taborsky, Edward. "Beneš and Stalin—Moscow 1943 and 1945,"*Journal of Central European Affairs* (Vol. XIII).

Williamson, Murray. "German Air Power and the Munich Crisis," *War and Society* (Vol. 2, London, 1977).

Williamson, Murray. "Munich 1938: the Military Confrontation," *Journal of Strategic Studies* (Vol. 2, December 1979, nr-3. Frank Cass, London).

Index

Aachen, 181
Adamów, 103
Adler, Victor, 127
Afghanistan, 270n, 328
Aggression, 7, 8, 19, 39; self-defense against, 47, 51, 79, 111, 127, 171, 212; Polish jurists on, 225–226; 227, 242, 331, 334
Agreements, international: Baltic countries-USSR, 243; DDR-Poland, 233; FRG-USSR, 234; Locarno Pact, 8, 18, 340; Nazi Germany-USSR, 77–79, 84, 93, 94, 107, 114, 124–125, 137, 155, 179, 198, 243, 257, 268–269, 282, 342; Poland-Germany, 65; Poland-USSR, 65, 201; Riga accord, 62–63, 114, 122, 140, 155–157; Sikorski-Maisky, 115, 122, 125, 128, 140; Treaty of Tartu, 241, 339; Treaties of Versailles, St. Germain, Neuilly, Trianon, 10, 18, 48, 49
AK (Home Army), 100–102, 127, 163, 164; and Warsaw uprising; 165–168, 170, 199; leaders on trial, 203, 216
AL (People's Army), 100, 102, 164
Alaska, 249
Alexander II, Czar of Russia, 315
Alliances. *See* Agreements
Alsace-Lorraine, 228
Anders, Władysław, 117–118, 120–122, 126, 131
Anti-Semitism, 16, 69–70, 118–120
Antrea, 297, 301
Appeasement, 13, 14, 15, 17, 21, 22, 39, 79, 116, 340
Arciszewski, Tomasz, 183, 193n
Ardennes, 181
Atlantic Charter, 139

Attlee, Clement, 207, 213
Austria, 8, 9, 18, 277
Austria-Hungary, 8, 59
Autonomy, 20

Baldwin, Stanley, 12
Balfour, Arthur, 144–145
Balkans, 122, 145, 283
Balkars, 150
Baltic Sea, 57, 61, 152–154, 169, 189, 211, 213, 227, 243, 282, 323
Baltic States, 62n., 79, 122, 124, 139, 220, 237, 243, 251, 268
Barbarossa, 111, 112
Bauer, Otto, 238
BBC, 114
BBWR, 66, 69, 170
Beck, Józef, 67–69, 72, 73
Beck, Ludwig, 43
Belgium, 200, 278, 279
Belorussia, 82–84, 154, 159, 162, 268
Belorussians, 58, 61, 62n, 63, 64; and National Assemblies, 83–84, 94, 125, 165, 270, 331
Bełz, 62
Bendzin, 103
Beneš, Eduard, 9, 17, 20–21, 24, 26, 35, 39; meets party and army leaders, 45–46, 48, 50, 155, 328
Berchtesgaden, 23, 34, 73
Berdichev, 59n
Berezyna, 61
Bergen, 287
Beria, Lavrenti P., 95, 111
Berlin, 76, 112, 207, 249
Berling, Zygmunt, 132

389

Bessarabia, 79, 220, 243, 268
Beuten (Bytom), 217
Bevin, Ernest, 223, 224
Białystok, 62, 82, 103, 123, 150, 170, 174, 188
Bierut, Bolesław, 162, 186, 193–194, 199, 211–215
Birobidzhan, 197
Black Sea, 136, 152
Blücher, Wipert, 281
Blum, Leon, 16
Bohemia, 10
Bohlen, Charles, 202
Bolshevism. *See* Communism
Bonnet, Georges, 17, 19, 90
Bor-Komorowski, Tadeusz, 163, 165, 168
Bormann, Martin, 97
Born, Ernst, 305
Bosporus, Straits of, 207
Bothnia, Gulf of, 268, 285, 310
Braclaw, 60n, 103
Brauchitsch, Walter, 81
Breslau (Wrocław), 189, 209, 217, 219
Brest-Litovsk, 82
Britain, 15; and appeasement policy, 20, 22; presses Czechs to agree to a "limited" German occupation, 26, 61, 77, 78, 86, 91, 99, 111, 113; wants to be sure that USSR will continue fighting, 116, 118; Lend Lease program to USSR from USA and, 135n, 138, 139, 145; in 1919 supported Curzon Line, 158, 169, 182, 203, 206, 249; aid to Finland, 279; volunteers from, 281, 295; Expeditionary Force, 308–311, 340
British Air Force, Army, Navy, 86, 167–168, 309n, 311
Brody, 103
Bukovina, 268
Buenos Aires, 132
Bug, river, 62, 81, 94, 153
Bukhara, 120
Bukharin, Nikolai, 238
Bulgaria, 111, 145, 153, 169, 201, 207
Bund, 127
Buzuluk, 119
Byrnes, James F., 213

Cadogan, Alexander, 157, 172

Cajander, A. K., 241, 255, 258, 270
Canada, 99, 135, 278
Čapek, Karl, 46
Case Green. *See* Fall Grün
Case White. *See* Fall Weiss
Catholicism, 69
Caucasus, 295
Carpathian Mountains, 62
Chamberlain, Neville, 19, 20, 22; declares Britain won't go to war for Czechosl., 23; 25, 26; quarrel in a far-away country, 27; "Munich" policy, 32–33, 34–35, 44; and German takeover of Czechosl., 74, 79, 91; declares war, 92, 107; and Winter War, 283–286, 312–313, 341
Chechens, 150
Cheka (*see also* NKVD), 123
Chełm, 162
China, 18, 138, 187
Chrobry, Bolesław, 60
Churchill, Winston S., 17, 23; and Poland's borders, 55–56, 59, 92, 103, 114, 116, 118; and Katyn Massacre, 129–131, 132, 133, 136; Teheran conference, 137–142; how to move Poland, 144; and percentage deal with Stalin, 145–146, 148, 150, 151, 157; controversy with Polish Govt.-in-exile, 157–160, 168, 171; and Mikolajczyk, 172–175; 177–180; Yalta Conference, 185–197, 198, 204–205; Potsdam Conference, 207, 209–212; replaced as PM by Hitler, 213, 214, 215, 228; mining of Norwegian waters, 286, 341
Ciechanowski, Jan, 159, 181
Clemenceau, Georges, 165, 187–188
Cold War, 198, 224
Comintern, 15–16, 110, 123, 137, 162, 261, 340
Communism, 18, 60, 67, 107, 112, 123–124, 152, 210, 234, 239, 258, 259, 330
Communists: Finnish, 261, 265, 272; French, 16; German 94, 98, 162, 199, 209n; Polish, 100
Cracow (Krakow), 103, 176
Crimea, 153, 185
Crimean Tatars, 150

Curzon Line, 61–63, 124, 125, 126, 148–150, 154–158, 160–161, 163n, 165, 171–178, 182, 187–188, 190–191, 206, 210, 214

Czechoslovakia, "an inimical thorn," 7, 9, 10; and German minority, 11, 19; and Western democracies, 24; mobilizes against German threat, 26; and Munich diktat, 32; "has ceased to exist", 36; democracy, industry, 40; and military option, 51, 62, 63, 72, 73, 74, 90; Red Army enters, 185, 201; Sovietization of, 208, 211, 213–214, 220, 226, 270n., 277, 323, 327

Czechoslovak Army, 15, 20; and fortifications, 41, 42, 43–44

Częstochowa, 103

Dairen, 192

Daladiėr, Edouard, 17, 19, 22, 23; and Munich conference, 32–33, 44, 65, 90, 107; and Winter War, 283, 286; and expeditionary force, 307–308, 311–312, 341

Danzig (Gdańsk), 61, 72–73, 91, 106, 157, 174, 189, 214, 227

Darlan, Jean, 90

David, Jozef, 45

De Gaulle, Charles, 193, 339n

Delegatura, 106, 156, 165

Democracy, 11, 12, 21, 51, 65, 105, 121, 151, 161, 179; Stalin on the principles of, 203, 210, 215; people's, 216, 251, 257, 277

Demography, 10, 58

Denmark, 242, 279, 280, 281, 309n

Dentz, Gen., 90

Derevyansky, Vladimir, 237, 248

Dewey, Thomas E., 181

Diplomacy, 107, 115, 153, 181, 210, 241, 330, 335–338

Disentanglement (see Transfer)

Dniepr, river, 61

Dniestr, river, 61, 153

Drohobycz, 160

Duff Cooper, Alfred, 34

Dzerzhinsky, Feliks, 123

Eastern Prussia, 43, 57, 61, 62, 72, 121, 150, 157, 160, 162, 163n., 174, 185, 190, 214, 219

Ecuador, 192

Eden, Anthony, 55–56, 114–116, 138, 146, 148; tries to persuade the Poles, 155, 156n, 157, 172, 173; defends Yalta resolution, 198

Eduskunta, 242, 251, 256, 264, 318

Eisenhower, Dwight D., 185, 340n

El Alamein, 136

Elba, 60

England (*see* Britain)

Enso, 310

Erkko, Eljas, 237, 251–253, 255, 258, 270, 280

Erlich, Henryk, 127

Estonia, 62n, 79, 94, 147, 169, 243, 253, 295, 302

Fagerholm, Karl August, 305

Fall Grün (Case Green), 20

Fall Weiss (Case White), 74

Fascism, 12, 15, 48, 69, 216, 277

Fifth Column, in Czechoslovakia, 11; in Poland, 70, 81, 88, 219

Finland, 62n, 79, 94, 123, 136, 153; and USSR, 206; Karelian refugees to, 228, 237, 238; civil war in, 239, 243; delegation to Moscow, 244, 253, 260; topography of, 266, 270, 272; winter in, 273, 278–280, 287, 292, 302; peace treaty, 316, 323, 327, 329–331

Finnish Army, 242, 250–251, 263–266, 274, 277, 290, retreats, 298, 301; casualties, 319

Finnish Parliament. *See* Eduskunta. *See also* Gulf of Finland

Finns, 238, 250, 257, 260

France, 7, 15, and Czechoslovakia, 17–19, 20, 22, 25; *see also* Guarantees; 48, 61; Stalin's suspicions of, 77, 78, 99, 108, 144, 153, 192, 203, 230, 278; aid to Finland, 279, 295, 309n, 310, 340

French Army, 43, 44; military protocol with Poland, 86, 311

Franco, Francisco, 27

Galicia, 160, 165, 182

Gällivare, 285
Gamelin, Maurice, 41, 44, 86, 90–91, 308
Ganeval, col., 290, 308
Georges, gen., 90
Germany, 9, 15; invades Rhineland, annexes Austria, 18, 35, 55; preventive war against, 65, 75, 79; occupies Poland, 97, 99, 107, 113, 118, 140, 148, 192; unconditional surrender of, 207, 212, 224, 226, 281; *see also* Ribbentrop; 282, 292, 331–332
Germany, Democratic Republic of, 233
Germany, Federal Republic of, 234
German Army (and Wehrmacht), 19, 20, 26; occupies Czechoslovakia, 37; in September 1938, 42–44, 73, 75, 81, 86–87; supremacy and innovations in tactics and technology, 88–89, 93, 97n, 108; prepares for attack on USSR, 111, 112, 113, 122, 136, 164; and Warsaw uprising, 166–168, and Finland, 240. *See also* Luftwaffe, OKW
Germanization, 230
German minority, 8, 11, 12, 21, 24, 63, 71, 228. *See also* Sudeten Germans
Germans, 55, 59, 61, 63, 127, 153, 154, 157, 189, 192, 210–214, 217–219, 220, 242, 250
Gestapo, 94
Glebokie, 103
Godesberg, 25–26, 34
Goebbels, Joseph, 11, 128
Gomulka, Wladislaw, 162, 186
Goering, Hermann, 27, 65n, 129, 167
Görlitz (Gorlice), 217
Gottwald, Klement, 45
Grabski, Wladyslaw, 176, 194–195
Grand Alliance, 207, 210
Greece, 111, 145–146, 185, 200, 226, 228
Gripenberg, Georg A., 284
Grodno, 62
Grzybowski, 82
Guarantees, international, 18, 19; France guarantees Czechoslovakia's "new borders", 25, 37, 49; French and British to Poland, 86, 90, 92, 93, 116, 339, 342
Gulag, 150
Gulf of Aquaba, 339n, 340n
Gulf of Bothnia. *See Bothnia, Gulf of*

Gulf of Finland, 241, 242, 244, 248, 250, 253, 295, 296, 299, 301, 302, 316
Günther, Christian, 295, 304

Hägglund, J. V., 267
Hague, The, 231
Halder, Franz, 81, 113
Halifax, Lord, 35
Hanko, 249, 246–251, 295, 301–302, 310, 318
Hannula, Uuno, 296, 305, 309, 311–312, 315–316, 319
Hansson, Per Albin, 280, 304
Harriman, W. Averell, 175–176, 183, 187n, 195–196, 201, 202
Heikkinen, P. V., 305
Heinrichs, gen., 267
Helsinki, 234, 237, 241, 243, 244, 247, 251, 252, 254–258, 263, 271, 284, 288, 295, 303
Henderson, Nevile, 12, 14, 20, 80
Henlein, Konrad, 11, 19, 20
Hitler, Adolf, 7; on Lebensraum, 7–8; 11, 14, 19; orders to smash Czechoslovakia, 20; at Nuremberg Party Rally, 22; receives Chamberlain, 23–25; replies to Roosevelt's appeal, 27–28; at Munich Conference, 32; orders liquidation of Czechosl., 36; meets generals' opposition, 43, 64, 65; with Beck on Danzig, 72, 73, 74. *See also* Fall Weiss, 79, 93, 97; on extermination of the "Jewish race", 98–99, 107; and Barbarossa, 111, 116, 122, 137, 138, 139, 151, 163; suicide of, 207, 257, 273; and the Finnish-Russian conflict, 282, 340
Hodža, Milan, 26
Holma, Harri, 290, 307
Holsti, Rudolf, 241
Homel, 59n
Hoover, Herbert C., 181
Hopkins, Harry, 192, 202–204
Hull, Cordell, 159
Hungary, 9, 18, 35, 47, 70n, 99, 111, 123, 145, 146, 153, 169, 185, 201, 207, 214, 220, 226, 270n, 279, 281

Ibn Sand, 197
IKL, 318

India, 228
Ingushi, 50
Ironside, Edmund, 86, 286, 311
Ismay, Hastings, 146
Israel, 228, 339n
Italy, 15, 35, 74, 135, 168, 226, 230, 279, 281
Izvestia, 126

Jaklicz, col., 90
Jakobson, Max, 248
Jankowski, Jan S., 165, 199
Janosz, Stanisław, 186
Japan, 9, 18, 77n, 136, 192, 207, 226, 328
Jerusalem, 102, 144
Jews, 58, 61, 63, 69, 75, 94, 98–99, 100, 118, 119–120, 131, 197, 216, 218, 222
Jodl, Alfred, 44
Johnson, Lyndon B., 340n

Käkisalmi, 297, 301, 316
Kalinin, Michail, 257, 260
Kallio, Kijosti, 255, 296, 304, 305, 312, 316
Kalmyks, 150
Karelia, 241, 249, 251–253, 255–256, 259, 262, 266–267, 274, 289, 295–296, 300–303, 310, 316, 320, 331
Kasprzycki, gen., 90
Katyń, 128–131, 170, 179
Kaunas (Kovno), 59n, 103
Kazakhstan, 121
Keitel, Wilhelm, 43–44
Kekkonen, Urho, 302, 305, 318
Kemijärvi, 274
Kennedy, John F., 338
Kerensky, Alexander, 254, 281
Kerr, Archibald Clark, 195–196, 201
Khrushchev, Nikita S., 77, 83, 84, 109, 113, 250, 256, 260
Kielce, 100, 216
Kiev, 60, 61, 136, 153
Klaus, Edgar, 137
Kleck, 103
Kleist, Peter, 137
Kobryń, 103
Koc, Adam, 67
Koivisto, 266
Kollontai, Alexandra, 293, 295, 304

Kon, Felix, 123
Königsberg, 150, 160, 174
Kosciuszko, Tadeusz. See also Polish Army, 131, 169
Kot, Stanisław, 117, 125, 161
Kozielsk, 129
Kraków. See Cracow
Krejči, Ludvik, 19, 46
Kremlin, 78, 94, 95, 117, 127, 145, 161, 163, 170, 248, 260, 261, 264, 270, 316
Krzemieniec, 103
Kuibyshev, 119, 125
Kukiel, Marian, 161
Kun, Bela, 123
Kurile Islands, 192
Kursk, 136
Kutrzeba, Stanislaw, 195
Kuusamo, 310, 316
Kuusinen, Otto, 123, 261, 265, 268, 270–272, 311

Laatikainen, O., 267
Lachwa, 103
Ladoga, 266, 274, 302, 310
Lane, Arthur B., 182
Lange, Oskar, 176, 203
Lansing, Robert, 13–14
Latvia, 62, 62n, 79, 94, 147, 169, 243
League of Nations, 18, 48–49, 61, 145, 277, 278, 280, 285
Leahy, William D., 147, 201
Lebensraum, 7, 8, 73
Lend-Lease, 135n
Lenin, Vladimir I., 8, 11, 13. See also Self-determination; 62, 165, 188; recognizes Finland's independence, 238, 239
Leningrad, 153, 241, 244, 248–253, 255, 259, 261, 262, 268, 274, 295, 316, 319
Lida, 103
Liebknecht, Karl, 123
Lignica, 216, 219
Ling, Robert, 290, 303
Lipski, Jozef, 70n, 72
Lithuania, 62, 62n, 79, 94, 162, 192, 243
Lithuanians, 63, 147, 165, 323
Litvinow, Maxim, 25, 127
Lloyd George, David, 144, 165
Locarno, Pact. See Agreements

Łódź, 64
Łomża, 174
London, 105, 127, 132, 161, 177, 178, 183, 227, 284, 287–288, 307, 308
"London Government" (Polish Government in Exile), 100, 103, 105–106; recognition of, 114, 121, 125; and Katyń massacre, 127–129, 132, 133, 140, 141, 143; accused by Stalin, 147, 153–155; under Churchill's pressure, 156–158, 161, 163; and Warsaw uprising, 164–168, 169, 170, 171, 172; refuses to concede, 179, 180, 181; protests of, 186, 193–195; Yalta seals the fate of, 196, 198, 204, 206, 336
Lublin, 94, 100, 162, 170, 186
"Lublin Committee", 162–166; consolidates its position, 169, 170, 171, 172, 174–175; recognized by USSR as Warsaw government, 186, 198. *See also* ZPP
Lubyanka, 203
Luftwaffe, 42, 81, 82, 112, 135
Lulea, 285–286
Luxemburg, Rosa, 238
Lvov (Lwów), 60n, 62, 63, 82, 83, 121, 124, 125, 148–150, 155, 158, 160, 170, 171, 172, 174, 176, 182–183, 187–188, 214

MacArthur, Douglas, 182
Maginot Line, 44, 91, 266, 320
Mainila, 262
Maisky, Ivan, 114–115, 131
Manchuria, 118, 128
Mandel, Georges, 17
Mannerheim, Gustav C., 240, 252, 254; warns against optimism, 258; appointed Commander-in-Chief, 259, 264, 265–268, 269, 271, 275, 279; assessment of military situation, 290–292, 295–297; orders retreat, 298, 300–301; recommends peace agreement, 305, 308–309, 311, 312; and nation's morale, 320–321
Mannerheim Line, 249, 252, 266–267, 297–298
Manteuffel, Hasso, 181
Marchlewski, Julian, 123
Marshall, George C., 223, 224
Marxism-Leninism, 84, 110, 151, 199, 238
Masaryk, Tomas G., 9, 49

Mastny, Voitech, 32
Matusinski, 82
McIntire, Ross, 182
Memel, 73
Meretzkov, K. A., 273, 297
Metz, 181
Mexico, 132
Mieszko I, Prince, 60
Mikołajczyk, Stanisław, 100, 141, 142, 143, 155, 157–159; received by Roosevelt, 159, 161, 163, 164; with Stalin, appeals for help for Warsaw uprising, 165–167, 169–173; and Molotov's remark, 174, 175–178, 180, 182; resignation of, 183, 188, 194–195, 203–205; in Potsdam as Deputy PM, 211, 216, 217
Mikoyan, Anastas, 257
Minsk, 60n, 153
Minsk, Mazowiecki, 103
Miory, 103
Modzelewski, Zygmunt, 231
Mohilev, 59n
Molotov, Vyacheslav M., 55, 75, 78; signs agreement with Ribbentrop, 79; *see also* Agreements; informs Amb. Grzybowski that the Red Army crossed Poland's border, 82, 83, 93, 95, 107, 108, 110; and Barbarossa, 112–113, 125, 131, 137, 146, 163, 172; on Roosevelt's support for Curzon Line, 174, 175, 176, 189, 190, 195, 196; opposes changes in Prov. Warsaw Govt., 200, 201, 203, 223, 230, 231; invites Erkko for talks, 237; and Finnish delegation, 243, 248, 245–251; responds to Roosevelt's letter, 260, 261, 268, 269, 271, 277, 279n, 282, 294, 295; and the Finnish war, 297, 301, 309–311; the "imperialist conspiracy" version, 319, 339
Moltke, Hans A., 68, 85
Moravia, 10
Mościcki, Ignacy, 67, 82
Moscow, 78, 113, 126, 129, 131, 132, 136, 145, 155, 161, 162, 163, 164, 169, 170, 172, 174, 177, 178, 183, 203, 204–205, 234, 237, 241, 242, 252–257, 259, 261, 270, 271, 292, 295, 307, 309
Munich, 7; conference, 32–34; diktat, 40, 51, 77, 79, 107, 242, 283, 307

Murmansk, 110, 249, 267, 274, 284, 310, 316
Mussolini, Benito, 31, 79

Namsos, 287
Napoleon Bonaparte, 108, 112n, 273
Narew, river, 79, 81
Narvik, 285–287, 209n, 311
Nazi propaganda, 13, 16, 65, 70, 129
Nazism, 12, 15, 18, 48, 59, 112, 277
Nazi terror, 22, 79, 92, 97–99, 136
ND, 69, 70, 105
Neisse, river (Glatzer-Eastern N.), 188
Neisse, river (Lausitzer-Western N.), 163n, 188, 209, 211–212, 213n, 223, 228, 231
Neutrality, 241, 242, 244–245, 250–251, 253, 269; Swedish policy of, 280, 282
New York Times, 103
Niemen, river, 153
Nieśwież, 103
Nimitz, Chester F., 182
Ninth Fort, 103
Niukkanen, Juho, 253, 255–256, 296, 305, 311–312, 315–316
NKVD, 84, 111; political guidance of, 132, 164, 166, 169, 170; repressions in Poland, 199
Normandy, 159
Norway, 242, 279, 280–281, 283, 285–287, 295, 303, 304, 308, 309n, 312–313
Nowogrodek, 103, 170
NSZ, 216
Nuremberg, 22, 43, 129–130
Nykopp, Johan, 244, 323

Obersalzberg, 23. *See also* Berchtesgaden
Oder, river, 60, 121, 147, 150, 157, 173, 185, 188–190, 209, 211, 213, 223, 228, 231
Oesch, Lennart, 252
Öhquist, Harald, 267
Okulicki, Leopold, 199
OKW, 42, 43, 75
O.N.R., 70
Oppeln, 150, 219
Orlemanski, 161
Oslo, 284, 288
Osóbka-Morawski, Edward, 166, 186, 193, 194, 199

Österman, Hugo, 267
Oulu, 267
Outer Mongolia, 192
Overlord, 146
OZN, 70

Paasikivi, Juho K., 244, 247–248, 251–252, 258–259, 269; joins Cabinet, 270, 290, 293, 296; favors peace talks, 303, 309, 311
Paasonen, Aladar, 244, 290
Paatio, 310
Pakistan, 228
Paldiski, 249
Paris, 105, 284, 287–288, 307
Paul-Boncour, M., 19
Parliament, 228
Parliament, Finland. *See* Eduskunta
Parliament, Poland. *See* Sejm
Pekkala, Mauno, 303
Persia, 118–119, 124
Peter, the Great, 248, 302, 310, 312, 316
Petsamo, 241, 259, 284, 302, 308, 310, 316
Philippines, 182, 260
Piast, dynasty, 231
Pinsk, 60n
Piłsudski, Józef, 62n, 65, 67, 70, 270
PKWN. *See* Lublin Committee
Poland, 9, 15, 18, 25; bites off Czechoslovakia's border district, 35, 47; Churchill and Stalin in Teheran on, 55–57, 58, 59, 65, 73, 78; under German occupation, 97, 99, 106, 108; renewing relations with USSR, 114–121; conflict of interests, 112, 138, 140, 141, 143, 148, 150; the Big Three and, 151, 153, 156, 160; and the dawn of liberation, 170, 171, 174–176, 182; and Yalta Conference, 186–187; Yalta communique on borders of, 190, 194, 202, 211; Potsdam establishes western border of, 213–216; Communist takeover of, 217, 224, 226; international recognition of borders of, 234, 249, 270, 277, 327, 329–332
Poles, 63, 97–99, 102, 117–119, 139, 148, 157, 158, 162, 164, 168, 187, 197, 203, 209–211, 217, 222, 223
Poles, in USA, 147, 180, 182

Polish Army, 68n, 81, 85, 87–89; new beginning abroad, 99, 101, 106; on Soviet soil, 114, 115, 117, 118, 121–122; Churchill praises, 194
Polish (People's) Army. *See also* Kosciuszko Division, 131, 132 *See also:* London Government; Lublin Committee; Warsaw Government
Polandization, 211, 217, 218, 219, 223
Polesie, 103, 170
Pomerania, 60, 61, 162, 217, 219
Pope (Pius XII), 79, 181, 211, 278
Porajärvi, 241, 249
Port Arthur, 192
Potemkin, Grigori, 248
Potocki, Jerzy, 70n
Potsdam, 59, 207, 209; Soviet troops remain in Poland contrary to resolutions of, 216, 218, 219, 221; final determination of borders, 223; German protests, 224–225, 228, 231
Poznan, 64, 176
PPR, 100, 170, 199, 216, 217
PPS, 100, 105, 183, 217
Prague, 26, 34, 37, 110
Pravda, 129, 135, 271
Prchala, Lev, 46
Pripet, Marshes, 62, 148, 169
Provisional Government of National Unity. *See* Warsaw Government
Prussia. *See* Eastern Prussia
Przemysl, 62, 149, 174
PSL, 217

Raczkiewicz, Władysław, 115, 117, 161
Raczynski, Edward, 138, 157
Radek, Karl, 238
Red Army. *See* Soviet Army
Red Cross, 128–129, 131
Reichstag, 71, 219
Renner, Karl, 238
Repola, 241, 249, 267
Rhineland, 12, 15, 18
Ribbentrop, Joachim, 27, 72, 75–76; signs agreement with Molotov, 78–80, 82, 92, 93, 95; and trade agreement, 108, 137, 243, 249; and the Russian-Finnish War, 281, 282. *See also:* Agreements, Nazi-Soviet

Riga, 62–63, 122. *See also* Agreements
Rio de Janeiro, 132
Rokossovsky, Konstantin, 169, 170, 185, 199, 216
Romania, 18, 25, 48, 62, 70n, 82, 99, 111, 145–146, 153, 169, 201, 207
Romer, Tadeusz, 157, 172, 175, 194–195
Roosevelt, Franklin D., 27–28, 55–56, 79; Poland praised by, 103; in view of Soviet-Polish rift, 132–133, 136; at Teheran Conference, 137–148, 150, 151; receives Mikolajczyk, 159–160, 161, 167, 171–180; re-elected, 181, 182, 183; goes to Yalta, 185–197; death of, 198, 207, 215, 231, 257, 260
Rowecki, Stefan, 101
Russarö, 255
Runciman, Lord, 20
Runeberg, Walter, 315
Rundstedt, Gerd von, 181
Russia. *See* Soviet Union
Russians, 59–60, 63, 68, 109, 110, 117, 165, 175, 187, 193, 202, 222, 242, 250, 253–256, 292–293
Rybachi Peninsula, 249, 253, 310, 316
Ryti, Risto, 270, 290, 292, 293, 294, 295, 296, 303, 305, 309, 310, 318

Saarinen, Eliel, 247
Sakhalin, 192
Salla, 267, 274, 310, 316
Salmijärvi, 310
San, river, 79, 81
Sapieha, Adam, 195
Saratov, 127
Scandinavia, 241, 242, 282, 302
Schacht, Hjalmar, 34
Schnurre, Julius, 108
Schulenburg, Friedrich W., 75, 82, 93, 111, 112–113, 243, 282, 295
Sejm, 66, 69
Self-defense, 26, 40, 46–47, 51, 219, 226, 228, 331, 334, 343
Self-determination, 8–9, 11, 14, 24, 29, 35; German demands for, 224; Polish arguments and legal principles on, 225, 228–230, 233; Lenin and, 238–239
Siegfried Line, 43, 266, 320
Siilasvuo, H., 274–275

Sikorski, Władysław, 66, 105, 114–115, 116; meets Stalin, 117–121, 124, 125, 126; and Katyn massacre, 129–130, 132, 138, 141, 150, 176, 177, 284
Silesia, 60, 61, 64, 157, 160, 162, 169, 189, 217, 219
Skoropadsky, Pavel, 281
Skworcew-Stiepanow, 123
Sławek, Walery, 67
Sławoj-Składkowski, Felicjan, 67, 70
Słonim, 103
Slovakia, 9–10, 36, 73
Smigły-Rydz, Edward, 67, 82
Smolensk, 128–129, 136
Sobibor, 103
Söderhjelm, 296, 305
Sörtavala, 304, 310, 316
Sosnkowski, Kazimierz, 66, 115, 117, 161, 164
Soviet Army, 61, 62; and the Great Terror, 67–68, 69, 82, 83; crosses Poland's border, 84–85, 97, 99; ordered not to return fire, 120, 122, 123; partisans, 123, 127, 131; victories in Stalingrad, Kursk, 136, 140, 143, 147, 151, 152; liberates Polish territories, 153, 154, 158, 163; and Warsaw uprising, 164–168; driving Germans out of Romania, Bulgaria, Hungary, Estonia, Latvia, 169, 170, 171, 185, 187–189; advances toward Berlin, 193, 199, 203, 207; needs friendly hinterland, 209–210, 213–215, 219, 226; in war against Finland, 243, 261, 263; equipment of, 264–265, 270, 271, 273, 275, 284, 289; reorganization of, 297; February offensive of, 298; casualties of, 319, 320, 328
Soviet Union, 7; and self-determination, 8, 9, 18, 56, 58, 60; and treaty with Poland, 65; purges and terror, 67–68, 75, 78, 79, 94, 97, 101; neutralized by Ribbentrop-Molotov agreement, 107; provides Germany with raw materials, 108–110, 114, 116; Polish POWs in, 118, 120; and Curzon Line, 124; and Slavic peoples, 125, 129, 133; Lend Lease and, 135, 138, 145, 146; and "London Govt.", 156, 165, 175, 177, 199, 202, 204, 206; and Oder-Western Neisse Line, 209–214, 215, 223, 241; security requirements of, 244, 248–249, 253, 258; and Finland, 260, 269, 270, 272, 277, 294, 302; peace treaty with Finland, 316, 323. *See also:* Kremlin and Moscow and Russians
Spain, 249, 277, 279
Speer, Albert, 41
Stachiewicz, gen., 68
Stalin, Joseph V., 15, 55–56, 59, 67, 76, 78, 93, 95, 103; and German invasion, 107, 108, 111; refuses to believe warnings, 112–113, 116; and Sikorski, 117–122, 123, 127, 128, 131, 135; at Teheran Conference, 137–142; and the percentage deal, 145–146; and Curzon Line, 149–150, 151, 155, 157; on the opening of the Second Front, 159, 160–162; and Mikolajczyk, 165–166; refuses assistance to Warsaw uprising, 167–168, 169, 170, 171, 177, 182; at Yalta, 185–187, 191–194; wants friendly Polish government, 200, 202, 205; at Potsdam, 207, 209–212, 219, 223, 234; and Finnish SD Party, 239, 243; receives Finnish delegation, 248–250, 252, 255, 260, 269; and the course of war, 297, 310, 330–331; and Tartu Treaty, 339, 341
Stalingrad, 122, 136
Stanislavov, 170
Stašek, Mgsr., 46
Stavanger, 287
Stefanik, Milan, 9
Stettin, 174, 189, 209, 211, 219
Stettinius, Edward R. Jr., 186, 187n, 196
Stockholm, 261, 280, 284, 288, 293–296, 307, 309
Stránský, Jaroslav, 45
Sudeten Germans, 11, 12, 13–14, 23, 24, 25, 35, 331
Sudentenland, 11, 23, 25
Summa, 298, 301, 302
Suomussalmi, 274, 275
Suursaari, 242, 244, 249, 253
Sweden, 27, 242, 257; aid to Finland, 279–281, 283, 285–287, 292, 295–296, 301; and the negotiations, 302, 303, 304, 312–313
Swinemünde, 211, 213
Syrový, Jan, 26, 33, 40, 46, 50

Tallin, 243, 249
Tanner, Väinö, 241, 252–254, 258, 269; replaces Erkko as FM, 270–271, 284, 290, 293–296; goes to Stockholm, 301, 302, 303; third meeting with Kollontai, 304, 313, 316
Tarnopol, 60n, 160, 170
Tarnów, 103
Tartu (Dorpat). *See* Agreements
Tashkent, 120
TASS, 154–156, 170
Teheran, 55, 59, 135–138, 143, 144–147, 152, 153, 157, 160, 171, 174, 175, 187–188, 191
Terijoki, 270
Thomas, George, 109
Thorez, Maurice, 16
Times (London), 23, 41, 103, 331
Timoshenko, Semën K., 297
Tobruk, 118
Tornio, 310
Transfer, 150, 158, 178, 183, 209, 214, 220–221, 223, 228
Trans-Jordan, 145
Treaties. *See* Agreements
Treblinka, 103
Trondheim, 287
Trotsky, Leon, 68, 123, 281
Truman, Harry S., 201, 202, 204; at Potsdam, 207, 209–210, 223; quoted by Polish jurists, 227
Tuominen, Arvo, 261
Tuompo, Gen., 267
Turkey, 192, 228, 323

UB, 199, 216
Ukraine, 82, 83, 84, 124, 125, 149–150, 154, 162, 268
Ukrainians, 58, 61, 62n, 63, 64, 83, 84, 94, 118, 121, 165, 172, 176, 270, 331
United Nations, 182, 192, 193, 200, 221n, 226, 328, 330
Unszlicht, Józef, 123
United States, 70n, 91, 99; with regard to Poland, 115, 118, 120; and Lend Lease, 135, 138, 156, 158, 160; Polish Community in, 182, 183, 202, 203, 206; and Potsdam resolutions, 224, 249, 277; and aid to Finland, 279; volunteers from, 281, 339n
United States Air Force, Army, Navy, 167–168, 181, 182, 328
USSR. *See* Soviet Union

Värtsilä, 310
Vasilevski, Alexander, 309
Vatican, 161
Vereker, Gordon, 303, 308
Versailles, 61, 83. *See also* Agreements
Vietnam, 328, 339n
Viipuri, 253, 267, 297, 300–301, 304, 310–311, 315–316
Vilna (Wilno), 60n, 62, 103, 148, 158, 160, 165, 170, 171, 176, 214
Virolahti, 310
Vishinsky, Andrei, 228
Vistula, river (Wisła), 79, 153, 163, 164, 169, 170
Vitebsk, 59n, 153
Voionmaa, Väinö, 309, 318
Volga Germans, 150
Volhynia (Wołyń), 170
Völkisher, Beobachter, 12, 128
Voroshilov, Kliment, 95, 297
Vuillemin, Joseph, 90, 91

Walden, Rudolf, 296
Warsaw, 61, 94, 95, 156; uprising in, 163–169, 170, 176; Rokossovsky's army enters, 185–186
Warsaw, Ghetto, 102, 103, 166
Warsaw Government, 186–187, 190, 191, 193–196, 199, 202, 204, 214, 224
Wasilewska, Wanda, 126
Wehrmacht. *See* German Army
Weimar, 60
Weizsäcker, Ernst, 282
Welles, Sumner, 115, 116
Westerplatte, 95
Wilson, Horace, 26
Wilson, Woodrow, 8–9, 13. *See also* Self-determination
Witos, Andrzej, 195
Wojciechowski, Stanisław, 64
Wuolijoki, Hella, 293

Yalta, 59, 135, 153, 169, 185, 186–188,
 191, 195, 197, 199, 200, 201, 204, 209,
 218, 231
Yartsev, Boris, 241, 242, 244
Yrjö-Koskinen, A. S., 237, 244
Yugoslavia, 18, 48, 111, 145, 201, 207, 226

Zaleski, August, 111, 117
Zay, Jean, 17

Zdołbunów, 103
Żegota, 102
Zhdanov, Andrei, 261, 297, 309
Zhukov, Georgi, 199
Zionism, 103, 120, 144, 197
ŻOB, 101–103
ZPP, 126, 127, 131, 162
Zuckerman, Itzhak ("Antek"), 101
Żymierski, Michał Rola, 170, 186, 211